Acclaim for Paula Fredriksen's

JESUS OF NAZARETH, KING OF THE JEWS

"Why was Jesus killed? . . . Fredriksen's search for an answer is almost a detective story . . . refreshingly independent of dogma and cant."   —*The Atlanta Journal-Constitution*

"Fredriksen's reconstruction of the events around the trial of Jesus is particularly brilliant. We can suddenly 'see' why the Romans . . . would decide he must become an object lesson for less disciplined Jews."   —*Providence Journal*

"*Jesus of Nazareth, King of the Jews* shows beyond any question Fredriksen's mastery of her sources and a level of insight achieved by firm command of the analytical tools she brings to bear."   —*The Boston Book Review*

"*Jesus of Nazareth* invites a general readership to forget everything it has learned about Jesus and to begin again."
          —*Mail on Sunday* (London)

"Fiercely argued . . . put together with great perceptiveness."
          —*The Daily Telegraph* (London)

"Fredriksen has made not only the world of first-century Palestine, but also the maze of Jesus scholarship, intelligible to lay readers."   —*Kirkus Reviews*

"Paula Fredriksen . . . does a masterful job of conveying what it must have been like growing up in Jesus' day."
—*The News & Observer* (Raleigh)

"The central question it asks—'Why did Jesus die the way he did?'—strikes to the very core of the debate over the historical Jesus . . . There is much new here." —*Publishers Weekly*

"An important contribution to the vast and proliferating literature on the historical Jesus." —*Booklist*

Paula Fredriksen

JESUS OF NAZARETH, KING OF THE JEWS

Paula Fredriksen currently holds the William Goodwin Aurelio Professorship of the Appreciation of Scripture at Boston University, where she has taught since 1990. An historian of ancient Christianity, Fredriksen holds degrees from Wellesley College (1973), Oxford University (1974), and Princeton University (1979). In 1988 she was awarded the Yale University Press Governors' Award for Best Book for her earlier study, *From Jesus to Christ: The Origins of the New Testament Images of Jesus;* in 1999 her *Jesus of Nazareth, King of the Jews* won the National Jewish Book Award. Fredriksen lived in Jerusalem in 1994–95 as a Lady Davis Visiting Professor at The Hebrew University. She is also the author of *Augustine on Romans* and many other studies on Paul, Augustine, ancient Jewish-Christian relations, and conversion in late antiquity.

ALSO BY PAULA FREDRIKSEN

From Jesus to Christ:
The Origins of the
New Testament Images of Jesus

Augustine on Romans

JESUS OF NAZARETH, KING OF THE JEWS

A JEWISH LIFE AND THE EMERGENCE OF CHRISTIANITY

Paula Fredriksen

VINTAGE BOOKS
A Division of Random House, Inc.
New York

For my mother, Erselia,
and my daughters,
Aliza, Noa, and Hannah

FIRST VINTAGE BOOKS EDITION, DECEMBER 2000

Copyright © 1999 by Paula Fredriksen
Maps copyright © 1999 by David Lindroth, Inc.

The Library of Congress has cataloged the Knopf edition as follows:
Fredriksen, Paula, 1951–
Jesus of Nazareth, King of the Jews : a Jewish life and the emergence of
Christianity / by Paula Fredriksen. — 1st ed.
p. cm.
Includes bibliographical references and indexes.
ISBN 0-679-44675-3
1. Jesus Christ—Biography. 2. Bible. N.T. John—Historiography. I. Title.
BT301.2F74 1999
232.9'01—dc21
[B] 99-31054
CIP

Vintage ISBN: 0-679-76746-0

Author photograph © Boston University Photo Service
Book design by Cassandra J. Pappas

www.vintagebooks.com

Printed in the United States of America
10   9   8   7   6   5   4   3   2   1

It often happens that those who live at a later time are unable to grasp the point at which the great undertakings or actions of this world had their origin. And I, constantly seeking the reason for this phenomenon, could find no other answer than this, namely that all things (including those that at last come to triumph mightily) are at their beginnings so small and faint in outline that one cannot easily convince oneself that from them will grow matters of great moment.

—Matteo Ricci, *Historia, Fonti Ricciane*
in Jonathan Spence, *The Memory Palace of Matteo Ricci*

CONTENTS

Contents

ILLUSTRATIONS

ACKNOWLEDGMENTS

HOW DOES the short-spoken, powerful exorcist-healer of Mark's Gospel relate to the loquacious hero of John's? Why does Matthew's Jesus revile the Pharisees, while Luke's Jesus virtually befriends some? How do these various interpretations of the figure of Jesus, all written in the final third of the first century, relate to the triumphant cosmic agent so blazingly announced by Paul some fifteen to forty years earlier? And how well do any of these later Greek documents afford a glimpse of the Galilean Jew executed by Rome around the year 30, whose mission and message inaugurated a movement that would ultimately transform the West?

I attempted to answer these questions in my earlier book, *From Jesus to Christ*. Most of my discussion there focused on the development of the New Testament's theological images of Jesus. The actual person whose Jewish life and Roman death stood at the source of these later Christian images, however, proved more elusive; and my chapter specifically on the historical Jesus was a scant four pages long. I felt that I needed to know more before I could say more.

In the ten years of reading and thinking that stand between that effort and this one, I have benefitted enormously from my encounters with a broad range of people variously engaged or interested in current historical research on Jesus of Nazareth. Senior colleagues in the field—particularly Marc Borg,

Dom Crossan, Ed Sanders, Geza Vermès, and Tom Wright—have made room for me in their fractious fellowship. Over the years we have commented on each other's ideas and presented our own in numerous panels, seminars, joint lectures, and professional meetings as we all work with common commitment (and occasional consensus) in the effort to reconstruct the Jesus of history. The passionate intellectual attention of the many different communities who have invited me to speak before them—churches of all different denominations, equally various synagogue groups, communities engaged in interfaith dialogue, intensive learning sessions for pastors, nonspecialist audiences intrigued by this period of history—has continuously renewed my own sense of the public importance of this research. Perhaps most of all, my own students at Boston University, undergraduate and graduate, both from the College of Arts and Sciences and from the School of Theology, have pushed me to reflect critically on and to think more clearly about the questions and issues that currently shape the quest for the historical Jesus. I am profoundly grateful.

More debts: Sandra Dijkstra, literary agent extraordinaire, first prodded me to shape my ideas into the sort of book that could bring the latest scholarship to the broadest reading public. Producer Marilyn Mellowes of WGBH, Boston's Public Broadcasting station, together with my colleague Mike White of the University of Austin, involved me intimately with their PBS special *From Jesus to Christ: The First Christians*. It was thrilling to see close up how effectively television can serve as an instrument of education. John Loudon, editor at HarperSanFrancisco, criticized an early draft and gave me many helpful suggestions, even though he knew I was taking my manuscript elsewhere: I deeply appreciate his intellectual and professional generosity.

Special thanks to Bill Green of the University of Rochester, whose invitation to spend the summer of 1994 digging at Yodefat in the Galil—the Jotapatha of Book 3 of Josephus' *Jewish War*—enabled me to plug a hole in my own text-based training with a season of remedial archaeology. My learned friend Oded Irshai of the Department of Jewish History at the Hebrew University walked me again and again, in wet weather and dry, through the ruins of Herod's Jerusalem. Guy Stroumsa and David Satran enabled me to spend 1994–95 in Israel as a Lady Davis Visiting Professor at the Hebrew University in the Department of Religion. Simply being in the country for a whole year sharpened my sense of its topography, its seasons, and the ways that the cycles of Shabbat and of the High Holidays, even in our own secular age, shape Jewish time and social life. Herschel Shanks and the staff at the Biblical Archaeological Society aided my search for pertinent photographs with enthusiasm and efficiency. When I began to conceive that the Gospel of John might in some ways surpass the Synoptics as historical evidence for the shape of Jesus' mission, I was abetted in my heresy by the valuable insights, knowledge, and wisdom of John Ashton and Brian Rice McCarthy. Ed Sanders interrupted his prodigious schedule of research and writing to read the penultimate version of my entire manuscript: he saved me from many errors, and forced me to sharpen my argument. My chairman at Boston University's Department of Religion, John Clayton, and my dean, Dennis Berkey, secured my leave of absence in the fall of 1998: without their understanding and active support, I would doubtless still be fighting with my first draft. The staff at Knopf fielded all my incoming phone calls, FedExes, and faxes with efficiency and good cheer. Finally, my editor, Vicky Wilson, with firmness, understanding, laser-keen scrutiny, and dry good humor, kept both me and my project on track. To all, my deepest thanks.

During the time that I worked on this book, the affection and support of friends and family steadied me in essential ways. For their loyalty and love I thank especially my mother, my daughters, and Zev.

CHRONOLOGICAL TABLE

167 Seleucid ruler Antiochus Epiphanes introduces pagan rites at Jerusalem Temple, triggering the Maccabean revolt.

Daniel

141 Victorious priestly Hasmonean family established as ruling dynasty of an independent Jewish kingdom. Origins of Dead Sea Scroll community.

63 Roman general Pompey conquers Jerusalem, penetrates Temple.

Hasmoneans now rule as client kings of Rome.

37 Herod becomes sole ruler. Expands Second Temple on a magnificent scale.

c. 4 Birth of Jesus according to Gospel of Matthew.

Herod dies, dividing his kingdom between sons Archelaus (Judea), Antipas (Galilee and Perea), and Philip (Transjordan).

COMMON ERA (C.E.)

6 Augustus deposes Archelaus. Judea becomes a second-grade province under a prefect (colonial governor) subordinate in turn to the provincial legate of Syria. The census for tax purposes entailed by this new administration triggers revolt led by Judah the Galilean.

Birth of Jesus according to Gospel of Luke.

26 Pontius Pilate appointed prefect of Judea; serves until 36.

c. 28 Jesus baptized by John. John executed by Antipas; beginning of Jesus' mission.

c. 30 Jesus crucified in Jerusalem around Passover; some followers experience resurrection appearances.

c. 33 Paul joins the Christian movement.

c. 36 Pilate dismissed as prefect following incident with the Samaritan prophet; Caiaphas deposed as high priest.

c. 39 Antipas deposed as ruler of Galilee; anti-Jewish outbreak in Alexandria. Caligula attempts to place his own statue in Jerusalem Temple; massive protest strike in Galilee and Judea.

41 Agrippa I rules Judea, which reverts to Roman administration under a procurator following his death in 44.

c. 45 Mass rallying to Theudas in Judea.

Crucifixion of the sons of Judah the Galilean.

c. 48 Christian assembly in Jerusalem to decide on halakic responsibilities of Gentiles in the Jesus movement; later controversy between Paul and other apostles over same issue in Antioch.

c. 50   Murder of Galilean pilgrims in Samaria.

The Egyptian and the signs prophets gather mass followings in Judea.

Period when Paul writes letters extant in the New Testament collection.

66–68   Judea and Galilee revolt against Rome; Josephus put in charge of the defense of the Galilee. Vespasian conquers the Galilee; later declared emperor.

Settlement at Qumran destroyed. Titus directs siege of Jerusalem.

70   Romans sack Jerusalem, destroy the Second Temple.

73   Romans overrun rebel outpost at Masada, ending revolt.

c. 80–100   Josephus writes *The Jewish War,* then *Jewish Antiquities.*

Period of composition of Gospels of Mark (>70), Matthew, Luke, and probably John; Acts of the Apostles, and other writings that will eventually comprise the New Testament canon.

132–135   Bar Kokhba revolt.

c. 200   Codification of the Mishnah.

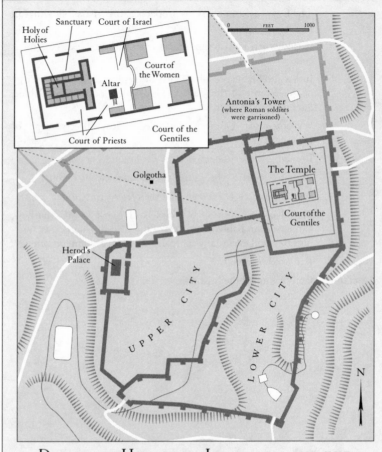

Holy of Holies · Sanctuary · Court of Israel

Altar

Court of Priests

Court of the Women

Court of the Gentiles

0   FEET   1000

Antonia's Tower
(where Roman soldiers
were garrisoned)

Golgotha

The Temple

Court of the Gentiles

Herod's Palace

UPPER CITY

LOWER CITY

N

DETAIL OF HERODEAN JERUSALEM AND THE
TEMPLE IN THE TIME OF JESUS

N

Sidon

SYRIA

Damascus

Tyre

PHOENICIA

Caesarea
Philippi

*Mediterranean
Sea*

GALILEE
(Antipas'
inheritance)

BASHAN
(Philip's inheritance)

Chorazin

Magdala

Capernaum

Sepphoris

Tiberias

Sea of Galilee

Nazareth

Gadara

Caesarea
Maritima

SAMARIA

DECAPOLIS

Gerasa

PEREA
(Antipas'
inheritance)

(Archelaus' inheritance)

Lydda

Jericho

Jerusalem

Bethany

Qumran

Bethlehem

JUDEA

*Dead
Sea*

DETAIL OF
EASTERN
MEDITERRANEAN
IN THE EARLY
FIRST CENTURY

IDUMEA

Masada

ARABIA

0   MILES   20

0   KILOMETERS   20

DACIA

DALMATIA

MOESIA

Rome

MACEDONIA

THR

ITALIA

ACHAEA

Athens

Corinth

CRET

Mediterranean Sea

AFRICA

CYRENAICA

EASTERN MEDITERRANEAN
IN THE FIRST CENTURY

0   MILES   200
0   KILOMETERS   200

Jesus of Nazareth,
King of the Jews

Introduction

THE HISTORY OF THE
HISTORICAL JESUS

C HRISTIANITY HAS always been concerned with the historical Jesus. The Gospels present their religious message through the medium of a life story, providing names and dates in their own narratives—the reign of Herod the Great or Augustus, the tenure in office of Pilate as prefect or Caiaphas as high priest—that orient their story in the flow of public time. Paul himself, though notoriously unconcerned with Jesus before the Crucifixion as opposed to the Risen and Returning Christ, nonetheless still incorporates a key moment in the life of Jesus into his proclamation when he invokes the teaching about the Last Supper: "On the night when he was handed over, the Lord Jesus took bread, and when he had given thanks he broke it and said, 'This is my body' " (1 Cor 11:23f.). The point, both for the evangelists and for Paul, was that Jesus, his elevated status as Redeemer, Lord, Messiah, or Son of God notwithstanding, had acted and operated in a human context, within human time.

Even as formal Christian theology developed and grew, and the language describing the person and work of Christ drew increasingly on the concepts and vocabulary of Greek philosophy, this historical dimension never disappeared. The same bishops who were caught up in endless controversies about the Son and the Trinity, about essences and substances, affirmed their faith in creeds whose content was largely narrative and, thus, historical: "I believe in God . . . and in Jesus Christ his Son our Lord, who was conceived of the Holy Spirit, born of the Virgin Mary, suffered under Pontius Pilate . . ."

The modern quest for the Jesus of history—the project here—was begun and pursued foremost in the university faculties of post-Enlightenment Germany. In part continuing the Reformation's protest against the theological formulations of Roman Catholicism, in part applying the developing methods of scientific historical research to the documents of the ancient church, German scholars blazed the path for critical work on the life of Jesus. Their efforts ended in an impasse almost a century ago, when these academic portraits of Jesus, sketched primarily from the palette of Mark, Matthew, and Luke, polarized around two options: Jesus imagined essentially as a teacher of religious ethics ("The fatherhood of God and the brotherhood of man"), or Jesus as self-designated apocalyptic Messiah (the hero of Albert Schweitzer's great classic *The Quest of the Historical Jesus*). Each interpretation emphasized different aspects of the Gospel tradition: the ethical Jesus, the Sermon on the Mount; the apocalyptic Jesus, those passages on the coming Son of Man, and God's kingdom. And both failed at the same point, namely, on constructing a convincing historical explanation (as opposed to a polemical or theological one) of why Rome would have moved to execute such an essentially religious figure in such a brutally political way.

One hundred years later, where are we? Jesus the charismatic leader; Jesus the existential religious thinker; Jesus the hypnotic healer; Jesus the witty, subversive sage; Jesus the passionate social revolutionary; Jesus the prophet of the End—all these diverse images of Jesus populate the most recent books; all are presented with the same flourish of authority; all are constructed by appeals to the same data. The paperbacks proliferate as the range of the portraits broadens. If this is progress, we might wish for less of it.

Whence this bewildering variety? In part, from the enormous gains made especially in the last fifty years in our knowledge of first-century Judaism, the historical matrix of both Jesus and the early churches. The recovery of the Dead Sea Scrolls, manuscript finds in Egypt and in the

Judean desert, energetic and sustained archaeological research in Judea and the Galilee pursued since the foundation of the modern state of Israel in 1948, and in Jerusalem, particularly around the Temple Mount, since the reunification of the city in 1967—all have contributed to increasing our knowledge and, hence, our interpretive options. In part, too, this variety comes of the new home for New Testament research created, particularly in the United States and Canada, within the religion faculties of liberal arts colleges and universities. Critical and comparative in principle, the modern liberal arts study of religion deliberately draws on the methods of other fields—social anthropology, cultural anthropology, sociology, political theory, literary criticism—to see familiar data through new interpretive prisms.

Proliferation of both data and analytic methods feeds the current superabundance of different images of Jesus. One clear example of the revolutionary effect of new data is the impact that the Dead Sea Scrolls have had on New Testament research. Some of the wildest arguments—that Jesus himself, or perhaps his brother James, was an Essene; that minute fragments of Christian texts can be seen in (emended) Scroll documents; that the Scrolls themselves speak of a crucified Messiah—routinely appear in popular media without seriously affecting the direction most scholars take. But the new knowledge gained through the Scrolls has permanently altered essential perceptions of Gospel material.

Before the Scrolls' recovery, for example, many scholars regarded the Gospel of John as presenting a very Hellenized, fundamentally non-Jewish image of Jesus. They consequently discounted this Gospel as both late and intrinsically nonhistorical, and they favored the synoptic tradition (Matthew, Mark, and Luke) when in search of the Jesus of history. The discovery of the Scrolls—whose place, date, and completely Jewish context is very secure—undermined this view of the Fourth Gospel. For the Scrolls, like John, speak the language of Children of Light and Children of Darkness; they, too, envisage struggle between the two realms. One need not posit, then, as earlier scholars did, that such language and thinking point to a late or non-Jewish origin for John's Gospel. The Scrolls incontrovertibly show that early first-century Judean Jews spoke and thought in similar ways. And an earlier, Jewish context of composition for John's Gospel then reopens the question of its historical value for reconstructing Jesus' life.

New methods complicate our efforts in other ways. Their very variety undermines any possibility of consensus about how to proceed; their

Photograph of the War Scroll from Qumran (1 QM)

"This shall be a time of salvation for the people of God, an age of dominion for all the members of His company, and of everlasting destruction for all the company of Satan. . . . At the season appointed by God, His exalted greatness shall shine eternally to the peace, blessing, glory, joy and long life of the sons of light." A page from the War Scroll (1 QM), part of the ancient sectarian library discovered in caves at Qumran by the Dead Sea. This Scroll gives the battle plan for the apocalyptic struggle between God and evil at the End of the Age. Its dualistic language—"sons of light"/"sons of darkness"—recalls similar phrasing and imagery in the later, Greek text of the Gospel of John.

respective orientations guarantee often disparate results. Do we emphasize political and economic theories on the organization of aristocratic empires? Then, unsurprisingly, we end up with a Jesus whose program addresses these economic and political problems, the inequalities of power, that such empires analyzed in this way are seen to embody and express. Do we look to anthropological studies of shamans in other cultures to understand spontaneous healings in first-century rural Palestine? Then we will analyze the Gospels' accounts of Jesus as exorcist and healer accordingly. Do we use literary methods to refract the evangelical narratives into the layers of tradition that putatively comprise them, isolate those layers that we consider the most ancient, and concentrate our efforts solely on those? If we argue that the earliest layer is sayings rather than story, word rather than deed, we will naturally conclude that Jesus was primarily a teacher. Our efforts then will turn to understanding what he taught, not what he did, since his actions (healings, for example, or exorcisms, or the scene in the Temple) are communicated not in sayings but in story. Narrative on this reading inevitably recedes in importance as primary evidence. In sum: Once method determines our perspective on our sources, *how* we see is really what we get.

All these diverse positions affect, indeed afflict, the current quest. Even though all scholars who work on Jesus look more or less to the Gospels as the mother lode to mine for data, a priori commitments to different methods mean that they actually read different texts. My colleagues who take Jesus' wisdom sayings ("Be wise as serpents and innocent as doves") as the earliest, most authentic tradition that the Gospels preserve portray a Jesus who seems much more like a Cynic philosopher—another purveyor of witty maxims in antiquity—than like a Jewish prophet. My colleagues who look to later rabbinic writings as the closest native context for traditions also visible in the Gospels will see Jesus as a charismatic Galilean Hasid, a pious layperson, beleaguered on that account by the Pharisees, since such men drew the scorn of the more learned and powerful in these later Jewish texts. And my colleagues who stay closest to Mark's story of a Jesus who goes to Jerusalem only once and stages some sort of action at the Temple inevitably see a Jesus whose religious business, in one form or another, essentially challenged the "official" Judaism of his day. The first group emphasize Jesus' sayings when they look at the Gospels; the second, a sketchier version of tensions that become more visible in the later Talmud; the third, the Markan narrative rather than the sayings. The methods introduced in quest of the historical Jesus, in short, have resulted in turn in a de facto quest for a historical Gospel. Once again, diversity—and controversy—dominate.

Do we have any polestar, then, by which we might navigate our way through this confusion? I think we do. Though the word is unfashionable in academic history right now, I shall breathe it anyway, here: We have facts. Facts about Jesus, and facts about the movement that formed after his crucifixion. Facts are always subject to interpretation—that's part of the fun—but they also exist as fixed points in our investigation. Any explanation, any reconstruction of Jesus' mission and message must speak adequately to what we *know* to have been the case. If it cannot, then no matter how elegant an application of interesting methods or how rousing and appealing its moral message, that reconstruction fails as history. It might conjure an image of Jesus that pleases or moves us as religiously meaningful, but that portrait will have only a glancing resemblance to the real person who lived, intact and entirely, within his own culture and in his own time, utterly without obligation to make sense to us in ours.

So let's put our facts up front in order to begin our search here. What do we *know* about Jesus of Nazareth, and how do these facts enable us to start out on the road to a solid and plausible historical portrait of him?

The single most solid fact about Jesus' life is his death: he was executed by the Roman prefect Pilate, on or around Passover, in the manner Rome reserved particularly for political insurrectionists, namely, crucifixion. Constructions of Jesus primarily as a Jewish religious figure, one who challenged the authority of Jerusalem's priests, thus sit uncomfortably on his very political, Imperial death: Pilate would have known little and cared less about Jewish religious beliefs and intra-Jewish religious controversy. The lines spoken in the Acts of the Apostles by Gallio, proconsul in Corinth, capture well the general Roman indifference to the particular religions of subject peoples and Rome's clear sense of where to invest its energies when running an empire. Addressing the group of Corinthian Jews who seek to arraign Paul before the tribunal, Gallio says, "If it were a matter of wrongdoing or vicious crime, I should have reason to bear with you, O Jews. But since it is a matter of questions about words and names and your own law, see to it yourselves: I refuse to be a judge in these things" (Acts 18:14–15).

This problem of linking Jesus' Jewish career with his Roman death challenges many, and extremely diverse, modern reconstructions of Jesus and his message. The more Jesus is imagined as a teacher whose message—be it the witty subversive aphorisms of the wandering Jewish Cynic, the existential ethics of the pious Hasid, or the antinationalist, anti-Temple proclamation of the Galilean visionary—essentially challenges Jewish religious authorities, the harder it is to explain Pilate's role. Explanations range from Jesus' having died by accident (caught up inadvertently by a police action against some sort of demonstration) or by mistake (Rome thought he was incendiary, but he really wasn't), to seeing the supposedly offended priests as the true initiators, who worked out a deal with Pilate for Rome to do what they could not, namely, execute him (this essentially expands the Gospels' view). Against these, other historians have speculated that Jesus actually did lead a more political, rebellious sort of movement than the Gospels dare portray, so that Rome responded rightly as Rome naturally would.

However, Jesus' cross is the stumbling block for all these reconstructions. Those who emphasize his offense to highly placed Jews rightly note that the former and current high priests named in the Gospels, Annas and Caiaphas, together held that office for seventeen of the first twenty years that Judea, hence Jerusalem, was under direct Roman rule: Presumably they had excellent working relations with whatever prefect was in power. If they decided they wanted Jesus out of the way, Pilate may indeed have been perfectly happy to oblige. This can explain Jesus' death at Rome's hand, but not, specifically, his crucifixion. Pilate could have disposed of Jesus easily and without much fanfare, murdering him by much simpler means. (The Gospels' emphasis on Jesus' popularity—"The chief priests and the scribes were seeking how to arrest him by stealth and kill him; for they said, 'Not during the feast, lest there be a tumult of the people' " [Mk 14:1–2]—makes Pilate's decision to crucify him that much odder.) And those who speak to the sharp contrast between Jesus' religious, Jewish message and his political, Roman death must claim that the Gospel stories are deliberately, egregiously misleading, either investing too much meaning, since Jesus truly died by mistake (Rome thought he was politically dangerous, but he wasn't), or obscuring the true meaning, since Jesus really was anti-Roman and political (so Rome was right, by its lights, to crucify him). But these latter theories collide head-on with a second incontrovertible fact we have from the earliest movement: Though Jesus was executed as a political insurrectionist, his followers were not.

Had Rome, mistakenly or not, truly thought that Jesus posed any sort of political threat, more than only Jesus would have died. Pilate never could have risked or tolerated the existence of what he would suppose to be a revolutionary group. Further, the earliest Christian evidence, Paul's letters, written midcentury, depict the disciples as ensconced comfortably in Jerusalem, directing a Mediterranean-wide mission without the slightest hint of constraint from Rome—or, for that matter, from Jerusalem's priestly hierarchy. Clearly, nobody in power was much worried by this movement. Why then did its leader die the way he did?

This is a crucial anomaly. Because it is established by two absolutely secure historical facts, it will serve as the driving wheel for my effort here to reconstruct the Jesus of history. I think that it forces us to conclusions about the Gospel evidence that run radically counter to the prime assumptions of all other current work on Jesus, most especially on the question of why he was killed. I emphatically include my own earlier book, *From Jesus to Christ,* in this group whose conclusions this book challenges. In the eleven years between that publication and this one, my contemplation of this anomaly has steadily eroded my conviction in my previous conclusions. The argument here, then, is my own *pentimento* as well as a fresh chapter in the current quest for the historical Jesus.

The opening two chapters necessarily delay the reader's plunge into the gospel material. The first is on the nature of history, the second on ancient religion, specifically Judaism. The peculiarities of our topic—the historical Jesus and the Jewish origins of Christianity—mandate these prior discussions.

For our knowing what Christianity's future would be makes its past harder to see. Because we seek causes, connections between events that explain them, patterns of meaning in the evidence that remains, we often run the risk of anachronism: Our knowledge of what ultimately happened affects our efforts to convincingly present the experience of those ancient agents whose actions we want to understand and explain. We see causes and impute motivations with a clarity that the actual historical characters could not possibly have had because, unlike us, they did not know what their future held.

In quest of the Jesus of history, this occupational hazard finds expression in the tendency of many scholars to impute to Jesus some thought or action that explains, in a concrete way, what Christianity ultimately became. By the time we have most of the texts that constitute the New Testament—say, by the late first or early second century—the Temple in Jerusalem was no more, Pharisees were emerging as notable sectarian survivors of the Jews' war with Rome, and the ethnic population base of the Christian movement had begun the momentous shift from its Jewish beginnings to its gentile future. Consequently, the ancient Jewish laws and customs enacted at the Temple had little practical application to late first-century religious life, whether Jewish or (to the degree that we can meaningfully distinguish the two communities so early on) Christian. The Pharisees, the most intact group of the post-destruction period, were also the most articulate in preserving and presenting their own particular interpretation of Torah. And Gentiles, whether as pagans or as Christians, had never been held by Jews, nor even by most Christian Jews, as responsible to and for the mandates of the Law. But now as Christians they had become worshipers of the God of Israel. What, then, was to be their relationship to his teachings as conveyed in biblical revelation?

The evangelists incorporate these postdestruction issues into their depictions of Jesus, the founder-figure for their communities. Thus their Jesus, too, exhibits a post-Temple religious consciousness; he, too, has his most charged arguments with Pharisees; he, too, seems turned away from his Jewish present, facing a gentile future. We have no option to drawing on the evangelists: Their writings represent the best body of evidence we have for reconstructing the historical Jesus. But we must be sensitive to the ways that their own historical context, some-time in the last third of the first century, shapes their presentation of Jesus and his: Jewish Galilee and Judea in the days of vigorous sectarian variety, oriented around the vibrant cult of the late Second Temple.

By considering the difficulties of anachronism and the complicated status of the Gospels as evidence (chap. 1), and by imaginatively locat-ing ourselves within the religious world of antiquity, and specifically Jewish antiquity (chap. 2), we can develop some critical purchase on the problems attending most current modern interpretations of Jesus. Our focus on the anomaly that stands at the heart of what we know past doubting to be historically true—that Jesus was executed by Rome as an insurrectionist, but that none of his followers were—together with our increased sensitivity to anachronism, will help us to formulate a new approach to the gospel material. And this approach, in turn, will enable us to see a new answer to that most ancient question that lies at the source of the Christian movement: Why was Jesus crucified?

Jerusalem

JERUSALEM WAS BURNING.

The fire fused with the dry August heat. A thick mass of sounds and smells signaled the end of the siege—stone and burning timbers crashing, soot and dust everywhere, the screams of victim and victor, the dense mix of sweat, blood, and fear from the bodies of the living, the stench from the unburied dead. Above, the white-blue bowl of heaven arched, remote and unmoved by the huge confusion below. Rome's legions—furious, implacable—consumed the ravaged Lower City.

For more than three years the Jews had defied the empire. Their hastily improvised defense of their country failed to hold the north, Galilee; but Jerusalem in Judea, to the south, had profited from the turmoil that followed Nero's death. Within that single year, three emperors had come and gone; the fourth, the general Vespasian, had had to quit the Jerusalem campaign for Egypt in order to secure the purple for himself. Meanwhile, subject peoples at the edges of the empire, encouraged by Rome's distraction, watched with keen interest the progress of the Judean war. Their attention sealed the city's fate: It had to be made an object lesson for others nursing similar dreams of revolt.

If the foreign siege outside the city walls pressed hard upon the people trapped inside, so did the civil war between rival Jewish rebel factions raging within. At first, Jerusalem's priestly aristocrats had directed the revolution, despite their initial opposition to it. They had led the nation for half a millennium, ever since Israel's return from Babylon: Whether as the designated mediators between their own people and some distant international power—Persia, Greek Syria and Egypt, now Rome—or as native priest-kings after the successful Maccabean revolt, these men had long wielded political as well as religious authority. In the beginning of this conflict they had tried, characteristically, to turn their countrymen from rebellion; but when Eleazar, the son of a high priest, called on those serving in the Temple to cease offering sacrifices for the well-being of Rome, the revolt in effect was declared, and the chief priests assumed responsibility for the defense of the city and the nation.

But the Galilee had crumbled before the Roman response, and Zealots and other ardent antiaristocratic revolutionaries, abandoning the debacle, fled south to the capital. They murdered their priestly competition and seized control. Assassination and intimidation kept the balance of power swinging madly. Even with the Romans at the gates, these nationalists paralyzed the interior, dividing Jerusalem into three warring camps, terrorizing the populace, murdering rivals; finally, suicidally, even burning the city's enormous stores of grain lest the other factions profit from them. They slaughtered those Jews who tried to flee. The hapless few who evaded the revolutionaries fell into the hands of the Romans. The soldiers crucified them within eyesight of the city, to further demoralize the Jews trapped within.

Even the beautiful white-and-gold Temple to the God of the Universe, the heart of the city and of the far-flung Jewish nation, finally succumbed to the devouring flames. The intense heat melted precious metals; even limestone burned and burst. The huge stone expanse of the Temple courtyards choked on carnage and confusion as priests, soldiers, terrorists, and civilians all surged toward the sanctuary, the Holy of Holies. In the austere emptiness of this innermost chamber abided the earthly presence of God: "He who swears by the Temple," as Jesus of Nazareth, some forty years earlier, had taught, "swears by it and by Him who dwells in it." Now it, too, perished; and in their grief, defying Rome to the last, two priests—Meir ben

Belgas and Joseph ben Dalaeus—flung themselves into its fires and so perished with it. The entire mountain that it had crowned—*Har ha-Bayit,* the Mountain of the House, God's House—was so "enveloped in flames from top to bottom," an eyewitness later wrote, that it "appeared to be boiling up from its very roots."

Herod the Great, some three generations earlier, had expanded the Temple area on a vast and lavish scale. Its outermost walls, taken together, ran a total length of nearly five thousand feet, almost nine-tenths of a mile. The space within—some thirty-five acres, or 169,000 square yards—could hold, when necessary, almost 400,000 pilgrims. During the great biblical festivals—Sukkot/Tabernacles in the fall, Pesach/Passover in the spring, Shavuot/Pentecost in early summer— the Temple teemed with myriad Jewish pilgrims and intrigued gentile tourists. From all over the world, in caravans overland from Babylonia, in ships traversing the Mediterranean, foreign Jews joined local Galilean pilgrims and the residents of the city so that the population swelled enormously, and so did the priests' duties. All action and attention focused on the Temple at these times, and the priests' chief responsibility was to see that everything ran smoothly and properly.

At Passover in particular, the press could be overwhelming. Priests and pilgrims would come together the week before the feast for the necessary rites of purification mandated by the Torah; and in a few hours on the afternoon leading into the fifteenth day of the month of Nisan, immediately before the holiday of Unleavened Bread began, a huge number of priests—perhaps as many as ten thousand— and an even greater number of worshipers would slaughter and prepare the Passover offering, the lamb or goat required for the sacred meal. So many Jews crowded into Jerusalem annually for these holidays that Roman prefects, who had controlled Judea since shortly after Herod's death, would march their troops from Caesarea, on the coast, up to the city, to control the holiday mob. Ringed round the Temple's perimeter, staring down from its porticoes at the surging crowds, the Roman armed presence encouraged prudence.

Nevertheless, excitement often turned to violence during these festivals. Once, after Herod's death, Jews who had gathered to celebrate Shavuot attacked an avaricious prefect's troops, and general slaughter ensued. At Sukkot seven years before the siege, one Jesus ben Hanan had disturbed other worshipers by suddenly, loudly declaiming the impending destruction of the sanctuary. Disciplined and punished by both Jewish and Roman authorities, he was released to continue his mournful prophecy, which he did most especially on the feast days. Only in the course of the siege was he finally silenced, killed by a Roman missile. But especially at Passover, given its great themes of redemption and national liberation, potential for political agitation was high, Roman nerves taut: It was during a Passover that Pilate, then prefect, had executed some Jews—nobodies, really—as political bandits and insurrectionists. The Roman presence could be as much a provocation as an inducement to order; and it ultimately, again, fell to the chief priests to keep everything moving, safeguarding the troubled peace between the wary Roman governor with his resentful troops and the excited holiday crowds.

Disease, starvation, slaughter—despite the huge numbers of Jews that had perished, huge numbers still remained. This, too, was due to Passover: These people had come to Jerusalem for the feast and been trapped there by the war. With its sanctuary crumbling and its defenses down, the ruined Temple mesa now served as a collecting point for what remained of the city's inhabitants. The Romans oversaw the postbattle triage. Those who had fomented rebellion they summarily executed. Others were sent off to slower deaths, in the mines by hard labor or in the arenas of urban centers, there by wild beasts or gladiatorial combat, for the amusement of the watching public. The tallest, best-looking young survivors were put aside for display in the triumphal procession back in Rome. Slave traders accompanying the army picked over those remaining, aged seventeen and under, for their stock.

The religious convictions that had nourished Jewish dreams of freedom seemed, in retrospect, sadly misconstrued. "Their chief inducement to go to war," wrote the historian Josephus of his own people, "was an equivocal oracle found in their sacred writings, announcing that at that time a man from their country would become the ruler of the whole world." Looking back on these things, Josephus knew that the prophecy actually referred to Vespasian, whose troops had acclaimed him emperor while he was still in Judea. But for those Jews who had put their faith in it, the prophecy had hailed the coming of the Messiah. And Josephus had seen a remarkable and wrenching example of the tenacity of this conviction. In the heat of the Roman assault, with frenzied legions surging about them and the

Arch of Titus in Rome celebrating his victory over Jerusalem

"Most of the spoils that were carried were heaped up indiscriminately, but more prominent than all the rest were those captured in the Temple at Jerusalem—a golden table weighing several hundredweight, and a lampstand similarly made of gold but differently constructed from those we normally use," Josephus, *Jewish War,* 7.149. Josephus here describes Titus' victory procession back in Rome, which celebrated his defeat of Jerusalem. This relief panel from Titus' Triumphal Arch, put up to commemorate that engagement, captures the moment that Josephus describes.

Temple collapsing in ruin, some six thousand Jews—a mixed crowd of men, women, and children—managed to climb to the roof of the last colonnade in the outer court. They had been encouraged by a "false prophet" (so Josephus, with the certainty of retrospect): This man claimed to have received a call from God himself to gather the group and mount the Temple, "to receive the signs of their deliverance." The soldiers, undeterred, fired the columns. None escaped.

The Upper City capitulated. Titus ordered everything razed to the ground. One legion remained behind; the rest moved off. Survivors trickled away in their different directions to slow death or servitude in Egypt, Asia Minor, or Italy. The massive gold table and menorah from the sanctuary, together with a captured scroll of the Law, made their way to Rome, spoils of the war. What was once Jerusalem stood at the smoking epicenter of a blasted landscape: The surrounding territory, devoured by Titus' need for war machines, had been stripped of trees for miles around. Hill and countryside, once green, now denuded, gave way to inevitable erosion. It was Rome's way with rebels. They make a desert, a Roman historian commented later, and they call it peace.

Chapter 1

GOSPEL TRUTH AND
HISTORICAL INNOCENCE

W HERE DO WE GO if we want to answer the question, Who was Jesus of Nazareth? Most historians begin at the same place as the traditional believer, namely, with the documents preserved in the New Testament. The four canonical Gospels—Matthew, Mark, Luke, and John—supplemented by the scattered references to Jesus in the Pauline Epistles, provide the basic building materials for any construction of the historical figure.

But even though the Gospels do provide valuable information, as historical sources for Jesus their status is complicated. For one thing, relative to their subject, they are late. Born, perhaps, in the last years of the reign of Herod the Great (who died in 4 B.C.E.; cf. Mt 2:1; Lk 1:5), Jesus died when Caiaphas was high priest, Pilate the Roman prefect, and Passover fell on a Thursday or Friday (all data suggested by the Gospels' Passion narratives)—that is, c. 30 or 33 C.E. But the Gospels seem to have been composed in the period between the destruction of the Temple or shortly thereafter (70 C.E.) and the close of the first century (c. 90–100 C.E.)—in other words, some forty to seventy years after Jesus' lifetime. As chronological gaps in the ancient historical record go (centuries, for example, yawn between the lifetime of Alexander the Great [d. 323 B.C.E.] and the documents speaking about him) forty to seventy years is not bad at all. Still, when we consider the mutagenic variety and intensity of the social, political, and religious forces bearing down on evolving Christian traditions in that period between Jesus' execution and the earliest narratives about him, we can better appreciate how complex the Gospel evidence really is.

For example, while the traditions they preserve ultimately extend back across the generation or two bridging their day and Jesus' own, the evangelists' narratives embody several important and fundamental differences between their subject and themselves. Jesus of Nazareth was a Galilean religious figure whose vernacular language was Aramaic (a close linguistic cousin to Hebrew) and whose teaching was exclusively oral (we have no writings from him, nor do early sources claim any existed). He apparently restricted his activity to the villages of the lower Galilee and to Jerusalem in the south, perhaps with brief excursions across the Jordan; he also would have traversed Samaria, which lies between the Galilee and Judea, when going to Jerusalem. This is another way of saying that Jesus' audience, like himself, would have been for the most part Aramaic-speaking Jews living in Jewish territory. But the language of the evangelists is Greek, their medium written, not oral. No one knows where the Gospels were composed, nor the identities of their authors—the traditional ascriptions ("Matthew," "Mark," "Luke," and "John") evolved only in the course of the second century: The original texts circulated anonymously. Most scholars assign locations of origin to somewhere in the Greek-speaking cities of the empire. Accordingly, the question of their communities' relations with Gentiles, with gentile culture, and with imperial government looms much larger for the evangelists than it could have for Jesus himself.

In brief, where Jesus' teaching was oral and his setting Jewish, Aramaic, rural, and Palestinian, the evangelists' is written, mixed (that is, Jewish and Gentile both), linguistically Greek, and probably within the matrix of the Diaspora city. Flung out over the gap between these distinctions, across time, space, culture, and ethnicity, are the human filaments of oral tradition. Ultimately, many stories and sayings presented in the Gospels probably do go back across these various frontiers to the original followers of Jesus. But eyewitness testimony is never scientific or objective, first of all because the witness is human. In this particular case, their conviction that Jesus had been raised from the dead, or that he was God's special agent working in history for the redemption of Israel and the world, would inevitably have affected the reports that these witnesses gave: Other witnesses, not so convinced, would and presumably did speak differently (cf. Mt 28:17).

Further, these stories would have been told and retold—by those of the original generation during their lifetimes; by the later, intervening generations for theirs—before achieving the relative stability of writing. Revision and amplification inevitably travel along this chain of transmission, again because its links are human. Since no way exists to compare later oral traditions to the earlier or earliest ones, the degree of change or distortion introduced into the tradition as it evolved, like the people themselves who received and passed it on, is lost, silenced by death.

Nor did the eventual achievement of written form fully stabilize these traditions from and about Jesus, as a simple comparison of these four Gospels shows. The Gospels differ among themselves. Sometimes the matter is undeniable but seemingly unimportant: for example, at Mark 8:27, Jesus asks his disciples, "Who do men say that I am?"; but at Matthew 16:13 he asks, "Who do men say that the Son of Man is?" But larger divergences exist. At the end of this scene, the Confession at Caesarea Philippi, Jesus rebukes Peter as Satan in Mark and Matthew (8:33//16:23); Luke's Jesus is silent (cf. Lk 9:22); John's Gospel lacks any corresponding scene (though cf. 6:68–69). While Mark's Jesus seems overtly hostile toward traditional Jewish observances (e.g., Mk 7:1–23, and Mark's comment at v. 19), Matthew's Jesus, in the Sermon on the Mount, actively endorses them ("Think not that I have come to abolish the law and the prophets; I have come not to abolish but to fulfill them," 5:17). And so on.

To make sense of such contrasting traditions, scholars have to devise interpretive strategies. Do we harmonize these conflicts somehow? Or do we acknowledge the conflict, and then favor one tradition over the other? If so, on what grounds?

Such weighing and choosing, and self-conscious reflection upon the reasons for making our choice, are all part of the process of historical reasoning. As we proceed through the Gospel material, then, the first task must be to become aware of its complications and difficulties as historical evidence. Only once we see, as clearly as possible, what its problems are, can we begin to take advantage of the tradition's virtues—those places from which, however obliquely, we are afforded a glimpse of the historical figure of Jesus. We discern such discrete vantage points in the ancient evidence wherever we can establish a correspondence of elements in Gospel material with other historical data derived independently from non-Gospel sources—from Paul's letters, written some fifteen years before the earliest Gospel, or from the vast body of material preserved in the work of the first-century Jewish historian Josephus, or from other near-contemporary Jewish sources, such as the Dead Sea Scrolls. Where these lines of evidence converge, where the data thicken, we can begin to construct a first-century Jewish historical context—the native environment of Jesus.

It is the contrast between this context and some of the claims made by the later Gospels that enables us to gauge their reliability. If the Gospels claim or depict something that cannot plausibly fit into what else we know about Jesus' period and culture, we have good reason to hesitate to accept the claim or depiction as historically authentic. Of course, both in terms of constructing this first-century context and in terms of amassing data about Jesus, we will never know as much as we would like to know. But we can still know quite a lot.

First things first. What are the problems with taking the Gospels as gospel?

The Synoptic Gospels

CONFLICTING EVANGELICAL TRADITIONS come, broadly speaking, in two types: conflicts between the first three Gospels (the so-called synoptic tradition); and conflicts between the synoptic tradition and John. Let's consider each of these, briefly, in turn.

Scholars refer to Matthew, Mark, and Luke collectively as the synoptic Gospels. This is because they can be "seen together" (Greek: *syn-,* with; *opsis,* visual object): That is, despite divergences, all three are clearly variations on a shared theme. For example, Matthew and Luke both begin with Jesus' birth (though their respective nativity stories differ strenuously with each other); both end with Jesus' post-Resurrection appearances, Matthew's on a mountain back north, in the Galilee, and Luke's in and around Jerusalem (Mt 28:16–20; Lk 24:33–43, cf. Acts 1:3–8). Mark's Gospel, much shorter, begins with Jesus' baptism by John and ends the first Sunday after the Crucifixion with the empty tomb (Mk 1:9, 16:8, this Gospel's original ending). Notwithstanding all the differences of detail, emphasis, style, and characterization both of Jesus and of his disciples, however, these three Gospels all take shape around a common narrative chronology. Once the story of Jesus' public mission is under way, all three present the same basic sequence of events; and for all three, Jesus' mission runs along a one-way trajectory, from the north, in and around the Galilee, to the narrative and theological climax in the south, in Jerusalem.

In all three Synoptics, Jesus comes to John the Baptizer and is himself baptized; the Spirit of God or the Holy Spirit comes down upon him while a voice from heaven declares Jesus "my beloved son" (Mk 1:9–11 and parr.). After a forty-day retreat into the desert during which he is tempted by Satan, Jesus begins his mission. He calls his disciples and begins to travel in the villages of the Galilee, casting out demons, healing the sick (sometimes, controversially, on the Sabbath), calling his disciples, debating with other Jews (most notably scribes and Pharisees) on the meaning of Jewish law, and pronouncing sins forgiven. And he teaches, often in parables, especially about the Kingdom of God and the Son of Man. Once Peter identifies him as the Messiah—"You are the Christ" (Mk 8:29 and parr.)—Jesus predicts his own impending death and resurrection, and soon thereafter, to Peter, James, and John, reveals himself gloriously on a mountain, conversing with Moses and Elijah, as a voice from a cloud again proclaims, "This is my beloved son; listen to him" (the Transfiguration, Mk 9:7 and parr.).

Finally, after spending most of his time in the north, Jesus turns south, to Jerusalem, for Passover. Through the device of the Passion predictions, Jerusalem has cast the shadow of the cross over the entire first movement of Jesus' story: we know that, once in Jerusalem, he will die. After his enthusiastic escort into the city by other Passover pilgrims, Jesus disrupts the sale of sacrificial pigeons in the Temple court and so earns the mortal enmity of the priests. Continuing to teach there in the days before the festival, Jesus predicts the Temple's coming destruction ("There will not be left here one stone upon another that will not be thrown down," Mk 13:2 and parr.) and describes events preceding the End of the Age and the glorious return of the Son of Man—a figure, the reader by now knows, for Jesus himself. Soon thereafter one of his disciples, Judas Iscariot, decides to betray Jesus to the chief priests: This must be accomplished on the sly, because Jesus is so popular with Jerusalem's crowds (Mk 11:18 and parr.; cf. Lk 22:6). At the seder Thursday night, Jesus presents the bread as his body and the wine, his blood, and again predicts his coming death: God's kingdom, he implies, is near (Mk 14:17–25 and parr.).

After their seder, out walking in the darkness, Jesus is identified by Judas and arrested by an armed crowd sent by the priests. Various authorities—the priests at their councils; Pilate, the Roman prefect; perhaps Herod (that is, Herod Antipas, the Jewish ruler of the Galilee and a son of Herod the Great; only Luke claims this, 23:6–12)—interrogate him. At the insistence of the Jewish authorities, who have a crowd on their side, Pilate orders Jesus crucified that Friday morning; by afternoon he is dead. Pilate then permits the body to be buried before the onset of the Sabbath that evening. When some of Jesus' female followers come to the tomb early Sunday morning, they find it empty (Mk 16:1–8 and parr.). Here Mark stops; Matthew and Luke elaborate various post-Resurrection appearances.

Looked at synoptically, the first three canonical Gospels represent a confluence of Christian tradition: they come together to present a reasonably unified picture of the life of Jesus. Looked at critically and analytically, however, their differences emerge, and as our awareness of their divergences grows, so does the need to have some sort of criteria to guide our reading. How do we choose between starkly contrasting, indeed occasionally mutually exclusive, evangelical accounts of the past?

For example, while nativity stories about Jesus do not predominate in the canonical material—two of the four Gospels, Mark and John, are completely silent on the topic—Matthew and Luke each have highly developed though divergent birth narratives. According to Luke, Mary and Joseph live in Nazareth, in the Galilee. They journey south to Bethlehem, the scripturally designated natal town of the Messiah, in time for Jesus' birth. The odd timing of their journey is explained by a Roman census: "In those days a decree went out from Caesar Augustus that all the world should be enrolled" (Lk 2:1. We know from other ancient sources that this tax occurred in the year 6 C.E.—but only in Judea, not in the Galilee). After the birth, they return home to Nazareth. In Matthew, however, Mary and Joseph already live in Bethlehem and so are in situ for the messianic birth. Because of Herod's murderous antagonism, the family then flees to Egypt, returning only once Herod has died (recall, Herod was dead by 4 B.C.E.). Only then do they move north to settle in Nazareth (Mt 1:18–2:23). Of course, neither story may be true. But if we choose to grant credibility to one, it comes at a cost to the other: *both* cannot be true.

Oral traditions and various lines of transmission, spoken and written, span the time between the writing of the Gospels and the life of their subject, Jesus of Nazareth. The different evangelists shaped these into their respective narratives. But the multiplicity of their sources implies a further datum about their nature, namely, that each Gospel in and of itself is really an assemblage, a collection of originally distinct stories or sayings, which each writer could deploy as he would. Hence, for example, Matthew's Jesus, during his Sermon on the Mount, teaches that "you cannot serve God and mammon" when discoursing about the dangers of split loyalties and the nullity of worrying about the future. His essential message is: Don't worry about tomorrow; put your trust in God (Mt 7:24–34). Luke's Jesus says no such thing during his (much briefer) Sermon on the Plain (Lk 6:20–49). But this teaching appears elsewhere, much later in Luke's story, in the course of a long and confusing parable about a dishonest steward (Lk 16:13); there, it sets up an insult to the Pharisees ("The Pharisees, who were lovers of money, heard all this and scoffed at him," 16:14).

Let us say that we are convinced that, behind the Greek, this verse preserves an actual teaching of Jesus. What did he mean by it? Context helps determine content, by providing an environment of meaning within which to place our interpretation. "I love you" means one thing when Juliet says it to Romeo, something else when Iago says it to Othello. So, too, with the different contexts here. If, as scholars conjecture, a contextless list of some sayings and stories about Jesus circulated, whether as oral tradition or as a (now lost) document, then *both* evangelists created *new* contexts that in turn effected a new interpretive content for the saying. Thus, if we think that Jesus of Nazareth did really say, "You cannot love both God and mammon," we need to know his situation when he said it to understand further what he would have meant. Was he uttering a generic human truth? Or was he moving into a specific polemic against another Jewish group? The evidence as it stands cannot help settle the issue. The same phrase, positioned differently, yields two different meanings.

Finally, crucial matters of fact are in dispute. This is nowhere more so than in the Passion narratives, which many scholars hold to have been one of the earliest and, because so important, most stable blocks of tradition. Matthew and Mark have Jesus appearing before two full sessions of a council, convened at night after the seder, and consisting of the high priest, chief priests, scribes, and elders (Mk 14:53, 15:1//Mt 26:57, 27:1). In both, also, the high priest and Jesus have a highly fraught exchange at the dramatic pinnacle of the hearing: "Are you the Christ, the Son of the Blessed?" "I am" (Mk 14:61–62; cf. Mt 26:63–64); and in both, the high priest pronounces Jesus' words blasphemy (Mk 14:64//Mt

26:65). Luke, however, has no night trial. A single conference is held in the morning, no dialogue between Jesus and the high priest ensues, no accusation of blasphemy pronounced (Lk 22:54–70). And John lacks a Jewish trial scene altogether. There, the action takes place on a different evening—still a Thursday, but with respect to the holiday, on the night *before* the night of the seder—and the high priest Caiaphas and his father-in-law, Annas, without any council, briefly and separately interrogate Jesus before passing him on, without comment, to Pilate (Jn 18:12–32).

We have no way, simply looking at these texts, to decide which is more reliable or even more plausible. To judge between the evangelists, we have to look at other types of historical evidence—histories of the period, such as those of Josephus; traditions of Jewish and of Roman law; records, where we can find them, of Rome's judicial practices in its provinces—and use those to reconstruct an early first-century historical context. Only once this general historical context is as clear as it can be do we have a standard of judgment, and an interpretive criterion, by which to sift the Gospel material.

This process of building up a context, a "thick description" of the immediate environment drawn critically from as many contemporary sources as possible is, again, fundamental to the process of historical reasoning in general, and to reconstructing the historical Jesus in particular. If something presented by the evangelists cannot be fitted into a responsible reconstruction of Jesus' own period, then there is reason to question its historical reliability. If one evangelist's story coheres better with a reconstruction of early first-century Palestinian Jewish concerns than another, then we have a reason to prefer the one to the other in our quest for the Jesus of history, himself an early first-century Palestinian Jew. This process of reconstruction and critical assessment, further, alerts us to anachronism, both in the evangelists' presentations and in our interpretations of them. Anachronism, the viewing of persons or events out of their own historical context, is the first and last enemy of the historian, and I will have more to say on it below. Here I simply want to emphasize that the Gospels in themselves cannot settle questions about their own historical authenticity.

So far I have emphasized conflict in this comparison of synoptic Gospels. But what about confluence? What accounts for the substantial areas of agreement between them?

Since the beginnings of scientific Gospel criticism in the modern period, scholars have speculated that the resemblances between the

Synoptics, especially their common chronology, echo some relation of literary dependency between them. Virtually every combination has been proposed and defended: that Luke used Matthew, or vice versa; that Mark used both, but condensed them; that Matthew's Gospel, originally Aramaic, was translated into Greek only later, and thus was the earliest.

Most scholars today accept the (not uncontested) view that Mark wrote first, that Matthew and Luke used Mark independently of each other, and that, besides Mark, these later evangelists also had access to another Greek source on Jesus that contained more of his sayings as well as some stories about him. Scholars designate this last "Q," from the German *Quelle,* meaning "source": Jesus' teaching on God and mammon is an example of such sayings material. This so-called two-source hypothesis thus addresses two questions. The first is: What accounts for the agreements between these three Gospels? Answer: Matthew and Luke each used Mark. The second question, then, concerns the agreement between these two later Gospels: If they are independent of each other, why do Matthew and Luke verbally replicate so much material not found in Mark? Answer: They also shared another source, the now lost Q. Was Q actually a document? Or was it a collection of sayings and stories that circulated orally? We cannot know. Its most secure existence is definitional: Q is that material common to Matthew and Luke that does not appear in Mark.

Their use of Mark and Q not only explains the patterns of resemblance between the two later synoptic Gospels; it increases our awareness of how these evangelists worked. Matthew and Luke were not only authors but also redactors, creative editors of earlier traditions that they changed even as they preserved. Further, to present their portraits of Jesus they also redacted a text much more ancient and prestigious than Mark. These later synoptists also edited biblical tradition in the form of the Septuagint (academic designation: LXX), a Greek translation of the Jewish Scriptures done by and for Greek-speaking Jews during the third and second centuries B.C.E.

All ancient Christians turned to the Bible in order to interpret and defend their understanding of the redemption that God had worked through Christ. Citations of and references to the Bible pervade the earliest strata of the tradition—indeed, its religious dependence on the Bible is the index of the early movement's intrinsic Jewishness. Thus when Paul refers his Corinthian congregation to Christ's death and resurrection, he says simply (and, alas, without naming what passages he had in mind), "Christ died for our sins, in accordance with the Scriptures" (1 Cor 15:3). Christ in the Epistle to the Hebrews—high priest, minister in the heavenly tabernacle, perfect blood sacrifice (5:5, 9:11–14)—is an assemblage of various Levitical images from the Torah. And without the words of Isaiah, Daniel, and Ezekiel, the Book of Revelation would be unimaginably different. At once both bedrock and building block, the Greek version of the Jewish Scriptures in fundamental ways formed early Christian proclamation.

But the evangelists' use of the Bible went boldly beyond such theological applications. In the Septuagint, the Gospel writers felt they had a third historical source for information about the life and especially the death of Jesus. We see this most clearly in Matthew, who often prefaces or concludes some action or story with the words, "This was done in order to fulfill the words which were spoken of by the prophet" (whether such a prophecy exists in Jewish Scripture or not). This creative usage of the Septuagint clearly shapes both synoptic birth narratives. The tradition that Jesus' mother was a virgin at the time of his birth, for example, draws on a prophecy available only in the Greek version of Isaiah 7:14: In the original Hebrew, the word that stands behind the Septuagint's *parthenos, *"virgin," is ʿ*aalmah,* "young girl." And this biographical usage of ancient Scriptures likewise shapes all four evangelists' presentation of the Crucifixion scene, where the continuous action of the Gospel narratives actually breaks down into a multitude of references to various lines from the prophets, Proverbs, and Psalms. In light of such dense citation, historians have to ask whether the existence of the scriptural image did not create the details or even the action of the story.

Put differently: The source for a Gospel story about Jesus might lie not in some transmitted tradition going back to a contemporary eyewitness in the early first century, when Jesus lived, but in the religious authority of the distant biblical past. The Gospel story thus may give information about the evangelist's reading of biblical tradition, and thus also about his theological interpretation of the figure of Jesus. We learn little, however, about Jesus of Nazareth himself. But the contrary also holds: Just because an evangelist refers to the Bible when presenting an episode in Jesus' life or an element of his teaching does not mean he necessarily constructs the episode or element himself. His biblical gloss of it notwithstanding, the tradition itself may be authentic. In light of these complexities, all Gospel material must be weighed and judged before it can serve as evidence for the historical Jesus.

The Synoptics and John

MARK SERVES AS the narrative linchpin of the two-source hypothesis: His is the Gospel that provides the sequence of events, and in some sense the basic plot, for Matthew and Luke. Since the turn of the twentieth century, however, scholars have grown increasingly aware of the degree to which Mark himself is also a redactor, an editor of earlier traditions. Mark, too, inherited his material from different sources, in different forms—miracle stories, parables, controversy stories, healings. Were these written or oral? How did he decide to organize what he had? Did he have access to some earlier, now lost, historically reliable chronology of Jesus' mission? Or did he himself assemble what he inherited, joining bits of tradition with the connective tissue of his own imagining, arranging them for his own purposes—polemical, theological, political—into the sequence that ultimately went on to shape the later Synoptics? To answer this question, we must consider Mark together with his canonical alternative, John.

Recall that Mark opens with John the Baptizer's mission (in Judea? 1:5, 9; cf. v. 14). John baptizes Jesus who, after a period of withdrawal, begins his own mission, taking the gospel message—"The Kingdom of God is at hand!"—to the villages of the lower Galilee. He calls his disciples, works exorcisms and cures, quarrels with other Jews over issues of observance, and wanders well east of the Sea of Galilee into Gentile areas (5:1–21) and northwest "to the region of Tyre and Sidon" (7:31). The content of Jesus' preaching, in other words, has nothing to do with his own identity. In fact, he is so notoriously reticent on this point, silencing demons when they recognize him (see 1:23–26), ordering those whom he cures to keep quiet (e.g., 1:40–43), that scholars have designated the "messianic secret" a major motif of Mark's Gospel. This reticence in turn highlights Peter's confession near Caesarea Philippi where, without any preparation in the story, Peter declares "You are the Christ" (8:29). (Typically, Mark's Jesus responds ambiguously. Matthew rewrites this scene in part to remove any doubt that Peter had identified Jesus correctly: cf. Mk 8:29–33 and Mt 16:16–23.) Peter's confession in turn prompts Jesus' first Passion prediction: "And he began to teach them that the Son of man must suffer many things, and be rejected by the chief priests and the scribes, and be killed, and after three days rise again. And he said this plainly" (8:31–32).

From this point on, Jerusalem exerts a gravitational pull over the rest of the story. (It is the arena of the "chief priests.") Jesus repeats this prediction two more times, the last explicitly when he and his disciples are on the way to the city for Passover. "Behold, we are going up to *Jerusalem,* and the Son of man will be delivered to the *chief priests* and the scribes, and *they will condemn him to death,* and deliver him to the Gentiles" (10:33).* Hailed as "Son of David" by a blind man on the Jericho road up to the city (10:47–48), Jesus is soon swept into Jerusalem by excited pilgrims who proclaim him the one "who comes in the name of the Lord" even as they hail "the kingdom of our father David that is coming! Hosanna!" (11:10). Jesus proceeds to the Temple area, then withdraws to the nearby village of Bethany, and returns to the Temple the next day.

In the Temple's courtyard, Jesus creates a scene that paralyzes all activity, driving out those buying and selling in the outer courtyard (Mark specifies those merchants selling pigeons for sacrifice and money changers, who would charge a fee for the service, 11:15–17). This alienates the chief priests and scribes, who "fear" him and resolve to kill him: They "sought a way to destroy him; for they feared him, because all the multitude was astonished at his teaching" (11:19). Nonetheless, Jesus continues going to the Temple, at one point predicting its utter destruction. When his disciples ask when this will happen, Jesus describes events that must occur first—false messiahs, wars, the persecution of his followers, the evangelization of the nations, an "abomination of desolation" set up where it should not be. (Mark here prompts his audience—"Let the reader understand!" (13:14)—to recall the reference that, drawn from Dn 9, implies the Temple.) It is after all these things occur that the Son of Man will return in glory to gather his elect. "Truly I say to you, this generation will not pass away before all these things take place" (13:30).

The priests meanwhile, Mark claims, have resolved to arrest Jesus by stealth and kill him: They know that they must be cautious because Jesus is so popular (the arrest must not take place "during the feast, lest there be a tumult of the people," 14:2). After the sacrifice of the paschal lambs, Jesus holds a Passover meal, offers the bread and wine as a sort of Passion prediction (the bread is his body; the wine his blood, "poured out for many"), and again predicts his own resurrection (v. 28). After the meal, he is ambushed by a crowd sent by the priests and led to their plenum assembly. "False witnesses" accuse him of threatening to

---

* Wherever *italics* appear in quotations, I have added them for emphasis.

destroy the Temple: "We heard him say, 'I will destroy the Temple that is made by hand, and in three days I will build another not made by hand' " (14:58). Jesus' refusal to respond prompts the high priest to ask, "Are you the Christ, the son of the Blessed?" At this point Jesus finally, publicly proclaims his true identity: "I am. And you will see the Son of man seated on the right hand of Power and coming with the clouds of heaven" (v. 62).

Accusing him of blasphemy (evidently on account of this identification), the priests hand Jesus over to Pilate, who, without enthusiasm, crucifies him as "The King of the Jews" (15:26). Passersby and the chief priests mock him and his prediction of the Temple's destruction. "Aha! You who would destroy the Temple and build it in three days, save yourself and come down from the cross! . . . Let the Christ, the King of Israel come down now from the cross that we may see and believe!" (15:26–32). Just as Jesus dies, Mark reports, the curtain of the Temple "was torn in two, from top to bottom" (v. 38). Seeing Jesus die, a centurion—significantly, a Gentile—suddenly declares, "Truly this man was the Son of God." The last scene is in Jerusalem, when women followers of Jesus discover the empty tomb. The angel who awaits them there reminds them of Jesus' earlier prediction: He is risen, and he awaits the disciples in the Galilee (16:6–7; cf. 14:28 at the Last Supper).

Now contrast John. Two differences from Mark's work leap out immediately: Jesus' itinerary and his character. The Johannine Jesus weaves back and forth between the Galilee and Jerusalem at least four times. When there, he invariably goes to the Temple, because he comes for the pilgrimage festivals, Passover (at least twice, chap. 2 and chap. 12) and Sukkot (7:10); once for the celebration of the Maccabees' purification of the Temple (the later tradition's Hanukkah, 10:22); and once for an unspecified feast (5:1). The text even implies that he lives in Jerusalem for a period of roughly four months, from the fall holiday of Sukkot (7:10) through to the winter holiday celebrating the Temple's purification (10:22).

Equally striking is John's placement of the incident in the Temple. His Jesus drives money changers and pigeon merchants (as well as sheep and oxen!) out of the Temple in the early stages of his mission (2:13–17). Mark, remember, had also placed this scene at the beginning of Jesus' entry into Jerusalem. But in Mark, Jesus' pilgrimage is the finale of his mission: He comes to Jerusalem only once, and this incident specifically mobilizes the fatal hostility of the priests: in this sense, Jesus' action is the trip-switch for Mark's Passion narrative. Mark must, therefore, place the scene toward the end of Jesus' mission. John's, on the contrary, comes so soon in his story that it cannot trigger the actions leading to the Passion: otherwise, the Gospel would be over before it were under way.

Still, John's Temple scene does refer to Jesus' coming Passion, and in a way that curiously recalls another Markan theme—the relation between Jesus' fate and that of the Temple. To select one out of a number of instances: Mark connected the ideas of destruction and restoration with the phrase "three days" in two dramatic, key contexts: in Jesus' predictions of his own Passion and Resurrection ("The Son of Man must *be killed* . . . and after *three days rise* again," 8:31, 9:31, 10:34); and in the accusation attributed to him before the priests' council ("We heard him say, 'I will *destroy* this Temple that is made by hand, and *in three days* I will *build* another, not made by hand," 14:58, mockingly repeated at the Crucifixion, 15:29). John's Jesus himself makes the connection explicit, though the agents of the Temple's destruction, in his rendering, shifts from Jesus to Jerusalem's Jews: "Jesus answered them [the Jews], '*Destroy* this Temple, and *in three days* I *will raise* it up.' . . . *But he spoke of the temple of his body.* When therefore he was raised from the dead, his disciples remembered that he had said this" (Jn 2:19–22). For John, the significance of the actual Temple is subsumed utterly by its Christological significance: The whole image of the destroyed Temple signifies the Passion. The Temple's function here is symbolic, not (as in Mark) dramatic.

Furthermore, Mark's Jesus had confided his Passion predictions only to his disciples; John, as we have just seen, publicly broadcasts the news to followers and enemies alike. This points to a second major distinction between the two Gospels, one that will affect any assessment of their respective order of events: the evangelists' different depictions of Jesus' character.

Mark's Jesus is a man of action: dashing, busy, driven in rapid motion from synagogue to invalid, from shore to grainfield to sea, commanding demons with authority, even ordering nature to obey his will. At his word, a sea storm calms and the fig tree withers (4:39, 11:14, 20). These demonstrations of power in turn underscore Jesus' twin message: the Kingdom is at hand, and the Son of Man has the authority to announce its advent. The story itself makes clear to the reader that this "Son of Man" is really Mark's Jesus; but Mark allows his protagonist to get no more specific about his own identity than this. In fact, Mark's Jesus seems to hide his identity in obscure speech even as he announces it in decisive actions. Though by "Son of Man" Mark's Jesus clearly intends himself (e.g., 8:31), he nonetheless speaks of this figure only in the third person; and he routinely demands silence from those who realize who he really is: the Son of Man, the Messiah (8:29, 14:61–62), the Son of God. "And whenever the unclean spirits beheld him, they fell down before him and cried out, 'You are the Son of God!' And he strictly ordered them not to make him known" (3:11–12). To the disciples, after Peter had identified him as the Messiah: "And he charged them to tell no one about him" (8:30); after the voice from the cloud names Jesus " 'My beloved son,' . . . he [Jesus] charged them [the disciples] to tell no one what they had seen" (9.9).

These three designations for Jesus—Son of Man, Son of God, Messiah—all come together only at the dramatic high point of Mark's story, the trial before the high priest. Right after the accusation that Jesus threatened the Temple's destruction, the high priest puts the question (14:61). Only here does Jesus openly affirm his identity, and it is his affirmation that leads directly to his sentence of death (vv. 57–64).

The two points to note here are that Jesus' identity is hidden at his own command until he gets to Jerusalem; and that his identity is bound up, through his death, with the destruction of the Temple. Mark structured his Gospel around this paradox of hiddenness and recognition, which he dramatically resolves by leading his main character, Jesus, along his deliberate one-way path from the north (hiddenness) to Jerusalem (revelation). Further, his Jesus predicts in chapter 13 that, once the Temple is destroyed, the Son of Man will return, glorious, to gather his elect. Jerusalem and the Temple thus play a key role in the revelation of the Son. As Mark presents his story, Jesus' very itinerary— the single, dramatic approach to Jerusalem—underscores this process of revelation. In other words, the sequence of events in Mark's story itself assists the theological message of his Gospel. Jesus' full identity as Messiah, Son of God, and suffering and triumphant Son of Man is revealed or (according to the prophecy in chap. 13) will be revealed only in Jerusalem.

John's eloquent, talkative Jesus is under no such constraint. From his opening dialogue with Nicodemus to the closing bel canto soliloquies on the night of his arrest, this Jesus proclaims his own high theological identity. He is the Son of God, the Son of Man, and the Christ. And his speeches also teem with a multitude of sacramental metaphors: "I am the bread of life . . . from heaven" (6:35–38), the light of the world (8:12, 9:5), the source of living water (4:7–15), the Sheepgate (10:7–10), the Resurrection and the Life (11:25), the Way and the Truth (14:6), the True Vine (15:1). Jesus is the only one who has come down from above, from the Father, to the world below; and therefore only those who acknowledge him can see beyond this lower world to the realm above; only they can know the Father (6:45–46, 8:21–58). And he speaks openly and frankly of his own extrahuman status: "Before Abraham was, I am" (8:58) and, yet more daringly, "I and the Father are one" (10:30).

John's Jesus, in other words, straightforwardly pronounces the evangelist's sophisticated theological beliefs about him. John's religious and literary interests center on and are showcased by the lengthy Christological monologues and extended discourses of his main character. His Gospel's choppy narrative structure, by contrast, serves mainly as a frame from which to hang Jesus' speeches: It is merely incidental to John's central concerns. And since his Jesus openly and from the beginning teaches his own elevated theological status, that self-identification cannot serve, as it did in Mark before the high priest, as the reason for Jesus' execution. Why, then, is he killed? John presents the priests together with the Pharisees determining to kill Jesus because they fear that his activities will somehow jeopardize the Temple and the people: "If we let him go on in this way . . . the Romans will come and destroy both our holy place [i.e., the Temple] and our nation." And Caiaphas the high priest adds, "It is expedient for one man to die for the people, and that the whole nation should not perish" (11:48, 50).

Perhaps we need not choose between these two different chronologies; perhaps we can fit the briefer timespan Mark depicts into the longer one of John. But then, what of the incident at the Temple? Could Jesus have made exactly the same dramatic protest *twice,* once early on in his mission and once at its end? Then we would have to account for the priests' motivation in arresting him: Why be offended and alarmed—even surprised—if such protest were a near-annual occurrence when Jesus was in town? Perhaps we should prefer John's depiction. Jesus' multiple pilgrimages to the city make historical sense. Galileans routinely went back and forth for the pilgrimage festivals; two-plus years (as implied) gives Jesus more time to establish his mission and proclaim his message. In light of his subsequent impact on history, a longer period during which his message could take root is, perhaps, intrinsically more plausible. Or maybe Mark's depiction is better: A short period of public activity conforms better to the itinerancy and poverty that Jesus evidently urged on his disciples. But Mark's chronology so immediately recapitulates his Christology: Could this really be incidental? If deliberate, then isn't Mark's narrative sequence itself evidence of his freedom and creativity as a redactor?

Again, perhaps the issue could be settled by a sort of majority vote: It's a three-to-one split in favor of one single, climactic ascent to Jerusalem. But Matthew and Luke do not represent independent traditions in this sense. Their chronologies support Mark's because Mark is the source of their own. The decision gets down to an even split: Mark or John.

Again, considering these Gospels by themselves cannot settle the issue. We need to assess their respective plausibility and coherence by setting them within their contemporary social and religious context, and against what we can reconstruct of Jesus' own context some forty to sixty years prior to the Gospels. It is this setting, constructed from other ancient sources, together with a careful reading of our primary evidence, that can help us gain some traction up the slippery slope of evangelical chronology. And figuring out when Jesus did what—the point of a chronology—will help us better perceive what he might have thought was the goal of his mission, and why the priests and the Romans stopped him.

Anachronism and Willed Innocence

Putting together a picture of Jesus' historical context requires no less interpretive work than does reading the Gospels in the first place. But for this project there are many more sources to draw on, both literary and archaeological. The literary sources themselves are richer: Simply taking the two main works of Josephus alone, *The Jewish War* (*BJ*) and *Jewish Antiquities* (*AJ*), increases by a significant order of magnitude the store of information about the Galilee and Judea than what we have from the evangelists alone. And Josephus himself stands no farther from the lifetime of Jesus than do the evangelists. Further, he was a participant in or an eyewitness to major events of his people and century. A young man at the outbreak of the rebellion against Rome in 66, he was from a well-connected priestly family in Jerusalem, where he served in the Temple. He attempted the defense of the Galilee; captive, later, he witnessed the siege of the city. We can augment his reports by appeal to some of the writings of Philo of Alexandria, an elder contemporary of Jesus and Paul who himself made the pilgrimage to Jerusalem. And we can build up a dossier of relevant data by gleaning the writings of pagan authors—Pliny the Elder, a first-century Roman naturalist who visited Palestine; or the late first-century Roman historian Tacitus, whose writings also treat the Jewish war. While these sources tell us little or nothing directly about Jesus himself, they help us to understand his world.

If these documents form one trajectory of evidence through the first century, then the assorted religious writings and documents specific to various forms of late Second Temple Judaism provide another. This specifically Jewish religious context, built up from a rich collection of texts and commentaries—the so-called Apocrypha and Pseudepigrapha, documents written in the late Second Temple or the early Roman period borrowing the name and prestige of ancient religious figures like Enoch or Moses or Solomon; the vast library preserved in the Dead Sea Scrolls; some of the letters and sermons collected in the New Testament—tells us how other Jews of Jesus' period interpreted the Bible, hence their own history and their place in it. The ideas of the Kingdom of God, the resurrection of the dead, the end of evil, the establishment of a new or renewed Temple, the universal acknowledgment of God's sovereignty—on the evidence of the Gospels, themes sounded by Jesus himself—shaped the hopes and convictions of many Jews in this period. By acquainting ourselves with their teachings, we gain an insight into the range of contemporary meanings of these terms, and hence into the meaning they might have held for Jesus as well.

Finally, there is the trajectory provided by specifically Christian evidence. The Gospels obviously figure as the prime source. But equally important, for different reasons, are the letters of Paul.

Paul stands as a sort of halfway point between Jesus of Nazareth and the later evangelists upon whose portraits we depend. Like the evangelists, and unlike Jesus, Paul's first language was Greek, his biblical tradition the Septuagint, his ambit the cities of the Mediterranean Diaspora. Like them, too, he is much more conscious than the Jesus of history ever would have had to have been about gentile culture and the consequences of the gospel message for Gentiles: Paul addressed his letters specifically, even exclusively, to gentile believers. And again like them—and presumably not like the historical Jesus—his gospel is informed by a post-Resurrection faith. Paul had seen the Risen Christ (1 Cor 15:8; Gal 1:16), and much of his good news, his *euangelion,* concerns what to expect at Christ's glorious, imminent return.

But like Jesus, and unlike the evangelists, Paul lived to the far side of the year 70. This fact, together with his conviction that God, through Christ, was about to bring human history to a glorious finale (1 Cor 15;

Rom 11), must caution us when we designate Paul a "Christian." Of course Paul was a Christian, and it is difficult to know what the term would mean at all if we did not use it for him: He believed that Christ was God's Son, his agent in Creation, and the key actor in bringing about the redemption of the universe (for example, Phil 2:5–11).

But Paul thought of himself as a Jew. He worked within a very condensed time frame: "The appointed time has grown very short . . . the form of this world is passing away" (1 Cor 7:29, 31). Upon him and his community "the end of the ages has come" (1 Cor 10:11). "Salvation is nearer to us now than when we first believed: the night is far gone, the day is at hand" (Rom 14:11–12). Such a time frame would scarcely allow him to conceive of his mission as establishing new communities separate from and independent of Jewish ones. When he argues with fellow apostles, also Jews, it is over typically Jewish concerns: lineage ("Are they Hebrews? So am I. Are they Israelites? So am I," 2 Cor 11:22; "of the people of Israel, the tribe of Benjamin; a Hebrew born of Hebrews," Phil 3:5); level of religious observance ("as to the law a Pharisee . . . as to righteousness under the law blameless," Phil 3:5–6; his opponents in Galatia "do not themselves keep the Law," Gal 6:13); religious authority ("the gospel which was preached to me is not man's gospel, for I did not receive it from a man, nor was I taught it, but it came through a revelation," Gal 1:11–12). When he organizes a major charity fund, it is for relief of the poor back in Jerusalem (1 Cor 16:1–3; 2 Cor 1:1–9:15; Rom 15:25).

But it is Paul's own words that most effectively make this point—namely, that his spiritual orientation centered on the Torah and Temple of his own time, pre-70 Judaism—when he describes his work as God's envoy (*apostolos*) to the nations bringing the good news of redemption in Christ. Paul conceived his apostolate on the analogy of the Jerusalem priests' service in the Temple. Thus, when urging his Gentiles in Corinth to understand that the material support of the community is an apostle's right, he drives home his argument by citing Deuteronomy:

> Do I say this on human authority? Does not the Law say the same? For it is written in the law of Moses, "You shall not muzzle an ox when it is treading out the grain." Is it for oxen that God is concerned? Does he not speak entirely for our sake? . . . If we have sown spiritual good among you, is it too much if we reap your material benefits?
>
> (1 Cor 9:8–11)

An apostle is as entitled to support from the community he serves as are the priests who serve the community in Jerusalem:

> Do you not know that those who are employed in the Temple service get their food from the Temple, and those who serve at the altar share in the sacrificial offerings? In the same way, the Lord commanded that those who proclaim the gospel should get their living by the gospel.
>
> (1 Cor 9:13–14).

In a later letter, writing to introduce himself to the gentile community in Rome, Paul enumerates the privileges and prerogatives by which God has distinguished Israel:

> They [Paul's people] are Israelites, and to them belong the sonship, the *glory,* the covenants, the giving of the Law, the *worship,* and the promises; to them belong the patriarchs, and of their race according to the flesh is the messiah.   (Rom 9:4–5)

So runs the translation in the Revised Standard Version (RSV). I have highlighted two words in Paul's list, "glory" and "worship," because the English obscures their immediate connection with the Temple. For "glory" Paul's Greek text has *doxa;* the Hebrew word that this translates is *kavod,* which in Jewish literature refers not to God's glory in general, but specifically to God's glorious *presence* that dwells on earth in the Temple in Jerusalem. As Matthew's Jesus says, "He who swears by the Temple, swears by it *and by Him who dwells in it*" (Mt 23:21). Further, behind "worship" stands Paul's Greek word *latreia:* this recalls the Hebrew *avodah,* the worship of God. And how is God worshiped? Through the cult he mandated for Israel through Moses that Israel preserved before God's presence in Jerusalem. "Worship" is a rather bloodless translation, for what Paul intends is "cult," specifically the cult of animal sacrifice (which in turn, as we saw above, provided food for God's priests) enacted at the Temple.

The Temple and the Jewish service to it stand for Paul as the acme of the human worship of God. Thus, when he speaks of his own role as an apostle, bringing the charity collected from the diaspora gentile communities in Christ for the poor in Jerusalem, Paul says that God has given him the grace to be "a *minister* of Christ Jesus to the Gentiles in *priestly service* of the gospel of God, so that the offering of the Gentiles may be acceptable" (Rom 15:16). Behind the English of the Revised Standard Version are Paul's words *leitourgos* ("minister") and *hierourgeo* ("priestly service"). In Greek, the first word means specifically "a priest's attendant," someone who assists with the sacrifices; the second, literally, means "priest's work," that is, making offerings at the altar. And since Paul in this passage names Jerusalem as his destination, we have a further clue that these images are not generically sacrificial, that is, related to just any first-century priestly service or priestly cult to any god, but they evoke specifically the cult of the God of Israel. For Paul, behind *hieros,* the Greek word for priest, stands the Hebrew *cohen,* the priest who in Jerusalem offers sacrifices to Israel's God.

If Paul, a diaspora Jew and active spokesman for the post-Resurrection faith in Jesus as Christ, so naturally and immediately esteemed the Temple and its cult, by that much more should we expect to see that same esteem evident in the pre-Resurrection mission and message of Jesus. But the Gospel sources complicate our view of him on this issue, because they are written after, perhaps in some sense in light of, the Jews' war with Rome. Thus, though the Gospels' narrative context is, roughly, the first third of the first century, from the final years of Herod the Great (d. 4 B.C.E.) to Pontius Pilate's term of office (26–36 C.E.), the Gospel writers' historical context is, roughly, the final third of the first century, c. 70–100 C.E. Between these authors and their subject yawned the unbridgeable breach in Israel's traditional worship. The evangelists' position as regards the Temple, then, is closer to ours, despite the nineteen centuries that intervene between us, than to that of those generations who immediately precede them. They, like us, *know* something that none of the historical figures about whom they wrote could have known: that is, that Jerusalem's Temple was no more.

This knowledge cannot but affect what the evangelists saw, and what we see, when we look backward. Both we and they are in the position of someone reading a novel or watching a film for the second time. Gestures and actions that the first time through seemed simply to give texture to the story now throb with heightened poignancy, because we know where things will end. Juliet's passionate outburst as Romeo prepares to leave Verona for exile—"O, think'st thou we shall ever meet again?"—heard in innocence, seems both to Romeo and to an unknowing audience an exaggerated anxiety in the face of traumatic separation. His assurances that all will be well—"All these woes shall serve / For sweet discourses in our times to come"—are a soothing and sensible response. But the second time through, her words take on a terrible accuracy, making his seem touchingly naive, even pathetic. We know too much to hear them the same way twice.

So, too, with the evangelists. Whatever the traditions they inherited about Jesus and Jerusalem, they received them in a period with a much-altered religious reality: the cult mandated by God to the Jewish people, whose details stretched through four of the first five books of Scripture, whose performance had been the particular responsibility of the Jerusalem priesthood, and whose manner of execution had fueled the wars of interpretation and the vigorous sectarianism of the late Second Temple period, had ceased to exist. Inherited sayings and stories about Jesus and the Temple, or about Jesus and the laws of purity concerning the Temple, or about Jesus and those groups whose piety focused especially on the Temple, accordingly acquired a dimension added by the evangelists' own, post-70 perspective: Jesus spoke about and interacted with an institution and its religious authorities that had vanished. How could he *not* have known what would so shortly happen? What could God have meant by permitting such a massive destruction? The evangelists' efforts to respond to these questions intimately affected their retelling of tradition.

So, too, with historical scholarship: It also is burdened with (in this sense) knowing too much. Our retrospective knowledge unobtrusively shapes what we see. *We* know that the Temple ceased being a focus of active Christian piety soon after the lifetime of Jesus; that most of the purity laws soon became irrelevant to the evolving movement; that the churches would become increasingly Gentile and, eventually, anti-Jewish. And this knowledge in turn can lend weight to those modern readings of New Testament material whereby Jesus himself seems alienated from or hostile or indifferent to the concerns and commitments of his Jewish contemporaries. The retrospect inevitable to the historical project can, ironically, threaten to collapse the distance between the present and the past. And such collapse in turn threatens the historical project both morally and intellectually.

Morally, this diminution of difference between present and past can lead us to project what is meaningful to us back onto and into our subject of inquiry. Especially when studying religious texts such as the Gospels or culturally central figures such as Paul and, even more, Jesus, the desire to have these ancient voices speak immediately to the present, to be spiritually and morally consonant with current concerns, too often pulls them out of their own historical context into territory familiar to later generations but foreign to them. We see the results in the Christ of the western Imperial church, depicted in a sixth-century Italian mosaic as a Roman army officer. We see them in the Jesus of liberal Protestant scholars in the eighteenth and early nineteenth centuries, who emerges from their weighty tomes as a religious liberal himself. We see them now, as the Jesus of the late twentieth-century academy battles nationalism, sexism, and social hierarchy. Such a Jesus is immediately relevant to the concerns shaping these later contexts. But his relevance comes purchased at the price of anachronism.

To do history both honorably and well, then, requires the moral discipline of allowing the gap of twenty centuries to open between us and our ancient subjects. What matters to us, what is meaningful to us, will coincide at best only rarely with what mattered to them. They lived in a different world. Some aspects of this world can be felt as well in ours: We, too, can understand the social consequences of oppression and poverty, the spiritual effects of prayer. But some aspects will remain obdurately other, forever outside our experience and our categories of meaning, precisely because the ancient past is ancient. It is not our own world at all, but a place where leprosy and death defile, where ashes and water make clean, and where one approaches the altar of God with purifications, blood offerings, and awe.

Respecting their historical integrity and moral autonomy, allowing Jesus or Paul or the evangelists as late Second Temple Jews or post–Second Temple Christians to be concerned with what concerned them and not with what concerns us—for which they had no responsibility and of which they had no knowledge—is the only way to see them in their full humanity. Anything less simply drapes disguised versions of ourselves in antique garb, presenting figures in a costume drama who comfortably inhabit a modern stage, not the ancient past. Thus, whether reading the Gospels themselves or assessing modern studies of them, we need to ask if later sensibilities affect the presentation of the past, the past as truly lived by Jesus and by his contemporaries—sympathizers, admirers, opponents, enemies.

The "backward" thrust of history also poses intellectual dangers. Again like the reader of the twice-read novel or the viewer of the twice-seen film, we cannot help knowing more than we should. Beyond the moral discipline of allowing for otherness, then, we need to cultivate as well the intellectual discipline of viewing the past as if we knew less than we know.

This is difficult precisely because history in its very nature is retrospective. We start from our vantage point in the present and work ourselves back into an imagined past. But though history is always done backward, life is only lived forward. We all move from our present into the radical unknowability of the future. If in our historical work we wish to reconstruct the lived experience of the ancient people we study, then we must forswear our retrospective knowledge, because it gives us a perspective on their lives that they themselves could not possibly have had. We, looking back now, know how their stories ended; they, living their lives, did not.

To understand our ancient people from the evidence they left behind, we must affect a willed naïveté. We must pretend to an innocence of the future that echoes their own. Only then can we hope to realistically re-create them in their own historical circumstances. Only by accepting—indeed, respecting and protecting—the otherness of the past, can we hope to glimpse the human faces of those we seek.

I propose that we start the search for Jesus of Nazareth by looking at an activity ostensibly common to both modern and ancient culture: the worship of God.

The Temple

THE BOY STOOD by his father very quietly, knowing how important this moment was. His father's hand rested on the ram's knobby head; his voice murmured something—the boy couldn't quite catch what—to the serious young priest who stood before them, on the other side of the low stone railing.

Was his mother watching? He turned, looking up and over his shoulder, at the rim of women and small children who leaned on the edge of the raised gallery that marked off the Women's Court. Somewhere up there, he knew, stood his mother and his older sister, his younger sister, and baby Shimon. But the sun was so bright, the shimmer dancing over the white limestone so brilliant, that all he could make out were dark figures silhouetted against the sky's light-drenched blue.

Once when he was younger, he remembered, God had made him so angry. What seemed like the whole village had left, just before the month of Nisan, to begin their walk down from the Galilean hill country, along the deep flatness of the river valley and then up, up to the city of David, Jerusalem; to *Har ha-Bayit*, the mountain of God's house. But Grandfather's illness had grown worse and worse, and finally, when the other families were completing their preparations for the trip, he had died. The other families in the village had helped his mother and father. They buried Grandfather and then came by with food and consolation. The boy had basked in the extra attention he'd received. But he had not expected his father's announcement that the family would remain in Natzerat that Pesach, and he had wept in frustration.

Ya'akov, his big brother, had tried to explain. Because Grandfather had died in their house, he said, because they had all washed Grandfather's body before bearing it to the village cemetery, all of them were *tameh,* impure. And because Grandfather was Grandfather, they had to sit and observe the period of mourning, which meant that they would never have enough days to finish travel preparations and then walk all the way to Jerusalem in time to fulfill the special seven-days' purification for the Passover. And if they missed the purification, they could not enter God's temple to bring the corban Pesach, the Passover sacrifice; nor could they eat it.

"Listen, Yehoshua. Moshe our teacher said that anyone who touches a dead person and then enters before the altar without first purifying himself makes the altar polluted too. You wouldn't want to do that."

"But Ya'akov—I know we could be in the city in time to bring the corban!"

"Yes. But we have to be there a week before that, to have the water sprinkled on us on the third day and the seventh day. Then we'd be clean." The water, he explained, had mixed in it the ashes from the *parah adumah,* a perfect red heifer that a priest had burned up and gathered just for this purpose. It was God's teaching, his torah.

"Well, we could be there in time for the second sprinkling. That counts."

Ya'akov had laughed at that point and shook his head. "No, little sage. God himself told Moshe what we have to do. We don't have to guess, and we can't change what he said. Seven days is seven days. Do you know," he said, leaning closer and dropping his voice; was he teasing? the boy wondered, "do you know that some people say that corpse-pollution is so strong that even the corpse's shadow, if it falls over a person or a vessel as we carry the corpse to be buried, is enough to make them *tameh*? What do you think of that?"

"I think that it's not fair that we can't go to the city, and I think that Grandfather would agree with me!" And he'd taken his argument to his father. Yosef had listened, half-smiling, and then hugged him tightly. "Death is a great change, child; it does not belong near the altar of the living God. Jews have made Pesach everywhere—even in Mitzra'im" (Egypt. The boy knew that some Jews still lived in Egypt, but he could not understand why), "even in Bavel" (Babylon! Yes, he even knew that they had cousins who lived in Babylon. But why would Jews want to live so far away, so distant from Jerusalem? The Galil, the boy thought, was already very far, a fair week's walk from the Temple). "We can certainly make Pesach in Natzerat. And next year, God willing, we will all go to *Har ha-Bayit,* and I will let you come with me and Ya'akov and Yosse and Yehudah into the men's court. You're getting so big now, you can help us bring our corban."

And so that year they made the feast at home. As they sat down around the flat bread of the holiday, their father—not Grandfather this time—began the story of their people. "A wandering Aramean was my father," recited Yosef. "He went down to Egypt and sojourned there . . . and he became a nation, great, mighty, and populous. And the Egyptians treated us harshly and afflicted us. . . . And we cried out to the Lord the God of our fathers, and the Lord heard our voice."

All that seemed so long ago now. He had come to Jerusalem many times since then. Once, they had been in the city for Yom Kippur and stayed through Sukkot in the early autumn. The city had teemed with tens of thousands of pilgrims, many of whom were farmers, free to celebrate now that their crops were gathered, happy to give the first fruits of their autumn harvest as part of their holiday offering. The songs and feasting in the booths everyone built, the sharp clean smell of the *etrogim,* lemonlike fruit carried by the worshipers into the Temple, all mingled in the boy's memory with the intensive study of the Torah that also marked the festival, and with his gratitude that God had brought his people out of slavery to freedom, to live in the Land. "You shall dwell in booths for seven days," Moshe had written God's word in *Vayikra,* the Book of Leviticus, "all that are native in Israel shall dwell in booths, that your generations may know that I made the people of Israel dwell in booths when I brought them out of the land of Egypt."

Once, his father had permitted him to come by himself, without the rest of his family, as the guest of one of the wealthy priests for whom Yosef did work in the nearby Galilean capital of Sepphoris. That trip had been for the celebration of the Feast of Dedication, when Judah Maccabee and his brothers—not so long ago, his father always reminded him—had chased the Greek idol-worshippers out of the Temple and cleansed and rededicated the sanctuary to the One God. But the weather had been windy and rainy—naturally, since the feast was in winter—and the Temple, so sparkling and white in sunshine, had seemed to the boy more like a huge manmade mountain, even harder to climb than a natural one because the rain, collected in numberless tiny invisible pools all over the smooth rock, made ascending the stairs and traversing the open plain of the Court of the Gentiles a slippery, treacherous business. The money changers, protected by the roof of the outer stoa from the worst of the weather, huddled around their braziers, exchanging foreign currency for the Tyrian shekel accepted as the silver standard by the Temple for donations. The boy wondered how the priests could stand to work barefoot for so many hours, and how they managed to keep the altar burning in all the gray winter wetness.

But the best, the very best, was always Pesach. The boy and his family would leave home weeks before the feast. When the holiday fell late, the plains of the Galil would dance with thousands of spring wildflowers. As they walked, the pilgrims from his village would join with families from other towns. Every night they would encamp, children roaming freely from one group's fire to the next; every day they would walk closer and closer to the city, and as they walked, they would sing the ancient pilgrim songs:

> I was glad when they said to me,
> "Let us go to the House of the Lord!"
> Our feet have been standing within your gates,
> O Jerusalem!
>
> Jerusalem, built as a city which is bound firmly together,
> To which the tribes go up, the tribes of the Lord,
> As was decreed for Israel, to give thanks to
> the name of the Lord.
> There thrones for judgment were set,
> The thrones of the house of David.
>
> Pray for the peace of Jerusalem!
> May they prosper who love you!

Peace be within your walls,
security within your towers!
For my brothers' and my companions' sake,
I will pray, "Peace be within you!"
For the sake of the house of the Lord our God,
I will seek your good.

The city was the biggest, the most beautiful place he had ever seen. As he climbed with his family out of the lowland plain of Jericho, turning right and upward away from the Jordan toward the hill country of Judea, he felt that his heart would burst with love and sheer excitement. The confluence of pilgrims made a mighty human river surging into the valley that spread out before the city's walls. In fact, outside the city another city spread, countless families from everywhere grouped by kin or village, clustered in tents and temporary shelters. The sky's deep nighttime indigo glowed with the silver luminescence of the increasing moon; the spring weather, sweet and beautiful, embraced them all.

When he was younger, it seemed that he hardly saw his family at all in the week before the feast. By day he would range around with a steadily growing pack of boys his own age, exploring the new universe about them. They would run down to the brook that flowed in the deep valley immediately east of the city. The drains of the Temple flushed into this brook; and once the men slaughtered their offerings, the boys knew, it would be off-limits, its waters thick with the blood of the victims. Or they would stroll around the stalls that ringed the lower market area near the Temple Mount, patting the heads of the fat yearling lambs, thousands and thousands of them, that stood, waiting to be selected as a family's corban. Or they'd play with other boys from faraway places who had come just for the feast. Sometimes this was difficult if the children had no language in common. The boy and his friends knew a few words of Greek, but the Greek-speakers, even the ones from Alexandria in Mitzra'im, knew absolutely nothing of Aramaic, and little more of Hebrew. The native boys teased them and called them "Hellenoi," Greeks; and the Alexandrians did clan together, more comfortable playing with the Greek-speaking Gentile boys who had also come for the holiday than they ever were with their Judean and Galilean cousins. Tired, dirty, at the end of the day he would return to the house in the city where his family rented space—the roof, actually—whenever they came to

Jerusalem. He'd stand with his father and brothers and the group of Galilean men staying nearby as they recited the evening *Sh'ma*.

Even with all his trips up to the city for Pesach, he had never actually seen the corban. Nor necessarily was it his father who brought the offering. "Oh no, son; believe me, I don't mind at all," Yosef had laughed when, late in the afternoon, he sat listening to some local Torah scholar expound the laws of Passover. The boy's uncle that year had been the one chosen to go to the Temple to sacrifice the sheep for the entire family-group of eight households. Didn't Yosef mind not being picked himself?

His father laughed. "You can't imagine what a scene it is. You have never seen so many men, nor so many animals, all gathered in one place! We can't do the sacrifice all at once; there's just no room. The priests prepare the inner courts so that we can offer there, too, not just around theirs. Levites stand at the entrance and let in one man with his beast each time one man with his pesach leaves.

"The animals panic because the smell of the blood is so strong, and the place is so crowded. We slaughter our corban as it kicks and struggles; one priest catches the blood in a bowl—a lucky thing if the animal doesn't first knock it out of his hands—and carries it to the altar. Another has to hang the carcass, skin it, gut it, and take the fat out for the Lord's altar. And then you have to fight your way back through the crowd. Everyone is in a terrible rush; everything needs to get done within a few hours." Yosef shook his head. "It seems like every Jew in the world is there. And the priests! They look like the survivors of a great battle, exhausted and flecked all over with blood. And just after the last men leave, they still have to make sure that the entire courtyard area is washed down before going home to their own families. No, really—your uncle could bring our corban for us every year as far as I'm concerned."

And in fact his uncle did seem even more tired than the other adults when they all sat down to the feast that night. But the excitement of the story eventually gripped them all. Slavery—then freedom; Pharaoh—but Moshe! God's strong arm and mighty hand, leading them out, out past the sea, out into the desert, out to the Jordan, finally into the Land. The songs and laughter of other households mingled with their own; all Jerusalem sang its prayers of praise as the sounds of the feast ascended up the valley, up the hillside, up into the starry silver night, the huge full moon, up, up to the throne of God himself.

But once, the day just before Pesach, when the boy and his gang played tag in the alleyways of the city, he felt as if Pharaoh had reached out through time and grabbed him with his cold, long arm. Rounding a corner, the boys had collided blindly with a group of Roman soldiers making their way up to the Temple Mount. The boy knew that these men now stood on the roof of the outer stoa and watched every movement of the people below them; but so much went on at his eye-level—thronging crowds, placid sheep or balky goats being led by worshipers and Levites up to a priest, native Jerusalemites directing lost pilgrims, the smell of blood and incense that wafted from the priests' court, the women murmuring to each other, shushing children as they all leaned to see the sacrifices enacted by their men in the court below them—that he forgot to look up and so did not see them. In the days of King Herod, no Roman soldiers had ever come near. But now here they were: huge, much bigger than his father, heavily muscled, short swords at their sides. He stood transfixed: He'd never seen a soldier this close before. None were in the Galil, since Herod's son ruled there; the only time he might have seen one was at a festival. One of them spat and said something in a language he could not understand at all; the rest had laughed and strode past the silent children. Yet the last one had smiled at the boy and ruffled his hair as he passed by—Yehoshua could still feel the man's large, hard hand on his head that evening, when his mother, with a similar gesture, had settled him down for the night.

As he had gotten older, this freedom decreased: Yosef insisted that he spend more of the time before the feast in study, learning the Torah on the different offerings and listening to learned men debate the correct interpretation of Moses' instructions. And once he started going with his father and older brothers into the men's courtyard, he had taken on the responsibility of purification. At first it had frightened him—standing pressed against so many other people as the priests sprinkled them with the water of purification; entering with his father and brothers into the area of the purification pools. The room had been so dark; the water, as he walked down the submerged, slimy steps into the basin of the pool, even darker, and so cold! But he had refused to be frightened by the cool gloominess. He had immersed and pronounced the blessing slowly and clearly. His brothers cheerfully thumped his back once he had dried off and dressed; and Yosef had smiled. That year, for the first time, he stood and saw close-up what earlier, with his mother and sisters, he had seen before only from a distance. He had felt wonder and awe.

A sudden movement startled the boy out of his thoughts. It was the Levite who, together with the boy's father, bent and lifted the ram, suspending its forelegs, breast, and head over the low parapet demarcating the priests' court. His father pulled back the animal's head and quickly slashed the arteries of its neck. The boy watched, his eyes fixed on the thin red line on its throat, which pulsed and swelled and then released a bright torrent. The young priest, bent slightly at the waist, caught this great gush in the basin that he stood holding in front of the suddenly placid animal. It was a source of wonder to the boy that God had placed such an enormous quantity of blood into such a small body. Now, he knew, the priest would give the blood back to God, splashing it around the base of his altar. God was the author of life, and the blood belonged to him alone.

> The life of the flesh is in the blood; and I have given it for you upon the altar to make atonement for your souls; for it is the blood that makes atonement, by reason of the life. Therefore I have said to the people of Israel, No person among you shall eat blood.
>
> (Lv 17: 11–12)

The priest came back to retrieve the animal's carcass, which he would flay and butcher, burning the fat upon the altar, eating, with the other priests serving at the Temple, the animal's flesh. This corban had been a guilt sacrifice—his parents had not told him for what—so all the flesh was given to God and thus remained in the Temple with his priests. Yosef had passed the rest of the offering—the oil, the flour, the wine—to another priest. The sacrifice was complete, but still they both stood there: Yosef, tranquil, thinking his thoughts, face turned toward the sanctuary; the boy, awed and moved by the silent beauty of the atonement, by his father's dignity, and by the Levite's strength (he had already moved off, assisting another worshiper). At the same moment, though no word passed between them, they both turned to go. His mother and the other children would meet them, as usual, at the eastern gate of the inner wall, and they would all walk down from the Temple together.

The boy and his family emerged into the heat and hubbub of the Gentiles' courtyard. Crowds coursed under the brilliant sun. They walked by a sight that no longer surprised him: a clutch of several men, clearly Gentiles (since they proceeded no further), standing to one side of the eastern gate by their boundary-marker, facing toward the sanctuary, chanting *tehillim*—psalms—in their musical Greek. Traffic toward the altar, people with their baskets of pigeons or their animal offering, streamed past him, walking in the opposite direction.

"Jesus!" The Greek name rang into his head. Yehoshua slowed and and looked around; so, he noticed, did three or four men who were walking near him. "Jesus of Nazareth!" Then he saw: Coming toward his family was a boy his own age, accompanied by several older men. The boy recognized him as one of his friends from years before, the child of an Alexandrian merchant. "Timotheus!" he called back.

The two groups slowed to face each other. Yosef, with a small smile, nodded his head in greeting to the other men. The two boys stood, at once shy and delighted; frustrated, too, that after all this time they could not say more to each other. Each desperately combed his own mind hoping to turn up a few words in the other's language. Finally the Alexandrian, with great feeling, simply grabbed both of Yehoshua's hands and said the one word he'd remembered. "Shalom, Jesus." Peace.

The boy struggled with the foreign words lying awkwardly on his tongue. *"Cháris kai eirēnē, Timotheus!"* Grace and peace.

The group moved on; the boy, grinning, took Shimon from his younger sister and continued walking across the courtyard, under the stoa—finally, in the shade!—down and out of the Temple area into the marketplace beneath. There he turned, as he always did, and looked up one last time at the steep shining surface of the Temple. And again, as he always did, he breathed a favorite blessing from his village's prayer service: *Baruch atah Adonai, shomea t'fillah.* . . . Blessed are you, O Lord, who hears prayer.

Chapter 2

GOD AND ISRAEL IN
ROMAN ANTIQUITY

W HAT IS the single biggest difference between the religious
sensibility of people in the modern West and our cultural
ancestors of twenty centuries ago? When I put this question to my students, they invariably name distinctions of religious
ideas: ancient people worshiped many gods, but we are monotheists;
ancient people saw demons or astral influences as causing disease, but
thanks to scientific medicine, we battle the virus, the bacterium, the
errant blood cell; ancient people followed the courses of heaven, the
stars and the planets, to understand the world and their place in it,
whereas we look to terrestrial realities—society, economics, politics—
to analyze ours.

These answers have their virtues—though I have too often encountered fellow moderns who cast star charts or dodge demons to be
entirely convinced. But I do not think that the biggest difference lies in
the realm of religious ideas. Ancient Jews were monotheists but also
fretted about planets and demons; for that matter, certain pagan

philosophies had their own forms of monotheism. What has changed, altered utterly, is religious behavior. Worship in antiquity involved blood sacrifices. Universally, the worship of a deity—virtually any deity—involved the slaughter of animals and the ritual redistribution of their bodies: some parts burned on the altar to the divinity, some parts eaten by the priests, other parts distributed to the worshipers. And since proximity to a god's altar meant, in some sense, proximity to holiness as well, all ancient peoples who offered at traditional altars, whether pagan or Jewish, underwent rites of purification. Purificatory rites helped prepare the worshiper for his or her encounter, through sacrifice, with the sacred.

Purity

PAGAN PURITY LAWS, like paganism itself, tended to be local, particular to the specific cult of a god. Their laws, when public (in mystery cults, silence was the rule), circulated much less widely than the Jewish scriptures: We find them inscribed in stone, on tablets associated with sanctuaries, or alluded to in ancient poetry and literature. Water rituals, abstention from sex, fasting or avoidance of certain foods—we might think of these as musical notes composing the scale of purification techniques. All ancient peoples concerned with purity expressed their religious culture by sounding these notes: Ancient pagan purification rites and sacrificial protocol, in technique similar to those observed by Jews, were thus particular variations played on this universal theme of worship. When commenting on what Jews did, pagans, whether admiring or hostile, would name circumcision or Sabbath observance or refusal to eat pork: These practices struck them as odd. Jewish purification and sacrifices, however, elicited no such comment, because in the religious sensibility of antiquity, such practices were simply normal. The thing most foreign to modern Western religiousness about ancient Judaism—the sacrifices and their attendant purity regulations—struck ancient observers as one of the few normal things Jews did.

We know much more about ancient Jewish laws regulating purity than we do pagan ones, because the Jewish laws are still published: Their establishment, together with the correct protocol for offerings, constitutes much of the matter between God and Moses in the opening books of the Bible. The biblical narrative specifies purity as a condition for a person's approaching the Divine Presence—in the language of the story, appearing before the tent of meeting; in Jesus' period, going to the Temple. *Impurity* in this context is an actual, objective, usually temporary state. It might be incurred through certain natural (and often involuntary) bodily processes, such as ejaculation, menstruation, childbirth or miscarriage, or various genital discharges. Certain defiling substances or objects—human corpses especially; also scale disease (the biblical "leprosy," which could afflict clothing, houses, and furniture as well as persons); the bodies of some animals—could convey their impurity through contact or even proximity. Scripture assumes that everybody at some point would be in such a condition some of the time—it was virtually unavoidable—and most people were in such a condition most of the time. But Scripture also prescribed the means to remove impurity. A system of "wash-and-wait"—immersion and observing a liminal time period (until sunset; seven days; forty days: it varied, depending on the case)—cleansed most impurities.

Many of these purity laws specifically regulated access to the Temple. They were in principle incumbent upon all Israel, though priests, given their special cultic responsibilities, had additional purity rules peculiar to their station. The High Holidays especially occasioned huge effort to ensure that pilgrims were in the appropriate condition of purity to stand before God: Beyond the descriptions remaining in ancient literature, our evidence lies embedded in the very stones of the Temple Mount itself, where today traces of a multitude of immersion pools stand in mute witness to the great numbers of Jews that used them on their way to the altar. The Temple was designed and prepared to accommodate great numbers of worshipers.

The sheer size of the Temple and the archaeological remnants of its purification technology point to another social and cultural fact about ancient Judaism that distinguishes it from traditional paganism. The religions of antiquity's majority culture were local; as one passed from sanctuary to sanctuary, from a grove sacred to one god to a valley or mountain sacred to another, one encountered the rules peculiar to that individual god's site. The priests of that cult would ensure that visitors acquainted themselves with and observed these particular rules, lest they pollute the altar and so incur the god's anger. The cultic worship of the God of Israel, similarly, stood localized in Jerusalem, around the altar, in the sanctuary; similarly, his priests (and their assistants, the Levites) supervised. But unlike paganism, Judaism was not restricted by locality, and consequently instruction in its cult did not depend on direct contact with its priests. Knowledge of its traditions, its sacrificial

etiquette, even the details of its sanctuary circulated widely because of its unique literary medium, the Bible. Thus Judaism could travel anywhere, everywhere, intact because it journeyed by book. And it was back from anywhere, everywhere, that Jews voluntarily sent their annual contributions or journeyed themselves. Jewish cult, too, was local; but instruction in the cult, thanks to the Bible, was universal.

Practice and Tradition

TWO INSTITUTIONS in particular enabled this wide transmission of Jewish religious culture. The first one, private, was the home and family; the second, public, was the synagogue.

If we define "home" functionally as the place where one cooks, eats, sleeps, and conceives and raises children, we see much of the do-

Photographs of a mikveh (ritual immersion pool) on the southern side of the Temple Mount.

"You shall keep the people of Israel separate from their uncleanness, lest they die in their uncleanness by defiling my tabernacle that is in their midst" (Lv 16:31). Much of the legislation given in Torah mandated purity for the Israelite who would approach the Divine Presence. This state of purity was attained in part through total immersion in water: "He shall bathe his whole body in water" (e.g., Lv 15:16, and frequently). Jews of the Second Temple period kept this commandment by immersing in prescribed immersion pools on their way up to the Temple. These photographs show one of these immersion pools just south of the Temple Mount, near the broad steps leading up to the entrance gate through which lay the Temple precincts.

mestic range of application of biblical law. The Jewish family was the most immediate environment within which one kept the food laws and the laws of purity governing permissible times for sexual intercourse (always understood as between married partners); where one prayed, instructed children, and kept the Sabbath. The *Sh'ma,* then as now a prime prayer within Judaism, recapitulates these defining aspects of Jewish life. The first part of the text of the prayer comes in Deuteronomy 6:4–5:

> Hear O Israel: The Lord our God, the Lord is one. And you shall love the Lord your God with all your heart, and with all your soul, and with all your might. And these words which I command you this day shall be upon your heart. You shall teach them diligently to your children and shall speak of them when you sit in your house, and when you walk by the way, and when you lie down, and when you rise up.

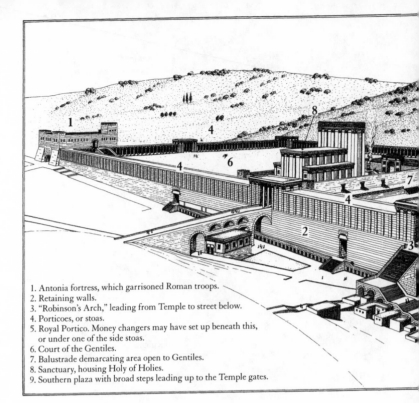

1. Antonia fortress, which garrisoned Roman troops.
2. Retaining walls.
3. "Robinson's Arch," leading from Temple to street below.
4. Porticoes, or stoas.
5. Royal Portico. Money changers may have set up beneath this, or under one of the side stoas.
6. Court of the Gentiles.
7. Balustrade demarcating area open to Gentiles.
8. Sanctuary, housing Holy of Holies.
9. Southern plaza with broad steps leading up to the Temple gates.

Line drawing of the Herodian Temple

"Then Jesus said to the crowds and to his disciples, . . . 'He who swears by the Temple swears by it and by Him who dwells in it' " (Mt 23:21). Jews held that their God was the Creator and Lord of the universe; no place was far from him, and prayer could be offered anywhere. Nonetheless, the Temple was in some special way God's *mishkan,* his "dwelling place." David consolidated the worship of Israel's God in Jerusalem around 1000 B.C.E.; his son Solomon built the First Temple, destroyed by Babylon in 586 B.C.E. Judeans returning from exile in Babylon built a much more modest sanctuary, which the Hasmoneans enlarged in their turn. But the Temple in Jerusalem achieved its greatest size and splendor under Herod the Great (ruled 37–4 B.C.E.). Herod lavishly expanded the Temple area, enlarging and beautifying its courts and improving the flow of human traffic through its precincts; the total length around its perimeter reached nearly a mile. This drawing gives a view of the Herodian Temple Mount from the southwest. Note the size of the human figures: They give a sense of its scale.

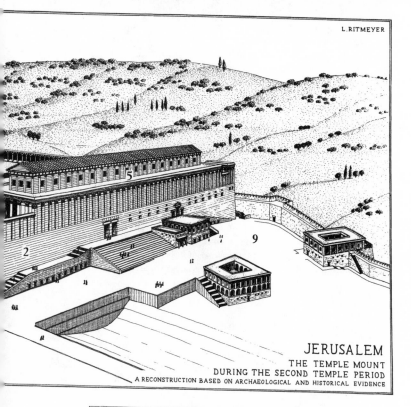

JERUSALEM
THE TEMPLE MOUNT
DURING THE SECOND TEMPLE PERIOD
A RECONSTRUCTION BASED ON ARCHAEOLOGICAL AND HISTORICAL EVIDENCE

L. RITMEYER

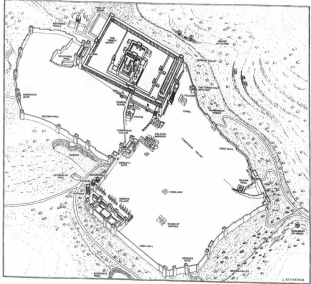

The synoptic Gospels themselves attest to this prayer's centrality in the first century. When he is asked by another Jew in Jerusalem, "Which commandment is the first of all?" Mark's Jesus replies, "The first is, 'Hear O Israel: the Lord our God, the Lord is one; and you shall love the Lord your God with all your heart and with all your soul and with all your mind, and with all your strength'" (Mk 12:29–30 and parr.). Jesus' words refer obliquely to the Ten Commandments, given in a passage preceding the *Sh'ma,* in Deuteronomy 5:

1. I am the Lord your God, who brought you out of the land of Egypt, out of the house of slavery. You shall have no other gods before me.
2. You shall not make for yourself a graven image. . . .
3. You shall not take the name of the Lord your God in vain. . . .
4. Observe the Sabbath Day, to keep it holy. . . . Six days you shall labor and do all your work, but the seventh day is a Sabbath to the Lord your God; in it you shall not do any work. . . .
5. Honor your father and mother. . . .
6. You shall not murder.
7. You shall not commit adultery.
8. You shall not steal.
9. You shall not bear false witness against your neighbor.
10. Nor shall you covet your neighbor's wife, or his house, or his field, or his servants, his ox or his ass, or anything that is his.

A broad range of ancient evidence in both Hebrew and Greek—Josephus, the Gospel of Matthew, early rabbinic traditions in the Mishnah (a late second- or early third-century text), the Dead Sea Scrolls, scraps of these verses found at Qumran—attests to how widespread, both in the land of Israel and in the Diaspora, the Jewish observance of these ordinances was, and how they were interpreted. The phrase in the *Sh'ma* that enjoins remembering God's word "when you lie down and when you rise up" led to the practice of reciting the *Sh'ma* twice a day in the home, upon awakening and before retiring. Putting "these words" upon the heart suggests study and contemplation.

The text of the *Sh'ma* continues with another directive about "these words": "And you shall bind them as a sign upon your hand, and they shall be as frontlets upon your eyes; and you shall write them on the doorposts of your house and on your gates" (Dt 6:6). This command was interpreted literally. Biblical phrases, copied out and posted on gates and doors of Jewish homes and buildings, are the *Sh'ma*'s *mezzu-*

zot ("gateposts"): Observant Jews in antiquity, as their modern counterparts, would post passages from the Torah on the entryway to their houses. Such passages bound by leather straps on the forehead "between the eyes" and on the arm are called tefillin (Hebrew) or phylacteries (Greek). Fragments of *mezzuzot* and tefillin have emerged among the texts from Qumran (thus giving us a definite date before 68 C.E., when the community was destroyed by the Roman Tenth Legion in the course of the war). And Matthew's Jesus implicitly instructs his followers on the correct size for their tefillin: They should not be as broad as those of the Pharisees (Mt 23:5). Tefillin, worn when one prayed, could thus be donned for devotions at home.

Deuteronomy specifically presumes religious instruction in the home. "When your son asks you in time to come, 'What is the meaning of the testimonies and statutes and ordinances which the Lord our God has commanded?' you shall say to him. . . ." (6:20); "You shall teach [my words] to your children, talking of them when you are sitting in your house" (11:18; the passage from vv. 13 to 21 served as the second paragraph of the *Sh'ma*). Such instruction in the commandments within the home would come, as well, through the rhythm of the week imposed by setting aside one day in every seven. On the Sabbath, no business was to be transacted, no work done. Cooking, also considered work, was done in advance of the day (which led many pagan observers to assume, wrongly, that the Sabbath was a fast day). The family would assemble for a day of rest and for learning the Law.

The study of the Law on the Sabbath brings us to a second, public institution of Jewish life, spread throughout the Diaspora as well as the land of Israel: the synagogue. The word means simply "congregation" or "assembly." It denoted primarily a gathering of people, not necessarily (as now) a particular building—though we do have archaeological remains of splendid public buildings in wealthy Mediterranean Jewish communities, and even an inscription from a synagogue by its founder, a Greek-speaking priest named Theodotus, uncovered near the Temple Mount. Jews gathered in synagogues at least once a week, on the Sabbath; and the community together heard and interpreted the Bible, most especially the Torah. "For from early generations Moses has had in every city those who preach him," says James, Jesus' brother, in the Acts of the Apostles, "for he is read every Sabbath in the synagogues" (Acts 15:21). The point of such weekly instruction, explains Josephus, was that every Jew ("the people") might "obtain a thorough and accurate knowledge of [the Law]" (*c. Ap.* 2.175). The importance of this

Photograph of the tefillin (phylacteries) discovered at Qumran

"And one of the scribes . . . asked him, 'Which commandment is first of all?' Jesus answered, 'The first is, "Hear, O Israel, the Lord our God, the Lord is one; and you shall love the Lord your God with all your heart, and with all your soul, and with all your mind, and with all your strength" ' " (Mk 12:28–29). The verse from Deuteronomy 6.4 that Mark's Jesus quotes here is the first line of one of the prime prayers of Judaism, the *Sh'ma.* God's command to bind His words "as a sign upon your hand, and they shall be as frontlets upon your eyes" (Dt 6:6) led to the development of tefillin (Hebrew) or phylacteries (Greek), small square boxes containing these biblical verses copied onto tiny sheets of parchment. These were (and are) bound with leather straps to the forehead and the upper left arm during daily prayers. This tefillin, for the head, was discovered in one of the caves at Qumran.

instruction accounts for the existence of the Septuagint: When Jews of the Western Diaspora shifted to the Greek vernacular, their scriptures shifted with them.

The existence of diaspora synagogues, their function as centers for community instruction, the biblical foundations of this instruction, and especially the fact that this instruction and the text of the Bible itself were available in Greek, all account for the existence of a special sort of Gentile, one whose presence affected the architecture of the Temple itself. Synagogues attracted interested outsiders who voluntarily affiliated themselves with Judaism to varying degrees. Jews in the Diaspora encouraged admiration for their religious cult and culture, and in general seem to have welcomed gentile interest. (Philo, for example, mentions a festival near Alexandria that celebrated the translation of the Torah into Greek, and he states that many Gentiles as well as Jews participated in that celebration, *Life of Moses* 2.41.) For pagan Gentiles, meanwhile, nothing was more normal than multiple religious allegiances: Paganism itself encouraged this sort of cultic ecumenicalism. Their worship of the Jewish God did not inhibit their normal participation in their own traditional cults. Nor did Jews themselves demand exclusive allegiance from interested Gentiles: In the Bible, God had addressed his demand for exclusive commitment only to Israel. Thus pagans *as pagans* were found worshiping Israel's God together with Jews both in the diaspora synagogue and, even more visibly, in the Temple. We'll return to this intriguing group later, when we look again at the letters of Paul: These sympathetic outsiders, the seedbed of the later gentile church, will figure prominently in the development of the post-Resurrection Jesus movement. Here we should note that so many came from the corners of the empire to worship in Jerusalem that they had their own courtyard, the largest one, which circumscribed the Temple area.

But synagogues and a vernacular Bible did more than inspire religious tourism. In disseminating the laws and serving as a place for discussion of them, synagogues also created a special kind of textual community. Whether in the Diaspora or in the homeland, the synagogue, precisely through its emphasis on public reading, diminished the need for literacy, and the monopoly a literate elite might exercise, when approaching the sacred text. The individual Jew did not have to be capable of reading in order to be involved in the interpretation of Scripture: Hearing the Law at least once a week, completing the cycle of the Torah time and again throughout one's life, provided text enough. The Bible, through community study, permitted the growth of a kind of secondary literacy, whereby Jews could be very familiar with a text without necessarily being able to read. And this secondary literacy encouraged and intensified community life: Everyone could (and for all we know, did) have a scriptural hook from which to hang his or her particular interpretation.

Jewish Diversity and Consensus in the Time of Jesus

THE RESULT, perhaps, was inevitable: The Jews were a nation of experts. "Should anyone of our nation be questioned about the laws," says Josephus, "he would repeat them all the more readily than his own name" (*c. Ap.* 2.175). Beneath the clannishness that so struck the watching eye of commenting pagans roared the full-throated feuds of family dissent. Jews everywhere—I generalize, but safely—expressed a broad consensus on what was religiously important: the people, the Land of Israel, Jerusalem, the Temple, and Torah. Behind these concepts and subsuming them stood their unique commitment to the imageless worship of the one God of the universe. The principled exclusiveness of their monotheism could strike pagan commentators as vaguely seditious and downright rude; their sanctuary empty of any cultic statue, at least odd. But within this broad consensus visible even to outsiders roiled vehement, interminable debate on virtually everything: not whether the Law was to be fulfilled, but how. Since God had been both detailed and extensive in his instructions to Moses, often specifying what should be done but not precisely in what way, the scope for interpretive debate stretched on forever. The vigorous sectarianism that characterized late Second Temple Judaism gives us the measure of how widespread instruction in the Law was, and how seriously it was regarded.

Purity laws in both their applications, domestic and communal, received a lot of attention. Even in the Diaspora, where distance from the Temple meant that many of these regulations were of little practical consequence, we find evidence that (some) Jews viewed purity as important in principle. For example, Philo of Alexandria, Jesus' elder contemporary, mentions nonbiblical sprinklings done for purification after a funeral or after sexual relations; perhaps before entering the synagogue, and perhaps before praying. The Jewish tendency to gather for prayer or to build houses of prayer near bodies of water (rivers, the seashore; see Acts 16:13) may be understood as an expression of this "purification" instinct: water was universally regarded as a purifying medium.

Closer to the homeland, we see an intensification and extension of these laws in the traditions ascribed to the Pharisees of evangelical notoriety. These lay interpreters of the Law seem to have been concerned with extending the scope and detail of biblical injunction, specifically on purity. Pharisees held in common among themselves certain beliefs and practices—Josephus specifies belief in resurrection, in the authority of their own tradition of interpretation (the "traditions of the fathers"), and in the interplay of free will and divine providence in human experience. But here as elsewhere, consensus never implies unanimity. Lay Torah scholars also divided between the houses of Hillel and Shammai, two sages of the generation before Jesus, who debated fiercely the correct way to fulfill the commandments of the Law. And they had their own views on how the priests should observe their laws, too.

Not that priestly ranks were joined. In the wake of the successful war of independence led by the Hasmoneans (166–142 B.C.E.), priests of the Zadokite family, for whom the high priesthood had been a hereditary domain, splintered when the Hasmoneans themselves assumed that office. One branch established their own temple in Leontopolis in Egypt; others found ways to continue the family vocation by setting up alternative temples in Samaria and in what is now Jordan. Another Zadokite established himself among a community of pious priestly separatists—"the keepers of the covenant of the sons of Zadok"—in the Judean desert outside Jerusalem. In the Dead Sea Scrolls, the library of this community, he appears as the "Teacher of Righteousness." His group, the Essenes, expanded the purity regulations elaborately (understandably, perhaps, given their priestly origins), eschewed worship in Jerusalem's current Temple (sullied, in their eyes, by unfit priests), and dreamed compensatory apocalyptic visions of a new or renewed Temple at the end of time, of gigantic proportions, run according to their view of the Law.

Still other Zadokites remained in Jerusalem, lending their prestige to the Hasmonean enterprise, and later to Herod's family. The term "Sadducee," used both by Josephus and by the New Testament writers for the sacerdotal aristocracy of the capital, may derive from their family name, "Zadok." But not all priests lived in Jerusalem, not all priests who lived in Jerusalem were aristocrats, and not all well-off Jerusalemite priests were "Sadducean" in their biblical interpretation. Josephus, for one, who came from this social stratum—the priestly Jerusalemite upper classes—nevertheless inclined toward the interpretive position of the Pharisees (*Vita* 1). Priests themselves were a clan rather than a sect or party. Whatever the interpretive persuasion of an individual priest, what mattered was the clan's obligation to serve in the Temple.

These are the three "philosophies" Josephus names when describing the main sects within the Palestinian Judaism in his day. Because of their role as Jesus' sparring partners in the Gospels, the Pharisees might seem to loom large in this period; because of all the media attention lavished recently on the Dead Sea Scrolls, the Essenes, also, take on added weight. To get a clearer view of things, we might contemplate some population figures. We must remember, however, that these figures are only estimates, and are therefore unreliable.

Some scholars estimate that as many as 2.5 million Jews lived in Palestine in the first century; others put the population at 1 million; still others at half that, at 500,000. Josephus himself provides membership numbers (which we have no more reason to trust or means to verify than we do the modern scholarly ones cited above) for the three groups—priests/Sadducees, Pharisees, and Essenes—that he details. Though untestable and unreliable, the relative proportion of discrete sect to general group that they suggest says something. During the reign of Herod the Great, Josephus claims, the Pharisees numbered about 6,000, the Essenes, 4,000 (*AJ* 17.42, 18.21). Even taking the very lowest estimate of the total population number—500,000 Jews in Palestine in the early first century—this means that the Essenes constituted .8 percent, the Pharisees 1.2 percent of the whole. If we assume a larger general population, then these percentages drop even lower. Neither the Pharisees nor the Essenes, then, represented a very large proportion of the Jews inhabiting Palestine.

Josephus put the figure for priests and Levites at twenty thousand (*c. Ap.* 2.108). Thus the priests, whatever their party affiliation (if they even had one), were clearly the largest group. They were concentrated in Jerusalem, and they held the most important job: running and overseeing the Temple. And despite the near-universal criticisms aimed against them by anyone who cared to have an opinion over the way they did what they did, the priests evidently (given the existence of the complaints) went on doing things their own way. Their critics and dissenters (some Essenes excepted) nonetheless continued to worship at the Temple. Whatever an individual priest's interpretive position on certain issues of Law, his right to teach and to serve came from a source of unquestionable authority, namely the Bible itself.

The Bible, then, together with the Temple, was at once an occasion for energetic divisiveness and a unique source of wide-flung unity. We need to be aware of both aspects of Second Temple Judaism. Jews of different sectarian orientations might criticize each other rancorously, but the vast majority of Jews belonged to no party, and the debate coexisted with consensus. Huge numbers of Jews everywhere within the empire and beyond voluntarily contributed the annual half-shekel tax for the Temple's upkeep. Huge numbers of pilgrims annually flooded the city to spend their second tithe money—a portion of the family's produce put aside to be spent specifically in Jerusalem—in celebration of the great pilgrimage festivals. Through their common religious culture they remained conscious of belonging to a single nation, no matter how widely dispersed: When the emperor Caligula, in the year 40–41 C.E., attempted to introduce a statue with his likeness into the Temple, he risked the resistance of Jews everywhere, who preferred death "in defense of the Laws" to tolerating such a desecration.

Living the Law: Sacred Space and Sacred Time

SABBATH, FOOD LAWS, sacrificial protocols; rules for distinguishing between holy and common, between pure and impure; sexual codes, instructions on animal husbandry and planting; torts and criminal law. All these come jumbled together as the great stories that open the Bible—God's Creation of the universe and of humanity; the saga of Abraham, Isaac, and Jacob, of Joseph and his brothers; Israel's bondage and freedom—transmute, about halfway through Exodus, into non-narrative directives and descriptions. God commands not only cultic and ritual observances, but affect ("Fear the Lord your God, walk in his ways, love him and serve him with all your heart and soul," Dt 10:12; "You shall love your neighbor as yourself," Lv 19:18), attitude ("Rise up before the hoary head, and honor the face of an old man," Lv 19:32), and ethical behavior ("Leave the fallen grapes in your vineyard for the poor and for the sojourner. . . . Do no wrong in judgment, in measures of length or weight of quantity," Lv 19:10, 35). The modern reader, accustomed to topical organization and a different logic of presentation, can come away confused and confounded by the sheer welter of instruction. (Those unfamiliar with biblical prose might glance now at a single chapter, Lv 19, and keep track of how many topics, unrelated by our categories, God manages to cover in a mere thirty-seven verses.) God's *torah*—the Hebrew means "teaching"—aims to instruct the people he chose as the unique bearers of his name in the proper way to live with each other and with others, and in the proper way to worship him, and he links the two endeavors intimately.

Biblical revelation thus represented not so much an external set of laws that one "obeyed," but an entire way of living, which one "guarded" or "kept." The Law structured life; it thereby also structured space and time. We will have a surer sense of the lived experience of the Law if we try to imagine these dimensions as ancient Jews did.

Space was understood to be ordered along a gradient of holiness, with "less holy" as the world beyond territorial Israel (the Diaspora), "more holy" the Land of Israel. Still more holy was the city of Jerusalem; and within the city, graduated zones of holiness ordered the

Temple Mount from least (the court of the Gentiles) to most (the sanctuary, which only the high priest could enter, and only once a year, on the Day of Atonement, Yom Kippur). "Holiness" in this system is not an abstraction: It is the measure of separation from the common, of being put apart for God. The organization of space calibrated proximity to the divine: Though all the earth was the Lord's, Jews held that, in some special sense, God dwelt in Jerusalem, in the sanctuary.

Along this gradient of holiness Jewish life was structured, from the sexual intimacy of marriage partners to the great communal celebrations of the annual pilgrimage festivals. God's instructions on permissible foods, for example, or on permissible times for sexual intercourse (forbidden during menstruation) obtained in all places. An observant family in Alexandria or Rome in principle would behave no differently from an observant family in Jerusalem. (I say "in principle" because variations in manner of observance and interpretation were inevitable, but both families would be concerned to keep the same mitzvah, divine command.) But in Jerusalem, the Temple added another dimension: The menstruating woman there would not enter the Temple area. Synagogue space was not ordered by purity codes because no sacrifices took place there: Their analogue would be the lecture hall or community center, not the Temple. Accordingly, a woman might go to synagogue as she wished, irrespective of purity. At the end of her period (determined variously: some Jews added another seven days to the time from onset of menses, meaning the period of sexual continence stretched from seven to fourteen days), the woman would reenter normal married life—and, depending on her custom, perhaps mark that transition with water, whether sprinkling or complete immersion.

Semen was another bodily effluvium that conveyed impurity. Men postcoitus or postejaculation thus had a low grade of impurity until the following sunset. Again, in the Diaspora, or any place distant from Jerusalem, this condition was of no practical consequence. If one had intended to go up to the Temple, however, entrance would have to be postponed to the following day. Priests on rotation in the Temple (where some would sleep during the period of their tour of duty), if they inadvertently incurred this impurity through nocturnal emission, would necessarily be excused from service for the duration of their impurity. A special stairwell allowed them to exit their area separately, without risk to other priests (since touching conveyed a secondary impurity). An understudy always prepared along with the high priest for Yom Kippur, to step in if the latter, because of impurity, became disqualified to serve.

Let's consider some of the implications of these two cases. First, these impurities lack all moral content: nothing can be inferred of the spiritual status of the impure person on account of his or her impurity. Put plainly: Impurity is not sin. There is nothing morally wrong with these people; they simply could not go into the Temple area. Still, we have evidence that Jews even far from Jerusalem went through some process to mark or make the end of the impure period. Allusions to ablutions of various sorts, remains of immersion pools for ritual cleansing (as opposed to common bathing), concern to have access to a water source: These remain in the literary and archaeological data as evidence for a general concern with maintaining purity. A second inference, then, that follows from the first: The remedy for impurity is purification and not (as some scholars, confusing impurity with sin, have argued) forgiveness.

Finally, there is a more subtle but extremely important observation we might make: Maintenance of these rules presupposes a high degree of internalization and self-regulation. How could an individual's observing the laws of sexual separation or semen impurity be monitored by anyone other than that person her- or himself? The fact that so many Jews interpreted the Law so variously, and had commitments to such a range of different interpretations, accounts for the unmistakable note of anxiety we can still hear in Pharisaic or Essene sources. Who could be sure that someone outside one's own group who thought of himself as pure was not, by the standards of the group, in fact impure? Hence the concern, in cases where control was possible—where and with whom one ate, from whom one bought foodstuffs or vessels—to stay within the group. Yet at the pilgrimage festivals, in the great press of humanity in the Temple's courts, everybody brushed up against and jostled against each other. Precisely at this moment when the concern for purity was highest, the tolerance for difference had to be highest, too.

One last aspect of our observation about internalization and self-monitoring to consider: A certain level of knowledge of and concern for the Torah on the part of those coming to the Temple was necessarily presupposed by its personnel, for the same reason noted above—only the worshiper monitored him or herself. No one checked to see whether some woman was menstruating; no one could know for certain whether the man just ahead or behind, who had journeyed from some corner of the earth to make a once-in-a-lifetime Passover pilgrimage, had *not* had a seminal emission during the night. Thus, despite the fiery debates over interpretation and the relentless sectarian attention to what might strike us as minute detail, the evidence of the sheer numbers thronging to the city at festival times indicates how much this whole huge, thick religious system managed to work as an effort of good faith.

These objective, and morally neutral, forms of impurity (occasionally designated as "ritual" or "levitical" purity) in principle restricted access to the Temple. But Scripture also named another type of impurity that resulted from certain sexual or cultic acts deemed sinful: illicit sexual relations (Lv 18:1–30, 20:10–21), ritual infanticide and magic (Lv 20:1–5; Dt 7:25), and especially idolatry (Dt 12:29–31). To distinguish these defilements from the first type, some scholars speak of "moral," "figurative," or "spiritual and religious" impurity. These defilements had to do with the morally polluting effect of sin.

Moral impurities worked differently from levitical impurity, both socially and ritually. Since such defilement was voluntary, it was sinful: One *chose* to perform the sinful and defiling act. Consequently (and unlike the levitical impurities discussed above) moral impurity was not contagious: Contact could not transfer it from the agent to a morally innocent third party. Interestingly, however, the contagion accrued around the altar. The sinner thus defiled not only him- or herself, but also the sanctuary and the Land: "Do not defile yourself by any of these things . . . lest the Land vomit you out when you defile it. . . . So keep my charge never to practice any of these abominable customs . . . and never to defile yourselves by them" (Lv 18:25, 28–30; cf. 20:3). The remedy for the impurity of immorality was cessation of the sinful activity, atonement, and a special day of purgation with its own specific sacrifices, Yom Kippur (Lv 16). Repentance and atonement purged the sinner, while the atoning sacrifice purged defilement from the sanctuary.

Sacrifice for sin was also part of a process that was at once psychological, spiritual, and practical. For example, God had specified a protocol for atoning for theft or fraud in Leviticus: The guilty party had to acknowledge his wrong and restore the amount "in full, and shall add a fifth to it, and give it to him to whom it belongs" (6:5). The final turn of this cycle was offering the sacrifice (a ram, v. 6): The penitent would put his hand on the animal's head and say to the priest before whom he stood what the sacrifice was for. The ram's throat slit, its blood poured out around the altar—this closed the process of repentance, restitution, and sacrifice by which the sinner atoned for his sin. The priest would then divide the animal's body—some to be burned on the altar, the rest to the priests. With other types of offerings, some of the meat would also return to the worshiper, to eat outside the Temple.

For personal sins, in other words, the Temple served as a means to effect atonement. It was not the sole means—too many Jews for too many centuries had lived too far from Jerusalem, and never got to the Temple at all, to have that be the case. Fundamental to atonement and God's forgiveness was the sinner's repentance. Sacrifice might add to this process, and, where practical, it should be added, but it was neither a substitute for nor the sine qua non of repentance. The blood of the sacrifice, again, did not cleanse the sinner, but the altar—on Yom Kippur, of the pollution from the sins of all Israel.

A final biblical category governing access to the Temple was the distinction between holy or sacred and common or profane. The distinction had to be made and kept by the priests, who in turn were responsible for teaching it to the people: Speaking to Aaron, God said, "You are to distinguish between the holy and the common, between the unclean and the clean; and you are to teach the people of Israel" (Lv 10:10). The two pairs of words correlate functionally—neither the unclean nor the common was to be brought close to the altar—but they are not synonyms. A priest with a physical defect, for example, could not serve at the altar: His impairment rendered him "common." But this did not affect his purity status at all: He could still partake of the food generated by the sacrifices, which had to be eaten in purity (Lv 21:6, 17–23).

This last distinction, taken together with the purity rules, can help us account for the layout of the Temple, and the ways that corresponded to sacred space. Jews viewed the Torah as the exclusive privilege and responsibility of Israel (so, e.g., Paul in Rom 9:4–5). Its commandments, accordingly, were incumbent only upon Jews. God's Torah to Israel was part and parcel of his election of Israel: They were, in the language of the Bible, a people whom he had set apart for himself, "a kingdom of priests and a holy nation." The later rabbis, in pursuit of their characteristic concern with interpretive precision, spelled this out in very practical ways. Only a Jewish corpse, they maintained, could convey corpse-impurity; a Gentile corpse did not. Similarly, only contact with Jewish menstrual fluid affected one's purity status. What if, walking past a public bath, a Jew stepped on a stain of menstrual fluid? Assume, said the rabbis, that it is gentile menstrual fluid, and so do not be concerned about impurity. In short, Gentiles were not subject to Israel's purity regulations.

We might have inferred this from the layout of the Temple: Gentiles had access to the largest, most exterior court within the complex. To gain access to their own sections within the Temple area, Jews had to walk through the crowds of Gentiles in the outer court. If Gentiles could convey impurity, Jews would have risked contracting it through contact precisely on their way to sacrifice, when they needed to be most concerned about being pure.

Gentiles were permitted in their own court, then. They were also restricted to it, just as women could penetrate only as far as their own area, and not enter that of the men, and just as the men could enter the court of Israel, but not the court of the priests, and just as the priests could work in their own court, but only the high priest could enter the sanctuary. Josephus described the court of the Gentiles as demarcated by "a stone balustrade, three cubits high [about 4.5 feet] and of exquisite workmanship. In this, at regular intervals, stood stone slabs warning, some in Greek, others in Latin, of the law of purification, namely that *no foreigner was permitted to enter the holy place,* for so the second enclosure of the Temple was called" (*BJ* 5.193–94). One of these inscriptions, recovered in the last century, reads:

> No man of another nation to enter within the fence and enclosure round the Temple. And whoever is caught will have himself to blame that his death ensues.

The objection to Gentiles entering could not have been, as we have seen, their impurity: They were not seen as subject to purity laws regulating access to the altar. The problem, rather, was more likely their status vis-à-vis Israel. Israel had been "set apart" by God: This is the meaning of "holy" or "sanctified." So also, for example, the formula spoken by the groom to his bride during the marriage ceremony: "I *sanctify* you to me according to the law of Moses and Israel"—the bride is set apart for her husband. The binary term with "holy" is "common"—which is what the Gentiles were, relative to Israel. And just as the impaired priest was "common" and could not serve at the altar, so with the Gentile: He stayed his appropriate distance from the altar, as the woman hers, and as the nonpriestly Jew his. But a Gentile could come closer to the altar than a menstruating or leprous Jew, who, according to Israel's purity laws, was debarred from the entire Temple area.

Purity laws and sacred space were one biblically based way that Jews structured community life in antiquity. Before turning to a look at the

Gospels, we should consider one more way: the monthly changes in the yearly calendar, the holidays, and, even more particularly, the Sabbath—sacred time.

Calendars are an extremely effective way to construct community across vast distances; conversely, calendrical differences demarcate different groups. We see both effects when looking at Israel in the Diaspora, where Sabbath observance especially stood out, and when looking at Jews themselves, when different groups measured different times. The Temple, and subsequent rabbinic Judaism, for example, ran on a lunar calendar, with months corresponding to the phases of the moon. But the community represented by the sectarian document *Jubilees* (a retelling of Genesis) and also the Essenes kept solar time, the emphasis of which is on the number of days in the year. The result was that calculations for holidays within these two different systems indicated different days. Still, discrepancies notwithstanding, all groups would follow the biblical script in determining and observing the times and seasons—Yom Kippur on the tenth day of the seventh month of the year (Lv 16:29); Passover on the fourteenth day of the first month (23:5); Shavuot/Pentecost, fifty days after (23:15); the festival of trumpets marking the first day of the seventh month (September/October: This corresponds to Rosh haShanah, Lv 23:24); Sukkot/Booths, the fifteenth day of the seventh month (23:33).

These days of holy convocation and solemn assembly, as God calls them in Leviticus, shaped the Jewish year. Within the land of Israel—the only setting presupposed in the Torah narrative—male Israelites were specifically enjoined to assemble to present offerings: in Jesus' time, of course, this would be construed as the Jerusalem Temple. Jews who lived outside the land—the majority by Jesus' period—developed various improvisations to compensate or substitute for Temple worship: The repetition of prayers at the approximate times of Temple offerings within the communal setting of the synagogue would be one way to achieve this. Or they would make the pilgrimage for the holiday from the lands of their dispersion. Or, most concretely, they would contribute the annual half-shekel Temple tax—mandated for male Israelites in the Land, thus voluntary in the Second Temple period for those outside—that went toward the Temple's overhead, especially the sacrifices on behalf of the community offered on the Sabbath and the festivals. Thus, shared holy time had a way, culturally and religiously, of shortening the distance between everyplace else and Jerusalem—holy space.

The ultimate temporal binder for Jewish life, family, and community was the Sabbath. Here the evidence both from the Diaspora and for the Land of Israel is beyond dispute. The Sabbath was one of the Jewish practices that pagan writers most commented on; and throughout the empire we have evidence of special legislation exempting Jews from serving in the army, or from appearing in court cases, because of their commitment to keeping the Sabbath. As the stories in the Gospels show, there was considerable scope for interpreting what "keeping the Sabbath" meant. But the principle of keeping the Sabbath itself was not in question: It was, as God said in the Book of Exodus,

> a sign between me and you throughout your generations, that you may know that I, the Lord, sanctify you. You shall keep the Sabbath because it is holy for you. . . . Therefore the people of Israel shall keep the Sabbath, observing the Sabbath throughout their generations as a perpetual covenant. It is a sign for ever between me and the people of Israel that in six days the Lord made the heavens and the earth, and on the seventh day he rested and was refreshed. (31:12–17)

The Sabbath was thus a special sign of Israel's unique dignity as God's elect nation. It condensed in a single symbol those elements of ancient Judaism that were at once broadly universalist and precisely particular. In its reference to God as Creator, the Sabbath implied the claim that God was a universal deity, the source of all Creation: He was, therefore, the proper object of Gentile as well as Jewish piety. (For a rhetorically lush statement of this position, see the first chapter of Paul's letter to the Romans.)

But this God who created was not a generic supreme being who stood in some vaguely causal relationship to everything else. The One God was specifically the God of Abraham, Isaac, and Jacob. The same God who made the heavens and the earth and everything in them was also concerned with the details of Israel's marital life, with the education of their children, with their just measures and fair law courts. Most specifically, he was the Redeemer of Israel, who realized his promise to Abraham by bringing his people out of bondage in Egypt. The God of all Creation was, at the same moment, the God of Jewish history.

This theme would be brought home repeatedly by the biblical story itself, invoked in the domestic and communal observance of the Sabbath, and recalled at each of the High Holidays, which came to be associated with specific moments in the creation of the people of Israel:

Sukkot, when Israel lived in booths in the desert; Shavuot, when Israel received the Law on Sinai; and, most especially, Pesach, with the liberation of the people from oppressive foreign dominion. And so, just as Judaism drew no distinction between "secular" and "religious" behavior or between "ethics" and "ritual"—both were the subject of divine concern and direction; God details with equal urgency how to care for the poor and how to worship at his altar—so, too, no firm distinction stood between the "religious" and the "national." Festival convocations drawing huge numbers together to celebrate God's redemption of Israel could very well embody what we would see as political as well as spiritual aims. Small wonder, then, that once Judea came under direct Roman authority, the prefect would march his troops up from Caesarea to Jerusalem. And the place most particularly guarded would be the Temple itself, where the soldiers would stand on the roof of the colonnade, staring down at the Jews massed below.

Chapter 3

TRAJECTORIES:
PAUL, THE GOSPELS,
AND JESUS

L IKE THE OLDER BIBLICAL TRADITIONS that they refer to and draw on, the Gospels present Jesus' teaching in a story relating his words and deeds. And since their stories are shaped by historical and religious traditions both from and about him, they share a similar narrative obligation: Whatever they claim about his activities and their venue, the evangelists must close on Jerusalem, at Passover, with the cross. Traditions before that point—what Jesus did and said where, to whom, in what circumstances—vary, as we shall see, from Gospel to Gospel; traditions after that point—Who saw what at the tomb? To whom (one woman? several women? Peter?) and in what place (Galilee? Emmaus? Jerusalem?) did the Risen Christ first appear?—likewise diverge. But Jesus' crucifixion is the cardinal point that all these Gospels share.

I want to start from this point and move both backward and forward; backward to a reconstruction of Jesus' mission and message; forward to a reconstruction of the earliest movement that formed in his name. In so doing, I am making a commitment to a position that the material itself can only support but not actually establish, namely, that we can draw causal and explanatory connections between *what* Jesus taught, *why* and *how* he died, and *why* and *how* the earliest Christian movement took the shapes it did.

Such a connected trajectory can be and has been challenged. Some scholars have argued that Jesus taught one thing (to love God and one another, for example), but was killed for another (priestly resentment, or Roman oppressiveness). Understanding his teaching, on this construction, sheds little light on why he died but does open up a road into Christianity's ethnically inclusive future (loving others means loving Gentiles).

Other scholars identify Jesus' message as some kind of social reform: Jesus, they say, a champion of social equality that he enacted especially through meals shared with all comers, taught against the sexual, political, and religious power hierarchies of his society. He accordingly fought against purity rules themselves (which operate by drawing distinctions between persons) and therefore especially opposed the priestly rulers in the Jerusalem Temple, in this view literally a monument to hierarchy.

The strength of this interpretation is its immediate linking of Jesus' teachings in the Galilee to subsequent events in Jerusalem. It thereby accounts for the traditions of priestly involvement in Jesus' death: How could the priests tolerate such a challenge to their authority? But it breaks any connection at the next two points on our trajectory, explaining neither why Pilate would have involved himself as he did (with an ugly public execution), nor what Jesus' teaching has to do with the earliest stratum of Christian material we have, namely, the letters of Paul (which evince no trace of any such social program).

Those who take certain strata of Q as the core historical material for Jesus argue even more strenuously and overtly against such causal linkages. Other gospel sayings and stories, as well as traditions in Paul, they urge, actually give the measure of distortion and loss of authentic Jesus material which, again on the evidence of Q, consisted chiefly of witty and culturally subversive sayings (as opposed to, for instance, teachings about the coming Kingdom of God) with nothing of Jerusalem or the cross. This Q-Jesus dies by misadventure, as such teaching has little to do with the Temple or with Rome. And the rest of subsequent Christianity, arising as it does around the proclamation of a crucified, raised, and returning Messiah, likewise has little to do with the Cynic-like figure who stands, obscured, at its beginnings.

All of these reconstructions syncopate links in the chain of ancient evidence for the origins of Christianity. In so doing, they emphasize the contingent or accidental quality of history familiar to all of us in our own lives. Intending one thing, we often end up with another. Our lives work out in ways that we neither anticipate nor plan. Events are not necessarily results caused by particular actions. What seems like causality is often just the rational webbing thrown out over the past by our own retrospection. In real life, often, things just happen.

Our individual experience of the truth of this perspective on life should not, however, persuade us of its usefulness when doing history. History is different from personal retrospection. The latter is individual, subjective, private, in many ways untestable: Its realm is memory. History, on the other hand, is social. It is public. Through debate, appeals to data, judgments about coherence and plausibility, history is in some sense testable. It is in its obligations to both evidence and testability that history as a discipline is scientific. Its relation to memory is thus different from that which memory shares with personal recollection, because history's realm is shared, public knowledge.

Thus, though we join here in the effort to retrieve an individual, Jesus of Nazareth, from his obscured past, since we do history, we necessarily seek to retrieve as well his culture, his religion, his social reality—the lived context of law, custom, practice, and attitudes surveyed before. Though the unique starting point of a new religious movement, Jesus would not have been Jesus without all the others standing around him and after him: his followers, his antagonists, pilgrims to and residents of Jerusalem, the Romans, Jews in the Diaspora, and, eventually, Gentiles. We cannot explain and understand him without likewise explaining and understanding them.

Again, the task is neither easy nor simple. The most direct evidence is complicated and therefore difficult to use, because it is late: The Gospels, as we have seen, are a stratigraphic record of various interpretations of Jesus, not reports of what he actually did and said. But unless what he did and said had made sense to his own contemporaries, we would have no object of study at all: Without his immediate followers, we would know nothing about Jesus, nor—since it is upon them that the existence of Christianity ultimately depends—would we have historical reason to care.

It is on this ground—the public coherence of his message to his own contemporaries—that we as historians gain our purchase on the confusing evidence of Jesus' past. Of the three points on our trajectory that I maintain are causally linked—his mission; his death; his subsequent movement—our evidence is best for the latter two. We know, if we can know anything, that Jesus died on a cross, hence in a context where Roman concerns about sedition must have figured significantly. And we know that his immediate followers, who were not likewise executed, began a mission soon involving Greek-speaking Jews of the Diaspora and extending, very early, to Gentiles as well. As the movement develops its data increase, until we arrive at Paul's letters and, later, the Gospels.

I propose, then, that we begin our first cycle of investigation in reverse, moving "backward" from our most secure data. Our historically latest point, the mission to Gentiles in the Diaspora, provides our chronologically earliest evidence, Paul's letters. In an attempt to isolate traditions in Paul's letters that he seems to share with the Gospels, we will pay particular attention to those traditions that he claims to have inherited: These will help us begin to build a trajectory backward.

The Gospel evidence cuts two ways. Since the evangelists wrote post-70 C.E., hence after Paul's lifetime, they testify in one sense to the sort of movement Christianity became in the period after the destruction of the Temple. But since they set their stories in the earliest period, Jesus' mission to Israel, they must inherit *some* aspects of their stories—characters, events, teachings—from the past. Where traditions in the Gospels (written c. 75–90 C.E.) seem similar to or supportive of themes in Paul's letters (written c. 50–60)—especially those that he identifies as traditions that he inherited from other Christians whose activity predates his own—we can gain, I shall argue, a glimpse into the earlier stages of the Jesus movement. And if any of these data match information about early Judaism from independent Jewish sources—Josephus' histories, for example; or the Dead Sea Scrolls; or various other intertestamental writings—then they can help to identify those aspects of earliest Christianity that may trace back to the lifetime and mission of Jesus himself.

Beginning our investigation with Paul means beginning with a contemporary of Jesus and his first followers. Though he did not compose the letters preserved in the New Testament until midcentury, information from Paul stands a good generation earlier than our next earliest source, the Gospel of Mark.

But "early" does not mean, in terms of evidence for Jesus, "most direct." For one thing, Paul's involvement in the movement came only *after* Jesus' death and, in a sense, because of it: Paul's point of contact is his response, at first negative and then positive, to the proclamation of the Resurrection (on this, especially Gal 1 and 1 Cor 15). Also, though Paul presumably knew many of Jesus' original followers, including and especially Peter, he had differences with them on important matters of principle. Thus, at some points, in other words, what he says represents something other than what Jesus' earliest followers were saying. And, finally, Paul occasionally insisted that the source of his gospel was *not* human—not the original apostles, and certainly not Jesus of Nazareth himself—but divine: What he had, Paul says, he had by revelation (Gal 1:12–22). Persuasive and even impressive as this last point may have been to an ancient audience, it rightly makes modern ones, in pursuit of the Jesus of history, mildly anxious: How much of what Paul says can actually be consonant with what Jesus might have taught, especially if he disagrees so pointedly with those who had known "Jesus according to the flesh"?

Paul's strongest assertions of his independence from Jesus' original followers come in his letter to the Galatians, where he argues vociferously for his own views on an issue—what observances non-Jewish followers of Jesus owe to Jewish law—that had never surfaced in the course of Jesus' own mission, since Jesus spoke primarily if not exclusively to fellow Jews. Elsewhere, with different issues in view, Paul insists equally strongly on his dependable knowledge of earlier Jesus traditions. Let's begin by reviewing his letters in their (probable) chronological order of composition, to see what of this we can glean.

"For this we declare to you by the word of the Lord": The Kingdom

THE FIRST LETTER to the Thessalonians, from our vantage point as historians, is very early evidence indeed, composed in the late forties or early fifties of the first century. But the letter itself conveys how late things already seemed to Paul's gentile audience. Having "turned to God from idols to serve a living and true God," they awaited "his Son from heaven, whom he raised from the dead, Jesus who rescues us from the wrath to come" (1:9–10). But these gentile Christians in Thessalonica had already waited longer than they had expected to. Evidently surprised that some of their number had died before Christ's return, they pressed Paul to know more clearly when this would be. These are the issues Paul deals with in chapters 4 and 5 of this letter, and for which, in 4:15, he invokes "the word of the Lord," that is, Jesus (cf. 4:1).

These two chapters give us a glimpse into the lively apocalyptic expectation of both Paul and this community. Their teaching corresponds in content and even in phrasing with traditions that occur a generation or so later in the synoptic Gospels. For instance, citing "the word of the Lord," Paul describes Jesus' glorious and imminent return:

> For this we declare to you by the word of the Lord, that *we who are alive,* who are left until the coming of the Lord, shall not precede those who have fallen asleep. For the Lord himself will descend from heaven with a cry of command, with the archangel's call, and the sound of the trumpet of God. And the dead in Christ will rise first; then *we who are alive, who are left,* shall be caught up together with them in the clouds to meet the Lord in the air; and so we shall always be with the Lord. Therefore comfort one another with these words.   (1 Thes 4:13–18)

Paul attributes his description of events at the Second Coming to a teaching of "the Lord." On the authority of that saying, he tells of Christ's impending descent from heaven. In the language of military engagement ("cry of command"; the archangel's "call"; God's "trumpet"), Paul then describes the resurrection of the dead, as well as the relocation "in the air" of "we who are alive."

Elsewhere in his letters, though without the invocation of the Lord's authority he gives here, Paul details this scenario further. (I shall italicize those items that he specifically repeats.) Thus in 1 Corinthians 15, after arguing that Christ's resurrection and the (future) resurrection of the dead are intrinsically linked, Paul continues:

> For as in Adam all die, so also in Christ shall all be made alive. But each in his own order: Christ the first fruits, then *at his coming* [Parousia, meaning "Second Coming"] *those who belong to Christ.* Then comes the End, when he delivers the Kingdom to God the father after destroying every rule and every authority and every power. For he must rule until he has put all his enemies under his feet. The last enemy is Death.
> (15:22–26)

Paul goes on from this passage to entangle himself in various moral exhortations. Several verses later, then, he returns to this theme, describing what the body of the raised dead will be like. "Sown" in the earth the way a seed is, as a physical or natural body, it will be raised a "spiritual body" (vv. 42–48). Whatever that might be, it is certainly *not* flesh and blood, which, says Paul, "cannot inherit the Kingdom of God" (v. 50). And more than the dead: The flesh of the living, too, will be likewise transformed. "*We shall not all sleep,* but we shall all be changed, in a moment, in the twinkling of an eye, *at the last trumpet. For the trumpet will sound, the dead will rise* imperishable, and we shall all be changed" (vv. 51–52). Further, in a later letter, Philippians, we find a more concise description: "Our commonwealth is in *heaven,* and *from it we await a Savior, the Lord Jesus Christ,* who will *change our lowly body to be like* his *glorious body,* by the power which enables him even to *subject all things to himself*" (3:20–21).

From Paul's core teaching on "the Lord's" authority about the sequence and substance of Endtime events, we have been able, by briefly canvasing his other letters, to thicken his description. It runs something like this: The Endtime, which Paul also identifies as the establishment of God's kingdom, will be inaugurated by the return from heaven of the raised and glorious Christ. He will descend to the noise of celestial battle to defeat the enemies of God: rules, authorities, powers, and finally even Death. The followers of Christ will also participate, both the quick and the dead. The dead will rise in special, nonphysical "flesh" to join the living (who are likewise transformed), so that their bodies, in the Kingdom, will correspond to that glorious body in which Christ himself was raised from the dead.

A further point to emphasize: According to Paul, the Second Coming is not infinitely distant. He expects to witness the Parousia himself ("we who are alive"). The Thessalonians' discomfiture at the death of some of their members in advance of Christ's return gives the measure of their time frame: They were surprised that these deaths had preceded the End, so soon did they expect Christ's glorious advent.

Indeed, the nearness of the End is a frequent Pauline theme. He sounds it repeatedly, and in many contexts. Unmarried Corinthians should stay as they are, he urges, "in view of the impending distress"— the travails, that is, before the establishment of God's kingdom (1 Cor 7:26. The travails are reminiscent of the "wrath" from which the Son delivers his faithful, 1 Thes 1:10 above). "The appointed time has grown very short. . . . The form of this world is passing away" (vv. 29, 31). It is upon *us,* he tells his congregation, that "the end of the ages has come" (10:11). And even in his final letter, Romans, Paul repeats his belief with undiminished conviction. Until the Son returns, all creation "groans in travail" (Rom 8:22). Nonetheless, Paul asserts—a decade, perhaps, after his correspondence to Thessalonica; more than two, perhaps, since his joining the movement—that "salvation is nearer to us than when we first believed. The night is far gone; the day is at hand" (13:11–12).

Yet in Thessalonians, his earliest extant letter, Paul had gone on to qualify what he had just said about Christ's advent:

> But as to the times and seasons, brethren, you have no need to have anything written to you. For you yourselves know well that *the day of the Lord will come like a thief in the night*. When people say, "There is peace and security," then sudden destruction will come upon them as travail comes upon a woman with child, and there will be no escape. But you are not in darkness, brethren, for that day to surprise you like a thief. (1 Thes 5:1–4)

Paul knows the End will be soon; he even has a fairly clear idea of the sequence of final events. Yet he cautions that believers cannot know its precise timetable in advance: Like the proverbial thief in the night, the End will come as a sudden surprise.

What in the later Gospels confirms or conforms to this earlier teaching which, Paul claims, itself goes back to Jesus? Let's look first at Mark, our next earliest source. (Q may represent earlier traditions; but since it appears solely in post-Markan documents—namely Matthew, Luke, and a later and noncanonical gospel, Thomas—we cannot know.) Like the other three New Testament evangelists, Mark begins his story about the public mission of Jesus with John the Baptizer. Immersing penitents—presumably Jews—coming to him by the river Jordan from Judea and Jerusalem, John also immerses Jesus, who arrives from Nazareth in Galilee, to the north. As he comes back out of the water, Jesus hears a voice from heaven (the trope indicates God) proclaiming him "beloved Son" (cf. 1 Thes 1:10, where Paul designates Jesus God's son). Thereafter, following John's arrest, Jesus begins his own mission in the Galilee, proclaiming, "The time is fulfilled, and the Kingdom of God has drawn near. Repent, and believe in the good news"—the good news, that is, of the Kingdom's closeness. Like Paul, though twenty years later, Mark's Jesus heralds the approaching Kingdom. Unlike Paul, Mark's Jesus neither defines nor describes it. We have to read further in Mark's story to find out what he means.

Mark is a while in getting to a description and explanation of what he (and, in his story, Jesus) means by God's kingdom. At first, through a mix of narrative description and teaching material, Mark simply trails his main character from Capernaum through the synagogues of the Galilee, where he performs exorcisms and healings on the Sabbath. Those in the synagogue exclaim at Jesus' "new teaching" (1:27), but again, Mark does not say what this is. The themes of God's kingdom and Jesus' sonship seem to disappear.

As the healings and exorcisms accrue, the atmosphere becomes charged with antagonism: Scribes and Pharisees grow hostile, and the latter even plot Jesus' death (3:6). Mark's Jesus does not again return to the theme of God's kingdom until he begins teaching in parables (that is, symbolic stories), likening the Kingdom to the way seed grows (4:1–34). The image this story evokes is very unlike the public, cosmic drama Paul had described. And we note another odd contrast to Paul's letter. Paul had spoken freely of Jesus as God's Son. In Mark's story of Jesus' mission, oddly, only demons or unclean spirits declaim this identity: "And whenever the unclean spirits beheld him, they fell down before him and cried out, 'You are the Son of God!' " (3:11; cf. 5:7, and 1:24, "the Holy One of God"). When Jesus speaks of himself as Son, he only does so obliquely, in the third person; and he calls himself the Son of Man (2:10).

Nevertheless, at two very dramatic moments in his story, Mark does present Jesus as speaking of the Kingdom in a way more reminiscent of Paul's. The first comes in 8:38–9:1. Here Mark presents a highly charged dialogue with Peter, during which (and for reasons utterly unexplained in the text) Peter identifies Jesus as "the Christ" (8:29). From this identification, Jesus goes on immediately to give a detailed prediction of his Passion, again couched indirectly in terms of the Son of Man (8:31). Mark's Jesus says:

> "Whoever is ashamed of me and my words in this adulterous and sinful generation, of him will the Son of Man also be ashamed when *he comes in the glory of his Father with the holy angels.*" And he said to them, "Truly I say to you, there are *some standing here who will not taste death before they see that the kingdom of God has come in power.*"

The italicized verses relay content similar to Paul's: God's Son will arrive with angels, and he will arrive soon—within the lifetime of the generation addressed by Jesus—to establish the Kingdom. But when? How can one know?

At several points in Mark's story, different characters—Pharisees at 8:11–13; Peter, James, John, and Andrew from among his disciples at 13:3–4—ask Jesus for or about "a sign." And at various points in this Gospel, Jesus had lamented his own generation: "Why does this generation seek a sign? Truly, I say to you, no sign shall be given to this generation," in evident reproach to some Pharisees (8:112). "O faithless generation! How long am I able to be with you? How long am I able to bear with you?" to a crowd asking for a cure (9:19; cf. the sinners and adulterers referred to above, 8:38). Nonetheless, he says, some from among his generation will live to see the Kingdom (9:1).

Once in Jerusalem just before Passover, however, Mark's Jesus fills in his prophecy in much greater detail. And he links the coming Kingdom, again tied to the lifetime of his own generation (13:30), to a sign—a specific, empirical, unmistakable public event: the destruction of the Temple. This is a crucially important passage for understanding the apocalyptic expectations of Mark and his post-70 community, and we will examine it in some detail. I give it here at length, italicizing those items that conform to those apocalyptic themes already identified in Paul:

And as he came out of the Temple, one of his disciples said to him, "Look, teacher, what wonderful stones and what wonderful buildings!" And Jesus said to him, "Do you see these great buildings? There will not be left here one stone upon another, that will not be thrown down." And as he sat down on the Mount of Olives opposite the Temple, Peter and James and John and Andrew asked him privately, "Tell us, when will this be, and *what will be the sign* when these things are all to be accomplished?" And Jesus began to say to them, "Take heed that no one leads you astray. Many will come in my name, saying, 'I am he!' and *they will lead many astray.* And when you hear of *wars and rumors of wars,* do not be alarmed, for *the End is not yet.* For nation will rise up against nation, and kingdom against kingdom; there will be *earthquakes* in various places, there will be *famines;* this is but the beginning of the birth-pangs.

"But take heed to yourselves; for they will *deliver you up to councils,* and you will be *beaten in synagogues,* and you will stand before governors and kings for my sake, to bear testimony before them. And *the gospel must first be preached among the nations* [Gk. *ethnē;* Heb. *goyim*]. . . . *You will be hated* by all for my name's sake. But he who endures to the end will be saved.

"But when you see *the abomination of desolation set up where it ought not be (let the reader understand),* then let those who are in Judea flee to the mountains. . . . For in those days there will be such *tribulation* as has not been seen from the beginning of the creation which God created until now, and never will be. And if the Lord *had not shortened the days,* no human being would be saved; but for the sake of the elect whom he chose, *he shortened the days.* And then if anyone says to you, 'Look, here is the Christ!' or 'Look, there he is!' do not believe it. False Christs and false prophets will arise and show signs and wonders, to lead astray, if possible, the elect. But take heed; I have told you all things beforehand.

"But in those days, after that tribulation, *the sun will be darkened, and the moon will not give its light, and the stars will be falling from heaven, and the powers in the heavens will be shaken. And then they will see the Son* of Man *coming in clouds with great power and glory.* And then he will send out *angels,* and *gather his elect* from the four winds. . . .

"From the fig tree learn its lesson: as soon as its branch becomes tender and puts forth its leaves, you know that summer is near. So also, when you see these things taking place, *you know that he* [i.e., the Son] *is near, at the very gates.* Truly, I say to you, *this generation will not pass away before all these things are accomplished. Heaven and earth will pass away,* but my words will not pass away.

"But of that day or that hour *no one knows,* not even the angels in heaven, nor the Son, but only the Father. Take heed. Watch. . . . What I say to you I say to all: Watch."

The cascade of apocalyptic images in this passage both recalls Paul's teaching and helps us to locate these ideas in broader contemporary Jewish tradition—as well, I shall argue, in first-century Jewish history. Mark, too, identifies travails, social as well as celestial, as marking the onset of the End. The End is on the way: The Lord, he says, has already shortened the days (v. 20); its arrival is predicted for the lifetime of those hearing the prediction (v. 30). And the Son again returns on clouds, in glory, with angels; again he gathers up those who are his (v. 26).

But Jesus' speech in Mark is also, unlike Paul's, self-consciously literary. Mark calls upon "the one reading" to understand the allusion he has just made when invoking the "abomination of desolation." Mark here refers his first-century audience to the Book of Daniel (13:14), a prophetic text now in both the Jewish and the Christian canons. The book's title refers to the historical Daniel, a Jew who had lived during the Judean captivity in Babylon in the sixth century B.C.E. (he is mentioned in Ez 14:14 and 28:3). But the author of this prophetic book only writes in the name of this earlier figure; in fact, he actually lived centuries later, during the second century B.C.E., when he described, in heavily symbolic language, political events in and around Jerusalem in the 160s. This pseudonymity was a common technique in the ancient world: The borrowed antiquity of false authorship enhanced the authority of a text.

It was during this decade in the second century B.C.E. that the religious and cultural struggle between cosmopolitan Hellenism and ancestral Jewish traditions reached a crisis. According to the First Book of the Maccabees, a near-contemporary history, certain Jews in Jerusalem desired to adopt Greek culture. They pushed to build a gymnasium, a cultural center for the study of athletics, literature, music, and philosophy; and some even endured surgery to remove the signs of circumcision. (Activities in the gymnasium were often conducted in the nude, and circumcision was viewed as a mutilation by the Greeks; 1 Mc 1:11–15). The cultural civil war that erupted turned quickly to actual combat once Antiochus Epiphanes, the Seleucid Greek ruler of this fragment of Alexander the Great's former territory, weighed in on the side of the Hellenists. First supporting the assimilationist position, then mandating it, Antiochus eventually ended by erecting an altar to Olympian Zeus in the Temple of the Jews' own high god in Jerusalem. The country, led by the priestly Hasmonean family under Judah Maccabee, erupted in open revolt. They routed the extreme Hellenists and purified and rededicated the Temple, celebrating its renewal in an annual festival thereafter. (This is the historical base of the modern celebration of Hanukkah; cf. John 10:22, when Jesus celebrates this holiday in Jerusalem.)

But the image of the "abomination of desolation" entered the bloodstream of Jewish apocalyptic tradition through the Book of Daniel, whose author associated Antiochus' profanation of the altar with the coming End of Days. Wars and desolation mark the introduction of the abominations (Dn 9:27, 11:31), "and there shall be a time of trouble such as never has been" (12:1). But eventually God will vindicate the righteous, raising them from the dead to everlasting life (12:2). When, asks the prophet, shall these things be accomplished? The text replies, When its words become known. "You, Daniel, shut up the words [of this prophecy] and seal the book *until the time of the End*" (12:4). The very act of reading, or hearing, the Book of Daniel thus "activates" its own prophecy.

It is this, when evoking the abomination of desolation, that Mark asks his reader to understand: the sign has been given that marks the beginning of the End (Mk 13:14). In "Daniel's" text, this had corresponded to Antiochus' altar, erected more than two centuries before Mark wrote. But what did it mean for Mark?

Here we have to read the passage attentively, and consider as well what we know of Mark's own period, for which we have other sources: Josephus' two histories, *The Jewish War* and *Jewish Antiquities;* Book 5 of the Roman Tacitus' *History;* and *Legatio ad Gaium,* midcentury, from Philo of Alexandria. The decades between Jesus' time and Mark's had seen increasing unrest and friction between Judea and its Roman overseers, often over the issue of introducing unacceptable religious images into Jerusalem. The region and the city were often unlucky in Rome's choice of prefects—on this Philo, Josephus, and Tacitus all agree, interestingly singling out Pontius Pilate (26–36 C.E.) as one of the worst provocateurs. Jews in Jerusalem had protested, sometimes violently, against real or imagined insults to their ancestral religious prerogatives. As the decades of direct Roman supervision wore on, charismatic religious figures predicting imminent redemption had gathered huge crowds and, cut down with their followers, been brutally suppressed; crowds in pilgrim-swollen Jerusalem had turned to riot; and finally the Temple itself, after a three-year standoff between the empire and Jewish rebels, was burned, torn down, utterly destroyed.

Mark 13, speaking the language of Jewish apocalyptic, lies on top of this historical terrain. Scholars variously match the figures and events he conjures to the ones discernible in the historical record. The audience of Mark's Gospel, shortly post-70, would have seen or known what Mark's narrative audience hears "prophesied," ostensibly c. 30: wars, rumors of wars, false messiahs, false prophets, social turmoil. And the apocalyptic image *par excellence,* the abomination of desolation, resonates precisely with two securely attested events. The first is the emperor Caligula's failed attempt, in 40–41 C.E., to introduce a cultic statue with his own features into Jerusalem's Temple—an episode that would have touched off massive Jewish protests. The second was a consequence of Titus' victory itself. The triumphant army at the finale of the siege would have carried its military standards onto the ruined Temple Mount. These standards served soldiers as a sort of mobile cultic altar.

Jesus' soliloquy in Mark's text thus ties all these religiously portentous events into a specifically Christian concern: knowing the time of the Parousia, the reappearance from heaven of Jesus Christ as the triumphant Son of Man. "When will this be, and what will be the sign when these things are all to be accomplished?" ask some apostles after

Jesus predicts the Temple's destruction. In so doing, they set up Jesus' apocalyptic discourse. He answers by detailing what must come first: false christs, wars, famine, persecution of those loyal to him, and the preaching of the gospel to Gentiles. (Note: this gentile mission did not get under way until some time after Jesus' execution. Mark demonstrates here the way his predictions have a double time frame: the narrative audience, Jesus' generation, c. 30; and the actual audience, Mark's, after 70.)

After these events come the abomination, which the understanding reader knows must mean the End; after these comes the Temple's total destruction ("no stone upon another"); after these, then—since the Lord has already shortened the days—will come the End, and the return of the Redeemer. Mark, in short, sees time stereoscopically. From the perspective of those around Jesus, "the faithless and adulterous generation," no sign had been given. But from the perspective of his own generation—a faithful generation who had witnessed to Christ before councils and governors, who had withstood the allurements of "false christs and false prophets" working signs and wonders, and who had preached the gospel to the Gentiles—the great and unmistakable sign of Christ's Second Coming had been given: the destruction of the Temple. The End, Mark thus knew, really was at hand; and some from Jesus' own generation were still alive to see it (13:30; cf. 9:1).

But Mark, like Paul, finally closes his apocalyptic discourse on a note of caution: Though the time is at hand, it cannot with greater clarity be known. One must remain discerning and alert: "Watch" (13:33, 37). In the two later Gospels that depend on him, Matthew and Luke, this counsel is preserved in a Q-saying that, again like Paul, invokes the proverbial nocturnal thief: "Watch, therefore, for you do not know what day your Lord is coming. But know this, that if the householder had known *in what part of the night the thief was coming,* he would have watched . . ." (Mt 24:43//Lk 12:39).

As time stretched on and history continued, this apocalyptic refrain in traditions about the Kingdom grows comparatively muted in the later Gospels. Q-sayings, or other traditions specific only to Matthew or Luke, speak of the Kingdom in various ways, some of which emphasize a present, nonapocalyptic quality. And where the two other Synoptics reproduce substantial sections of the Markan Apocalypse, they feel free to alter or delete parts of Jesus' speech. One of Matthew's alterations, however, interestingly picks up a vivid detail that we saw in Paul: the sound of the celestial trumpet. When the Son of Man returns in glory, says Matthew's Jesus, he will send out his angels *with a loud trumpet call*" (Mt 24:31). And Matthew and Luke repeat a Q-tradition that conforms to Mark's outlook: When teaching his followers, Jesus instructs them to pray, "Thy Kingdom come" (Mt 7:10//Lk 11:2, the Lord's Prayer).

But other changes soften Mark's urgency. Whereas in Mark's Gospel the Lord had already shortened the days till the End, in Matthew that still lies in the future ("For the sake of the elect, those days *will be* shortened," 24:22), and Luke drops the passage entirely. Indeed, Luke's Jesus even preaches specifically against the kind of kingdom that Mark's Jesus, and Paul before him, had heralded. "Because he was near Jerusalem, and *because they supposed that the Kingdom of God was to appear immediately,* he proceeded to tell them a parable" (Lk 19:11); "Take heed that you are not led astray; for *many will come in my name saying, 'The time is at hand!' Do not go after them*" (21:8). This sits oddly with Jesus' very first line in Mark: "The time is fulfilled, and the kingdom of God is at hand!" (Mk 1:15), which is possibly why Luke dropped it from his Gospel (cf. Lk 4:15). The Kingdom, urges Luke's Jesus, is a present reality, not a future event: "Behold, the Kingdom of God is in the midst of you" (17:20).

The Gospel of John, another source for our investigative efforts, cannot help us much here. John's presentation of Jesus' character and teachings is utterly different from that of the Synoptics, and his own highly characteristic theology dominates much in the speeches his Jesus gives. The Kingdom of God, a major theme in the teaching of the synoptic Gospels (where the word or phrase appears a total of 123 times), is hardly in evidence in John (who gives it 5 times). And the Synoptics' temporal eschatology—"Now" and "Then," or, as with Mark especially, "Now" and "Soon"—gives way in John to moral and metaphysical eschatology, an absolutizing of abiding oppositions: Light and Dark, Above and Below, Upper World and Lower World, "of God" and "not of God." On this aspect of Jesus' teaching, John's points of contact with both Paul and with the synoptic tradition are minimal.

Predictions of an imminent End generally tend in one of two directions: Either they age gracelessly, or interpreters contrive to have them stay forever young. We see evidence of these tendencies in another New Testament writing, the Second Epistle of Peter. Written in Greek at the end of the first or beginning of the second century, this pseudonymous letter openly acknowledges the Parousia's belatedness and offers an explanation for its delay.

You must understand this, that scoffers will come in the last days with their scoffing, following their own passions and saying, "Where is the promise of his [Christ's] Coming? For ever since the fathers fell asleep, all things have continued as they were from the beginning of creation"... Do not ignore this one fact, beloved, that with the Lord one day is as a thousand years, and a thousand years as one day. The Lord is not slow about his promise, but is forebearing toward you, not wishing that any should perish, but that all should reach repentance.

(2 Pt 3:3–9)

Deliberately echoing Paul, whose letters this author knows (3:15–16), "Peter" then adds: "*But the day of the Lord will come like a thief,* and then the heavens will pass away with a loud noise, and the elements will be dissolved with fire" (3:10).

"Peter" in his way repudiated the obvious meaning of the Gospel proclamation of the Second Coming by arguing for a vastly expanded view of time: Each of God's days is like 365,000 of ours. This is why, he could then explain, the End was late: It only *seemed* late. His Christian contemporary John of Patmos, on the contrary, stimulated perhaps by the outbreak of local persecutions, inferred from current events that ancient prophecies were falling due. Creating a pastiche of images from Isaiah, Ezekiel, Daniel, and various Christian traditions, he insisted that the End was indeed at hand: "The time is near." "Behold," says the revealing angel, speaking on behalf of the Lord God and the Lamb (that is, Christ), "behold, I am coming soon" (Rv 1:3, 22:7).

Christian apocalyptic prophecy would go on to have a long, continuous, and tumultuous career. As our own era moves to the year 2000, we hear its noisy enthusiasts still. But in the ancient canon we can trace its "official" diminution as the tradition itself perdures and changes. Within the New Testament, along the antiapocalyptic gradient, we see a rough inverse correspondence: The later the writing, the lower its level of commitment to an imminent Apocalypse; the earlier the writing (i.e., Mark and, before him, Paul) the higher. Can we ride this trajectory backward into the documentary void that surrounds the historical Jesus? I think so. But we need more evidence, first, before making the case.

"He appeared to Cephas, then to the Twelve": The Twelve

PAUL WAS a contemporary of Jesus' original followers, and in his letters he provides glimpses of his dealings with them. In Galatians, he specifically names Peter ("Cephas"), James (Jesus' brother), and John: Interestingly, they have all relocated from their home region, Galilee, to Jerusalem—a fact we shall have to consider later on (Gal 1:18, 2:9; cf. Mk 16:7 and Mt 28:7–20, where they are last seen in the Galilee). And though in Galatians, Paul insists on the authority of his own gospel and so deliberately emphasizes his independence from this original group, in 1 Corinthians he speaks otherwise. Invoking precisely the authority of their witness and his place in the apostolic chain of transmission, he shores up his own teaching on the resurrection of the dead and coming of the Kingdom:

> For I delivered to you . . . what I also received, that Christ died for our sins in accordance with the scriptures; that he was buried, that he was raised on the third day in accordance with the scriptures, and that he appeared to Cephas, *and then to the Twelve.* Then he appeared to more than five hundred *brethren* . . . then to James, then to all the *apostles.* Last of all . . . he appeared also to me.   (1 Cor 15:3–7)

Paul seems to name three distinct groups here: the Twelve, the brethren, and the apostles. The "brethren" may refer to that group who had received Jesus' message but did not as a matter of course travel with him: The masculine plural noun, *adelphoi,* encompasses grammatically and thus can attest socially to a mixed group of women and men both. The later Gospels reflect this sort of social organization in the group that formed around Jesus in his lifetime. Some wandered with him; others—among whom women, settled in villages—received and cared for the itinerants. These, then, are perhaps the "more than five hundred" brethren of Paul's account.

Apostoloi is the Greek word for envoys or messengers, and Paul routinely so designated himself ("Paul an apostle of Christ Jesus"). These followers of Jesus would have worked on the road, disseminating the gospel message to others after Jesus' death and even, according to the evangelists' stories, before.

And then there are "the Twelve." Who were they? What did they do? The Gospels provide more detail. Mark relates a story that he sets at the start of Jesus' mission after his baptism and the forty-day retreat in the wilderness. Back in the Galilee, walking along the Kinnerit (the large inland lake referred to in Gospel stories as the "Sea of Galilee" or "Sea of Tiberias"), Jesus calls his first followers. These are the fishermen Simon (that is, Simon Peter, the "Cephas" of Paul's letter), his brother

Andrew, and two sons of Zebedee, James and John (1:16–20). At a later point, this group expands to "the Twelve" (3:14), whom Jesus eventually commissions to travel two by two to expand his own mission. These men also are to exorcise unclean spirits, heal the sick, and preach repentance (6:7–13). These twelve, Mark says, are *apostoloi* (6:30). Whether they are identical with Jesus' "students" or "followers" (Gk. *mathētai,* Latin *discipuli,* "disciples") Mark leaves unclear (cf. v. 35). But whatever the vagaries of these designations, "the Twelve" themselves are clearly a core group. Jesus had specifically appointed them (3:14). It is they who share Jesus' final Passover meal with him in Jerusalem, and they to whom he gives the commemorative teaching, "this [bread] is my body," the wine "my blood of the covenant" (14:17–24).

Matthew, Luke, and John all echo these traditions. Matthew, too, names "Simon who is called Peter," Andrew, James, and John as comprising Jesus' initial following (4:18–22); later, he simply refers to "the Twelve" and repeats Mark's list of their names: Besides the initial four, Philip, Bartholomew, Thomas, Matthew, another James ("son of Adelphas"), Thaddaeus, Simon the Cananaean, and "Judas Iscariot, who betrayed him" (10:1–4; cf. Mk 3:13–19). Luke edits Mark differently, dropping Andrew and moving the call of Peter, James, and John well into Jesus' mission in Galilee (5:5–11). From a larger, unspecified number of disciples Jesus designates twelve "whom he called apostles": These are Peter, now with his brother Andrew; James and John; Philip, Bartholomew, Matthew, and Thomas; James, son of Adelphas; Simon the Zealot; Judas, son of James; and Judas Iscariot (6:13–16; cf. Acts 1:13): Though coincident, Luke's list of names does not exactly match Matthew's. At some point thereafter, Jesus appoints seventy others to travel two by two and commissions them to heal and preach (Lk 10:1–12). John's version, too, is different. Andrew, originally a disciple of John the Baptizer, decides to follow Jesus and subsequently brings along his brother Peter (1:40–43); thereafter, returning to the Galilee, Jesus calls Philip, who in turn calls Nathanael. The fourth evangelist never relates any further details about Jesus' filling out this group, though he does refer to "the Twelve" (6:71, 20:24).

Finally, these later Gospels depict the post-Resurrection Christ as charging his core group to continue and even enlarge his mission, taking the gospel to the Diaspora and thus to Gentiles ("the nations") as well as Jews. Matthew's Jesus, when he had sent out the Twelve from the Galilee, specifically limited their mission to Jews. "These twelve Jesus sent out, charging them, 'Go nowhere among the Gentiles, and enter no town of the Samaritans, but go rather to the lost sheep of the house of Israel. And preach as you go, saying the Kingdom of Heaven is at hand' " (Mt 10:5-7; cf. 15:24). It is the Risen Christ, appearing to them again in the Galilee, who alters this charge. "Go therefore and make disciples of all nations" (28:16). Mark had implied as much, but since his Gospel ends with the empty tomb, not the Risen Christ, he folded this new mission field back into the lifetime of Jesus. Thus Jesus during his apocalyptic soliloquy in Jerusalem explains to Peter, Andrew, James, and John that the Temple will be destroyed and the Son will return only after the gospel has been "preached to all the nations" (Mk 13:10). Luke's Risen Christ, appearing in Jerusalem, also commands an international mission, claiming that such had been prophesied in Jewish scripture. "Thus it is written, that the Christ should suffer and on the third day rise from the dead, and that repentance and forgiveness of sins should be preached in his name to all nations, beginning from Jerusalem" (24:45-46; cf. Acts 1:1-8). The charge is, again, to this core group (v. 33).

On the evidence of Paul's letters—thus within twenty years of Jesus' death and well before these Gospels were written—we already see a wide-flung network of Christian communities in Damascus, Antioch, other cities in Asia Minor, and Rome. Their members, some of whom Paul names when closing his letters, seem energetically committed to the work of spreading "the gospel" (e.g., Rom 16:1-16; 1 Cor 16:10-20). Some in these communities are Gentiles, not Jews (e.g., Titus, Gal 2:3), though these *ekklēsiai* are found in cities with significant Jewish populations. Peter himself, one of the original group who apparently settled in Jerusalem (Gal 1:18), also ventured out into the Greek-speaking Diaspora, certainly as far as Antioch (Gal 2:11), perhaps as far as Corinth (1 Cor 1:12), perhaps beyond—the ancient evidence runs out there. And whatever the Galilean roots of this movement, it had clearly relocated to, and directed its mission from, Jerusalem (Gal 1:18-2:12).

The familiarity of all these data—that Jesus had apostles and a core group of twelve; that they spread his mission in the Jewish homeland and later, after his execution, took it into the Diaspora; that the central community, comprising many of his original followers, stayed in Jerusalem—should not dull us to their historical import, and thus to our obligation to explain them. They in fact reveal much that is unusual about the movement.

It is true, for example, that teachers in antiquity, whether pagan or Jewish, routinely gathered "students" or "disciples." Schools of philosophers in the Greco-Roman world established themselves in this way, as in the Jewish world a rabbi's teachings would be preserved, repeated, and reinterpreted by his students. The Gospels allude to the disciples of the Pharisees, and of John the Baptizer. Josephus speaks of Jewish teachers in the prerabbinic period whose students acted on their instruction. Two he names, Judas and Matthaias, "unrivalled interpreters of the ancestral laws," taught against a huge golden eagle that Herod the Great had placed over the great gate of the Temple: As a result, some of their students tore it down (Herod executed them all; *BJ* 1.651–5; *AJ* 17.149–67).

But Jesus seems to have commissioned disciples to travel for the specific purpose of spreading his particular message. On the evidence of the Synoptics, he and his core group of twelve traveled widely throughout the villages of the Galilee, east to Transjordan, north near the coastline, south through Samaria, and in Jerusalem. According to John, Jesus taught repeatedly in Jerusalem, particularly in and around the Temple during the pilgrimage holidays. He charges those he commissioned to spread the gospel exactly as he had, indeed to enact before others what he had enacted before them: healings and exorcisms coupled with the announcement of the Kingdom's advent. Yet Jesus seems to operate at cross-purposes, sending disciples out on the road while demanding that they be ill prepared for long-term travel. Teach for free, he tells them; and travel absolutely without provisions, "for the laborer deserves his food"—in other words, depend on those you teach to feed you. (Years later, in the Diaspora, the mission was evidently still trying to operate on these terms. Paul repeats this teaching, on the authority of "the Lord," who "commanded that those who proclaim the gospel should get their living from the gospel," 1 Cor 9:14. It seems that, as the mission spread and time wore on, this arrangement caused some resentment; Paul points out to the Corinthians that, despite this entitlement, he has never demanded provision from them, v. 15.) Do not take money with you, Jesus instructs his disciples, nor a change of clothes; travel without a bag, staff, or sandals; announce the coming of the Kingdom, exorcise demons, and heal (Mt 10:5–42; cf. Lk 9:1–6). This combination of impractical missionary etiquette and principled itinerancy needs to be explained.

We might do so, paradoxically, by first considering other, more firmly established aspects of the early Christian movement that also need to be explained—for example, the fact that the early movement after Jesus' death spread out from territorial Israel to the Diaspora, where it also embraced Gentiles. To be sure, by midcentury, debate had broken out between members of the movement over the terms under which Gentiles might join—this is the central issue of Paul's letter to the Galatians—but evidently no one denied that they could be and should be included. During Jesus' lifetime, Gentiles scarcely figured at all in his mission: How, then, and why so soon after his death does the Jesus movement come to see the Gentiles' inclusion as a natural extension of itself?

Another fact: The movement, almost immediately after Jesus' death, settled in Jerusalem. Why? If Jesus' message had conformed essentially to the peculiarities of Galilean society—if he spoke to its grinding rural peasant poverty, to land reform and radical sharing, or to a social program of radical egalitarianism; or if he taught an ethic of compassion pitched against the distinctions of purity that regulated access to Temple and even table, as some scholars have recently argued—then this relocation is all but impossible to explain. Why Jerusalem, if the peasants are back in Galilee? Why Jerusalem, where the prestige, antiquity, and centrality of the Temple would work directly against the principled opposition to purity that some scholars see in Jesus' message?

And, finally, there is the very odd fact that this early evidence—Paul and Mark overtly; Matthew and Luke more guardedly—proclaims and affirms that the Kingdom is coming, even as time drags on. How is this possible? Why would Paul, years after the Thessalonians had already grown alarmed at the Kingdom's delay, assert that he was even more confident "than when we first believed" that it was at hand (Rom 13:11)? Why would Mark, twenty years further along, assert the same thing? Why would Matthew and Luke, despite their lengthening perspective, also both repeat Mark's Jesus saying, "This generation will not pass away before all these things take place" (Mk 13:31//Mt 24:34//Lk 21:32)? Those who argue that Jesus himself was non- or even antiapocalyptic explain these later stages as a misrepresentation of his teaching. But then we need to ask: Why would the later tradition repeat something *already* seen not to be true? Why invent a tradition that would already be an embarrassment?

To recapitulate: We know that Jesus did have an inner core of followers; in Galatians, Paul names some of "those who were apostles before me"; in 1 Corinthians he speaks specifically of "the Twelve." After the Crucifixion, these people traveled to spread the gospel even into the Diaspora, where they welcomed Gentiles in as well (Paul's letters; Acts; Tacitus; Josephus). The movement did relocate to Jerusalem

(Paul; Acts), where it remained at least until the years preceding the revolt. And written sources well after Jesus' lifetime continued to attribute to him a teaching that the Kingdom of God was at hand.

All of these facts can be brought together under the umbrella of Jewish apocalyptic expectation. A strand within traditional Jewish apocalyptic thought anticipated the Gentiles' turning to the God of Israel as one of the events at the End of Days. (We will examine the sources for this tradition in detail later in this chapter.) Such traditions routinely featured Jerusalem as the center of the Kingdom. God's Redemption radiates out from Zion; exiled Israel and newly pious Gentiles come to Jerusalem, to worship at God's house. And the redeemed Israel would include more than those Jews currently living in the Diaspora. It would include as well those who, centuries earlier, had been lost: not just the two tribes, Judah and Benjamin, which had survived the Babylonian Captivity in the sixth century B.C.E., but also the ten lost tribes of the Northern Kingdom that had been swallowed up by Assyria after 722 B.C.E.

These themes appear variously in different intertestamental writings, but all can be found in the classical and authoritative source from which their authors, Paul, and the evangelists all drew: the prophet Isaiah. At the End, foresees the prophet, the mountain of God's house will be raised as the highest mountain and will draw all the nations (Heb. *goyim*) to it, to the worship of the God of Jacob (Is 2:2–4). And God will work a still greater miracle. "There will be a highway from Assyria for the remnant which is left of his people, as there was for Israel when they came out of Egypt" (11:16). "In that day the Lord will extend his hand . . . to recover the remnant which is left of his people, from Assyria, from Egypt, from Pathros, from Ethiopia. . . . He will raise an ensign for the nations, and will assemble the outcasts of Israel, and gather the dispersed of Judah from the four corners of the earth" (11:11–12). At the End, God will restore Israel to the Land—*all* Israel. All twelve tribes.

More: At this time "there shall come forth a shoot from the stump of Jesse" (v. 1). God will establish a son of David's house as the eschatological king. This Davidic king will preside not only over the twelve tribes of the restored Israel, but also over the nations: "Him shall the nations seek" (v. 10). At the End, God will make a feast for all peoples; all humankind will converge at the Temple, in the city, Jerusalem (25:6, and often).

How does consideration of Jewish apocalyptic tradition help in evaluating this data? It makes visible both the internal importance of the

Gentile mission to the earliest Christian movement, especially as time wore on, and the internal logic of this (ostensibly Galilean) movement's relocating permanently to Jerusalem. Gentiles turning from idols to God would have made sense to these Jewish apostles, since this event was one of those foretold for the Endtime in apocalyptic tradition. Whatever the ultimate social trauma these Gentile adherents eventually occasioned, the basic fact of their allegiance to the movement confirmed the movement's own message: that the Kingdom was indeed at hand. This is perhaps why, even decades after Jesus had first pronounced it, both Paul and, even later, Mark could with conviction repeat his prophecy.

It also accounts for what might otherwise seem like an odd choice for headquarters: Jerusalem. If the church chose to relocate, why not go someplace more sensible (especially in view of its vigorous penetration of the Diaspora) with easy access to sea travel, like Caesarea? Why indeed not stay in the Galilee, near the important overland routes? Why Jerusalem? Because Jerusalem stands at the heart of this ancient redemptive myth. "The word of the Lord goes forth from Jerusalem" (Is 2:4).

What then of the New Testament's traditions about "the Twelve"? Were it not for Paul's witness, we might be tempted to question the group's actual existence. After all, the list of their names varies from Gospel to Gospel, which itself indicates shaky information. And the concept itself is too conveniently metaphorical: To the degree that Christian tradition will eventually conceive itself as the New Israel, these men might simply stand as ciphers for the twelve "new tribes" of the church.

However, considered otherwise, these slippages in this tradition might argue in fact for its historical authenticity. For example, even though all four evangelical narratives, in light of the betrayal by Judas Iscariot, drop the total number of the core group from twelve to eleven *before* the death of Jesus, the number "twelve" itself still remains the symbolic touchstone. Hence Matthew speaks of a post-Resurrection (thus, logically, postbetrayal) moment when "the Twelve" will play a role in the coming Kingdom: "When the Son of Man shall sit on his glorious throne, you who have followed me will also sit on twelve thrones, judging the twelve tribes of Israel" (19:28). Paul, as we have seen, also speaks of the Twelve as a post-Resurrection group. (Some ancient copyists, aware of this problem, "corrected" 1 Cor 15:3 to read "the eleven.") That the number twelve is insisted upon despite the awkwardness of retaining it may be construed as the strength of the early tradition. In light of the betrayal, the number twelve would have to go back before the Crucifixion; if so, then perhaps to Jesus himself.

To what end? Here we have to retrieve one of our observable facts, that later tradition continues to attribute to Jesus an already disconfirmed prophecy; and one of our interpretive conjectures, that much of our scattered evidence can be coherently brought together by an appeal to broader Jewish apocalyptic tradition.

To the New Testament evidence first. Moving backward along a trajectory from later text to earlier text to, finally, Jesus himself, we might hypothesize a gradient of increasing apocalyptic intensity. Matthew and Luke had Jesus proclaim the coming Kingdom, though they both defined "kingdom" in nonapocalyptic as well as apocalyptic ways, and they linked the Kingdom to Jesus' glorious Second Coming. In this they follow Mark, whose Jesus proclaimed the coming Kingdom, conceived apocalypticly: That is, the Kingdom was an event that would happen or a stage that would arrive, not a state that somehow existed concurrent with normal reality. This Kingdom would arrive within the lifetime of Mark's generation, at the edges of the lifetime of Jesus'. And it would begin with the return of the triumphant Son.

Mark's tone of confident immediacy matches that of Paul, a generation earlier. Paul, too, had proclaimed the imminent return of the Son, the resurrection of the dead, and the establishment of the Kingdom within *his* own lifetime. Paul said that he inherited this tradition: He has it as a "saying of the Lord" (1 Thes 4:13; the passage is cited in full on p. 79). Might not some version of this teaching go back through those who were apostles before Paul to the teaching of Jesus himself? Jesus' messianic, triumphant appearance as the vindicated, militant Son most easily coheres, it is true, with post-Crucifixion developments. It compensates for the disappointment of Jesus' crucifixion and clearly stands as a specifically Christian embellishment on earlier Jewish traditions of Messiah and Kingdom.

But the Kingdom itself, the belief that it is coming, that it will particularly manifest in Jerusalem, that it will involve the restored nation of Israel as well as Gentiles who have renounced their idolatry—all these beliefs predate Jesus' death by centuries and are also found variously in other Jewish writings roughly contemporary with him (some Pseudepigrapha; the Dead Sea Scrolls). Predicting his own Second Coming may indeed be historically implausible. Preaching the good news of the coming Kingdom of God, not at all.

Here, then, is our historical purchase on traditions concerning the Twelve. Symbolically the number recalls the plenum of Israel. By Jesus' day, ten of those twelve tribes had long since ceased to exist. If, nonetheless, Jesus did commission a core group of twelve disciples, and saw them as spreading the good news of God's coming kingdom, then he, too, was thinking symbolically. If he sent them out on the road deliberately, consciously underprepared for sustained travel, then perhaps this gives the index of his expectation: The Kingdom was coming soon; their underpreparedness embodied their conviction.

And if Jesus indeed taught that ultimately these twelve would judge the twelve tribes, then he was thinking eschatologically. To assemble the twelve tribes so many centuries after the Assyrian conquest would take a miracle. But that, I think, is what Jesus was expecting.

"To the married I give charge, not I but the Lord": Ethics and the End

NOT MUCH in their respective depictions of Jesus overlaps between Paul's letters and the Gospels. If all we had were the Epistles, we would know precious little about Jesus of Nazareth: not where or whom he taught, little about his activities and his teaching, scarcely anything about the circumstances of his death—precisely that information that the evangelists are concerned to relate. Paul's burning commitment focused not on the past but rather on the near future; his gospel proclaims the coming or returning Christ, whose Resurrection signaled the imminent redemption and transformation of the world (Rom 8:19 ff.).

It is with some surprise then that we see reflected in Paul and Mark virtually identical versions of an ethical teaching that both attribute to the historical Jesus. In his letter to the gentile community at Corinth, working through a lengthy exhortation to moral behavior, Paul finally turns to matters "about which you [i.e., the community] wrote," specifically on sexual discipline (1 Cor 7). Paul first advises a temperate and periodic sexual abstinence within marriage. (Had his congregation, more absolutist, pushed for more?) Marriage partners have mutual conjugal rights, and extremes of abstinence might lead to sexual temptation: "Do not refuse one another except perhaps for a season, that you might devote yourselves to prayer; but then come together again, lest Satan tempt you through lack of self-control." Total abstinence from sexual activity, Paul readily admits, is the higher path; but it is not for everybody. "I say this by way of concession, not of command. I wish that all were as I myself am. But each has his own gift from God, one of one kind and one of another" (1 Cor 7:1–7). Those not married or no longer married should remain as they are, with the same proviso: If passion tempts, wed (vv. 8–9). And then:

> To the married I give charge, *not I but the Lord,* that the wife should not separate from the husband (but if she does, let her remain single or else be reconciled to her husband)—and that the husband should not divorce his wife.   (1 Cor 7:10–11)

Some twenty years later, Mark anchored a longer version of this same teaching in a story about Jesus' mission:

> And he left there [i.e., Capernaum in Galilee] and went to the region of Judea and beyond the Jordan, and crowds gathered to him. And again, as his custom was, he taught them. And Pharisees came up and in order to test him asked, "Is it lawful for a man to divorce his wife?" He answered them, "What did Moses command you?" They said, "Moses allowed a man to write a certificate of divorce, and to put her away." But Jesus said to them, "For your hardness of heart he wrote you this commandment. But from the beginning of creation, 'God made them male and female.' 'For this reason a man shall leave his father and mother and be joined to his wife, and the two shall become one flesh' [Gn 1:27, 2:24]. So they are no longer two but one flesh. What therefore God has joined together let no man put asunder." And in the house the disciples asked him about this matter. And he said to them, "Whoever divorces his wife and marries another, commits adultery against her; and if she divorces her husband and marries another, she commits adultery."   (Mk 10:1–11)

The message is the same in both sources: No divorce, period.

Luke later repeated Mark's version of Jesus' instruction, though he shifted emphasis slightly: "Everyone who divorces his wife and marries another commits adultery; and he who marries a woman divorced from her husband commits adultery" (Lk 16:18). Perhaps this last phrase is a Q-version, because Matthew in his turn alters Mark's meaning and phrase in the same way. Matthew repeats this teaching twice, in two different settings: the Sermon on the Mount, in the Galilee; and his recapitulation of Mark's whole scene, during the mission in Judea. Both times, he adds a significant modification: "I say to you, that everyone who divorces his wife, *except on the grounds of unchastity* (Gk. *porneia*), makes her an adulteress; and whoever marries a divorced woman commits adultery" (5:31–32); "I say to you, whoever divorces his wife, *except for unchastity,* and marries another commits adultery" (19:9).

The more extreme version of this prohibition is doubtless the earlier one: Matthew alone of these four sources permits the exception. Yet his narrative extension of this story—an M-tradition, a unit unique to his Gospel—sounds a note that brings us back to a central theme in Paul. Matthew's Jesus in this passage goes on to endorse celibacy in view of the coming Kingdom:

> The disciples said, "If such is the case of a man with his wife, it is not expedient to marry." But he said to them, "Not all men can receive this saying, but only those to whom it is given. For there are eunuchs who have been so from birth, and there are eunuchs who have been made eunuchs by men, and there are *eunuchs who have made themselves eunuchs for the sake of the kingdom of heaven.* He who is able to receive this, let him receive it." (Mt 19:10–12)

This verse would have a long and scandalizing effect in subsequent Greco-Roman Christianity when some men, gripped by their enthused dedication to its ethic of moral perfectionism, voluntarily had themselves castrated. Justin Martyr in his *Apology* (c. 150) approvingly relates the story of a young man's petition to the governor for permission to have himself castrated. A century later, Origen of Alexandria's great reputation for chastity was belittled by rumors that he, too, had interpreted literally this injunction given in Matthew. In context, however, this teaching seems to relate not to surgical procedures but to ethical resolve: The voluntary forswearing of sexual activity was an index of commitment to the Kingdom.

In 1 Corinthians 7, Paul continues in this vein. In verses 12–16, he addresses the issue of "mixed" marriages—marriages, that is, between Christian Gentiles who as part of this movement have at least in principle forsworn their native religious practices and worship solely the God of Israel (cf. 1 Cor 5:11), and pagan Gentiles who still worship traditional gods. This is a circumstance specific to the Diaspora mission, and Paul's prefatory remark—"To the rest I say, not the Lord"—names only himself as his authority. Those in mixed marriages should stay in them, just as generally "everyone should remain in the state in which he was called" (v. 20). But clearly, Paul repeats—this time from the instance of unmarried men vis-à-vis their "virgins"—the preferred state is celibacy. What is truly important is staying focused on the imminent redemption in Christ:

> Now concerning the virgins, I have no command of the Lord, but I give my opinion as one who by the Lord's mercy is trustworthy. I think that *in view of the impending distress it is well for a person to remain as he is.* Are you bound to a wife? Do not seek to be free. Are you free from a wife? Do not seek marriage. But if you marry, you do not sin, and if the virgin marries, she does not sin. Yet those who marry will have worldly troubles, and I would spare you that. *I mean, brethren, the appointed time has grown very short. . . . The form of this world is passing away.*
>
> (1 Cor 7:25–31)

We see this same combination of sexual austerity and moral commitment to preparedness in the face of coming redemption in another ancient Jewish apocalyptically minded community: the Essenes. The first-century writers Pliny the Elder, Philo, and Josephus all comment on this community's custom of celibacy, and this behavior seems of a piece with other aspects of their perfectionist ethics. They also disallowed private property, holding all things in common; they shared common meals; out of piety, they rejected taking oaths—man should not need to call on God to secure his word. Some Essenes, Josephus mentions (and this has been confirmed by the *Damascus Document,* one of the codes for communal behavior discovered at Qumran), also married and had children. This social reality afforded another opportunity where their teachings resembled those of Jesus: Essenes, too, were absolutists on the issue of forbidding divorce.

The Essenes in the perspective of these three outsiders seem a sort of philosophical school, which is indeed the word—*haerisis*—that Josephus' Greek text gives (*Vita* 2). The community's own long-buried library, however, provides a clearer view of how it saw itself: as the true Israel, uniquely instructed by their master, the Teacher of Righteousness, to understand the meaning of God's revelation. "Sons of light," they lived in the final days, at the very edge of time before God redeemed his people; and their whole way of life was dedicated to preparing for the coming Kingdom of God.

Very direct connections between the Dead Sea Scrolls and early Christian writings, or between the two communities that they represent, cannot and indeed should not be drawn. The Scrolls are the lush literature of highly educated, priestly, separatist, mostly Hebrew- and

Aramaic-speaking Judean sectarians. Much of their literary production was for internal consumption. Their library was vast in size and scope: It has yielded, in whole or in part, ancient Hebrew manuscripts of virtually every book in the Jewish Bible, as well as commentaries on these. This library attests to the profound literacy and learning of this sect; the intensive development of the halakah of purity that we see in the commentaries, to its specifically priestly origins.

The movement around Jesus, by contrast, was lay, not priestly, both in his lifetime and later. (This probably accounts for its indifference to intensification of purity rules: more on this below.) Nor in its beginnings was it traditionally erudite or even in any important sense literate (though in Paul's letters we see both his Pharisaic education in his scriptural expertise and his Greek cultural literacy). Its literature—by the time we begin to have one, arguably post-70 (Paul wrote letters, not treatises)—was lightweight by comparison with the Scrolls: spare and mobile, exclusively Greek, missionary in intent and effect, built for the road.

All the more striking, then, is the sensibility shared by the Essenes and the early Christians in their respective ethical traditions. Both prohibited divorce, both repudiated the taking of oaths (Mt 5:33–37), both promoted an ideal of celibacy (seen, on the Christian side, in Paul and in Matthew, cited above; and in the combined narrative depictions of Jesus himself as an unmarried adult male), both idealized the renunciation of personal property for members of the community ("Go, sell all you have, give to the poor, and you will have treasure in heaven; and come, follow me," Mk 10:21 and parr.). And both groups—the Essenes while it still stood; the Christians after it was destroyed—had complicated and critical relations with the Temple.

An overarching framework of apocalyptic conviction, further, unites both. In the specifically apocalyptic texts of the Qumran community such as the *War Scroll* and the *Messianic Rule,* we see variations on the themes of final battle, angelic armies, the overthrow of Satan, and the coming of a variety of messianic figures—a priestly messiah (cf. the image of Jesus in the New Testament's Epistle to the Hebrews), a Davidic warrior messiah (cf. New Testament descriptions of the Son's activities at the Parousia in the Gospels and Paul), a prophet-messiah. These last items of course particularly resonate within primitive Christian tradition. *Meschiach—christos* in Greek—is so early and so forcefully ascribed to Jesus that it comes to function less as a title than simply as his name: Jesus Christ, not Jesus *the* Christ.

From this apocalyptic promontory in first-century Judaism, then, we can survey and evaluate those ethical traditions imputed to Jesus in the Gospel material and reflected also in Paul. Several strong themes appear in the didactic passages of the Gospels. Jesus is drawn especially to the poor, whose very poverty enriches them spiritually (Mt 5:3–12; cf. Lk 6:20–23); indeed, as we have just seen, he enjoins care of the poor and an ethic of voluntary poverty on his followers. Jesus puts membership in and obligations to his group above normal ties to family and property (much material here: Mt 8:21 f.//Lk 9:59 f.; Mk 13:12 and parr.; Mt 10:34–39//Lk 12:51–53 and 14:26–27; cf. Mk 3:31–35 and parr., where Jesus repudiates his own family). Evil is to be met with nonresistance; the enemy loved rather than hated (Mt 5:38–6:4//Lk 6:27–36). Yet alongside this ethic of perfectionism is also a message of divine leniency. Sinners need not fear exclusion from the Kingdom: Indeed, the most notorious among them, toll collectors (renowned for living by graft, thus overtaxing those under them) and prostitutes, if they follow Jesus, will precede even the priests into God's kingdom (Mt 21:31). And according to evangelical depiction, Jesus did not demonstrate his authority to teach through traditional erudition or textual expertise. He thereby "astonished" his listeners, because he taught "as one who had authority" (which is to say, on his own authority), "and not like the scribes" (who would typically present their interpretations by appeal to authoritative teachers or texts: "Rabbi X said in the name of Rabbi Y." Mk 1:22 and parr.).

What of all this ethical instruction in the New Testament texts might trace back to the very earliest movement? Quite a bit, I think. The evidence of Paul, independent of and converging on this later Gospel material, implies a common source: primitive Christian tradition, and so perhaps Jesus himself. Paul repeats, as we have seen, specific teachings on such issues as divorce, celibacy, and the subordination of normal family relations to preparations for the coming redemption. Persecutors, Paul likewise says, should be blessed, vengeance eschewed, injustice tolerated, taxes to governing authorities paid (Rom 12:9–13:14; cf. 1 Cor 6:7; on the last point—taxes—see also Mk 12:14–17 and parr.: "Render to Caesar the things that are Caesar's"). And the poor back in Jerusalem are the special responsibility of his gentile communities, who on this account should give cheerfully to their support (1 Cor 16:1–3; 2 Cor 9; Gal 2:10; Rom 15:25–29).

Other first-century Palestinian Jews, as we know from the Dead Sea Scrolls, thought similarly on these topics. And as with these others, so with Jesus: The fervent conviction that redemption was at hand served as incentive for the intensification and extension of the teachings of Torah. The Dead Sea sect, as we might expect of a priestly group, extended and intensified especially the rules of purity. Jesus also, if we can judge by some synoptic passages and from the Q material surviving in the Sermon on the Mount, extended and intensified the Torah's commands. But—as we should expect of the lay leader of a lay movement—he focused on those given to all Israel, the Ten Commandments, and he concentrated on the moral aspects of these. Thus Torah condemns murder; Jesus, even anger (Ex 20:13; Dt 5:17; Mt 5:22). Torah condemns adultery; Jesus, even the feeling of lust (Ex 20:14; Dt 5:18; Mt 5:28). Torah condemns swearing falsely, taking God's name in vain; Jesus, swearing itself (Ex 20:7; Lv 19:12; Mt 5:34). And when a scribe asks, "Which commandment is first of all?" Jesus replies by referring to those commands directed to the entire people: Deuteronomy (the first line of the *Sh'ma*) and Leviticus: "The first is, 'Hear O Israel, the Lord our God is One. And you shall love the Lord your God with all your heart, and with all your soul, and with all your strength.' And the second is this: 'Love your neighbor as yourself.' There is no other commandment greater than these" (Mk 12:28–31 and parr.).

Here we must pause to consider what Jesus' ethical teaching can tell us more generally about his attitude toward the Law. It should be noted that his teaching in the Sermon on the Mount is not presented as an alternative to Torah, despite the way we might hear Matthew's rhetoric ("You have heard it said. . . . But I say. . . ."). Jesus here does what the later rabbis will term "building a fence around the Torah"; that is, he prescribes rules of behavior that extend the prohibition, thus ensuring that the biblical command cannot be broken. Someone who will not permit himself even anger is that much less likely to commit murder. Someone who does not allow himself even unexpressed desire—"lust in the heart"—is that much less likely to actually commit adultery, and so on. So, too, with his teaching on divorce. Jesus by forbidding divorce is not speaking "against Torah," because the Torah does not mandate divorce, but simply permits it. Jesus' teaching, rather, reinforces marriage—perhaps, as with Paul, in view of the short time remaining until the Kingdom comes.

In the immediately preceding example, Mark's scribe goes on to say, "You are right, teacher; you have truly said that he (God) is one, and there is no other but he; and to love him with all the heart, and all the understanding, and all the strength, and to love one's neighbor as one-self, *is much more than whole burnt offerings and sacrifices*" (Mk 12:32–33). The correct knowledge of God and love of God and neighbor is more important, Mark implies, than the Temple cult mandated in Torah. This teaching sits in the middle of Mark's description of events in and around Jesus' entry into and sojourn in Jerusalem for Passover, events that at least imply Jesus' antagonism to the Temple. For example, when he goes up to the Temple the week before Passover, Jesus curses a fruitless fig tree ("May no one ever eat fruit from you again!" 11:14). Mark uses this act as a kind of commentary on what Jesus does next: "Cleansing" the Temple, he overturns the tables of the money changers and chairs of pigeon sellers, condemning getting and spending in the Temple courtyard (vv. 15–17). Then, passing by the tree the next morning, his disciples see that it had "withered away to its roots" (v. 20). Finally, in the chapter following this dialogue, Jesus predicts the Temple's utter destruction. "Do you see these great buildings? There will not be left here one stone upon another, that will not be thrown down" (13:2). The accusation that Jesus threatened to destroy the Temple weaves in and out of the scenes of his trial and crucifixion (14:58, 15:29). The impression is overwhelming: Mark's Jesus repudiates traditional Temple worship.

Earlier Markan passages also present and develop a general theme of Jesus' opposition to traditional practice during his mission in the Galilee. Scribes and/or Pharisees dispute with Jesus over other aspects of Jewish piety: healings on the Sabbath (2:1–12, 3:1–6); dining in questionable company (the proverbial tax collectors and sinners, 2:15 f.); not fasting when the disciples of the Pharisees and of John the Baptist fast (2:18–20); sitting loose of Sabbath observance (2:23–28). In a single, highly fraught episode related in chapter 7, Mark presents Jesus disputing with Pharisees over washing—that is, purifying—hands before eating, over tithes and oath-taking, and finally, according to Mark's editorial gloss, over the very principle of clean and unclean foods (7:1–23).

These controversies heat Jesus' opponents to homicidal rage. After a healing on the Sabbath, "the Pharisees went out, and held counsel with the Herodians against him, on how to destroy him" (3:6). Mark foreshadows Jesus' fate through the device of the Passion predictions, wherein Jesus, describing with precision the events to unwind in Jerusalem, names his opponents, representatives of "traditional" Judaism: elders, chief priests, scribes (8:31; see also 9:31, 10:33). In this way Mark ties Jesus' teachings in the Galilee to his fate in Jerusalem: Jesus died, Mark suggests, because of hostility to his teaching and acting against certain traditional interpretations of Torah and Temple.

Mark's Jesus thus can be read as standing against the Judaism of his time, represented on the one hand by his scribal and Pharisaic opponents (particularly in the Galilee), and on the other by the Temple and its priests (particularly in Jerusalem). So powerful is this impression, and so powerfully reinforced by the way that Christianity in fact developed—as a Gentile movement after Jesus' lifetime and, indeed, as a post-Temple movement well after Mark's—that it is easy to read the evangelist as, in these instances, historically reliable: These episodes attest to Jesus' true hostility, not just toward certain practices, but toward the Law itself.

But it was Paul, not Jesus, who insisted on freedom from (most of) the mandates of Torah, and this made good sense in light of his audience. Paul spoke not to Jews but to Gentiles, whom no stream of Jewish tradition ever regarded as responsible to and for Torah. Their elective observances were exactly that: optional. Should a Gentile convert to Judaism—if male, receiving circumcision—then he, like the born Jew, "is bound to keep the whole Law" (Gal 5:3), the peculiar sign, as Paul states in Romans, of Israel's election (9:4). But even Paul nowhere argues that Jews in principle were free to drop Torah. To do so would have put him outside the entire idea of the Biblical covenant that he in fact invokes when accounting for Jesus' role in salvation (e.g., Rom 15:1–12. We will shortly examine this passage in some detail). What Paul, midcentury, said to Gentiles makes no sense as a message that Jesus, some twenty years earlier, would have said to fellow Jews.

The prima facie unlikelihood of a Jesus so removed from his own social and religious context is compounded by a further historical fact: If Jesus during his own lifetime had abrogated the Law, evidently neither his own disciples nor Paul himself knew. On the evidence, again, of the Gospels and Paul, Jesus' earliest followers continued to keep the Sabbath. This alone accounts for the lag between Jesus' burial before Friday evening and the women's discovery of the tomb only on Sunday morning. Luke makes this explicit: Returning from the tomb early Friday evening, "on the Sabbath they rested according to the commandment" (Lk 23:56).

After Jesus' death, the early church in Jerusalem continued to worship in the Temple (Lk 24:53; Acts 2:46, 3:1); in the Diaspora, they moved within synagogue communities (cf. 2 Cor 11:24; Acts passim).

The kosher status of food and drink continued to be of lively importance not only to the Jewish members of the movement (Gal 2:11–12), but also to its Gentiles, whose concerns on this score Paul had to address (1 Cor 8:1–13; Rom 14:2–4 and passim). And Paul himself, his so-called Law-free mission to Gentiles notwithstanding, praised precisely those aspects of traditional Judaism that Mark's Jesus supposedly condemned: the presence of God in the Temple (Gk. *doxa,* the "glory" of divine presence at the altar), the covenants, the giving of the Law on Sinai, and the mandated cult of sacrifices and offerings (Gk. *latreia,* translated weakly into English as "worship"). These, Paul states, number among the privileges that God had given to his "sons," Israel (Rom 9:4).

This is not to say that Jesus did not dispute with other Jews over the correct way to be Jewish. As our brief survey of Second Temple Judaism has shown, few things are so antecedently plausible, even probable: This is what Jews did. By comparison with what some of the Qumran texts and later rabbinic literature have to say about the Jerusalem priesthood, or what the houses of Hillel and Shammai, debating points of Pharisaic interpretation, occasionally say about each other, what passes between the scribes and Jesus is fairly mild. Further, the very fact of argument implies the opposite of rejection or indifference. Argument here implies mutual involvement, common concern, shared values, religious passion. If one party or the other had thought the issues unimportant, there would have been no fight. But even Mark's Jesus, responding with the *Sh'ma* and Leviticus to the scribe, does not say, "And you can forget the rest of the Torah," or, "Love God and neighbor, then, and skip the offerings." He says, rather, "No other commandment is greater than these." All are great or important; none is greater or more important.

Mark shapes these controversy traditions polemically, to provide the greatest contrast between Jesus and his challengers. The scribes and Pharisees fuss over imagined Sabbath infringements (in fact, none is actually presented; it is the tone of Jesus' activity that offends), oblivious to the splendid healings; miffed by a question and a miracle, they plot his murder. In their anxiety to ensure universal conformity to their own standards of observance, they follow Jesus everywhere, watching his house to see whom he eats with and how (Mk 2:13–17 and parr.), patrolling grainfields on the Sabbath hoping to catch him out (2:23–24), checking to see whether his disciples first wash their hands before eating (7:2). This is polemical caricature, not realistic portraiture. As such, we can scarcely use it directly for realistic reconstructions of the past. The first step, rather, is to identify Mark's polemical hobbyhorses, and then try to correct for these when reading what he has to say.

For example: Consider the long and contrived controversy story given in Mark 7. In protesting that Jesus' disciples do not purify their hands before eating, Mark's Pharisees in effect complain that Jesus' disciples are not Pharisees (since such a purification practice seems to have characterized specifically this group). Should this surprise them? As we noted in our earlier survey, even taking Josephus's number of six thousand Pharisees in the first century, they would have constituted at the most 1.2 percent of the total population of Palestine. Didn't they know that they were a small minority, and that their customs were hardly universal? Jesus' teaching that what comes out of a man defiles him— "evil thoughts, fornication, theft, murder, adultery, coveting, wickedness, deceit, licentiousness, envy, slander, pride, foolishness"—not what goes into him (7:14–23), is reasonably uncontroversial. Jesus in this passage overstates his case to make his point, prioritizing the moral pollution of sin over levitical pollution from external defilement. He is hardly endorsing the consumption of shellfish and pork here. It is Mark's heavy-handed gloss—"thus he declared all foods clean" (v. 19b)—that flamboyantly relates Jesus' teaching in this passage to the biblically mandated food laws.

Mark's gloss intrudes in this passage. Stylistically, it is the equivalent of a film actor's stepping out of character and narrative action and, speaking directly into the camera, addressing the viewing audience ("Now watch this part closely!"). The addition makes Mark's point, not his main character's (cf. Matthew's retelling, 15:1–20). And finally, we must take into account the controversy in Antioch, years after this supposed encounter between Jesus and the Pharisees, when Peter, the men sent from James, and Paul disputed about mixed Gentile-Jewish meals taken in community (Gal 2:11–13). If Jesus during his mission had already nullified the laws of kashrut, this argument never could have happened.

Mark dismisses the concerns of Jesus' opponents—Shabbat, food, tithing, Temple offerings, purity—as the "traditions of men." To these he opposes what Jesus ostensibly propounds as "the commandment of God" (7:8). The strong rhetoric masks the fact that these laws are biblical and, as such, the common concern of all religious Jews: It is God in the Torah, not the Pharisees in their interpretations of it, who commanded these observances.

Indeed, running like an undercurrent in Mark's narrative, obscured by the immediacy of his polemical concerns, is Jesus the traditionally religious Jew. He frequents synagogues on the Sabbath, certainly a normatively pious practice. The ill grab ahold of "the fringe of his garment" (6:56); the term, *kraspedon* in Greek, translates the Hebrew *tzitzit*. These fringes are not decorative but ritual. God had instructed Moses on them in a passage in Numbers that was incorporated into the *Sh'ma*. "Speak to the people of Israel and bid them to make tassels on the corners of their garments throughout their generations . . . to look upon and *to remember all the commandments of the Lord, to do them*" (Nm 15:38–39). Pious Jews would (and do) wear these; if Jesus did, too, it would be small surprise. Mark's Jesus celebrates Passover in Jerusalem, with its special mandated evening meal. In brief, and Mark's conscious efforts to the contrary notwithstanding, Jesus appears even in this Gospel as a recognizably observant Jew.

Mark's polemical position, picked up to a greater or lesser extent by the other evangelists (and, alas, by centuries of New Testament scholars), urges that ethical concerns override or oppose halakic ("ritual") concerns. In considering this position, we must realize, first, that Mark writes after 70 C.E., in a period when many of the cultic purity laws were simply moot, because the Temple was no more. Few things could be safer than having his main character, whose prediction of the Temple's destruction he dramatically showcased in his Gospel, proclaim that Temple ritual was not essential to true piety.

But this dichotomy of "ethical" vs. "ritual" is itself intrinsically anachronistic. It is a modern distinction, resting on the perceived externality (hence moral superficiality) of ritual in favor of (implicitly more authentic) ethics. But people in antiquity did not distinguish these behaviors in these terms. In broader Greco-Roman culture, ethics as such—self-conscious reflection on right behavior—was the concern of the philosopher. Cult rules and revealed ritual—what the gods told to men in dreams, visions, traditional stories, visitations—correspond roughly to what we think of as "religion." But when Paul urges his Gentiles to behave in a way consistent with his gospel, he forbids them (for instance) not only to drink to excess or to fornicate ("ethical" behavior), but also, equally adamantly, to have anything to do with the worship of idols ("ritual" behavior). For a Jew, both ethics and ritual stand on the same continuum, because both are equally the revealed will of God. (Remember Leviticus 19.)

This polemic can distract us from noticing an actual, practical aspect of this ethical instruction in the Gospels and Paul, an aspect that coheres with the foreshortened time frame of vivid apocalyptic expectation. I speak of its sheer impracticality. No normal society could long run according to the principles of the Sermon on the Mount. Total passive nonresistance to evil—indeed, compliance with injustice (Mt 5:38–48//Lk 6:27–36)—and an absolute refusal to judge (Mt 7:1–2//Lk 6:37–38) would simply lead to the exploitation of those abiding by such rules by those who do not. Voluntary poverty ultimately only increases the absolute numbers of the poor. Not worrying about tomorrow—a principled refusal to plan—can be disastrous: Lilies of the field live one kind of life, but humans another.

And as we see already from Matthew's emendation, society, in the long run, cannot tolerate an absolute prohibition of divorce. To live by their stringent codes, the Essenes formed their own society, withdrawn from the rest of the world. Much later Christianity, acting on some of these injunctions to poverty and sexual abstinence, of necessity did much the same, variously institutionalizing monasticism and the practice of celibacy, collecting those who would live out their religious commitment in this way into their own settlements.

But the earliest followers of Jesus did not retreat into separate communities and did not establish institutions. Why not? Because these early Christians, and Jesus before them, did not expect a long run. The Kingdom was at hand. In the intense and idealized ethics of this new community we see literally embodied, through the way they led their own lives, their utter commitment to this view. Perhaps, too, they viewed their own behavior as a proleptic enactment of eschatological society, bringing into the present what life would be like in the Kingdom.

"The one spirit gives the gifts of healing": Works and Power

CONVOCATIONS OF the Gentile *ekklēsia* in Corinth must have been quite a scene. Paul's letter gives us a glimpse: divisiveness and competition ("I belong to Paul!" "I belong to Cephas!" 1 Cor 1:12); disputes about whether one could eat food previously offered to idols—some thought yes, others no, still others felt morally queasy (8:1–13); refusal to share food at the community eucharistic meal ("Don't you have your own houses to eat in?" 11:22). So bad was their behavior, Paul heatedly warns, "that is why some of you are weak and ill, and some have died" (11:30). Some members, secure in the wisdom revealed to them, continued in old behaviors even after baptism, drinking to excess, fornicating, thieving, worshiping the old gods ("Do not even eat with such a one!" 5:11). While some prophesied, others overflowed with unintelligible charismatic speech, *glossolalia* ("If the whole group assembles and all speak in tongues and outsiders or unbelievers enter, will they not say that you are mad?" 14:23).

Their failings and confusions notwithstanding, these Gentiles, Paul maintained, had been filled with God's spirit. Inspired, they were likewise empowered:

> To each one is given the manifestation of the spirit for the common good. To one is given through the spirit the utterance of wisdom, to another the utterance of knowledge according to the spirit, to another faith by the same spirit, to another *gifts of healing by the one spirit, to another working of miracles* [literally, "works of powers"], to another *prophecy,* to another *the ability to discern between spirits.*
>
> (1 Cor 12:6–10)

The spirit had come to these Gentiles through baptism, said Paul, thereby incorporating them into the "body of Christ" whose individual members they were (12:13). And it is this spirit, from God, through Christ, that enabled them to perform these charismatic acts.

In Matthew's Gospel, perhaps forty years after Paul's letter, we find a similar collocation of actions attributed to later followers of Jesus. Interestingly, these actions do not attest to their membership in the true community. Quite the opposite: In this episode, toward the close of the Sermon on the Mount, Matthew's Jesus warns of what he is going to say to certain Christians, charismatic deeds notwithstanding, when he encounters them at the final judgment:

> Not everyone who says to me, "Lord, Lord," shall enter the Kingdom of Heaven, but he who does the will of my Father who is in heaven. On that day many will say to me, "Lord, Lord, *did we not prophesy* in your name? And *cast out demons* in your name? And *do mighty works* in your name?" And then I will declare to them, "I never knew you; depart from me, you evil doers."   (Mt 7:21–23)

The power to heal, prophesy, and do miracles is not self-authenticating, as it might seem from the passage in Paul. Here Matthew says, rather, that this power—which he, or his Jesus, does not dispute (the passage does *not* run, "Lord, did we not do mighty works in your name?" "No; you thought you did, but you really didn't")—settles nothing. The person's religious or spiritual status must rest on other criteria.

The scribes in Mark's Gospel had thought similarly about Jesus (Mk 3:22–27. When Matthew repeats and edits the same story, the "scribes" become "Pharisees"; Luke simply says "some," Mt 12:22–37; Lk 11:14–23). According to Mark, Jesus had been traveling throughout the Galilee casting out demons; healing the feverish, the possessed, and those suffering from various diseases; curing a leper, a paralytic, and a man with a withered hand; and finally appointing "twelve" to preach and cast out demons in their turn (3:14–15). The scribes were unimpressed. "By the prince of demons [Beelzebub] he casts out demons" (cf. Jn 8:48, 8:52, 10:20, where Jesus' audience simply assumes that "he has a demon"). Again, no dispute arises about whether Jesus works these cures and exorcisms—indeed, the scribes' statement acknowledges that he does. But their challenge means that having such powers, in and of itself, establishes nothing more.

I mention these passages to make a larger point about the way that New Testament authors viewed miracles. Such occurrences are extraordinary yet, at the same time, not unusual in the sense of unprecedented or unique. Nor do they in and of themselves say anything about the person performing them. More than just Jesus, certainly, can work them. Paul's Gentiles can, according to his first-hand testimony. Paul himself can and does, thus (in his view) establishing his authority as an apostle ("signs, wonders, and mighty works," 2 Cor 12:12; his apostleship to the Gentiles wrought in "word and deed, by the power of signs and wonders, by the power of the Holy Spirit," Rom 15:19). The Gospel traditions develop their portrait of Jesus, most centrally and importantly, as an exorcist, healer, prophet, and author of mighty works or signs; but such powers are also attributed to his disciples (Mk 6:13), to those who do not follow him but simply cast out demons in his name (Mk 9:38), and even to those followers whom Jesus, at the End, will repudiate (Mt 7:21–23). In their efforts to deceive the elect, false christs and false prophets also "will show signs and wonders" (Mk 13:22). And Jesus in Matthew's retelling of the "Beelzebub" controversy imputes successful exorcisms to the "sons of the Pharisees" as well (Mt 12:27).

When we turn to broader streams of evidence—various pagan traditions; other Jewish writings—we again find reports of miracles and miracle workers, healers and exorcists. Ancients would "incubate"—

that is, sleep in at a cult site—in order to receive visions of or favors from a god. We have evidence of this practice from the cult of Asclepius, the god of healing. His worshipers, receiving cures, left a record of his miracles in inscriptions around his shrine. So also the pagan holy man Apollonius of Tyana had numerous miracles attributed to him: spectacular healings, exorcisms, even once raising someone from the dead. And in the Greek Magical Papyri—books for professionals consulted for cures and different kinds of help (in love or in betting on races, for example)—we can read recipes for conjuring demonic aid to achieve some of these ends. If these practices were not thought to be effective, if the miraculous and the wonderful were thought not to happen, we would not have so much ancient evidence that they did.

Biblical and extrabiblical tradition, on the Jewish side, also speak of powerful prayer, miraculous cures, signs, and wonders. Scripture relates the deeds of prophet Elijah and his younger protégé, Elisha: Elijah, for example, raised a widow's son from the dead (1 Kgs 17:17–24). Elisha, too, raised a child from the dead (2 Kgs 4:18–37) and cured the foreign general Naaman of leprosy, specifically on his authority as a prophet: "Let him now come to me, that he may know that there is a prophet in Israel" (5:1–27). He also blessed a widow's jar of oil, so that it "filled many vessels" (4:1–7), and later fed one hundred men from only a few loaves: "they ate, and had some left" (4:42–44). Such miraculous acts echo in the Gospels' stories about Jesus.

Josephus and later rabbinic texts also speak of wonder-workers. Some, such as Honi the Circle-Drawer ("Onias" in Josephus) and his grandson Hanan had reputations as rainmakers, and thus commanded nature. A certain Eleazar (so Josephus, giving an eyewitness account) expelled demons from those possessed, while Hanina ben Dosa worked cures from a distance. (Interestingly, later rabbinic sources associated some of these men specifically with the Galilee.) References to such activity remain in Essene literature also. In their retelling of Genesis, the Genesis Apocryphon, Abram drives an evil spirit, responsible for sickness, from Pharaoh and his men. The *Prayer of Nabonidus,* a Scrolls fragment, connects sin and sickness, health and forgiveness of sin, when King Nabonidus tells how he was "afflicted with an evil ulcer for seven years. . . . and a *gazer* [exorcist?] pardoned my sins. He was a Jew." And in *The Jewish War* and *Antiquities,* Josephus speaks of charismatic leaders who gathered followings while promising to work great signs: One Theudas promised to part the Jordan River; another Jew, from Egypt, to collapse the walls of Jerusalem by his command; others, to perform marvels out in the desert. My point is not whether these men did or did not work these miracles, but rather—as the great numbers of their followers attests—that their contemporaries clearly thought they could. And, finally, Josephus refers to Jesus of Nazareth as such a wonder-worker: He was, says Josephus, a "wise man" who performed "startling deeds" (*AJ* 18.63).

I review these sources for two reasons. The first is to make the point that people in antiquity, unlike most people today, evidently had little difficulty either perceiving certain events as miraculous or attributing what we think of as supernatural powers to human beings. While miracles and healing were not common occurrences (if they were, they would not be mentioned as attesting to power), they were common enough so that the simple ability to perform such deeds was not seen in itself as establishing the wonder-worker's authority. The second point refines this one, and relates it specifically to Jesus: His ability to work miracles might enhance his status but could not of itself establish it.

Jumping from Paul's testimony of the charismatic deeds worked by his Gentiles-in-Christ to those traditions about Jesus himself, we note that Jesus as exorcist, healer (even to the point of raising the dead), and miracle worker is one of the strongest, most ubiquitous, and most variously attested depictions in the Gospels. All strata of this material—Mark, John, M-traditions, L-traditions, and Q—make this claim. This sort of independent multiple attestation supports arguments for the antiquity of a given tradition, implying that its source must lie prior to its later, manifold expressions, perhaps in the mission of Jesus himself. Such reasoning establishes only that traditions about Jesus' working miracles are early: They cannot answer the question—a modern concern, not evidently an ancient one—whether he actually did them.

Did Jesus of Nazareth, then, perform miracles? Here I as a historian have to weigh the testimony of tradition against what I think is possible in principle. I do not believe that God occasionally suspends the operation of what Hume called "natural law." What I think Jesus might possibly have done, in other words, must conform to what I think is possible in any case. (Those who have no trouble accepting these miracle accounts as reliably, factually descriptive may skip this paragraph and the next. They should also be aware, however, that Jesus, on the evidence, was hardly unique in performing such acts.) So, to answer my own question: Yes, I think that Jesus probably did perform deeds that contemporaries viewed as miracles. Those I have least trouble imagining his working conform to those also named by Paul: healings and exorcisms. Modern culture, too, is familiar with charismatic cures worked by suggestion. Our explanations differ from those given in ancient sources—where we use the language of psychosomatic disease and suggestion, people in antiquity spoke of demons and special powers—but the phenomenon observed seems identical.

An ability to work cures, further, coheres with another datum from Jesus' mission: He had a popular following, which such an ability helps to account for (see Mark 1:23–28, 32, 39, 45: "But he [a former leper] went out and began to talk freely about it [i.e., Jesus' curing him of leprosy], and to spread the news, so that Jesus could no longer openly enter a town . . . and people came to him from every quarter"). To take as much as I can as historical, I would also include the Synoptics' stories about Jesus raising the dead within this category. I think of "death" in these instances as something like coma: These instances would represent an extreme type of healing. But such healing abilities, in an age of so many healers and miracle workers, would confer no unique distinction upon Jesus: Again as we see in the Gospels themselves, the same ability is imputed to other contemporaries. The Gospels use this material, rather, to make a particular point about Jesus, as we shall shortly see. The miracles in and of themselves are not the point.

The other wonders attributed to Jesus—walking on water (Mk 6:45–52//Jn 6:16–21); calming the storm (Mk 4:35–41 and parr.); causing a miraculous catch of fish (Lk 5:1–11; Jn 21:1–14); withering a fig tree with a curse (Mk 11:12–14, 20–21); changing water into wine (Jn 2:1–11); feeding a multitude (Mk 6:32–44)—cannot be rationalized so readily. I see them function in the tradition more as ways of proclaiming Jesus' power than as reports of remembered events. Within this category I would include the raising of Lazarus, found solely in John's Gospel. That Gospel insists that Lazarus had been dead for four days, and that the corpse already stank (11:17, 39). The whole incident pronounces the evangelist's theological message about Jesus. "I am the Resurrection and the Life," this Jesus tells Lazarus's grieving sister; "who believes in me, though he die, yet he shall live" (v. 25). As this Gospel's Jesus himself remarks, when hearing the news of his friend's extremity, "This illness is not unto death; it is for the glory of God, so that the Son of God may be glorified by means of it" (v. 4), which is precisely how this story in this Gospel works.

The synoptic Gospels themselves put Jesus' wonderworking within the larger framework of his prophetic authority: Miracles demonstrate Jesus' authority to announce the coming of the Kingdom. Responding to an inquiry from John the Baptizer ("Are you he who is to come, or shall we look for another?"), Jesus, according to this Q-tradition, says to John's disciples, "Go and tell John what you hear and see: the blind receive their sight and the lame walk, lepers are cleansed and the deaf hear, and the dead are raised up, and the poor have the good news preached to them," and he goes on to speak about the Kingdom (Mt 11:2–24//Lk 7:18–35). The miracles speak to the power of God breaking into the present, in advance of the Kingdom's full arrival.

Here the evangelical interpretation of Jesus' miracles provides a glimpse into the way that Jesus of Nazareth himself might have understood them; for both they and he stand within the larger context of Jewish views on power and prophecy, the authority to announce God's message.

The miracles should not be regarded in isolation, then, but together with Jesus' moral message and his call to prepare for the coming Kingdom. Miracles would not demonstrate his personal power, but rather— as with the wonder-workers of Talmudic lore—his intimacy with God, the true source of such power. Miracles as deed reinforce the authority of word: They enhance and support Jesus' reputation as authoritative prophet of the Kingdom. "If it is by the finger of God that I cast out demons, then the kingdom of God has come upon you" (Mt 12:28//Lk 11:20). The miracles are the medium; but the Kingdom is the message.

Our speculation here about Jesus' own view of his miracles returns us by another road to our earlier observation about his perfectionist ethics, and also to our point of origin in this cycle of research, namely, the diaspora mission and the letters of Paul. Christian eschatology as such, as distinct from its matrix, Jewish eschatology, expresses at its earliest and most vibrantly apocalyptic strata—Paul and Mark—the paradox of "Now" vs. "Not yet." Paul's Kingdom—with the Son's Parousia, the defeat of death, the resurrection of the dead, and transformation of the living—lay just over the historical horizon; and until those things are accomplished, he insists, the Kingdom has not arrived. Yet within the *ekklēsia,* the turning of the ages is in some sense realized. The Spirit has been poured forth, so that Gentiles-in-Christ have already renounced their idols and acknowledged "the living and true God"; already they, too, can work charismatic deeds of power. Spiritually if not physically, redemption has already been won, because Christ, "the first fruits of those who have fallen asleep" has already been raised from the dead (1 Cor 15:20; cf. 2:14–16, 3:16, chaps. 12–14; Gal 4:3–9; Rom 8:10–17, etc.).

So, too, with what we can discern of the movement around Jesus. He spoke of a Kingdom still to come; yet the measure of his authority as its spokesman was broadcast in the defeat of evil, sickness, and death already actualized in his own mission through his exorcisms and heal- ing miracles. Those who accepted him and his message of impending salvation—the restoration of Israel and the redemption of the world— were in a privileged position: they could prepare for the event they knew was coming by living according to the intensified, internalized precepts of Torah that Jesus preached, forswearing not just sin (murder, adultery) but the very emotions that precede sinning (anger, lust); returning good for evil (Mt 5:17–48); perhaps—if they would imitate Jesus himself—forswearing the false security of property, embracing poverty, living on the road, taking to others the message of the King- dom (Mk 6:7–13, specifically of the Twelve; cf. 9:42–47, 10:17–22, the rich man; Lk 10:9–11, the commission to the Seventy).

The perfectionist ethical teachings and the miracles, then, are all of a piece, both in Jesus' own mission, and even twenty years after his execu- tion, in the Diaspora, with Paul's Gentiles. Both *together* attest to the nearness—now but not yet—of the Kingdom.

" 'This is my body, which is for you' ": The Lord's Supper

COMMUNITY ETIQUETTE was lacking in Corinth. Among his many complaints about their deportment, Paul names the Corinthians' fractiousness and rudeness: Rather than a communal event, the meal taken together by the *ekklēsia* was closer to a free-for-all. "When you eat together, it is not the Lord's supper that you eat. For in eating, each one goes ahead with his own meal, and one is hungry and another is drunk!" (1 Cor 11:21). To recall them to their purpose, Paul reminds them of the origins of this practice: Jesus himself.

> For I received from the Lord what I also delivered to you, that the Lord Jesus on the night he was handed over *took bread, and having given thanks, he broke it* and said, "*This is my body which is for you.* Do this in remembrance of me." In the same way also the cup, after sup- per, saying, "*This cup is the new covenant in my blood.* Do this, as often as you drink it, in remembrance of me." For as often as you eat this bread and drink this cup, you proclaim the Lord's death *until he comes.*
>
> (1 Cor 11:23–26)

Paul anticipates here by some twenty years a tradition that we find, later, in Mark. I italicize the particular elements they have in common:

> And as they were eating, he *took bread, and he blessed it and broke it,* and gave it to them and said, *"This is my body."* And *he took a cup,* and when he had given thanks he gave it to them, and they all drank of it. And he said to them, *"This is my blood of the covenant,* which is *poured out for many.* Truly I say to you, I shall not drink again of the fruit of the vine *until that day when I drink it new in the Kingdom of God."*
>
> (Mk 14:22–25)

In the Gospel narrative, Jesus celebrates the Passover meal together with the Twelve (though Mark does not actually depict a seder). Shortly thereafter, Judas Iscariot, who had arranged to betray Jesus to the priests (14:10–11), leads a crowd to Gethsemane to ambush Jesus after the meal (vv. 43 ff.). The preceding Passion predictions have prepared the reader for these events: betrayal and death in Jerusalem.

Paul's version, by comparison, has none of this narrative context (though in deference to the Judas story, modern translations give the verb he uses in 11:23, *paredidoto,* "handed over," as "betrayed"). Yet the "words of commission" in both versions presuppose that (1) Jesus anticipated his own impending death and (2) interpreted it himself as a kind of expiatory sacrifice (his body "for you"; his blood "poured out for many"). Finally, Paul, in his version, and Jesus in Mark's, tie the commemorative meal into the coming Kingdom: The Corinthians are to keep the meal as a way to "proclaim the Lord's death until he comes"— that is, comes again; Mark's Jesus will not drink wine again until "I drink it new in the Kingdom of God."

What historically might stand behind this tradition? Both versions attest, first, to the celebration of a common meal, in anticipation of the Kingdom, as an early and prominent feature of primitive Christianity. Sayings of Jesus elsewhere in the Gospels likewise speak of the Kingdom as a banquet (e.g., Mt 8:11). The idea is further attested in Judaism contemporary with Jesus. The Essenes, too, predicted such a feast, to be presided over by the priest and the Messiah; and they observed a communal meal in anticipation of this Endtime "messianic banquet." Later Jewish apocalyptic texts—Baruch, Enoch, the Apocalypse of Elijah— speak both of a superabundance of food at the End and of dining with the Messiah. Had Jesus himself, perhaps at his final Passover in Jerusalem, likewise spoken of the impending Kingdom, he may have enacted such a feast with his twelve disciples, whose company symbolized the restored, eschatological Israel.

It is the details of the eucharistic formula, however, that engage speculation. We know, again from Paul, that Jesus' followers early on saw his death as in some sense vicarious and expiatory ("Christ died for our sins in accordance with the Scriptures," 1 Cor 15:3). We must wait until we consider, in more detail, events surrounding Jesus' last week in Jerusalem before we can gauge the plausibility of Jesus himself being the source of this idea in Christian tradition. But the coincidence of our two earliest witnesses, Paul and Mark, demonstrates at the very minimum that this formula, and the practice of this communal meal, was very early on regarded by these communities as a teaching of Jesus himself.

God's "Son, who was descended from David according to the flesh": Jesus the Christ

"CHRISTOS," the Greek translation of the Hebrew *meshiach* or "messiah" ("anointed"), is Christianity's designation of choice for Jesus. The word is so firmly established in the tradition so early on that, by the time we have Paul's letters, "Christ" functions most simply as Jesus' name. In other words, the understanding of Jesus as Messiah did not originate with Paul, but was inherited by him. To reconstruct its prehistory, then, we need to consider the following questions:

> *What* was the meaning of the term in this period?
> *When* was it attached to Jesus of Nazareth?
> *Why?*

THE MEANINGS OF MESSIAH

The Hebrew Bible is the fundamental source for the term *meshiach*, though the word itself occurs there only thirty-nine times. Most usually it designates the current ruler of the Jewish kingdom whose assumption of office was marked by anointing with oil (e.g., 2 Sm 5:3; 1 Kgs 1:39; Ps 89:20). In a few cases, "anointed one" refers to the holder of priestly office (e.g., Lv 4:3, 5, 16), and anointing could evidently figure in the investiture of prophets (1 Kgs 19:16; cf. Is 61:1). But at one point the entire people of Israel is called "God's anointed" (Ps 105:15; 1 Chr 16:22); and, more surprisingly, Isaiah uses the term to designate the Persian ruler Cyrus, who defeated Babylon and permitted the Jews exiled there to return to Jerusalem and rebuild the Temple (Is 45:1; cf. 2 Chr 36:23).

This free use notwithstanding, the prime historical referent of this term was the warrior king David. In Jewish tradition, David appears as the ruler who especially loved God (authorship of the Psalms is attributed to him) and who in turn was especially loved by God. For this reason God promised eternal sovereignty to the kings of his line:

> The Lord declares to you that the Lord will make you a house. When your days are fulfilled and you lie down with your ancestors, I will raise up your offspring after you, who shall come forth from your body, and I will establish his kingdom. He shall build a house for my name, and *I will establish the throne of his kingdom forever. I will be a father to him, and he shall be my son.* When he commits iniquity, I will punish him with the rod of men, with the stripes of the sons of men; but *I will not take my steadfast love from him,* as I took it from Saul whom I put away from before you. And your house and your kingdom shall be made sure forever before me; *your throne shall be established forever.*   (2 Sm 7:11–17)

But it was precisely when royal power was torn from the kings of David's line, when God's house was destroyed and the people of Israel driven off the land, that this promise was reaffirmed in prophetic oracles. In the wake of the fall of the north to Assyria (722 B.C.E.), and the capture of Jerusalem and exile in Babylon under Nebuchadnezzar (586 B.C.E.), Isaiah, Jeremiah, and Ezekiel confirm the hope of a future, idealized kingdom. Thus Isaiah 11 anticipates a "shoot coming forth from the stump of Jesse," David's father. This "shoot" is a future monarch whose reign will be marked by righteousness and peace (extending even to the animal kingdom, vv. 6–8), when "the earth will be full of the knowledge of the Lord" and the outcasts of Israel reassembled; even the Gentiles will seek this messianic king (11:1–15).

"The days are surely coming, says the Lord, when I will raise up for David a righteous branch," prophesied Jeremiah, "and he shall reign as king and deal wisely, and shall execute justice and righteousness in the land" (Jer 23:5). Amplifying this promise later in his book, Jeremiah continues: "Thus says the Lord: David shall never lack a man to sit on the throne of the house of Israel"; he goes on to compare the certainty of this promise with the certainty of Creation itself (Jer 33:17–22).

To Ezekiel, God swears that he will establish "over them one shepherd, my servant David, and he shall feed them . . . and be their shep-

herd. And I, the Lord, will be their God" (Ez 34:23). Surveying the Dry
Bones ("Son of man, these bones are the whole house of Israel," 37:11),
the prophet receives God's promise of resurrection and restoration: "I
will open your graves and raise you from your graves, O my people; and
I will bring you home into the land of Israel" (37:12). Further, at that
point God will "set up over them one shepherd, my servant David"
who will be their king (v. 24). Israel will then dwell in the land forever,
always under the Davidic prince. God will restore his sanctuary, the
Temple, and establish with his people an everlasting covenant of peace.
And with the restoration of his sanctuary even the Gentiles will
acknowledge "that I the Lord sanctify Israel" (vv. 25–28).

These prophetic promises were spoken in the teeth of brutal disconfirmation of the covenant: defeat, destruction, exile. The prophets'
invocation of the ultimate Davidic king served to affirm God's general
and continuing commitment to Israel and to his covenant promises.
Israel *was* broken, but its brokenness was temporary: God would
redeem.

And, in fact, the Exile did come to an end. In the closing decades of
the sixth century B.C.E. (c. 538–510), with their defeat of Babylon, the
Persians permitted the exiles to return to Judea and rebuild their city
and temple. But the days of a native monarchy were over. Under the
Persians, leadership ultimately devolved to the high priests, who governed from Jerusalem while serving as the intermediary between their
own people and the empire. This ruling priest was (or was considered
to be) a Zadokite, that is, a descendant of the ancient house of Zadok,
whose historical prominence was intertwined with that of the Davidic
monarchy: the biblical Zadok had endorsed Solomon as David's heir
and anointed him king (1 Kgs 1:28–45). Long after Persian power
waned, this form of government persisted. After Alexander the Great
conquered Persia, Jerusalem's high priests mediated variously between
the Greek Ptolemies of Egypt and the Greek Seleucids of Syria, and so
the situation continued until the outbreak of the Maccabaean revolt
(167 B.C.E.).

The cultural civil war that led to the revolt expressed a split within
the Zadokite family itself. In 175 B.C.E., Jason, brother of the current
high priest, bought the office for himself by bribing the Seleucid ruler
Antiochus, whose permission he sought to turn Jerusalem into a Hellenistic city (hence the gymnasium mentioned in 1 Mc 1:14; cf. 2 Mc
4:7–22, on Jason). Various Zadokites divided their political loyalties
between the perennially warring Ptolemies and Seleucids; but most

endorsed, to one degree or another, the cultural and religious Hellenization of Jewish life. The priestly family of the Hasmoneans who took charge of the revolt ultimately led the forces opposed to radical Hellenization to victory. In recognition of their power and authority in Judea, Seleucid monarchs thereafter appointed one of their number to the office of high priest. Later (in the 140s or 130s), as political autonomy increased, the Hasmonean high priest assumed the role and even the title "king."

Should Jews worship foreign gods as well as their own? Ignore biblical laws on food, sacrifice, Sabbath? Cease—or disguise the marks of—circumcision (1 Mc 1:14f., 43–49)? The success of the revolt answered all these questions with a clear "No." Extreme Hellenization was out, and the Law of Moses, however variously interpreted, would be the law of the land.

But the political independence established by the Hasmoneans, together with the post-Seleucid freedom of practice, complicated, for some Jews, precisely this issue of interpreting and living the Law. The problem was exacerbated and in a sense exemplified by the Hasmoneans themselves: High priests but not Zadokites; kings, eventually, but clearly not of the house of David (who had been a layman); they lacked the correct biblical pedigree for either job, and this troubled some Jews. Others simply preferred the older form of government as under Persia or the Greeks: a high priest (whose position, in comparison to the Hasmonean consolidation of royal and priestly offices, was relatively unpolitical) serving under an empire remote from and uninterested in the day-to-day life of the country. For some, in brief, the new order chafed.

Politically (and thus religiously), matters continued to grow ever more complicated. Israel became increasingly drawn into pan-Mediterranean politics, which naturally affected both the government and, accordingly, the Temple. Tangled up in the civil wars marking Rome's transition from republic to empire, Jerusalem was besieged and the Temple's inner sanctum violated by the Roman general Pompey (63 B.C.E.). Then Hasmonean rule ceded to Herod the Great (37–4 B.C.E.), a third-generation convert to Judaism. Unable to serve as high priest himself, Herod used the position as a blatantly political appointment, assigning (and later assassinating) his Hasmonean brother-in-law to the office, and later bringing in foreign nobodies completely beholden to him to fill the position temporarily. (Traditionally, it had been a life appointment.) When he died, Augustus as executor of Herod's will divided the country between his three surviving sons: Archelaus took Judea and Samaria; Antipas, the Galilee and Perea (on the east bank of the Jordan); Philip, parts of Transjordan. Archelaus proved controversial, and in 6 C.E., partly at the request of some Judeans, Augustus sent him into exile and brought Judea directly under Roman authority. Herod's other two sons retained their lands and their autonomy as client kings.

The prefects in Judea kept the peace with varying degrees of success, while high priests continued to come and go, now mostly at the pleasure of Rome. The war against the empire in 66–73 C.E. devastated Jerusalem and Judea; and the final, unsuccessful revolt in 132–135 C.E. led by Bar Kokhba (designated messiah by no less a religious authority than Rabbi Akiva) sealed the political and military desuetude of the country. The people and the religion would continue; but kingship, priesthood, Temple—those religious-political ideas and issues that had so charged the Hellenistic and Hasmonean period—were, by the changed realities of rabbinic times, transposed into a new key.

The Hasmoneans' biblically irregular execution of high priestly office and restoration of the monarchy, coupled with a contentious freedom of religious practice, had incubated the various religious parties—Sadducees, Essenes, Pharisees—enumerated by Josephus. They also contributed to the highly charged apocalyptic convictions that gave the intertestamental period its mutagenic religious intensity.

Stimulated by this climate, the messianic paradigms of earlier scriptural tradition altered, grew, proliferated. In the Qumran library alone, alongside the more familiar image of the royal Davidic messiah, the future warrior/prince of peace, we also find other messianic figures. The messiah also appears as the perfect priest. Or he might be the eschatological prophet, who will teach righteousness and interpret Torah correctly at the End of Days. Moses himself had foreseen his coming: "The Lord your God will raise up for you a prophet like me from among you, from your brethren. Him you shall heed, just as you desired of the Lord your God. . . . And the Lord said to me: 'I will raise up for them a prophet like you from among their brethren, and I will put my words in his mouth, and he shall speak to them all that I command him" (Dt 18:15–18). In an even more radical divergence from earlier types, the Scrolls also speak of a messianic figure (angelic? human? the text is fragmentary) enthroned in the heavens as final redeemer.

These figures from Qumran encode critiques of circumstances specific to the aftermath of the Maccabaean revolt. The insistence on a Davidic messiah bespeaks a negative response to the non-Davidic Hasmonean kingship; the notion of an Endtime priestly messiah, dissatisfaction with the current running of the Temple; the division of messianic authority between priest and king ("Aaron and Israel," as the Scrolls have it), a criticism of the Hasmonean combination of the two offices. That the texts of a single community exhibit such a striking variety of these messianic figures gives a good indication of the degree of interpretive diversity that apocalyptic hope could accommodate generally. And when we broaden our perspective to take in some of the various apocryphal and pseudonymous revelations circulating in this period between Judah Maccabee and Bar Kokhba—Daniel, 2 Esdras, 1 Enoch, who spoke of a coming Son of Man; 2 Baruch and the Psalms of Solomon, of a kingly messiah; the Assumption of Moses, of the final Kingdom but no messiah at all—we see that none of the details of the coming cosmic drama were fixed. What mattered was the final triumph of Good over Evil, in universalized fulfillment of God's promises to Israel.

This diversity of messianic figures and their function should not obscure the prime importance of the Davidic messiah. Messianic expectation was not universal; but those who chose to speculate in this vein had, in the classical prophetic texts and later apocalyptic interpretations of them, a readily available body of tradition to draw on. The Messiah son of David is the best and most widely attested figure, cutting across sectarian as well as temporal lines: We can trace him from the classical Jewish biblical histories and prophets through the multitudinous intertestamental texts just reviewed on into rabbinic prayers and benedictions. His role in history's final drama was clear. "See, Lord, and raise up for them their king, the son of David," prayed the author of the pseudonymous Psalms of Solomon sometime in the first century B.C.E., "at the time that you have knowledge of [i.e., the Endtime], and gird him with strength, so he may smash those who rule without justice" (17:23). Executing judgment, defeating the enemies of God, reigning over a restored Israel, establishing unending peace, this eschatological prince epitomized the military prowess, valor, and virtues of his royal ancestor, the warrior king David.

All the more mysterious, then, that earliest Christian tradition would choose this figure as a way to express and proclaim the religious identity of Jesus of Nazareth.

"Christ" in Paul

Paul typically identifies Jesus as "Christ": the term occurs more than 140 times in the seven letters of his extant correspondence. Since he writes to already established communities, Paul nowhere offers an elementary, catechetical explanation for his or the tradition's use of the word—the sort of "since Jesus did thus-and-so, he must be the Christ" instruction that we find in the later Gospels. Only in his last letter, to the community at Rome, do we find two fleeting but formal declarations of Jesus' identity that link him with the broader, biblically based redemptive myth. The first occurs as Paul introduces himself:

> Paul, a servant of Jesus Christ, called to be an apostle, set apart for the gospel of God which he promised beforehand through his prophets in the holy scriptures, the gospel concerning his *Son, who was descended from David according to the flesh,* and designated Son of God in power according to the spirit of holiness by his resurrection from the dead, Jesus Christ our Lord.   (Rom 1:1–4)

The second appears in a cento of biblical quotations from Psalms, Deuteronomy, and Isaiah as Paul moves into the closing of his letter. He again invokes Jesus' coming as the fulfillment of biblical promises, "for whatever was written in former days was written for *our* instruction, that by steadfastness and by the encouragement of the Scriptures we might have hope" (15:4). These promises, he says, had always had in view a double goal: the redemption of Israel ("Christ became a servant to the circumcised to show God's truthfulness in confirming the promises to the patriarchs") and of the nations ("in order that the Gentiles might glorify God for his mercy," v. 8). Naming Isaiah, Paul then adds: " 'The *root of Jesse* shall come, he who rises to rule the Gentiles; in him shall the Gentiles hope' " (Is 11:10 LXX).

These allusions are brief but pregnant with biblical significance. In his opening sentence, for example, Paul names Jesus as the physical descendant of David and thus David's "son." But Paul also introduces Jesus first of all as God's Son. This idea of sonship—that the king (thus "son of David") is also in some sense God's Son—pertains, as we have already seen, to ancient Jewish traditions of kingship. God when speaking through the prophet Nathan to David had promised sovereignty to David's house, saying of the future ruler, "I will be a father to him, and he shall be a son to me" (2 Sm 7:14; the full passage is quoted above, p. 120). The kinship language expresses the abiding bond of affection between God and king.

But, in light of the metaphysical claims that later, trinitarian Christianity will make for Jesus, we should note here that this biblical tradition also affirms the king's earthly, physical paternity: The descent from David as human father is precisely the point of God's promise of permanence to his royal line. "Your house and your kingdom shall be made sure forever before me; your throne shall be established forever" (7:17). David as messiah and, therefore, God's son, appears similarly in Psalm 89: "I have found David, my servant, with my holy oil I have anointed him; . . . He shall cry to me, 'You are my Father' " (89:20, 26). So also Psalm 2, the so-called Enthronement Psalm: "You are my son; today I have begotten you" (v. 7).

"Son of God," in other words, is an ancient phrase native to Jewish tradition for designating the human messiah. Such a phrase signals the intimate relationship between God and the designate. It is also used in the Bible for other close relationships between God and select beings. Angels, prophets, particularly just or righteous men, the entire nation of Israel (as Paul at Rom 9:4)—all could properly be called "son(s) of God." Used of a figure of David's house, the phrase indicates a monarch. Transposed into an apocalyptic key, the phrase indicates the final eschatological king.

Paul gives no explanation for his identifying Jesus as such a royal figure—"Christ" (that is, Messiah) "descended from David." However, no matter what Paul's reasons are for identifying Jesus in this way, the Resurrection is not one of them. Jesus' resurrection designates a special sonship—"son of God *in power*"—but not the Davidic one, which Paul distinguished earlier as depending on physical descent ("according to the flesh"). Paul states here what scholars know from their study of broader Jewish tradition, namely, that the Judaism preceding and contemporary with ancient Christianity knew no tradition of a resurrected messiah, and thus nothing of a dying messiah. Where an "anointed one" does die—in Daniel 9:26, for instance, "after sixty-two weeks, the messiah will be cut off and be no more"—he is a human political figure. But he is not, ipso facto, the final eschatological Redeemer-King.

The only hint of Paul's reason for viewing Jesus as the Davidic Messiah comes in chapter 15, when he refers explicitly to Isaiah 11:10, the "root of Jesse" ruling over and bringing hope to the Gentiles (15:12). To see the point he is making more clearly, we must step back to view it within its larger context: Jewish speculations on the role of the Gentiles in the final days.

Such speculations form an element within more general Jewish apocalyptic hopes. These hopes express the fundamental biblical conviction that God is good, that he works in history, and that he is true to his promises. The fundamental promise—which Paul alluded to in Romans 15:8—goes back to the calling of Abraham, which in the tradition's view was the beginning of the Jewish people:

> Now the Lord said to Abram, "Go out from your country and your kindred and your father's house *to the land that I will show you. And I will make of you a great nation, and I will bless you and make your name great, so that you will be a blessing. I will bless those who bless you and curse him who curses you, and through you shall *all the families of the earth be blessed.*"   (Gn 12:1–3)

The story of Abraham thus begins with God's pledge that the Land of Israel awaits Abraham and his family, and that their unique relationship will benefit all humankind. God later makes other pronouncements to Abraham. His descendants will be enslaved in a foreign land, but God will redeem them from slavery and bring them to their promised home (15:12–20). Abraham and his family must walk before God and be blameless (17:1), sealing their covenant in the flesh with circumcision (17:10–13), keeping God's ways by doing righteousness and justice (18:19). The pledge of the Land repeats throughout the rest of the Genesis, recurring in God's dealings with Isaac and Jacob; invoked by Joseph, dying in Egypt, in the book's closing lines:

> And Joseph said to his brothers, "I am about to die; but God will visit you and bring you up out of this land to the land which he swore to Abraham, Isaac and Jacob."   (Gn 50:24)

From Genesis 12, with God's call to Abraham, to the close of Deuteronomy, with Moses dying as the twelve tribes prepare to cross over the Jordan, the entire Torah tells this story of how God made good on his promise of the Land—"the land which I swore to Abraham, to Isaac, and to Jacob, 'I will give it to your descendants' " (Dt 34:4). The final collapse of the northern Jewish kingdom to Assyria in 722 B.C.E., and the fall of the south to Nebuchadnezzar in 568 B.C.E., must be viewed within this perspective. Exile from the Land was a traumatic disconfirmation of God's promise, of his covenant, of Israel's election as God's people.

It was the genius of the prophets that made it otherwise. Out of all the families of the earth, they urged, God had chosen Israel alone to know and serve him: "Only you [Israel] have I chosen from among all the nations." Israel's suffering and exile thus actually expressed God's continuing commitment: "Therefore I will punish you for your sins" (Am 3:2). Suffering was punishment, and punishment was not rejection. God used calamity to call Israel to repentance. By rededication to fulfilling her covenant obligations—ritual, moral, economic, as the modern mind parses them—by returning to Torah, Israel would also return to the Land. "Zion will be redeemed by justice, and those in her who repent, by righteousness" (Is 1:27). God is just and merciful; his love is steadfast; his word unchanging; his promises, therefore, sure— or, as Paul put it in Romans, "The gifts and the call of God are irrevocable" (11:29).

In the prophets' view, the confrontation of Babylon and Jerusalem embodied in historical idiom the two poles of a spiritual and moral reality: exile and return, slavery and redemption, sin and repentance, repentance and forgiveness. Later generations, traumatized in their turn by the cultural and religious confusions of the Greek and Roman periods, looked to this prophetic tradition. They amplified its urgency and universalized its claims: Prophecy became apocalyptic eschatology. The assured redemption no longer lies simply in the future. That future impinges on the present: It is imminent, and one can know its approach by reading the signs of the times.

And the surest sign was how bad things had become. If Hellenizing priests controlled the Temple; if a foreign idol stood at the altar of God; if Jews apostatized and idols polluted the Land; if the high priesthood were torn from the house of Zadok; if everything, in brief, were as terrible as it could be, then surely God was about to intervene. How bad things were or what exactly "bad" was depended, of course, on one's particular viewpoint: What was terrible for an alienated Zadokite priest might seem just fine to a Maccabaean partisan. In brief, the particular situation or event stimulating the apocalyptic response varied from person to person and community to community. But common to all was the mentality of urgency, coupled with intense religious conviction: The worse things got, the better they were about to become. God—just, good, almighty—would not let history drift indefinitely.

Thus what in the prophets was to be a historical event in the life of the people of Israel—the return to the Land and restoration of the Kingdom—became in its apocalyptic mode what God would bring about at the End of Days, changing the nature of historical reality itself. Both the preceding extent of evil and the final extent of good wax universal, as Israel's redemption from Babylon and return to the Land expand to a huge scale: the cosmic defeat of evil, the ingathering of the entire people (living and dead), and the universal worship of the God of Israel. As Israel returns from the lands of her dispersion, she will be escorted by the nations to Zion: "In those days ten men from the nations of every tongue shall take hold of the robe of a Jew, saying, 'Let us go with you, for we have heard that God is with you' " (Zec 8:23). Both the city and God's house will be rebuilt in splendor, "for all generations for ever, just as the prophets said of it," wrote Tobit, an apocryphon of the second century B.C.E. "Then all the Gentiles will turn to fear the Lord God in truth and will bury their idols" (Tb 14:5–6).

Here, then, is the clue to understanding Paul's view of Jesus as the Davidic Christ. That in the final days, to effect Israel's redemption, God would send his Messiah, the branch of Jesse, was *not,* as we have seen, a universally held Jewish belief; but, clearly, Paul and the other members of the Christian movement were among those Jews who did hold it. And that in the final days God would turn the gentile nations from their false gods to his own worship was *not* the only apocalyptic role assigned the Gentiles. We also find less generous speculations (many also in Isaiah): The unrighteous nations would be destroyed, their cities desolate (Is 54:3); their wealth would flow into Jerusalem (45:14); the kings of the Gentiles would bow down to Israel (49:6); the nations would lick the dust at Israel's feet. But it is the inclusive tradition anticipating gentile participation in Israel's final redemption that sounds increasingly in intertestamental writings, in later synagogue prayers, and in rabbinic discussion. And, clearly, this is the tradition shaping the convictions and activities of the earliest Jewish Christians—James, John, Peter, Barnabas, and most especially Paul (see Gal 2).

If we consider the place of Gentiles in antiquity's diaspora synagogue communities, we see more clearly the impact of this apocalyptic notion on Christian gentile life. Interested outsiders had long been accommodated by the synagogue and would continue to be for centuries after this period. Such Gentiles were free to assume as much or as little of Jewish practice as they wished, while continuing in their ancestral practices. This open attitude was consistent with the religious ecumenicalism that marked pagan culture generally. For the Jews' part, encouraging the interest and even the admiration of the host gentile majority simply made good sense. Further, since Jewish tradition regarded keeping Torah as the defining privilege of Israel, the synagogue would have little reason to impose its own standard of monotheism on these neighbors. If Gentiles in the Diaspora chose to join with Jews in worship of Israel's God, they were free to, just as in Jerusalem they were free to fund offerings at the Temple. Abundant literary and inscriptional evidence reveals considerable Gentile-Jewish interaction. And, much to the annoyance of later Christian bishops, gentile Christians well into the fourth century and after continued what their pagan ancestors had begun, frequenting synagogues and keeping Jewish fast or feast days as they would.

Conversion to Judaism, which entailed circumcision for men, was another matter entirely. A Gentile who chose to become a Jew would thereby take upon himself the obligation to observe Torah. "Every man who receives circumcision," as Paul wrote in Galatians, "is bound to keep the whole Law" (5:3). Conversion accordingly meant ceasing traditional pagan worship altogether, thus cutting oneself out of the social and religious fabric of the ancient city. This was a serious and consequential step. Virtually all civic activities involved sacrifices. Failure to participate in the cults of the city and of the empire (which mandated homage to the emperor and to the genius of Rome) could easily result in at least resentment, if not actual criminal charges. An exclusive allegiance to the Jewish god would therefore necessarily affect aspects of the convert's life well beyond what we as moderns (and particularly Americans, given our legally protected distinction between church and state) think of as "religious."

Born Jews had to negotiate exemptions from the cults of majority culture, and these exemptions were written into the laws of the cities where they lived. Their religious exclusivism angered some pagan writers, who considered it "atheist," the derogatory term describing refusal to worship the gods. Commenting resentfully on Jewish "atheism," these writers particularly reproached those (former) Gentiles who had converted to Judaism: Such conversions seemed a form of sedition, a rank disloyalty to and betrayal of one's own people, country, ancestors, and gods.

This resentment highlights the oddness of the idea of conversion in antiquity. What we now think of as "religion" had a clear genealogical nexus then: People worshiped the gods native to them. To undergo a rite that would turn a pagan into a Jew would make as little sense to

Photograph of the synagogue at Sardis

"From early generations Moses has had in every city those who preach him, for he is read every sabbath in the synagogues" (Acts 15:21). In the ancient world, "synagogue" might mean simply a "gathering" or congregation, not necessarily a building. But in the cities of the Diaspora, Jews sometimes erected large and stately public buildings to serve as a gathering place for their community. Interested Gentiles might drop by at will. The fourth-century remains of the synagogue at Sardis (in modern Turkey) attest to a wealthy and well-integrated Jewish community whose public building stood in the heart of their city, in the same structure as the marketplace and the baths. The floor of the synagogue runs along the entire lower edge of the structure.

most ancient pagans as would a modern person's undergoing a ritual by which she would somehow be transformed from being, say, actually, culturally English to actually, culturally Italian. A modern can convert from Anglicanism to Catholicism but still be English; or she can legally change her citizenship, trading in her U.K. passport for an Italian one, but still be Anglican. Our distinction of legal and cultural nationality, or religious versus cultural status, is not native to antiquity. To "become" a

Jew meant to become part of another people or nation, somehow to undo one's own past.

Absent conversion, however, no such change in religious allegiance seems to have been demanded or expected by these diaspora synagogue communities: Sympathetic Gentiles could and most often did remain pagans. Further, diaspora Jews themselves do not seem to have promoted missions as such to these Gentiles: Given the religious social fabric of the ancient city, and pagan resentment at Jewish cultic exclusiveness, such a mission, had diaspora Jews ever conceived it, might very well have jeopardized the well-being of their own community, a minority in whatever city they lived.

Consider then, within this context, what Paul is telling his Gentiles. He urges them to worship *only* the God of Israel. "You have learned from us," he tells the Christian Gentiles of Thessalonica, "how you ought to live and to please God," now that they have "turned to God from idols, to serve a living and true God" (1:9). The Corinthians must completely renounce idolatry; anyone still indulging must be put out of the community (1 Cor 5:1–13). Even if they know that " 'idols have no real existence' and that 'there is no God but one' " (Paul, quoting them, 8:4), eating meat from an animal sacrificed to idols puts some members at risk: "Weak in conscience," they might slip back through this old cultic activity to thinking that such gods really exist (8:7–12). Better then that they not eat meat at all (v. 13)—in effect, completely absenting themselves from civic ritual. Again and again Paul repeats his point: "Shun the worship of idols" (10:14; see the entire chap.).

But this is not to say that these Gentiles should become Jews: This is the whole point of Paul's argument in his letter to the Galatians. They need not convert—indeed, Paul argues heatedly, they *should* not convert, because God in Christ had saved them graciously, without the works of the Law. It is enough, says Paul, that Gentiles-in-Christ love one another and repudiate the "works of the flesh." (Paul then lists the usual condemned behaviors: fornication, impurity, idolatry, drunkenness, and so on: "I warn you, as I warned you before, that those who do such things shall not inherit the Kingdom of God," Gal 5:14, 19–21). In sum, according to Paul, Gentiles-in-Christ should repudiate their traditional worship and commit exclusively to the God of Israel. They should hold themselves aloof from the social and religious holy days of their city and native culture. *And* they should not become Jews.

No precedent in normal synagogue practice explains his demands. They are drawn, rather, from various Jewish apocalyptic traditions.

Paul urges his Gentiles to precisely that behavior that other Jews who thought about such things would have anticipated only once the Kingdom came. We find the theme of the Endtime pilgrimage of Gentiles to Zion already in the classical prophets. Thus Isaiah:

> It shall come to pass in the latter days that *the mountain of the house of
>   the Lord* shall be established as the highest of the mountains,
> and shall be raised above the hills.
> And *all the nations shall flow to it,*
> and *many peoples shall come* and say,
> "Come, let us go to the mountain of the Lord,
> to the house of the God of Jacob;
> that he may teach us his ways,
> and that we may walk in his paths."
>
>   (Is 2:2–3)

This theme develops into the expectation that Gentiles at the End will make an exclusive allegiance to God and repudiate their idols. "At that time I will change the speech of the peoples to a pure speech," says God through the prophet Zephaniah (seventh century B.C.E.?), "that all of them may call upon the Lord and serve his with one accord" (Zep 3:9). Turning to God in the final days, Gentiles "will bury their idols," prophesies Tobit (Tb 14:6; second century B.C.E.). Journeying to the Temple, contemplating the Law of the Most High God, these Gentiles will see idols destroyed by flames (Sibylline Oracle 3.616, 716; mid–second century B.C.E.). And we see this theme repeated later in a synagogue prayer, the *Alenu:* When God finally reveals himself in glory "all humankind" (Heb. *kol benei basar,* "all the sons of flesh") will turn from their idols to worship the Lord. And we see this theme, mid–first century C.E., in Paul.

Pagan culture and the sort of moral, sexual, and religious behavior it tolerated (or in Paul's view, produced) were not topics of general Jewish enthusiasm. Paul fully shared the views of his fellow religionists on this topic, as his roiling condemnation of pagan culture shows:

> Claiming to be wise, they became fools, and exchanged the glory of the immortal God for images resembling mortal man or birds or animals or reptiles. Therefore God gave them up in the lusts of their hearts to uncleanness, to the dishonoring of their bodies among themselves, because they exchanged the truth about God for a lie and worshiped and served the creature rather than the Creator, blessed forever, Amen! . . . God gave them up to a base mind and improper conduct.

The inscription at Aphrodisias

This third-century Jewish inscription from Aphrodisias (in modern Turkey) provides an intriguing glimpse into the nature of Gentile-Jewish interactions in the Diaspora. In its list of names (perhaps commemorating donors), it gives inter alia fifty-four *theosebeis* or "God-fearers," pagans who chose also to worship the God of Israel. Nine of these were listed as members of the city council, which means that as part of their civic office they would have been responsible for presiding over public sacrifices to their traditional gods, for example, when convening sessions of the council. Evidently their public religious activity inhibited neither their interest in the God of Israel nor the Jewish community's recognition of that interest.

They were filled with all manner of wickedness, evil, covetousness, malice; full of envy, murder, strife, deceit, malignity. They are gossips, slanderers, haters of God; insolent, haughty, boastful, inventors of evil, disobedient to parents. Foolish. Faithless. Heartless. Ruthless. (Rom 1:22–31)

Thus the Apostle to the Gentiles! To Paul, the fact that his Gentiles-in-Christ were able to renounce their idols and the behaviors that Jews associated with idolatry must have seemed like a miracle, and that is precisely what he says. Their turning to God, their embrace of idealized Jewish ethics—sexual modesty, monogamy, support of the poor, and so on—is the measure, he says, of God's spirit, or Christ's spirit, working in them (Rom 8:9, and frequently elsewhere; Gal 4:6). Christian Gentiles, for Paul, embody in their new behavior the proof that the Kingdom was indeed about to dawn, that the Messiah truly had in fact come, and was about to come again.

But herein lay the awkwardness, too. For though the Messiah had already come, he still needed to return to complete the work of redemption. In this brief in-between, from the Resurrection to the Parousia, Paul's Gentiles, empowered by the spirit, were to live *as if* they were already in the messianic age. In terms of life within the *ekklēsia,* this was so: There the Spirit was poured forth, believers prophesied and spoke in tongues; people healed and worked mighty signs; they had, through Christ, received adoption and become children of God. But the larger world still ran as it had before, unaware that in Paul's view it seemed to be passing away.

Here, then, we see most clearly the measure and the consequences of Paul's foreshortened perspective on time. By insisting both that they *not* convert to Judaism (thus maintaining their public and legal status as pagans) and that they nonetheless *not* worship the gods (a protected right only of Jews), Paul walked these Gentiles-in-Christ into a social and religious no-man's-land. In the time before the Parousia, they literally had no place to be. And in the long run, their position would prove untenable: It is precisely this Gentile group who fall victim to anti-Christian persecutions in the long centuries until the conversion, in 312, of Constantine. But Paul, again, did not expect a long run. The Messiah had not only come already; he was coming again. Soon. His Gentiles were for Paul exactly the proof of this.

It is in Paul's descriptions of Jesus' Second Coming that we see, finally, the strength of traditional Jewish expectations about the role and function of the Davidic Messiah. Jesus' first appearance had not been messianic, and Paul knew it. He even emphasized it: Paul preached "Christ crucified, a stumbling block to Jews and folly to the Gentiles"; God had deliberately chosen to work through "what is foolish and weak." But divine foolishness was wiser than the wisdom of the world; divine weakness stronger than human strength. Through Christ's cross, God worked redemption (1 Cor 1:18–31).

But that redemption, Paul equally insisted, would not be fully, publicly realized until the Parousia. Only at that point would redemption be manifest. To the sound of trumpets and the war cry of angels (1 Thes 4:16), the returning Son would destroy God's enemies (1 Cor 15:24–28), assemble the quick and the dead (1 Thes 4:16 f.; 1 Cor 15:23, 42, 51–52; Phil 3:21; Rom 11:15), and gather in scattered Israel (Rom 11:12 full inclusion of Israel, 11:26 all Israel saved). When Christ came again, said Paul, he would come the way the royal Messiah was supposed to come: in power.

Paul's vision of Jesus as the Davidic Messiah thus corresponded intimately both with his understanding of his own calling and with his views on the surprising way in which God was realizing his biblical promises to Israel. God, Paul said, had set him apart even before he was born for the purpose of calling the Gentiles through his Son (Gal 1:15–16). Paul claimed that even the pillars of the Jerusalem community who had known Jesus according to the flesh—Peter, James, John—had recognized him as the apostle to the Gentiles *par excellence* (2:7–9). He held that the interim between Christ's resurrection and his Parousia corresponded roughly to the length of his own mission: As soon as he had reached "the full number of the Gentiles," the final events could unwind (Rom 11:25; cf. vv. 11–24). Jesus was the Christ, the root of Jesse foreseen by Isaiah, whom the Gentiles would seek (15:12). Paul did his part to bring them in. And as far as he was concerned, by midcentury he had done nearly all there was to do. "From Jerusalem as far round as Illyricum I have fully preached the gospel of Christ. . . . I no longer have any room for work in these regions" (Rom 15:19, 23).

Paul was not the only Jewish apostle to go to Gentiles in this first generation, though it is easy to come away from his letters with that impression. Peter himself had gotten involved; there was Barnabas and, in Antioch, "the rest of the Jews" (Gal 2:11–13). Somebody had gotten to Rome before Paul had, because he writes ahead to that *ekklēsia,* largely if not totally Gentile, by way of introduction. He closes the letter by sending greetings to the apostles ("fellow workers in Christ Jesus") already there: Some among them were Jews (Rom 16:1–16). Did these others, too, construct Jesus' Davidic messiahship around this idea of the eschatological turning of the Gentiles?

We can't know, of course, because Paul's letters are the only evidence we have from this generation. But if this group were the first to identify Jesus as Messiah for this reason, then the designation would back only as far as the diaspora mission, the earliest point at which significant numbers of Gentiles became involved. Before it spread to the Diaspora, on the evidence of the Gospels, the movement had been confined for the most part to the villages of the Galilee and to Jerusalem. Gentile participation had been negligible.

Paul's list of witnesses to the resurrected Christ suggests, however, the designation's origin in pre-Diaspora days. Christ "appeared first to Cephas, then to the Twelve, then to almost five hundred . . ." (1 Cor 15:5–6). But if Jesus as Christ dates to the Resurrection events—however we chose to interpret them—we still have no understanding of the reason for the claim. Nothing in pre-Christian Judaism anticipated a resurrected Messiah. Whence, then, this identification, already well established by the time that Paul, c. 33, joins the movement?

The fact that Jesus died on a Roman cross pushes the point of origin for this messianic designation back from the diaspora mission, back from the Resurrection, back into his own lifetime. The essential meaning of "messiah" coheres well with Jesus' manner of death. A royal title long before it acquired its eschatological significance, "messiah son of David" indicates, at the very least, a king of Israel—a political claim that any competent Roman colonial governor would want to discourage. The favored Roman means of discouraging sedition was crucifixion. The way Jesus died is our surest evidence that a claim for his Davidic messiahship dates from his lifetime, not after. Did he claim this title for himself? Did others so acclaim him? Why? To address these questions, we must turn to the Gospels.

"Christ" in the Gospels

IN WAYS DIFFERENT than Paul's letters, the Gospels also move us both closer to the historical Jesus and farther away. Closer because, whatever the vicissitudes of the various traditions that the Gospels preserve, at least some of these must ultimately trace back to Jesus' original followers—either that, or the Gospels tell us absolutely nothing about the historical Jesus at all. His earliest followers are the necessary middle links in the chain between Jesus and these later stories about him.

But they also move us farther away because, unlike Paul's letters, the Gospels are composite documents. Their period of formation stretches forward from the oral inheritance of the earliest disciples to the evangelists' own time, a gap of some forty to seventy years. In this interim, events of tremendous consequence had unwound. First, the Christian movement itself had evolved into a distinctive sect within Judaism, and so taken its place in the fractious debates that characterize intersectarian relations in this period. (Hence, for example, the high polemic against Pharisaic Jews that marks all these stories.) Second, as they increasingly lived on the Diaspora side of the linguistic frontier between Aramaic and Greek, these Jews and their Gentile adherents looked to the Scriptures in their Greek translation, the Septuagint, rather than the Hebrew, as their biblical authority. (Whence, for example, Matthew and Luke's nativity stories, where Mary's virginity rests on the *parthenos* of Is 7:14 LXX.) And, finally, Israel had fought, and lost, the war with Rome.

Each of the four evangelical narratives ostensibly describing the mission of Jesus thus actually offers us a mix of material from the full stretch of these years: inherited sayings and stories from and about Jesus; contemporary polemics against other Jews; biographical "facts"

about Jesus mined from various readings of the Septuagint; convictions—mined from the same quarry—about the religious significance
of the Temple and its destruction; creative theological interpretations of
Jesus as Christ, Son of God, Son of Man. The Gospels can no more be
approached directly for information about the historical Jesus than a
"historical" film by Oliver Stone, for example, can be approached
directly for information about JFK, Nixon, or the war in Vietnam.
Both genres present a mix of fact, reasonable conjecture, creative filling in of holes, and flat-out fiction. As historians, we have to sort
through.

The evangelists, all later than Paul, wrote from within a tradition
that already proclaimed Jesus as Christ. I propose that we read their stories to see how they present that claim, and then test how well their presentations can fit credibly into Jesus' lifetime.

We begin, again, with Mark. One of the great curiosities of this
Gospel, noted earlier, is its reticence precisely on the issue of Jesus' identity. Commanding silence from those who recognize him, forbidding
those he cures to speak of it, Mark's Jesus never names himself Messiah,
and but for one dramatic exception, never clearly accepts the title either.
Mark's designation of choice for Jesus is, rather, the Son of Man. The
Son of Man will suffer rejection and death in his First Coming, Jesus
teaches, but will soon return, vindicated and glorious, at his Second
Coming. In other words, it is through his use of this term "Son of Man,"
and not "messiah," that Mark articulates his Christian convictions
about Jesus. He weaves these into his narrative about Jesus, a theological retelling of known elements of his mission—miracles and exorcisms, itinerant preaching about the Kingdom of God, disputations
with other Jews, death in Jerusalem by crucifixion—in terms of Jesus'
actions as suffering Son of Man.

Where and how does the term *christos* figure in all of this? Messianic
terms—Christ, Son of David, king of Israel—appear only seven times
in Mark's Gospel. The first simply opens his story: "The beginning of
the gospel of Jesus Christ" (1:1). The next occurrence, highly dramatic,
occurs when Jesus himself abruptly demands an answer to a question
he has never addressed: "Who do men say I am?" (8:27). His disciples
respond, John the Baptist, Elijah, one of the prophets. Jesus presses
them further: What do they think? Peter answers, simply, "You are the
Christ" (8:29).

It is instructive to read Mark's scene here, 8:27–33, in tandem with
Matthew's revision of it, Matthew 16:13–23. Matthew clears up the con-

Mark 8:27–33	Matthew 16:13–23
And Jesus went on with his disciples to the villages of Caesarea Philippi; and on the way he asked his disciples, "Who do men say that I am?" And they told him, "John the Baptist, and others say, Elijah; and others one of the prophets." And he asked them, "But who do you say that I am?" Peter answered him, "You are **the Christ**."	Now when Jesus came into the district if Caesarea Philippi, he asked his disciples, "Who do men say the **Son of Man** is?" And they said, "Some say John the Baptist, and others say Elijah, and others Jeremiah or one of the prophets." "But who do you say that I am?" Simon Peter replied, "You are the **Christ, the Son of the living God**."
	And Jesus answered him, "Blessed are you, Simon bar Jonah! For flesh and blood has not revealed this to you, but my Father who is in heaven. And I tell you, you are Peter [Gk. *Petros*], and on this rock [Gk. *petra*] I will build my church, and the powers of death shall not prevail against it. I will give you the keys to the Kingdom of Heaven, and whatever you bind on earth will be bound in heaven, and whatever you loose on earth will be loosed in heaven." Then he strictly charged the disciples to tell no one that **he was the Christ**.
And he charged them to tell no one about him. And he began to teach them that the **Son of Man** must suffer many things, and be rejected by the elders and the chief priests and the scribes, and be killed, and after three days rise again. And he said this plainly.	From that time, Jesus began to show his disciples that **he** must go to Jerusalem and suffer many things from the elders and the chief priests and the scribes, and be killed, and on the third day be raised.
And Peter took him, and began to rebuke him.	And Peter took him and began to rebuke him, saying, "God forbid, Lord! This shall never happen to you!" But he turned and said to Peter, "Get behind me, Satan! You are a hindrance to me; for you are not on the side of God, but of men."
But turning and seeing his disciples, he rebuked Peter, and said, "Get thee behind me, Satan! For you are not on the side of God, but of men."	

Matthew, by carefully editing Mark, brought greater clarity to this scene, the dialogue between Jesus and Peter outside of Caesarea Philippi. Matthew makes unambiguous Jesus' acceptance of Peter's answer ("You are the Christ"): Matthew adds "Son of the living God," and then a long passage where Jesus praises Peter and confers authority on him. He likewise clarifies the reason Peter rebukes Jesus (he is prompted by concern; in Mark, by comparison, the reason is not clear). Further, Matthew drops Mark's confusing reference to the other disciples ("But turning and seeing his disciples, he rebuked Peter. . . "), having his Jesus simply reprimand him.

fusion Mark leaves in his wake. Where Mark's Jesus persistently speaks of the Son of Man in the third person, leaving the reader to infer an identity, Matthew makes the identification explicit: His Jesus, posing the same questions to his disciples, uses "Son of Man" interchangeably with "I" (16:13, 15). Still more helpful, where Mark's Jesus had responded to Peter's identifying him with a demand for silence ("And he charged them to tell no one about him," v. 30), Matthew's bursts out in approval at his answer ("Blessed are you, Simon bar Jonah!" vv. 17–19). Only after this does Jesus ask for silence, phrased by Matthew in such a way that no doubt remains that Jesus accepts the designation ("Then he strictly charged the disciples to tell no one *that he was the Christ*," v. 20).

In Mark's passage, by comparison, questions linger. Without acknowledging Peter's answer, demanding the disciples' silence, Mark's Jesus abruptly goes on to teach about the suffering Son of Man (8:31 f.). Peter then rebukes Jesus (Mark isn't clear why) and Jesus rebukes Peter as Satan (Why? Evidently because the disciples overheard Peter rebuking him, v. 33). Again, Matthew smooths this out. He provides Peter with a clear and laudable motive for rebuking Jesus—"God forbid, Lord! This shall never happen to you" (16:22)—and removes Mark's confusing one for Jesus' rebuke of Peter (v. 23).

The point here is not to ponder whether it is Mark or Matthew who gives the more plausible depiction of a conversation between Jesus and Peter. We have absolutely no way of knowing whether anything like such a conversation ever took place, in Aramaic, some forty to sixty years earlier. Matthew's version smooths over rough spots in Mark's so precisely that good editing, rather than more reliable historical tradition, seems the likely reason for his greater clarity. This dialogue in Matthew's Gospel accords with one of his strongest themes, namely, that Jesus *is* the Messiah from the house of David. Mark on the same issue is more complex.

Mark uses messianic terminology more straightforwardly in the three episodes that follow. Preaching in Capernaum, his Jesus says, "Whoever gives you a cup of water to drink because *you bear the name of Christ* will by no means lose his reward" (9:41). Next, on their way up to Jerusalem through Jericho, Jesus and his disciples together with a "great multitude" (other pilgrims also going to the city for Passover) pass by the blind beggar Bartimaeus, who abruptly addresses Jesus as "*Son of David*" (10:47, 48—the second time over rebukes to silence from the crowd). Jesus cures his blindness, presumably in acknowledgment of his address to him ("Go your way; your faith has made you well," 10:52). And finally, as the crowd approaches Jerusalem, Jesus seems almost to provoke a messianic incident by riding a colt into the city (another scene that Matthew's editing will clarify, 21:2–11). The crowd responds by spreading their garments before him, waving leafy branches, and crying out, "Hosanna! Blessed is *the kingdom of our father David that is coming.* Hosanna in the highest!" (11:10).

His apparent approval of these Davidic designations notwithstanding, Mark's Jesus challenges the traditions they are based on:

> As Jesus taught in the temple, he said, "How can the scribes say that the Christ is the son of David? David himself, inspired by the holy spirit, declared:
> 'The Lord said to my Lord,
> Sit at my right hand,
> till I put your enemies under your feet.'
> "David himself calls him 'Lord'; so how is he his son?"

Mark here refers to Psalm 110:1 LXX. His Jesus uses it to teach the superiority of the Messiah to David. David, in the spirit, calls the (future) Messiah "Lord"—by implication, his superior, and therefore not his "son." We do well here to recall that Mark, unlike the later two Synoptics, has no birth story providing Jesus with a link to Bethlehem. His Jesus is, without apology, a Galilean: Jesus of Nazareth. In this context—with no reason in the narrative, in other words, for the reader to associate Jesus with David's house—Mark's Jesus seems to refute as unnecessary the Davidic pedigree of the Messiah. This passage subtly asserts Jesus' messianic status despite his not being David's "son." Mark's Jesus cites David himself to make his case.

The next time this Gospel explicitly identifies Jesus as Christ is at the moment of highest drama at his night trial before the Sanhedrin. The high priest finally demands to know, "*Are you the Christ,* the son of the Blessed?" For once, Jesus' reticence—or Mark's—completely disappears, and he responds with a simple and powerful affirmation: "*I am.*" But Jesus immediately goes on to qualify this statement, speaking in terms of the apocalyptic Son of Man: "And you will see the Son of Man seated at the right hand of Power [God] and coming with the clouds of heaven" (14:61–62; cf. 13:26). The high priest pronounces this blasphemy, and the council condemns Jesus to death. Convening again once more at dawn, they lead Jesus, bound, to Pilate.

Throughout the rest of the Passion—the dialogue with Pilate, the roaring mob, the Crucifixion—this royal designation repeats consistently and ironically. Pilate (unprompted in the narrative) asks, "*Are you the King of the Jews?*" and Jesus answers evasively, "You have said so" (15:2). Pilate then asks the hostile mob, appearing out of nowhere, if they want him to release "*the King of the Jews*" (v. 9). No. "Then what shall I do with the man *whom you call the King of the Jews?*" (Odd— they haven't; v. 12). The crowd demands his crucifixion. Roman soldiers then proceed to mock Jesus—"Hail, *King of the Jews!*" (v. 18)—and they crucify him under an inscription of the crime he was charged with: "*The King of the Jews*" (v. 26). Mocked further by the two robbers hanging with him, by passersby, and finally by the chief priests ("Let *the Christ, the King of Israel,* come down now from the cross, that we may see and believe!" v. 32), Jesus finally dies.

The theme of Jesus' messianic identity appears in Mark in complex ways. Mark shapes his narrative around his project of redefining "messiah" to conform to his convictions about Jesus of Nazareth, whom he knew had been crucified and whom he expected to return. Thus after Peter's confession ("You are the Christ," 8:29) Jesus goes on to speak of the suffering Son of Man; and after the high priest's query ("Are you the Christ?" 14:61), Jesus affirms his identity and then speaks further in terms of the glorious and returning Son of Man. This presentation of Messiah as suffering-and-vindicated Son of Man expresses Mark's own theological creativity as a Christian. By contrast, at other points in his story he presents Davidic messiahship in a more traditionally Jewish— hence arguably pre-Christian—way. These cluster specifically around events in Jerusalem. Jesus parades into the city before Passover like a king (11:7–10); and he is executed by Pilate as if he had, indeed, claimed to be one (15:2–26).

In John's Gospel, as in Mark's, we also find this interesting combination of a seeming disavowal of traditional Davidic dimensions of messiahship with an insistence, ironically and especially stressed in the hearing before Pilate, that Jesus is, indeed, the royal Messiah, King of the Jews. In the very first chapter of this Gospel, Jesus' titles accrue rapidly: John the Baptizer and eventually his own disciples identify him as Lamb of God (1:29, 35), Son of God (v. 34), "the Messiah (which means Christ)" (v. 41). Finally, dramatically, Nathaneal proclaims, "Rabbi, you are the Son of God! You are the King of Israel!" (v. 49).

Yet John seems at pains to repudiate any traditional connection to David, especially via Bethlehem. He emphasizes that Jesus comes from

Nazareth. The *Ioudaioi* ("Jews" or "Judeans")—unknowing, some-times hostile crowds, usually in Jerusalem, who function rhetorically as a kind of chorus to emphasize aspects of Jesus' teachings—are inca-pable of knowing who Jesus is in part because of their attachment to this Davidic tradition. John seems to argue for the sort of disavowal we also saw in Mark's use of Psalm 110 LXX. Thus while Jesus teaches in the Temple during the Feast of Tabernacles, some people in Jerusalem ask, "Can it be that the authorities really know that this is the Christ? Yet *we know where this man comes from;* and when the Christ appears, no one will know where he comes from" (7:26–27). On the last day of this weeklong feast, some assert that Jesus is the Christ, but others respond,

> "Is the Christ to come from Galilee? Has not the scripture said that the Christ is descended from David, and comes from Bethlehem, the village where David was?" So there was a division among the people over him.   (Jn 7:41–43)

As the final events begin to unwind in Jerusalem, John's promotion of this title grows stronger. Pilgrims parade Jesus into the city, crying out, "Blessed is he who comes in the name of the Lord, even the King of Israel!" (12:13), and John specifically refers this scene to Zechariah 9:9: "Daughter of Zion, your King is coming." Jesus' kingly status domi-nates John's presentation of his audience with Pilate: The words "king" or "kingship" appear fifteen times within twenty-eight verses. Roman soldiers crown Jesus with thorns and place a purple robe on him, hail-ing him as King of the Jews (19:2–5), and thus, also, Pilate presents him to the people: "Behold your king! . . . Shall I crucify your king?" (vv. 14–15). The prefect composes the titulus himself—"Jesus of Nazareth, King of the Jews"—in Hebrew, Latin, and Greek, broad-casting the message as it were in three linguistic frequencies (vv. 19–20). The joke, of course, is actually on Jesus' mocking tormentors, for John's readers know what the characters in his story do not: Jesus *is* the Mes-siah, he is the King of the Jews (cf. 1:49).

Unlike John, Matthew and Luke both clearly draw on Mark; unlike both Mark and John and similar to each other, the two later Synoptics are at pains to affirm that Jesus is exactly the fulfillment of traditional expectation, the Davidic Messiah. Both avail themselves of the mes-sianic future that Mark had created for Jesus when he combined (as Paul had before him) the coming of the Kingdom with the return of the

Son of Man, who would then do messiah-like things—end the period of travails, gather in the elect, and so on. But by using the Septuagint for biographical information about him, these later Gospel writers also provided Jesus with a messianic past. Even at his First Coming, they each argue, Jesus of Nazareth was, demonstratively, the Messiah son of David, and thus the realization of Israel's ancient hope of redemption.

In sharp contrast to the other two Gospels, which each begin their stories with John the Baptizer, these later Synoptics both open with elaborate birth stories (Mt 2:1–23; Lk 2:1–39). These tie Jesus the Galilean to the messianically correct natal town in Judea: Bethlehem. "And you, O Bethlehem, in the land of Judah, are no means least among the rulers of Judah; for from you shall come a ruler who will govern my people Israel" (Mi 5:2, cited in Mt 2:6 as a prophetic proof-text). Both offer genealogies tracing Jesus' lineage back, through Joseph, to King David (Mt 1:1–16; Lk 3:23–39). In their respective accounts of the nativity, Matthew through his introduction of the foreign magi, Luke through Simeon's recognition of the infant Jesus in the Temple, both foreshadow the inclusion of Gentiles in the Christian move-ment—a fact of history by the time each writes, c. 90. This theme picks up the prophetic idea of the nations turning to the eschatological "root of Jesse" heralded in Isaiah and invoked at the close of his letter to the Romans by Paul: "The root of Jesse shall come; . . . in him shall the Gentiles hope" (Is 11:10 LXX; Rom 15:12). "Where is he who has been born *king of the Jews?*" ask Matthew's wise men (Mt 2:2). "Mine eyes have seen your salvation," Luke's aged Simeon prays to God, "which you have prepared in the presence of all peoples; *a light for revelation to the Gentiles, and for glory to your people Israel*" (Lk 2:31–32).

But Matthew and Luke explicitly postpone any inkling of a Gentile mission until after the Resurrection. Matthew's Jesus goes so far as to positively prohibit any efforts with Gentiles during his lifetime ("Go nowhere among the Gentiles . . . but go rather to the lost sheep of the house of Israel," 10:5–6; cf. 15:24; cf. the Gospel's finale, 28:19). Luke's story, a two-volume work, has more room: his apostles do not actually go to Gentiles until well into the Diaspora at Antioch (Acts 11:20). Nei-ther Matthew nor Luke, then, can use the Gentiles' reception of the gospel, as Paul had, as proof of Jesus' status as Christ: it falls outside the time frame of their stories about his mission. Yet they both want to pro-mote Jesus' identity as Davidic Messiah during his mission. They must find other ways to make their case.

Though the details differ between them, their strategy is the same.

Matthew and Luke both conform—and occasionally create—incidents in the life of Jesus of Nazareth to particular readings of the Septuagint. This technique gives a deep biblical resonance to their stories. The evangelists, and sometimes the characters in their stories, can then proclaim Jesus as Christ on the basis of this matching-up of ancient prophecy to biographical incident.

Thus Matthew interprets Jesus' healings and exorcisms in prophetic perspective, specifically quoting Isaiah: "He took our infirmities and bore our diseases" (Mt 8:17; Is 53:4). Characters in the Gospel simply address Jesus as "Son of David," an appellation he never denies (Mt 10:27). They infer his messianic status from the fact that he cures ("And all the people were amazed and said, 'Can this be the Son of David?' " Mt 12:23). Presumably because she knows of his healing powers, even a Canaanite, unprompted, recognizes him: "Have mercy on me, O Lord, Son of David!" (15:22; no such address appears in Matthew's source, Mk 7:24–30). For the same reason—his curing the blind and the lame in the Temple—even children cry out, "Hosanna to the Son of David!" (21:14–15). His disciples know that Jesus is "the Christ," an identification that he approvingly accepts (16:13–20; cf. 20:30–31). And Matthew edits Mark's version of the triumphal entry by explicitly quoting Isaiah 62:11 and Zechariah 9:9, identifying Jesus as Zion's prophesied king (cf. Jn 12:15):

> Tell the daughter of Zion,
> Behold, your king is coming to you,
> humble, and mounted on an ass,
> and on a colt, the foal of an ass.

Determined to depict Jesus fulfilling these prophetic visions to the letter, Matthew resolutely presents him as riding on *two* animals, both an ass and a colt, at the same time (21:7). The crowds of Passover pilgrims who parade him into Jerusalem praise Jesus as the Messiah: "Hosanna to the Son of David!" (v. 9), and he assents to their acclaim, to the irritation of the chief priests and scribes (vv. 14–17). Following Mark, Matthew's Jesus tells the Pharisees that the Messiah is greater than David; he is David's Lord, not his son (22:41–46). In light of Matthew's framing of the nativity story, the passage here does not refute the importance of Davidic descent, but rather simply asserts the superiority of the Messiah.

Matthew's Gospel, in brief, has Jesus recognized and proclaimed the

Messiah son of David in his own lifetime. His Jesus approves of and embraces this designation publicly. The tension between hiddenness and revelation that shapes the irony and suspense of his source, Mark, disappears: Matthew has written the "messianic secret" out of his story. In so doing, he also achieves a nice interpretive sleight of hand. The biographical particulars of Jesus' life, in Matthew's accounting, provide a narrative definition of the term "messiah." The prophets, argues the evangelist, had foretold a messiah coming who would do what Jesus did; therefore Jesus is the Messiah.

The familiarity of Matthew's story should not mask his creativity here, or his accomplishment. Through his depiction of the mission of Jesus, Matthew gives new, precisely Christian definition to the term "messiah," while presenting it as deeply traditional. Hence his strategy of composition, matching prophetic verse to biographical event. The phrase "this took place to fulfill what was spoken by the prophet" repeats constantly, verbally highlighting and dramatizing the entire text. Matthew thus ties the life of Jesus intimately into Israel's ancient history of salvation.

With different details, and with an appropriation of the Septuagint equally deep though more subtle, Luke's Gospel makes a similar point: His Jesus, too, is recognized as the Messiah Son of David in his lifetime. The angel Gabriel speaks to Mary saying that the child she will conceive, the Son of God, will sit on "*the throne of his father David,* and reign over the house of Jacob forever" (1:32–33). Later the priest Zechariah, father of John the Baptist in Luke's story, blesses God for having "raised up a horn of salvation for us in *the house of his servant, David*" (1:69). At Jesus' birth, angels announce to shepherds "to you is born this day *in the city of David a savior who is Christ* the Lord" (2:11). Simeon praises him as "the Lord's Christ" (2:26 ff.). And Luke later repeats Mark's story of the blind man at Jericho who asks for healing by addressing Jesus as "*son of David*" (18:35–43). Once the post-Resurrection mission is under way, Jesus' disciples routinely preach that he was "the Christ" (e.g., Acts 3:19–21, 5:42, 17:3, 18:5, 28).

Further—and utterly unlike Mark, his source, and Matthew, his contemporary—Luke integrates Jerusalem profoundly into the preaching of the Gospel. Herald angels notwithstanding, Jerusalem, not Bethlehem (a village in any case), was the "city of David," hymned as such in psalms and prophets. Luke thus opens his story not by the banks of the Jordan, as did Mark, but in Jerusalem, at the altar of the Temple (1:9). It is to the Temple that Jesus' parents bring the new baby in the weeks after his birth, and where he is first recognized as Savior (2:22). There Anna the prophetess speaks in terms of "the redemption of Jerusalem" (v. 38). Jesus' family, pious observant Jews, go to the city "every year at the feast of Passover" (v. 41); and the young Jesus, teaching in the Temple, refers to it as "my father's house" (v. 49).

Luke also locates Jesus' post-Resurrection appearances in and around Jerusalem, rather than in the Galilee (as Mark and Matthew; Lk 24:34–52). The disciples, having seen the Risen Christ, praise God at the Temple, where they continue worshiping as the movement itself develops (Lk 24:53; Acts 3:1). The earliest community relocates to Jerusalem permanently (2:12), and for the rest of his story, Jerusalem serves as the site of the mother church. For Luke, redemption literally comes out of Zion. His clear emphasis on the city is his original way of weaving the earlier traditions of the Messiah son of David into his presentation of Jesus.

But Luke also uses another messianic idea to articulate the biblical dimension of Jesus' mission: not just the king-messiah, but the prophet-messiah. Dramatically, right at the beginning of his preaching in the Galilee, Jesus enters the synagogue at Nazareth on the Sabbath "as was his custom." Handed a scroll of the prophet Isaiah, Jesus reads:

> The spirit of the Lord is upon me, *because he has anointed me* to
>   preach good news to the poor.
> He has sent me to proclaim release to the captives, the recovering of
>   sight to the blind,
> To set at liberty those who are oppressed,
> To proclaim the acceptable year of the Lord.
>
> > (Is 61:1,2, 58:6)

Jesus then refers the passage to himself and immediately invokes two scriptural episodes—Elijah and the widow from Sidon; Elisha and Naaman the Syrian—when Gentiles, rather than Israelites, had received the benefit of a prophet's powers (Lk 4:14–27). By so crafting this scene, Luke combines this non-Davidic idea, the prophet-messiah, with the (ultimately Davidic-messianic) theme of Gentile inclusion.

John and Matthew also identify Jesus as a prophet. For the fourth evangelist, this is a major theme, often appearing in tandem with kingly notions of messiah. Thus at 6:14 we find Jesus hailed by crowds as "the prophet who is to come into the world," and immediately thereafter going into hiding "perceiving that they were about to come and take him by force to make him king" (v. 15). Conflating Davidic traditions of messiahship with prophetic ones, other characters in John's story protest that, because he is from Nazareth and not Bethlehem, Jesus cannot be a prophet: "search [the scriptures] and you will find that no prophet is to rise from Galilee" (Jn 7:52). But the powerful and great "signs" that Jesus does justifies his identification as a prophet (9:17). In sum, while John makes much broader claims for Jesus and his true theological status than do the other Gospel writers, the evangelist clearly approves of "prophet" as one of the suitable designations.

Matthew invokes this theme more rarely than John, but dramatically nonetheless. Just after Jesus' Triumphal Entry into Jerusalem for Passover, toward the end of the Gospel, the pilgrims who have just hailed Jesus as "Son of David" explain to the crowds in the city, "This is *the prophet Jesus from Nazareth* of Galilee" (Mt 21:10–11). The chief priests fear to move against him openly because "when they tried to arrest him, they feared the multitudes, because *they held him to be a prophet*" (v. 46). In comparison to Matthew, Luke, however, really emphasizes this theme, by placing this prophet-messiah quotation from Isaiah in such a dramatic episode right at the beginning of his story. He further draws attention to the idea's importance by having Jesus, not the crowds around him, name himself a prophet. So also when using the Q-source lament over Jerusalem—"Jerusalem! Jerusalem! killing the prophets and stoning those who are sent to you!"—Luke's Jesus adds, "It cannot be that a prophet should perish away from Jerusalem" (13:33–34; cf. Mt 23:37–39). And this is how his followers identify him too (24:19).

Finally, by statement rather than by story, Luke simply asserts that the Messiah was always supposed to suffer and die exactly as Jesus had. This teaching comes dramatically at the very close of Luke's Gospel, made explicit by the Risen Christ himself:

> "These are my words which I spoke to you while I was still with you, that everything written in the law of Moses and the prophets and the Psalms must be fulfilled." Then he opened their minds to understand the scriptures, and said to them, "Thus it is written, that *the Christ should suffer and on the third day rise from the dead.*"   (Lk 24:45)

What historical sense can we make of the Gospels' presentation of Jesus as the Messiah? We might note as a general tendency that the earlier the Gospel, the less prominent this theme seems to be; or, making the same observation in reverse, the more these evangelical traditions about Jesus develop, the more prominent this theme becomes. And as this theme moves to the foreground, the more distortion, in two directions, that we find. Either biographical particulars of Jesus' past are made to fit the biblical paradigm, or the original meaning of the term, "messiah"/*christos,* is stretched to fit biographical particulars of his life. In the first instance, we have the creation of the Bethlehem birth stories; in the second, the identification of certain activities from the biographical tradition (healings and exorcisms, for example; and, ultimately, crucifixion) with scriptural characteristics of "messiah"—the speech of Luke's Risen Christ, above, being the most succinct and extreme example.

Still, all these evangelists do is tell a story that fills in the claim made already midcentury by Paul: that Jesus was the son of David *kata sarka*—"according to the flesh," that is, by physical descent (Rom 1:3). Where they clearly redefine "messiah" to bring it into line with their religious convictions about Jesus (as in the quotation from Luke just above: the Messiah is someone who suffers, dies, and rises after three days), we may justifiably credit their own theological creativity, and/or the traditions shaping the commitments of their late first-century Greek-speaking communities. Where the concept even as they present it nonetheless coheres with other, independent data from the period around the lifetime of Jesus (c. 6 B.C.E.–c. 30 C.E.), we may find some purchase for further historical investigation.

A prime datum is Jesus' crucifixion itself. Coupled especially with his offense, written on the titulus over the cross—"the inscription of the charge against him read, 'The King of the Jews' " (Mk 15:26 and parr.)—this execution coheres precisely with known Roman responses to a subject's claim to autonomy, in territorial Israel or anywhere else. Here Josephus provides our best evidence specifically for Judea. In 6 C.E., Varus, the Roman legate of Syria, crucified two thousand rebels as part of his effort to pacify the rebellious Jewish countryside (*BJ* 2.76; *AJ* 17.297). James and Simon, sons of the Galilean rebel Judah, were crucified c. 46–48 C.E. by the procurator Tiberius Alexander (*AJ* 20.102). Under Cumanus, a later Judean governor (48–c. 52), a murderous skirmish between Samaritans and some Galilean pilgrims passing through Samaria on their way to Jerusalem for a festival escalated into a round of crucifixions once the tumult threatened to spread (*BJ* 2.241; *AJ* 20.130). The Roman historian Tacitus, who also speaks of this event, mentions specifically the fear that the initial incident might have ignited armed rebellion engulfing all of the Galilee and Samaria (*Annals* 12.54). Finally, in the violent convulsions just preceding the outbreak of the war in 66 C.E., the procurator Florus responded to provocations in Jerusalem by rounding up many citizens, even those of high Roman rank, and first scourging and then crucifying them (*BJ* 2.306–8). And intermittently throughout the siege, Titus's soldiers nailed captured Jews to crosses visible to those watching from the city, "hoping that the sight would terrify the rest into surrender" (*BJ* 5.290). Jews caught in desperate forays outside the walls as the siege heaved to a close—"every day five hundred, sometimes even more, fell into his hands"—were tortured, scourged, and "finally crucified in view of the wall:" Titus hoped

> that the sight of it would perhaps induce the Jews to surrender in order to avoid the same fate. The soldiers themselves through rage and bitterness nailed up their victims in various attitudes as a grim joke until, owing to the vast numbers there was no room for crosses, and no crosses for the bodies.   (Josephus, *BJ* 5.450)

Thus the titulus on the cross and the repeated imputation of messianic kingship that runs throughout all the narratives of Jesus' hearing before Pilate fit well into this context that Josephus provides. As with these other Jews, so with Jesus: Crucifixion broadcast Rome's zero-tolerance policy toward a perceived threat of sedition. We must return to consider the issue of Rome and sedition later, because certain anomalies complicate Jesus' case. Here, however, it can serve as a point of departure for understanding that other, nonkingly messianic idea attached to Jesus: the title or role of "prophet." Once more, we turn to Josephus.

In the period before the war, charismatic popular leaders appeared, gathering crowds and promising to work signs: They claimed, says Josephus, to be prophets. Thus under the procuratorship of Fadus (c. 44–46 C.E.), the prophet Theudas led a large following to the Jordan, which he said would part at his command (*AJ* 20.97–98). Under Felix (52–59 C.E.), prophets arose—"deceivers and imposters" in Josephus' view—who agitated Jerusalem by "fostering revolutionary changes" under "false claims" of divine inspiration. Attracting large crowds, these prophets led their followers out into the desert to receive from God "tokens of deliverance" (*BJ* 2.259; cf. *AJ* 20.168). Another who "gained for himself the reputation of a prophet," a Jew from Egypt, led a multitude to converge on Jerusalem: At his command, he promised, the walls of the city would collapse (*AJ* 20.170; *BJ* 2.261–63).

These various prophetic figures share three important characteristics. The first is that they all evidently construed and constructed their missions from ancient biblical episodes harking back to the foundational history of the Jewish people. Theudas' parting the Jordan recalls God's parting the waters for Israel to leave Egypt and, more proximately, Joshua leading the tribes across the river and into the promised Land (Ex. 14:16 ff.; Jos 3:13–14). Wandering in the desert awaiting deliverance recalls the period of the liberation from Egypt, the giving of Torah on Sinai. And the miraculous collapse of Jerusalem's walls would recapitulate a similar miracle: the fall of Jericho's, where Israel entered into the Land (Jos 6:20).

Second, common to these men is their popularity. Josephus speaks of "multitudes" and "crowds" of followers, and sometimes gives swollen numbers—thirty thousand came to the Egyptian, he claims (*BJ* 2.262; Acts 21:38 gives four thousand). In Josephus' retrospect these men seemed clearly "imposters" and "false prophets"; in evangelical retrospect, perhaps, too. "False prophets will arise," warns Matthew's Jesus in his apocalyptic discourse, "and show great signs. . . . They shall say to you, 'Behold, he [i.e., the Christ] is in the wilderness,' " (Mt 24:24 ff.). To many of their contemporaries, however, on the evidence of their committed response, the message of these prophets was compelling, their promise sure. The times were such that not only did men with such conviction in their own message appear, but they also drew many who were prepared to believe them.

Third, these men and their movements all met with the same response from Rome: immediate, definitive repression. Troops dispatched after Theudas slaughtered many of his followers and brought his head back to Jerusalem. Felix saw in the crowds streaming out to the desert "but a preliminary to insurrection," and dealt with them accordingly: Cavalry and heavy infantry put them down. Most of the Egyptian's followers met the same fate: slaughter by heavy infantry.

These prophets were manifestly speaking to religious hopes, not practical insurrection; their followers were civilians, not guerrillas preparing to combat Roman force. What need for arms anyway, since God was about to step in? Yet Rome deposed them nonetheless. It took a dim view of crowds massing around charismatic native leaders and would have little patience distinguishing apocalyptic hope from seditious action.

No ruler in antiquity looked kindly on unsanctioned mass gatherings of their subjects: Given the steep social- and power-pyramid of ancient society, such gatherings could easily seem—and perhaps become—threats to those in power. A pertinent example here is John the Baptizer. The Gospels present John as Jesus' herald, a sort of Elijah figure to Jesus' Messiah. Preaching an apocalyptic message of repentance and coming wrath, John receives penitents by the Jordan. Matthew transposes Jesus' message to John: "Repent, for the kingdom of heaven is at hand!" (Mt 3:2; cf. Mk 1:15). All four evangelists depict John as a popular figure with disciples of his own and many hearers: "all the country of Judea and all the people of Jerusalem," says Mark (1:5); "multitudes," says Luke (3:7, 10). He was beheaded by the Jewish ruler of the Galilee, Herod Antipas, Mark claims, for offending Antipas by criticizing his marriage to his niece (Mk 6:14–29).

Josephus tells the story differently. Narrating Antipas's defeat in 39 C.E. by his eastern neighbor and former father-in-law, the Nabatean king Aretas, Josephus "flashes back" to the year c. 28, to John.

> To some of the Jews, the destruction of Herod's army [in 39] seemed to be divine vengeance, and certainly a just vengeance, for his treatment of John, surnamed the Baptizer. For *Herod had put him to death,* though he was a good man, and had exhorted the Jews to lead righteous lives, to practice justice toward their fellows and piety toward God, and so doing to join in baptism [that is, immersion]. In his view this was a necessary preliminary if baptism was to be acceptable to God . . . as a consecration of the body implying that the soul had already been cleansed by right behavior. When *others too joined the crowds around him, because they were aroused to the highest degree by his words, Herod became alarmed.* Eloquence that had so great an effect on people *might lead to some form of sedition,* for they looked as if they would be guided by John in everything they did. Herod decided that it would be much better to strike first and be rid of him before his work led to an uprising. . . . John was brought in chains to the stronghold Machaeras . . . and there put to death. But the Jews were of the opinion that the army was destroyed to avenge John, since God wished to inflict harm on Herod.
>
> (Josephus, *AJ* 18.116–19)

Certain differences distinguish the case of John the Baptizer from the other prophetic figures in Judea. One big difference is their location. Jerusalem and the Judean desert, where the signs prophets gathered their followers, were immediately under Roman jurisdiction. John worked and roamed "in the wilderness" of the rocky desert next to the Jordan River before it spills into the Dead Sea. He immersed people coming to him on both sides of the river, the western bank in Judea, the eastern bank in the region of Perea, part of the Jewish Antipas' territory. The other prophets promised to deliver "signs"—divinely wrought mighty works—while John seems to have limited himself to a call to moral reform and bodily purification, a prophetic mission of a different sort.

Further, John's mission seems to have been established for some time, and the people who received his message, both disciples and others, evidently came and went. But the other prophets Josephus describes massed and mobilized large followings at one time in anticipation of a spectacular miraculous event. We may suppose that the level of nervous energy, disruptive anticipation, and popular enthusiasm was much higher among the latter group.

Finally, Herod Antipas arrested John, withdrew him to an isolated prison, and beheaded him there—a relatively quiet and orderly execution, again attesting to an absence of a single huge assembly of followers. The signs prophets and their followers, by contrast, were the targets of decisive Roman military actions, and many more than the leaders suffered. From the latter cases, then, we can infer that a prophet's hearers, massed all at one time, called forth a much stronger and more destructive response from those in power. But fear of sedition, stimulated by the leader's popularity—as with John—seems common to the response of both Rome and Antipas. A popular following would not endear a prophetic figure to any ruling authority.

WE BEGAN OUR EFFORT to understand why Paul would call Jesus the Messiah son of David by surveying the term's range of meanings in the period between the Maccabees and the Mishnah, roughly 200 B.C.E. to 200 C.E. The cultural and political confusions of the Hellenistic period stimulated a number of various conceptions of the role: We saw that "messiah" might be imagined as a pure priest, as a final eschatological prophet, and, perhaps, as a heavenly nonhuman redeemer figure. But the most widespread meaning of the term harkened back to its biblical source: The Messiah was the Son of David, the eschatological warrior, the prince of peace.

Paul himself indicates his reasons for ascribing this title to Jesus only in his letter to the Romans. In that context, Paul seems to name the Gentiles' turning through Christ to worship the God of Israel as the eschatological event confirming Jesus' status as (Davidic) Messiah.

Hence his closing this letter with the quotation from Isaiah, "The root of Jesse shall come, he who rises to rule the Gentiles; in him shall the Gentiles hope" (Is 11:10 LXX; Rom 15:12). But the Gentile mission was a post-Resurrection phenomenon. Its eventual successes cannot account for the original apostles' proclamation of Jesus as Christ, nor for Paul's initial acceptance, c. 33, of their claim. And on the evidence of Jesus' crucifixion alone we may infer that, at least just shortly before his death, Jesus either claimed this title for himself or others claimed it for him, and in a way public enough that Rome got involved. The Gospels' evidence itself, however, provides no clear view of these events, in part because their narratives are so theologically freighted with specifically Christian revisions of the term *christos,* matching it to various particulars, fictive and factual, of Jesus' life.

Three questions opened this cycle of inquiry: What were the various meanings of the term "messiah" in this period? When was the term used of Jesus? Why? We have examined the New Testament sources' own reasons for this identification and so have a sense of why and how these Christians between c. 50 and c. 100 thought that Jesus was the Christ.

But we need to push back earlier in time to the period of Jesus' own life and mission. This means leaving Paul behind as our guide and plunging into the historical territory of Jesus himself: early first-century Judea and Galilee. "Christ" was ascribed to Jesus at some point during his mission. Our two questions remain: When? Why?

Chapter 4

CONTEXTS: THE GALILEE, JUDEA, AND JESUS

SCANNING THE EVIDENCE by moving from Paul's letters "back" into the Gospel material and then "forward" again into the gentile mission, elements of early Christian tradition emerged that might conceivably trace back to Jesus of Nazareth. The far greater part of this evidence was textual: Whether from New Testament documents, Jewish Scriptures, Josephus or other ancient historians, the Scrolls or various Pseudepigrapha, data were mediated through writings, and interpretation turned upon how to read a text.

The project here is different. Though again texts play a key role—and Josephus, once more, often provides the premier evidence—the goal is the reconstruction not so much of ideas (Kingdom of God, Messiah, and so on) but of social context. "Social context" means the collective human environment of Jesus and his contemporaries: their work, their significant material culture, their communal economic and religious lives, their perceptions of and responses to various situations and events. This effort at reconstructing a specific social context leads the investigation into some new types of evidence and some new types of arguments. In brief, the quest now turns to archaeological artifact and to questions of social theory and method.

Archaeology, in comparison with the ambiguities of textual interpretation, might at first seem comfortingly empirical; and, in a sense, it is. Objects have a kind of given reality that texts do not. And material evidence can settle certain arguments. Excavations around the Temple Mount, for example, can help decide whether to rely on Josephus or the Mishnah for a description of its physical layout. On this issue, Josephus usually wins. Rather than extrapolating from texts that may simply preserve the views of a religious elite on what common people *should* do, physical evidence helps make visible what common people actually *did* do. Thus, the numerous stepped pools dug into bedrock that pock the land of Israel reveal a widespread concern with purity, for these *mikvaot* are man-made pools for ritual immersion. Or inscriptions can correct what is otherwise obscured by overtidy reconstructions. The old argument that synagogues as particularly Pharisaic institutions somehow either challenged or competed with the Temple (as if that were exclusively a "priestly" institution—and as if priests could not also be Pharisees!) is more difficult to maintain in light of the first-century Greek synagogue inscription, discovered near the Temple Mount, proclaiming its foundation by the priest and synagogue-leader Theodotus.

Interpreting an object, however, is no less dependent on context than is interpreting a saying in a text. Objects rarely convey their own interpretation. For example, many ossuaries (bone boxes used in secondary burial) give the names of the deceased in Greek. Is this evidence that Greek was a current vernacular in Palestine? Or evidence for the reburial of returning diaspora Jews? The ossuaries themselves cannot settle the issue.

Social theory and comparative methods brought from other fields to bear on the various data of first-century Judaism and earliest Christianity also hold out the promise of improving investigative results. If studies of millenarianism in other cultures show that perceived economic deprivation contributes to the mentality of the movement, for example, they can be used to provide an interpretive grid on which to map the social realities of ancient Palestine. On this theory, members of Jesus' audience, to the degree that they received his message of the impending Kingdom, would have been or felt themselves to be economically or socially deprived, too: hence his particular appeal to the sinner, the toll collector, the prostitute, and the poor. Or, if aristocratic empires run on

Photograph of the Theodotus inscription

"Theodotus the son of Vettenus, priest and ruler of the synagogue, son of a ruler of the synagogue, son's son of the ruler of the synagogue, built the synagogue for the reading of the law and for the teaching of the commandments, also the strangers' lodging and the chambers and the conveniencies of waters for an inn for them that need it from abroad, of which [synagogue] his fathers and the elders and Simonides did lay the foundation." This first-century inscription, found in Jerusalem, attests to the concern of a priestly family (three generations of which are invoked here) to establish a synagogue reasonably near the Temple as a place providing instruction in Torah (presumably in Greek, the language of the inscription) and housing for Greek-speaking Jewish pilgrims to the city.

the systematic and ruthless exploitation of their peasants, and the Roman Empire had exactly this sort of class structure, then peasants within the empire—all peasants, not just Jewish ones—must have been exploited too. In this reconstruction, Jesus, when speaking to (Galilean) peasants, would address not just the poor, but the powerless and destitute. Or, if the texts and institutions of a Great Tradition—knowledge of Torah, literacy, sacrifices, or access to the Temple in Jesus' culture and period—rest with an identifiable elite (aristocratic priests, scribes, and Pharisees), those disempowered by this power structure will combat their oppression with subversive countertraditions that are naturally not as visible in the data, because texts and buildings are remnants from the elites. On this construction, Jesus as peasant teacher would have spoken and acted in ways subversive of the Great Tradition's institutions. And his followers would have responded because they, too, felt alienated—by the Temple, for example, or the laws of purity, or by literate scribal traditions when their own, the "little" tradition, were popular and oral, and so on.

The method we choose, in other words, by organizing our sparse data according to its criteria, could help to unveil motives or meanings or social dynamics that are disguised, only implied, or perhaps otherwise invisible in the record once the positive evidence runs out. The method's application provides a kind of "plot" by which data can be organized into a story: The attractions of Jesus' message, or the reasons for his execution, can accordingly be explained by appeal to the method's criteria of meaning—class antagonism, hostility between a subversive peasant teacher and the representatives of the Great Tradition (priests, Pharisees), and so on. The danger, of course, is that, absent evidence, we have little way to test the conclusions the method offers us. If theory organizes data to begin with, arguments for its validation can easily start running in circles.

This combination of ancient texts, archaeological data, and models of social interaction drawn from other disciplines has only multiplied interpretive choices. Appeals to the exact same data often defend precisely opposed reconstructions. Not only do scholars have difficulty discerning even the broad outlines of Jesus' mission and message; they also cannot agree, quite simply, on a description of the social, cultural, and religious context in which he acted and spoke. The quest for the historical Jesus has thus given rise to equally fraught, equally contentious quests for the historical Galilee and the historical Temple.

Attending to those traditions in the Gospels that are not confirmed or supported by Paul greatly increases the amount of biographical material we have to work with: Jesus' early contact with John the Baptizer, his various itineraries during his mission, his reception by contemporaries, his activities in Jerusalem, his fatal confrontation with the chief priests and with Pilate once there. Again, we will have to weigh and test these against other things we can know, whether from Josephus, from other Jewish or early Christian documents, from Tacitus or other pagan writers, or from archaeological findings. The goal is to situate Jesus realistically and plausibly within his early first-century context, in order to see when and why he might have been hailed as Messiah in his own lifetime. And the test of our reconstruction will be its explanatory power, the way it illumines the three facts that stand unambiguously in the historical record: that Jesus was crucified, that his followers were not, and that, within years of his execution, Gentiles, too, took their place within the Jewish movement that subsequently formed around his message and memory.

Economics, Politics, and Power

ALL FOUR GOSPELS present Jesus as initiating his mission in the Galilee; two, Luke and John, specifically set some of the mission in Samaria; and all four bring it to a close in Judea, in Jerusalem at Passover. Distilling Jesus' social context from evangelical tradition requires that we have some grasp of the history that shaped these three regions. We must go back again, then, to events under Assyria and Babylon.

The Northern Kingdom of Israel finally capitulated to the Assyrian invasion in 722 B.C.E. Assyria skimmed Israelite elites off of their native territory, settling them elsewhere within the empire and relocating other peoples there (2 Kgs 17). The empire incorporated these regions—both the Galilee and Samaria—as provinces. Some scholars assume that the larger part of the Israelite population in these areas remained behind; others, that a new population resettled this entire area. On this issue debate continues.

Ancient unresolved conflicts between King David (who c. 1000 B.C.E. had sought to consolidate worship of the God of Israel in Jerusalem) and the northern tribes (who had worshiped at various scattered—and biblically attested—cultic sites) resurfaced in the subsequent history of the region. When in the late sixth century B.C.E. Persia released the Judeans exiled to Babylon and permitted them to return to Jerusalem and to rebuild the Temple, Israelites who had remained in the province of Samaria protested: They already had their own site of worship at Shechem. Later, following Persia's defeat at the hands of Alexander the Great (d. 323 B.C.E.), these Israelites built a splendid temple on Mount Gerizim that rivaled Jerusalem's (*AJ* 11.297; 307–11. Some disaffected priests left Jerusalem and installed themselves in Samaria's temple). The Gospels catch the echo of this old rivalry. "Our fathers worshiped on this mountain," the Samaritan woman tells Jesus, "and you say that in Jerusalem is the place where people ought to worship" (Jn 4:20). And in Luke, Samaritans refuse to receive Jesus, "because his face was set toward Jerusalem" (Lk 9:53).

Samaritan religious autonomy suffered and relations with Jerusalem worsened drastically in the period of Judean expansion following the successful Maccabaean revolt. The Hasmonean John Hyrcanus subdued Samaria's capital city, destroying the temple on Mount Gerizim in

128 B.C.E. before turning south to Idumea (the biblical Edom), which he likewise subdued, forcing the Idumeans to accept Judaism (*BJ* 1.62–63; *AJ* 13.254–58; this conquest was the occasion of Herod's family's conversion). Later, Hyrcanus' son, pushing north, secured the Galilee and forced conversion on the Itureans (*AJ* 13.318–19). This phase of the Hasmonean military and cultural consolidation around Jerusalem went more smoothly than it had in Samaria: The Galilee had no comparable rival cultic site. Nor, evidently, were forced conversions required, perhaps because those Galileans who worshiped the God of Israel, like the Samaritans earlier, represented that Israelite remnant that the Assyrians had left behind.

THE GALILEAN CONTEXT

By the first century of our era, the overall population in the Galilee, as in this region generally, was mixed. Gentiles and Jews in varying proportions cohabited certain cities. The chief of these in the immediate area of Jesus' activity were Sepphoris and Tiberias. Ten other cities, called the Decapolis, formed a federation. One city was geographically within the Galilee, the others ringed round it in Transjordan. These had been founded in consequence of the conquest of Alexander the Great: By culture, politics, and population, they were largely Gentile. (When Mark wants to prefigure the mission to the Gentiles within his Gospel, he speaks of Jesus' going to the eastern shore of the Sea of Galilee and thence to a site within "the country of the Gerasenes," 5:1. The herd of swine into which he drives the demon "Legion" indicates a pagan settlement: Jewish villagers would have had no reason to keep them. And the cured Gentile demoniac then proclaims "in the Decapolis how much Jesus had done for him," 5:20.)

Awareness of these cities, increased by archaeological research, has recently led to talk of the "urbanization" of the Galilee and, consequently, its "Hellenization" as represented, most especially, by the penetration of the Greek language. Architectural remnants, inscriptions, coins; the commercial opportunities that a comfortable command of Greek would have offered; the human traffic borne on the major trade routes running from areas farther east to the cities on the Mediterranean coast: All these suggest the routine interaction of different groups that Greek alone could have facilitated. Already by Jesus' day, thanks to Alexander the Great, Greek had been well established in the neighborhood for some three centuries.

With their Hellenized public architecture (theaters, baths, stadiums, and the like), their regional administrative and commercial functions, and their mixed populations, Sepphoris and Tiberias particularly focus this question of the urbanization and Hellenization of the Galilee. Destroyed by the Romans during the revolts that followed the death of Herod the Great in 4 B.C.E., Sepphoris had been splendidly rebuilt by Herod Antipas, who as tetrarch ("ruler of a fourth," functionally a minor client king) governed this portion of his father's former kingdom from 4 B.C.E. to 39 C.E. He made Sepphoris "the ornament of all Galilee" (*AJ* 18.27) and used it as his first capital city. It was easy walking distance to the village of Nazareth, fewer than four miles away; and this fact, combined with the period of its reconstruction, has led some scholars to speculate that Jesus' father and/or Jesus himself, since they were (perhaps) craftsmen or carpenters, would have been involved in its rebuilding. In that case (so goes the argument) Jesus would have been exposed throughout his formative years to spoken Greek and this urban culture.

Tiberias, the new capital that Antipas built and moved to c. 26 C.E., was situated on the western shore of the Sea of Galilee. This could have affected Jesus, too, because at some point before he began his mission, he seems to have moved from Nazareth to Capernaum, a lakeshore village just north of Tiberias. According to Mark and Matthew, Jesus made his home in Capernaum (Mk 2:1; cf. Mt 4:13), and Mark opens his public activity there (Mk 1:21). Once again, on the basis of simple proximity, Jesus can be seen as operating at least in the penumbra of a major urban, Hellenized site, where for commercial as well as cultural reasons Greek would have been spoken. Some scholars argue further that the existence of these cities helps to explain the prominence of the poor in Jesus' missionary activity, because of their effect on Galilean economic life. Centers of taxation, dependent on peasant productivity for foodstuffs, indeed (in this view) parasitic on the countryside around them, these cities would oppress and deplete those upon whom they depended.

Add to this picture the Hellenization of a city we know Jesus to have taught in: Jerusalem. Jerusalem had been the focus of efforts to Hellenize since at least the second century B.C.E., when aristocratic priests turned to the Seleucid Antiochus for support in their efforts to "modernize" their cult. This effort was checked by the successful Maccabaean revolt, but the aristocratic Hasmoneans themselves were likewise politically and temperamentally bicultural. Once Herod the Great took over, his massive and ambitious building program, especially focused on the Temple, broadcast the monumental Greco-Roman architectural style throughout the country. Further, as its status as Judaism's major pilgrimage site suggests and the first-century synagogue inscription of Theodotus attests, Greek would certainly have been one of the major languages spoken in Jerusalem. The aristocratic priest Josephus, raised in Jerusalem, in fact speaks specifically of his bilingual education: Besides learning the traditions native to his people in Hebrew and Aramaic, he also studied Greek grammar, prose, and poetry (*AJ* 20.263).

Can we move from these archaeological data from material culture, and the inferences we draw from trade and government in Judea and the Galilee in this period, to conclude that Jesus himself would have had a comfortable command of Greek and a reasonable familiarity with Gentiles and their urban culture? Some scholars have proposed this, which has opened up new interpretive possibilities in the current quest for the historical Jesus. First, Jesus' hypothesized command of Greek closes the linguistic gap between his mission and the Gospels. The Aramaic residuum in the Gospels—*Talita, cumi!* (Little girl, get up! Mk 6:40); *Ephphatha!* (Be opened! 7:34); *Abba!* (Father! 14:36)—indicates one of Jesus' languages, but not the sole one; and when he went into marketplaces and, most especially, to cosmopolitan Jerusalem, he could and would have spoken Greek as well.

Some push the implications of this view further. Greek language plus Hellenized urban culture in the Galilee, taken together with certain traditions still visible in the Gospels, support a specific interpretation of Jesus as a teacher and a specific redaction history of the stories told about him. Of all the types of popular teachers in antiquity (so goes this theory), Jesus was actually most like a Cynic philosopher. The Cynics had inhabited the Hellenistic urban landscape from the fourth century B.C.E. Itinerant, voluntarily poor, they taught through caustic wit and aphorisms, thereby "subverting" the values of majority culture. Their dress—ragged cloak, knapsack, staff—was as particular as their homeless lifestyle, though similar to what the Gospels depict Jesus mandating for his own disciples ("he ordered them to take nothing for their journey except a staff; no bread, no bag, no money," Mk 6:8f.). Given the Greek-style urbanization of the Galilee, and the aphoristic Wisdom teachings retrievable especially from the sayings in Q, some scholars have posited that Jesus himself is best understood as a sort of Cynic sage. This hypothesis then suggests a redaction history for the Gospels. Evangelical narrative, the "story" part of the story, is not as authentic as the "sayings" part of the story, because Jesus as a Cynic-type, countercultural teacher would have taught through aphorisms and witty, troubling short stories. The apocalyptic Q-sayings, on this reading, would represent later, conservatively Jewish accretions to the earlier, authentic "sapiential" or Wisdom layer.

This interpretation rests in part on its inference from material culture to linguistic and intellectual culture, that is, from the archaeology of the region to the conclusion that the Galilee in Jesus' period was Hellenized and urbanized. But how well can this foundation support the argument? Yes, Sepphoris, Tiberias, and Jerusalem were architecturally Hellenistic, and yes, their respective administrative roles did ensure some use of Greek. But what does this mean for the living culture of their residents? The populations of the two Galilean cities were mixed, but in both, Jews made up the significant majority, and the population of Jerusalem was overwhelmingly Jewish. The use of Greco-Roman styles, particularly for monumental architecture, no more attests to Hellenized Jewish *culture* (speech, literature, habitual activities, patterns of thought, indices of meaning, and so on) than do Monticello's Palladian windows attest to Jefferson's being culturally Italian.

Nor does inscriptional evidence necessarily give the gauge of its human medium. Today, every sign in Milan's railroad station appears in Italian and English. An archaeologist, several millennia hence, could make the argument that the population of Milan was therefore demonstrably bilingual: How else explain the signs? Any Anglophone tourist who has actually tried to get other information from the railroad's native employees knows how false this conclusion would be. Greek inscriptions in Jerusalem (like English signs in Milan) simply tell us what we already know: that the city was a magnet for large numbers of foreign visitors.

Comfortable familiarity with Greek most likely varied from area to area, from trade to trade, and from class to class. We might imagine that at least the Jewish aristocrats, like their Roman counterparts, would use Greek with each other in the way that, say, the mid-nineteenth-century Russian nobility used French. But here again Josephus provides us with an interesting case to contemplate. He was literate in Greek, learning the language as a child; and we know his histories in Greek. Nonetheless, the spoken language remained difficult for him, even after decades in Rome: "The habitual use of my native tongue has prevented my attaining precision in pronunciation" (*AJ* 20.263). He wrote *The Jewish War,* his history of the revolt, originally in his native tongue (probably Aramaic), and translated a Greek version only with the help of assistants (*c. Ap.* 1.50). Further, during the siege itself, Titus employed him as a special emissary: While Titus would try to persuade the Jews to surrender in Greek, Josephus, ensuring the message got through, would do the same "in the language of their forefathers" (again, most likely Aramaic, with Hebrew the less likely alternative; *BJ* 5.361).

If even an educated, literate, upper-class Jerusalemite found Greek an effort; if even Jerusalem's Jews were most comfortable carrying on negotiations in Aramaic, then it is difficult to imagine Jesus, a Galilean craftsman, running a successful mission to fellow Galileans in Greek. Perhaps Jesus had tradesman's Greek—a rudimentary command of numbers, a simple knowledge of elements of the spoken language. But does that mean that he could teach in Greek, expounding concepts whether philosophical (as sapiential sage) or biblical (as charismatic prophet)? We cannot know for a fact that he did not, but it seems to me extremely unlikely.

Besides, the Gospels are utterly silent on even the existence of Sepphoris and Tiberias. The places they name on Jesus' itinerary, Jerusalem excepted, consist overwhelmingly of Jewish villages—Capernaum, Cana, Chorazin, Nazareth. A rich agricultural area, the Galilee itself was dominated by villages—according to Josephus, approximately two hundred (*Vita* 235). "The cities lie very thick and the very many villages that are here are everywhere so full of people because of the richness of the soil, that the very least of them contained about 15,000 inhabitants" (*BJ* 3.43; Pliny's *Natural History* speaks similarly, 5.75). That last is a classic, impossible Josephan number. But modern research, and specifically calculations of feasible population density per unit of farmland needed to support it, sustain the *impression* that Josephus' estimate gives: The Galilee in Jesus' period was fertile and well populated, its social life organized chiefly around villages housing low-level craftsmen (such as Jesus' own family), freeholding peasants (those who owned their own land), and tenant farmers (those who worked land belonging to others). Estimates of ancient population figures are notoriously unreliable (not that modern ones are much better), but they can give us at least some imaginary range. Some scholars, then, think that Nazareth's prewar population would have stood roughly between sixteen hundred and two thousand people; the Galilee's two large cities, perhaps ten times that; most small villages, at least several hundred.

What was the economic life of this village patchwork like? Here scholarship once more diverges widely. Some speculate that Sepphoris and Tiberias would have drained the surrounding country people of their resources through taxation or appropriation of goods. Others argue, on the contrary, that the cities "heated up" the Galilean economy. Construction would have provided jobs, the urban populations markets and employment, so that their net effect was positive. Exactly the same archaeological data inform both reconstructions: Only their interpretive contexts differ, because their economic models differ, too. And appeal to the Gospels cannot settle the matter. It is true that some of Jesus' preaching did particularly concern the poor, but this does not provide a clear view of the actual living conditions of his audience or followers. Care of the poor is a deeply traditional theme and articulate index of piety in Judaism generally. And if some of Jesus' followers had not, on the contrary, been fairly comfortable, his exhortations to voluntary poverty would make no sense.

Perhaps the best clue to the overall tenor of life in the Galilee is what did not happen. Under Herod Antipas—which is to say, from 4 B.C.E. to 39 C.E., virtually the entire period of Jesus' life—the Galilee was quiet. Both the Gospels and Josephus tell of his executing John the Baptizer, and this fact in turn (to speculate for a moment) might hint at why Jesus, evidently, never took his mission into the two Herodian foundations of Sepphoris and Tiberias: Perhaps, after John's experience, he thought it best to give the tetrarch wide berth (though such discretion had not helped John). But Antipas never had to suppress a popular revolt by force of arms, nor did the Romans have cause to assist him in containing unrest by marching their legions down from Antioch. Excessive taxation, harsh rule, or, in such a Jewish area, flagrant violation of religious law would have fanned unrest: Again, we have no evidence of any. In contrast to his brother Archelaus in Judea, Antipas enjoyed a long and largely untroubled reign.

THE JUDEAN CONTEXT

Judea was different. It was harder to govern precisely because of Jerusalem, which was always a magnet for unrest. Also, administratively, the new Roman province from 6 C.E. on also contained Samaria, with all the potential for conflict that implied. And its transfer to Archelaus in 4 B.C.E. was traumatized by repercussions from a series of bloody incidents that had marred the closing years of the reign of his father, Herod the Great. In 5 B.C.E., Herod burned alive some protesters who had destroyed the great golden eagle that he had placed over the great gate of the Temple. He also executed their two well-known and well-loved teachers, Judas and Matthias, and deposed the current high priest for permitting the situation to get so out of hand (*BJ* 1.651–55; *AJ* 17.149–67). Ever fearful for his own security, just months before his death in 4 B.C.E. he ordered the execution of one of his sons (*AJ* 17.187); two others—his last by his Hasmonean wife Mariamne—he had executed for conspiracy just three years earlier. Archelaus, Herod's named successor, inherited along with Judea the unhappy and destabilizing aftermath of Herod's repression.

Before Augustus could ratify Herod's will and confirm the successions of his remaining sons, more violence broke out. Jerusalemites, angered at the deaths resulting from the incident of the golden eagle, demanded that Archelaus remove Herod's last appointment to the office of high priest. They were "indignant at having been deprived of those dearest to them during Herod's lifetime and at having been deprived of their revenge for this after his death" (*AJ* 17.211). Passover approached, the city filled with worshipers, and Archelaus worried that these people still mourning Judas and Matthias would encourage unrest among the pilgrims gathering at the Temple for the feast. He sent out a cohort of soldiers to police the crowd, which the crowd in its fury stoned to death. Confusion escalated; Archelaus then sent out "his whole army including the cavalry" to prevent the pilgrims encamped outside the city from helping the Jews in the Temple. Some three thousand casualties, Josephus claims, resulted; and Archelaus summarily suspended the rest of the weeklong festival. On this inauspicious note, he sailed to Rome to secure his inheritance (*AJ* 17.213–19).

While Herod's heirs contested his will before Augustus, unrest and rebellion broke out throughout the country. Within fifty days of the Passover debacle, at the next pilgrimage feast, Shavuot/Pentecost, a huge throng of Jews ("tens of thousands")—"Galileans, Idumeans, a multitude from Transjordan and from Judea itself"—staged a pitched battle against the temporary Roman overseer, Sabinus, again in the Temple complex. The Roman legate in Syria, Varus, had to bring the army south in an effort to contain the confusion; engaged later against rebels in the Galilee, he burned Sepphoris. In Judea, veterans of Herod's former army fought with those still in arms. Two different royal pretenders, Simon, a former slave, and Athronges, a shepherd, both characterized by Josephus as exceptionally strong men, wreaked havoc in the countryside, Simon by plundering royal palaces, Athronges and his brothers, together with their armed bands ("for a large number of people gathered around them") by slaughtering troops of Romans. The country, says Josephus, filling with brigands, stumbled into anarchy and highway robbery. Varus finally asserted order in Judea only after combing the countryside for insurrectionists, eventually crucifying some two thousand of them (*AJ* 17.250–89).

In the aftermath of these convulsions, Varus permitted a delegation of fifty Jews to leave the country for Rome to add their voices to the wrangling over the disposition of Herod's will. Their position was supported there, says Josephus, by more than eight thousand Roman Jews. These men reviewed for Augustus the long misrule (from their perspective) of Herod, and, pointing to Archelaus's recent slaughter of thousands of Jews at Passover, pleaded that rather than be subject to his son the country instead be granted *autonomia,* "autonomy" (*AJ* 17.295–314).

"Autonomy" did not mean in this context what we would take it to mean in ours, and this fact should alert us to how poorly the modern concept "nationalism" serves for understanding Jews in antiquity, or, for that matter, ancient people generally. These Judeans were *not* seeking political independence for their country: That was clearly beyond possibility. Their request was simply to no longer be governed by Herodian kings, but rather by Roman administration as part of the province of Syria (*AJ* 17.314). This may seem counterintuitive: Why prefer foreign, indeed pagan dominion to Jewish? In fact, their petition gives the measure of the appeal of the good old days *before* the Hasmoneans took over. This earlier form of government—incorporation into an empire with local rule left in the hands of the high priest—had persisted relatively uncontroversially for centuries under Persian rule, and even for most of the period under the Seleucids. In the view of these dissident Judean Jews, a remote Gentile political ruler would go farther toward guaranteeing the peace of the land, and the integrity and independence of the Temple and, accordingly, of the high priesthood, than would a Herodian king.

Belatedly, and only in part, these men got their way. After ratifying Archelaus as ethnarch ("ruler of the people") in 4 B.C.E., Augustus deposed him in 6 C.E. on account of misgovernment. At that point he indeed added Judea, Samaria, and Idumea to the Roman province of Syria. Unlike the northern and eastern parts of Herod's old kingdom, still governed by his two sons Antipas and Philip, the south would be ruled by Rome. To administer locally, Augustus appointed a colonial

governor from a lower stratum of the Roman governing class than that
of the senatorial legate of Syria. This colonial officer, called a "prefect"
or (after 44 C.E.) a "procurator," was to oversee Archelaus' former
domain. But here Augustus mandated a procedure probably unanticipated by the Jews who petitioned him to make Judea a province in 4
B.C.E. To understand Augustus' action, we have to understand as well
those of Herod and, before him, the Hasmoneans.

The Hasmoneans as *cohanim* had been able to doubly consolidate
their power and authority by serving as both high priests and kings.
Herod as an Idumean Jew—that is, from a line of converts—naturally
did not belong to this clan, the sole one biblically designated to serve in
the Temple. Once he seized the Hasmoneans' power he could not exercise their option. Herod clarified any lingering confusions about his
own control by blatantly treating the office of high priest as a political
appointment. Even more to the point, he retained control of the high
priestly vestments. These had tremendous religious significance. The
details of their construction and appearance had been mandated by
God himself in the Torah (see Ex 39); in a certain sense they embodied
the holiness, dignity, and authority of the office and its function.
Herod's in-laws as high priests had guarded these garments themselves,
since they were the sole ones to wear them and were responsible for
them. The garments' purity as well as their physical maintenance were
of paramount importance, since the high priest had to wear them when
standing before the altar of God as representative of the whole people
on the high holy days and on the day of atonement (Yom Kippur).
When Herod took over as king he took over, as well, the vestments,
"believing that for this reason the people would never rise in insurrection against him" (*AJ* 18.92). Josephus' remark conveys the measure of
the prestige and authority of the office itself, irrespective of the particular and contingent officeholder. So holy and important was the *role* of
the high priest that his garments, too, also holy and important, commanded respect.

But after 6 C.E., the Roman governor was to serve in the place of the
Jewish monarch. Augustus accordingly ruled that he should also exer-
cise Herod's old prerogatives. The prefect would appoint or remove the
Jews' high priest, and supervise control of his sacred vestments, too.

The Romans understood full well the religious significance of this
administrative decision: their religious culture, too, mandated sacrifices, offerings, and rules of purity. Accordingly, they handled the gar-

ments carefully and cooperated with the temple personnel in maintaining them. Again, Josephus:

> When the Romans took over the government, they retained control of the high priest's vestments and kept them in a stone building, where they were under seal both of the priests and of the custodians of the treasury and where the warden of the guard lighted the lamp day by day. Seven days before each festival the vestments were delivered to the priests by the warden. After they had been purified, the high priest wore them; then after the first day of the festival he put them back again in the building where they were laid away before. This was the procedure at the three festivals each year and on the fast day.
> (*AJ* 18.93–94)

Nonetheless, both for the Romans and for the Jews, this arrangement signaled an unprecedented level of foreign involvement in Jerusalem's cult. In time, it would become a source of friction.

Another change imposed on Judea because of its new political status was the Roman tribute. The necessary first step in subsuming the southern region to Roman control was thus the assessment of property for this tax. Whether in cash or (more likely the greater part) in goods, the tribute itself may never have left the country, since its function was to defray the costs of maintaining the army in the province.

We should think neither of a massive number of troops nor even of troops dispersed, however thinly, throughout the countryside. Rome did not *occupy* Judea the way that modern armies occupied conquered countries in World War II. The major concentration of troops was in Syria, under the Roman legate. He commanded four legions—approximately twenty thousand men—and about five thousand cavalry; in time of emergency, should he need more, he could count on contributions of auxiliary troops from the local clients of Rome (such as Agrippa or Philip; see *BJ* 2.500–503). The Judean prefect, by contrast, had approximately three thousand troops garrisoned with him on the coast at Caesarea.

Finally, a small number of forces were stationed in the country's fortress strongholds and particularly in Jerusalem, where the army maintained a small but permanent presence as a police force. Garrisoned close to the Temple, these troops were intended to encourage its uneventful operation. During the three major festivals, the prefect together with his troops would march in from the coast to reinforce this contingent, "for it is on these festive occasions," as Josephus remarked, "that sedition is most apt to break out" (*BJ* 1.88).

Augustus' enrollment of Judea—wrongly presented in Luke's nativity story as affecting the Galilee also—in fact threatened to trigger another round of rebellion. With the rallying cry, "No king but God!" Judah the Galilean and Zadok the Pharisee encouraged Judeans to revolt. From Josephus' report we see, once again, two extremely prominent characteristics of late Second Temple Jews and Judaism: first, their mingling—or, really, identifying—what moderns would think of as distinctly separate political and religious aspirations; and, second, their violent mutual fractiousness.

These popular leaders framed the rebellion in utterly religious terms. It would be impious as well as servile to cooperate with the tax, they argued; refusal was so religiously correct that surely God would come to their aid. "Heaven would be their zealous helper . . . [in] furthering their enterprise until it succeeded—all the more if with high devotion in their hearts they did not shrink from the bloodshed that might be necessary" (*AJ* 18.5). Josephus continues that the populace "responded gladly" to this call to arms—some, that is, but not all. Looking ahead to the war in 66 against Rome, he continues that this tax revolt sowed the seeds of civil strife and "the slaughter of fellow citizens" (*AJ* 18.8). Commenting in his history of that war, he states:

> Judas . . . induced multitudes to refuse to enroll themselves, when Quirinius was sent as censor to Judea. For in those days Sicarii ["dagger-men"] clubbed together against those who consented to submit to Rome and in every way treated them as enemies, plundering their property, rounding up their cattle, and setting fire to their habitations; protesting that such persons were no other than aliens who so ignobly sacrificed the hard-won liberty of the Jews and admitted their preference for the Roman yoke.   (*BJ* 7.253–55)

The *autonomia* so heatedly sought by the Judean delegation to Rome in 4 B.C.E. was precisely the treason so violently repudiated by these insurrectionists in 6 C.E. As with events under Antiochus Epiphanes in the second century B.C.E., so again, now, with Rome: The ostensible fight against a foreign power served at the same moment as the vehicle for Jewish civil war. The paying of the tribute accordingly remained a religiously as well as politically charged issue. This is the point of the

Gospels' story, correctly set in Jerusalem, of Jesus' being asked what he thinks of it. "Is it lawful to pay taxes to Caesar or not? Should we pay them, or should we not?" (Mk 12:14–15 and parr.). Supporting the payment would insult popular religious sentiment; denying the payment would seem a counsel to revolt. Hence, in Luke's Gospel, the priests' accusations to Pilate: "We found this man perverting our nation and forbidding us to give tribute to Caesar" (Lk 23:2).

Rome prevailed and completed the census. It also appointed a new high priest. Judea began paying the tribute, which defrayed the costs of the prefect's troops in Caesarea. The "system," such as it was, began its work of governing the new province.

These various authorities and their interrelations made the government of Judea the complicated affair it was. The high priest was particularly responsible for maintaining the peaceful functioning of the Temple and Jerusalem. To this end, he himself commanded several thousand Temple guards, who served as Jerusalem's police force. Together with those who served on his council, the high priest was also responsible for overseeing the collection and delivery of the tribute (*BJ* 2.407). In principle he reported to the prefect, whose appointment he was.

The prefect in turn was directly answerable to the emperor and to the Syrian legate, who himself maintained close contact with Rome. And the brief period of restored Jewish monarchy during the short reign of Agrippa I (41–44 C.E.) introduced yet another complication. Command of the armed forces of troops transferred from the prefect (since now there would be none) to the Jewish king (*AJ* 19.356–66). Upon Agrippa's death, Rome granted his brother Herod, king of Chalcis (a tiny area in southern Lebanon) authority over the Temple, its funds, and the selection of the high priest (*AJ* 20.10–14). However, the newly reinstalled Roman governor, now called procurator, had military command transferred back to him.

These concurrent and occasionally conflicting lines of authority did not make governing the region any easier. Worse: This awkward administrative balance could at any time be arbitrarily destabilized by the personal character of the prefect. Pontius Pilate (c. 26–36 C.E.) serves as an excellent case in point. Reproducing a summary of Pilate's character given by the prefect's contemporary, Agrippa I, Philo of Alexandria describes him as a man of "inflexible, stubborn and cruel disposition," whose administration was marked by his "venality, thefts, assaults, abusive behavior, and his frequent murders of untried prisoners" (*Legatio* 38.302). His first act in office was knowingly provocative. Ignoring

Jerusalem's traditional exemption from Imperial images, he ordered some of his troops, under cover of darkness, to carry standards bearing the image of Caesar into the city. This stirred up both town and country, as a large number of Jews followed him to Caesarea and sat outside his residence in protest for five days. Summoning them to the tribunal, Pilate surrounded them with his soldiers whom he ordered to draw swords. At this the Jews "extended their necks and exclaimed that they were ready rather to die than to transgress the Law" by tolerating Pilate's action. He backed down and withdrew the standards (*BJ* 2.169–74; *AJ* 18.55–59).

Pilate later provoked fresh protests when he used funds given in dedication to the Temple (Heb. *corbanot,* "offerings") in order to build an aqueduct for Jerusalem. In his view this probably seemed appropriate. The Temple used a tremendous amount of water and would only have benefited from an increased supply; and thanks in no small part to Jewish donations of the Temple tax, it held huge deposits of wealth. Many Jews saw the issue differently. These funds had been vowed to God and dedicated to his service in the Temple. Pilate's act—using pledged sacred monies for municipal projects—in their eyes was sacrilege. Again they flocked to his tribunal, this time in Jerusalem. But Pilate was prepared and did not back down. He interspersed armed soldiers in civilian clothing throughout the crowd; at his signal, they beat the Jews. Many died, some from their blows, others from the panicked stampede that ensued (*BJ* 2.175–77; *AJ* 18.59–62).

Finally, at a later date—perhaps regretting his giving in to Jewish demands in the matter of the standards—Pilate brought up to Jerusalem votive shields bearing the emperor's name (but no image) and hung them in his residence there. The Jews once more protested, this time joined by four of Herod's sons who were also in the city (probably for one of the feasts). Pilate remained firm. These princes, together with important men of the city, then addressed a petition to the emperor Tiberius. Tiberius himself ordered Pilate to remove the shields to Caesarea (Philo, *Legatio* 38.299–306).

Samaria, not Jerusalem, finally precipitated Pilate's removal from office, and in a sense from history. In 35 C.E., a Samaritan prophet gathered a huge crowd at Mount Gerizim with the promise of producing sacred vessels buried there by Moses. Pilate dispersed the group with cavalry and heavy infantry, taking prisoners and executing the principal leaders. The Samaritans then complained to the Syrian legate, Vitellius, that Pilate had slaughtered unarmed pilgrims, not massing rebels. Vitellius placed a friend in charge as acting prefect and ordered Pilate to Rome, to be heard before the emperor (*AJ* 18.85–89). With this, information about Pilate ceases. Coming into Jerusalem at Passover, Vitellius smoothed things over by remitting some taxes and returning the high priestly vestments to the keeping of the priests. Finally, he deposed Joseph Caiaphas, the high priest who had served under Pilate's entire tenure of office. For a while, Judea settled down again.

ROME AND THE JEWS

As this brief overview has revealed, Roman dominion in the first century and in this part of the empire was not uniform. Rome had no military presence in the Galilee and slight presence in Judea. The largest collection of troops stayed for the most part in the seaside city of Caesarea. The Imperial presence would inevitably have been felt, however, at the High Holy Days, because the attention necessarily concentrated on the Temple inevitably enhanced its visibility. And although the emperors from Augustus on were personally involved in all decisions of regional import—adjudicating royal inheritances, receiving petitions to intervene in local disputes—this same procedure necessarily cushioned their effect, because it slowed everything down. Rome could be reached only by letter, and the speed of seaborne correspondence varied widely according to weather, season, and happenstance. The usual sea route, running counterclockwise from Rome to Alexandria and then up the eastern Mediterranean coast, was unreliable, and communications consequently slow.

Also, Rome's interests were fairly circumscribed: The empire wanted internal peace, secure borders, and steady tribute. As long as these conditions were met, its myriad subjects and clients were by and large left to their own cults, to observe what they would as they would. Despite its entanglement in the Jewish cult because of the specific issues surrounding government and the Temple, the empire maintained this policy toward Judea also. Pilate's belligerence—and certainly Caligula's, when he attempted to place his own statue in the Temple—were exceptional in the extreme. For practical reasons both administrative and religious (who would want to provoke the ire of another nation's gods?), Rome had small wish to upset regional observances and usually went out of its way to accommodate Jewish sensibility. Consider the example of Vitellius, the Syrian legate mentioned above, who came to Antipas's aid in 39 C.E. when Antipas was attacked by his former father-in-law, the Nabatean king Aretas.

> Vitellius got himself ready for war against Aretas.... Since he had
> started to lead his army through the land of Judea, the Jews of the
> highest standing went to meet him and entreated him not to march
> through their land. [Note: Vitellius had mobilized to assist a Jewish
> ruler.] For, they said, it was contrary to their tradition to allow images,
> of which there were many attached to the military standards, to be
> brought upon their soil. Yielding to their entreaty, he abandoned his
> original plan and ordered his army to march through the Great Plain
> while he himself, together with Herod the tetrarch and his friends,
> went up to Jerusalem to sacrifice to God during the traditional festival.
>
> (*AJ* 18.120–22)

Claudius, who succeeded Caligula as emperor in 41, publicly and
pointedly denounced the "great folly and madness" of his predecessor.
In the early empire, precedent was for the emperors to be deified upon
their death; Caligula's demand to be worshiped in life had disgusted his
own people, and his attempt to erect his own statue in Jerusalem's temple provoked a crisis for Jews. Claudius wasted no time in sending out
edicts, both to the city of Alexandria in Egypt and also "to the rest of the
world," reasserting the empire's traditional policy of religious tolerance.
According to Josephus, Claudius first addressed the Greek Alexandrians, who had violated Jewish civic rights during the turmoil caused by
Caligula. Claudius proclaimed his desire that "the several subject
nations [in that city] should abide by their own customs and not be com-
pelled to violate the religion of their fathers." Learning of the Greek
Alexandrians'

> insurrection against the Jews in their midst in the time of Gaius Caesar
> [Caligula], who through his great folly and madness humiliated the
> Jews because they refused to transgress the religion of their fathers by
> addressing him as a god, I desire that none of their rights should be lost
> to the Jews on account of the madness of Gaius, but that their former
> privileges be preserved to them; and I enjoin both parties to take the
> greatest precaution to prevent any disturbance arising after the posting
> of my edict.

His second edict pronounced the same principle generally. He
explained that he had acceded to the request of his friend, the Jewish
monarch Agrippa I, who asked that the privileges enjoyed by Alexandrians Jews be maintained also for Jews throughout the empire.

I very gladly consented, not merely in order to please those who petitioned me, but also because in my opinion the Jews deserve to obtain their request on account of their loyalty and friendship to the Romans. In particular, I did so because I hold it right that not even Greek cities should be deprived of these privileges, seeing that they were in fact guaranteed for them at the time of the divine Augustus. It is right, therefore, that *the Jews throughout the whole world under our sway should also observe the customs of their fathers without let or hindrance.* I enjoin upon them also by these presents to avail themselves of this kindness in a more reasonable spirit, and not to set at nought the beliefs about the gods held by other peoples, but to keep to their own laws.

To ensure that his will was broadcast, Claudius closed by ordering the ruling bodies of all cities and colonies in Italy and beyond, and all client kings through their own officers, to inscribe his edict and post it for at least thirty days "in a place where it can plainly be read from the ground" (*AJ* 19.283–91).

This practical and principled religious tolerance contrasts markedly with most people's sense of the Roman Empire. Majority culture in the modern West is Christian. This means that whether because of school-day surveys of ancient history, elementary instruction within traditional churches, or the lurid depictions of Hollywood epics, Rome's anti-Christian persecutions loom large.

This impression of Rome as religious persecutor obscures both the ancient notions of cult and the practical realities of running an empire. "Rome" as such had no policy of persecuting Christians up until the emperor Decius in 250 C.E. Before that time, some Christians in the various cities of the empire might be the targets of local resentments and fears because they as Gentiles were not honoring their ancestral gods, upon whom the community's well-being ultimately depended. As Tertullian, a late second-century Latin Christian complained, "If the Tiber overflows to the walls, if the Nile does not rise to the fields; if the sky doesn't move or the earth does; if there is famine or plague, the cry goes up at once: 'The Christians to the lion!' " (*Apology* 40.2). And Jewish Christians were not so persecuted, because as Jews their exemption from public cult was ancient, traditional, and protected by law. Ancestral obligation was what mattered.

Further, when in 250 Decius mandated participation in public cult for all residents of the empire (again, Jews and, thus, Jewish Christians excepted), he did not forbid the practice of Christianity. Rather, he simply ordered that gentile Christians, in addition to their peculiar personal religion, also observe the traditional cults of their own people and of the empire. His goal was not religious uniformity, but preserving the well-being of the empire, which was superintended by the gods.

Finally, Rome's principled ecumenicalism reflected the tolerant pluralism most typical of ancient paganism with its "if-some-is-good-more-is-better" attitude toward other gods (which in turn explains some of the enduring gentile interest in the synagogue). More than just culturally congenial, such religious pluralism was also politically pragmatic. What mattered most was peace and security—which explains why Decius took the unprecedented step he did. In the mid–third century, inflation raged and invading armies had penetrated the empire's frontiers. Decius' edict was meant to enroll everyone in persuading heaven to protect Rome once again.

But to be proactively concerned with all the countless ancestral practices of its subject peoples would simply have interfered with the smooth operation of the empire. Outright illegal activities such as cultic murder, cannibalism, or castration aside, the emperors wasted little time on what was literally not their concern. The cult of the goddess Roma and the Imperial feast days honoring the deity of deceased emperors simply took their place in the liturgical calendars of the empire's wide-flung municipalities. Jewish communities meanwhile prayed for Rome's well-being and, in Jerusalem, offered sacrifices on its behalf.

Our second conclusion simply sums up what we saw presented in detail above: The political and social experience of the Galilee in this period contrasted substantially with Judea's. Unlike Judea, with its complex and conflicting governing administrations, the Galilee enjoyed the long, unbroken, and stable regime of Herod Antipas. No Roman soldiers appeared in the Galilee during Jesus' lifetime, nor did the region ever undergo census or pay tribute to Rome. And despite the tetrarch's concerns over John the Baptizer, no popular rebellions or protests marred his reign. Compared to Judea, the Galilee was peaceful and quiet.

Third and finally, we should note that Judea and the Galilee, political experiences aside, were nonetheless united *religiously,* so that events seemingly affecting only Judeans might nonetheless move Galileans to action, and vice versa. Their intense interaction expressed the binding power of their unique religious culture, which generally distinguished Jews from their neighbors and identified them with each other no matter how widely scattered they were. This last point, too, needs to be emphasized, because the recent scholarly focus on Galilean regionalism, or on its peasant culture supposedly alienated from and hostile to the (elite, Judean) Torah and Temple, has made Alexandria, Rome, or even Babylon seem religiously and culturally closer to Jerusalem than the Galilee was. Let's review once more what can be culled from the ancient evidence.

That Jews no matter where they lived comprised a single people seemed true both in their own eyes and in the eyes of their gentile contemporaries. They were united both through kinship and through cult—which in antiquity, as we have noted again and again, correlated closely. "Eight thousand" Jews resident in Rome at the time of Augustus involved themselves immediately with the visiting delegation's petition for Judean "autonomy": What concerned the homeland, and especially the Temple, concerned them (see p. 167). Further evidence of the Diaspora community's concern with Judea can be seen in the bizarre story that Josephus relates concerning a Herodian pretender (*BJ* 2.101–10; *AJ* 17.323–38). After Augustus had carried out the provisions of Herod's will in 4 B.C.E., a young man appeared claiming to be Alexander, one of Herod's sons by the Hasmonean princess Mariamne. The real Alexander, together with his brother Aristobulus, had actually been executed for conspiracy by their father three years earlier. But so strong was the physical resemblance of this man to the dead prince that Jews in Crete, Melos, Puteoli, and Rome thronged to him, opening both hearts and purses. Some of these supporters, Josephus remarks, were simply hoping to receive a return for their patronage when "Alexander" became king (*AJ* 17.327). But many others ("the whole Jewish population" of Rome) welcomed him joyfully "because of their racial tie with his mother" (17.330: the translator's "racial" is the text's *genos*, "ethnic"). These Jews, though far from Jerusalem, kept very much involved.

The religious unity of this scattered people was equally evident to outsiders: For this reason Josephus depicts the emperor Claudius' publicizing the principles of his decree concerning Alexandrian Jews throughout the empire. This fact also explains the pattern of some of Herod the Great's benefactions to pagan foundations in the Diaspora. As king of the Jews, Herod funded projects in diaspora cities with large Jewish populations. Besides enhancing his own prestige, he intended these projects to purchase the goodwill of his gentile beneficiaries for the resident Jews.

The Bible, the knowledge of Torah mediated through the synagogue, the near-universal concern with the Temple in Jerusalem—all these were both expressions and agents of the singular identity of the Jewish people in antiquity.

> Our books, those which are justly accredited, are but two and twenty, and contain the record of all time. Of these, five are the books of Moses, comprising the laws and the traditional history from the birth of man down to the death of the lawgiver. . . . From the death of Moses until Artaxerxes, who succeeded Xerxes as king of Persia, the prophets subsequent to Moses wrote the history of the events of their own times in thirteen books. The remaining four contain hymns to God and precepts for the conduct of human life. . . . We have given practical proof of our reverence of our own Scriptures. For, although such long ages have now passed, no one has ventured either to add, or to remove, or to alter a syllable; and it is an instinct with every Jew, from the day of his birth, to regard them as the decrees of God, to abide by them and, if need be, even to die for them.   (Josephus, *c. Ap.* 1.38–42)

Their universal acknowledgment of the sanctity of the Law and their consequent "perfect uniformity in habits and customs," Josephus states—without irony!—is the cause of the Jews' "admirable harmony" (*c. Ap.* 2.179). This, obviously, we must take with several large doses of salt: After all, this writing—his reply to calumnies published by the Greek Apion, who had drawn on the works of a number of other anti-Jewish authors—was Josephus' most fulsome apology for his people. Elsewhere, in his histories, his details of fratricidal frictions and sectarian wrangling provide abundant evidence refuting his claims of "admirable harmony" here.

But his basic point—that Jews in general knew their ancestral laws; that they kept Sabbath, circumcision, and food laws; that they loyally supported the Temple—is amply borne out by non-Jewish evidence as well. Emperors drafted laws protecting the Jewish observance of the Sabbath, the sanctity of the scrolls of the Law, and the monies they dedicated to the Temple (e.g., *AJ* 16.162–66). Gentile observers from a broad spectrum of periods and places, whether hostile or admiring, whether pagan or Christian, whether in Greek or in Latin, comment on the same characteristic beliefs and behaviors as Josephus does.

Perhaps the best index of the widespread Jewish loyalty to the Temple is the money that Jews throughout the world voluntarily contributed toward its upkeep, the so-called Temple tax of one half-shekel or two drachmas. Matthew in his Gospel simply assumes that the tax will be familiar to his readers. When Jesus and his disciples returned to Capernaum, he writes, "The collectors of the half-shekel tax went up to Peter and asked, 'Does not your teacher pay the tax?' He said, 'Yes' " (Mt 18:24). Jews throughout the empire sought to have the Imperial government legally guarantee their right to collect and send this donation. Thanks again to Josephus, the language of several of these Imperial decrees survives. They asserted as legal principle that the Jews' "sacred monies shall be inviolable and may be sent up to Jerusalem and delivered to the treasurers in Jerusalem" (so Augustus in his role of *pontifex maximus,* "greatest priest" and guardian of all legitimate cults in the empire, to the cities of proconsular Asia, *AJ* 16.163). The cities of their residence, tempted by this quantity of cash, had sometimes seized it, or appropriated it for more local use. Hence this proconsul's decree:

> Gaius Norbanus Flaccus, proconsul, to the magistrates and council of Sardis, greeting. Caesar has written to me, ordering that the Jews shall not be prevented from collecting sums of money, however great they may be, in accordance with their ancestral custom, and sending them up to Jerusalem. I have therefore written to you that you may know that Caesar and I wish this to be done. (*AJ* 16.171)

And another:

> To the magistrates, council and people of Ephesus, greeting. When I was administering justice in Ephesus on the Ides of February, the Jews dwelling in Asia pointed out to me that Caesar Augustus and Agrippa [a Roman noble, not the later Jewish king of the same name] have permitted them to follow their own laws and customs, and to bring the offerings, which each of them makes of his own free will and out of piety toward the Deity, travelling together under escort to Jerusalem without being impeded in any way. And they asked that I confirm by my own decision the rights granted by Augustus and Agrippa. I therefore wish you to know that in agreement with the will of Augustus and Agrippa I permit them to live and act in accordance with their ancestral customs. (*AJ* 16.172–73)

This tax generated so much income that the Romans, in the wake of the Jewish war, insisted on continuing to collect it. Their Temple was no more, the tax no longer voluntary, and Jerusalem no longer its destination, but still the Jews paid: Papyrus scraps from Egypt let us glimpse some actual local rolls. Now, however, Rome rerouted the funds so that the Jews' tax supported the temple of Jupiter on the Capitoline hill.

Both the Gospels and Josephus speak of the Galilean presence at the Temple during the pilgrimage holidays. Galileans had shown up in force at Shavuot/Pentecost, fifty days after Archelaus's dismal first Passover as Herod's heir designate in 4 B.C.E. They and the others with them—Josephus names Idumeans, people from Jericho and Transjordan, and most of all, naturally, Judeans—were inflamed by "the reckless insolence of Sabinus," the prefect temporarily installed to oversee the country while Archelaus appeared before Augustus in Rome. This Sabinus provoked local and regional outrage by using his soldiers and his own slaves to harass the Jews, and by seeking to help himself to the royal treasury (*BJ* 2.40–46; *AJ* 17.253–54). Accordingly, "it was not the customary ritual so much as indignation which drew the people in crowds to the capital" (*BJ* 2.42).

The point to note here is that Galileans, specifically, cared about what went on in Judea. The same point is made by the Judean tax revolt in the year 6 C.E., protesting Augustus' census of and levy on Judea. Its chief instigator was Judah the Galilean. He saw such tax for tribute as a religious offense and did not hesitate to attempt to rally Judeans to his view (*BJ* 2.117–18; *AJ* 18.4–10). And finally the murder in Samaria of Galilean pilgrims passing through on their way to Jerusalem confirms both that there was such traffic between north and south and that the Judeans for their part cared what happened to their northern coreligionists (*AJ* 20.119–36).

But the most dramatic and certainly the largest demonstration of religious solidarity between Judea and the Galilee occurred in 40 C.E., provoked by Caligula. The emperor had already begun to insist that his divinity be acknowledged, a demand that his non-Jewish subjects in the Greek East and in Egypt had little difficulty complying with. When Philo together with a small band of other Alexandrian Jews came as a delegation to Italy to seek redress for the anti-Jewish violence in their city, Caligula snubbed them. The pagan Alexandrian delegation led by Apion (against whose calumnies Josephus would later direct his apology) had goaded the emperor, saying that the Jews alone of all his subjects refused to honor him as they should.

Caligula abruptly resolved to correct this situation. He ordered the Syrian legate, a man named Petronius, to take half of his fighting force—two legions, or between ten thousand and twelve thousand troops—and embark for Judea. Evidently Caligula was prepared to exercise violent force to achieve his goal: to set up a statue of himself in the Jews' temple in Jerusalem. In order to execute his mission, Petronius had first to march through the Galilee; and that, it turned out, was as far as he got.

Early in the summer of 40 c.e. at Ptolemaïs (a northern port city and point of entry to the Galilee), and again, during the autumn sowing season, at Tiberias, Petronius was met by huge crowds of Jews bent on passively resisting Caligula's order. "Slay us first before you carry out these resolutions!" (*AJ* 18.264). The people were not going to budge.

> "On no account would we fight," they said, "but we will sooner die than violate our laws." And falling on their faces and baring their throats, they declared that they were ready to be slain. They continued to make these supplications for forty days. Furthermore, they neglected their fields, even though it was time to sow the seed. For they showed a stubborn determination to die rather than to see the image erected.
>
> (*AJ* 18.271–72)

Petronius finally openly petitioned the emperor to rescind his order. Caligula responded by ordering Petronius to kill himself. But death overtook the emperor himself shortly thereafter, when he was assassinated in January of 41. Petronius received the news of Caligula's death in the beginning of March—approximately four weeks before receiving the emperor's prior letter ordering his suicide (*AJ* 18.307–8). The earlier letter had taken three months to reach him, slowed by bad weather: The unreliability of the sea route had worked to Petronius' advantage. He happily abandoned both of Caligula's directives.

No Jew anywhere in the empire was indifferent to Caligula's plan. Philo speculated that unless the emperor changed his mind, he would face eruptions of Jewish protest from one end of the empire to the other (*Legatio* 214–20). The point to note here is the strong, committed, joint response of Galileans and Judeans in particular to this threat to the Temple. Protesters poured out of Jerusalem and the rest of the country, Philo says (*Legatio* 222–49). Josephus notes the concern of the nobles and leading men, who warn Petronius that "since the land was unsown, there would be a harvest of banditry, because the requirement of tribute could not be met" (*AJ* 18.274)—a clear reference to the Judean identity of some of the strikers, because only Judeans paid tribute. These

Judeans joined with the Galilean Jews to persuade Petronius not to continue with his orders. Other Galileans must have assisted such a large body—"tens of thousands," in Josephus' view—as they sat in Tiberias striking for forty days.

As we review the Gospel stories of Jesus' mission, this, then, is the general social context we should keep in mind. The Galilee in Jesus' lifetime was politically stable and, especially when compared with Judea, relatively untroubled. The land itself was fertile and thickly populated, and these two go together: Absent sufficient food, populations thin. This in turn implies that the economics of the region, by whatever modern method we choose to construe them, did not compromise its basic fecundity. The two large and new cities in Jesus' part of the Galilee—Sepphoris and Tiberias, both built in Jesus' lifetime—most likely, therefore, did not have an overwhelmingly negative effect on village life around them, for the sources say nothing of peasant protest movements, unrest, famine, or riot.

Social life in the Galilee was organized primarily around villages, as we should expect in a heavily agricultural area; on this Josephus, the Gospels, and the archaeological data all agree. Family observance and group religious life would coincide at the village's weekly assemblies on Shabbat (the "synagogue"). These were marked by public reading (and hence, for the majority of those gathered, public *hearing*) of the Torah; instruction in and interpretation of its precepts from those with the knowledge and therefore the authority to teach (a *cohen* resident in the village, perhaps; or a scribe; or learned laymen, maybe Pharisees); prayer (whether communal or individual); and perhaps also lessons from some of the other authoritative traditional writings, such as those that Josephus lists, cited above: prophets, Psalms ("hymns"), Proverbs.

The villagers' agricultural calendar flowed together with seasons of spiritual and historical significance in the life of the nation through the annual cycle of biblically mandated pilgrim holidays. Sukkot/Booths, after the fall harvest was in, celebrated the fruits of the Land while recalling Israel's period of wandering, landless, in the desert. Pesach/Passover in early spring, in many ways the nation's fundamental festival, looked back to the redemption from Egypt, when God had brought Israel out of slavery "with a strong arm and a mighty hand." And Shavuot/Pentecost, which fell after the first barley harvest in late spring or early summer, celebrated the people's hearing and receiving the words of God on Sinai, his "instruction," his Torah. Measuring their lives by this cycle of planting, harvesting, and enacted recollection, the people would walk from their villages in the Galilee to celebrate at the Temple, singing pilgrim psalms in praise of Jerusalem. The rituals and traditions of the holidays themselves, like the singing, prayers, and special holiday foods (such as the unleavened bread of Passover) all served as a means of religious instruction and spiritual orientation. Thus, while Sepphoris and Tiberias dominated the region geographically, spiritually, and religiously (to use a modern distinction that would make little sense to the people of antiquity), the chief city of the Galilee was Jerusalem.

Walking from the Galilee to Jerusalem would bring these pilgrims into contact with the supreme governing power of their period: Rome. When they went up for the major holidays, so, too, would the prefect, marching up from Caesarea with the greater part of his three thousand troops to post guard at the Temple. The weeklong period of purification, plus the seven- or eight-day run of the holiday, would mean that the city's population would stay bulked up for some two weeks at a time. Some pilgrims would find lodging within the city; many others would encamp in the valley just below; others would seek temporary lodging in villages nearby. (According to Mk 11:12, for example, Jesus lodged in the village of Bethany during his final Passover; Jn 7:10 implies that Jesus stayed in the city for Sukkot.) Jewish police of the Temple guard would keep order in Jerusalem itself; the Roman soldiers, garrisoned near the Temple, would patrol its perimeter from the roof of the stoa. Their contact with the crowds, if all went well, was minimal: Their visibility itself was meant to deter any popular commotion.

The time leading up to the festival would be punctuated by the ceremony of purification from corpse-pollution. (For the biblical description, see Nm 19.) On the third and seventh days of this week, worshipers would be sprinkled with the special "water of cleansing" that was mixed with the ashes of a red heifer. Once he or she completed these sprinklings, the worshiper would immerse, likewise immersing his or her clothes. Thereafter the worshiper, purified, was prepared to enter the Temple area for the holiday offerings that were part of the feast. The first and last days of the festive week itself were "high" holidays, with their particular protocols. Except for Shabbat, the intermediate days of the holiday, like the time during the preparatory week, were stretches of unstructured leisure: learning, socializing, enjoying the respite from daily life's usual demands. With the conclusion of the feast, the city's population would ebb as pilgrims began their return home. The prefect, too, together with his army, would turn back to Caesarea.

For the next while, if all went well, Jerusalem, too, would be quiet.

The Mission of John

THE GALILEE and Judea provide the widest contexts—geographical, political, societal, economic—for understanding the message and meaning of Jesus' mission. Two historical figures who stand at the extreme ends of his mission provide a more focused and personal context: John the Baptizer at the beginning, Pontius Pilate at its end.

Why take the Gospel stories of Jesus' encounter with these two men as historically reliable? First, they are multiply attested in the sources. Not only the Gospels, but also Josephus and Tacitus name Pilate as the Roman authority responsible for Jesus' execution; Mark and John both speak of the Baptizer's mission as preceding, and in some sense initiating, Jesus'. Further, both pass a rough test for authenticity that historians use on this material, known as the "criterion of dissimilarity" or "discontinuity." In its classic formulation, this criterion states that if a saying or story about Jesus is dissimilar both to contemporary first-century Judaism and to teachings about him by the later church, then it may be authentic. Applied mechanically, of course, this criterion will yield nonsense. In privileging a definition of "authentic" as "unique," it can in effect present Jesus as a man without a native historical and religious context, or a teacher whose teachings had no effect on the movement that later formed around his memory. Applied judiciously, though, it can help to clarify the data. For example, nothing in early Judaism speaks of a baptized or crucified messiah; therefore, the evangelists would have little reason to invent such stories. Where, then, might they come from? Perhaps from remembered events.

The criterion of embarrassment, a modified version of dissimilarity, holds that a tradition that is clearly *not* in the interests of the later church—disparaging remarks about Gentiles, for example; or explicit pronouncements of the imminent End—*may* indeed be authentic. Why would the later community have invented stories that only created difficulties for itself? The source of such awkward material, again, may be historical reminiscence. We can trace the increasing awkwardness that Jesus' baptism and crucifixion caused later communities in the way that the evangelists treat these traditions. Thus, Mark's simple statement that Jesus came to John for baptism prompts explanatory speeches in

Matthew's retelling ("John would have prevented him, saying, 'I need to be baptized by you, and do you come to me?' " Mt 3:13–15; cf. Mk 1:9). Luke passes over the baptism in great haste in a subordinate clause, obscuring John's agency (Lk 3:21); the Gospel of John drops the baptism scene entirely. And as the narratives of Jesus' Passion evolve, we see their increasing tendency to exculpate Pilate and inculpate Jewish authorities—a sensible allocation of hostility and blame since, by the time the evangelists write, Jerusalem's priestly authorities were no more, and the new movement had to find its place in a world ruled by Rome. Had the evangelists been completely free to invent their stories of Jesus, we can only suppose that they would have spared themselves these difficulties that John and Pilate both posed.

According to blocks of tradition preserved in Q, John himself preached a message of repentance in view of the impending arrival of God's kingdom, and he addressed toll collectors and sinners who responded to his call. He, too, died violently, executed by a governing authority. And beyond the fact of their historical synchronicity and these shared similarities in their missions, John stands in some sort of initiatory relation to Jesus: only after his immersion "for the forgiveness of sins" (Mk 1:4, 9, and parr.) did Jesus himself undertake to bring the message of the Kingdom to Israel. The more clearly we understand John, then, the more clearly we might understand Jesus.

Evidence about John collects in several different sources: in some brief narrative passages in Mark, which Matthew and Luke repeat; in Q, which contains some of John's teachings (Mt 3:7–12//Lk 3:7–9, 15–18) as well as remarks by Jesus about him (Mt 11:2–19//Lk 7:18–35); in other, independent traditions in the Fourth Gospel; and finally in the passage from the evangelists' contemporary, Josephus, in *AJ* 18.116–19 (cited on p. 152).

Mark's introduction of John fits with the information in Josephus:

> John the baptizer appeared in the wilderness, preaching a *baptism of repentance for the forgiveness of sins.* And there went out to him all the country of Judea and all the people of Jerusalem; and they were *baptized by him in the river Jordan, confessing their sins.* Now John was clothed with camel's hair, and had a leather girdle round his waist, and ate locusts and wild honey.   (Mk 1:4–6)

The italicized snippets in Mark's passage cohere well with Josephus' summary of John's preaching: John, Josephus says, "had exhorted the

Jews to lead righteous lives, to *practice justice towards their fellows and piety towards God,* and so doing *to join in baptism.* In his view, this [behavior] was necessary if baptism was to be acceptable to God." This immersion, Josephus explicitly states, did not confer forgiveness of sins, but served rather "for the *purification of the flesh* once the *soul* had previously been *cleansed by right conduct.*" Repentance and sincere contrition before God, John and his contemporaries believed, would gain forgiveness. The former sinner, having harkened to John's call to repentance, would then amplify his new moral purity by immersion for bodily purity. In short, both Mark and Josephus describe a ritual of purification so immediately associated with John's mission that the activity itself was how he was known: John the Immerser, or Baptizer. The water of the Jordan purified the bodies of the former sinners only once their prior acknowledgment of sin and consequent repentance had already "purified" their souls.

Mark's description of John's clothing and diet in this passage may further cohere with Josephus' report of John's concern with bodily purity. Cloth of camel hair, a loosely woven fabric, would easily allow water to completely penetrate the garment during immersion, thus ensuring the body's full contact with water (a desideratum of immersion for purity). Purity concerns, too, might account for the details of John's diet. True, locusts and honey fit first of all with his venue in the wilderness: Such would be readily available in the desert. But Q adds to our knowledge of John's eating habits, claiming that he "came eating no bread and drinking no wine" (Lk 7:33//Mt 11:18). In other words, the Baptizer evidently did not eat man-made or cultivated foods. This, too, may reflect his purity concerns: Such food—locusts, honey, water— runs no risk of being impure, that is, of violating in any way the laws of kashruth.

Why was John "in the wilderness"—specifically, in the Judean desert, wandering on both banks of the Jordan near the Dead Sea? His immersions for purity obviously required abundant water, so John's working by the river itself is easy enough to understand. But if abundant water were his only concern, he might just as easily have chosen some bank of the Sea of Galilee: Instead, he chose the wilderness of Judea. This choice of venue was shared by other Jews whose religious devotion was also particularly marked by purity concerns and immersions: the community at Qumran, and also the solitary holy man, Bannus, with whom Josephus lived between ages sixteen and nineteen. In his autobiography, Josephus wrote that he studied variously with Sadducees, Pharisees, and Essenes:

> I thought that, after a thorough investigation, I should be in a position to select the best. So I submitted myself to hard training and laborious exercises and passed through the three courses. Not content, however, with the experience thus gained, on hearing of one named *Bannus, who dwelt in the wilderness, wearing only such clothing as trees provided, feeding on such things as grew of themselves, and using frequent ablutions of cold water, by day and night, for purity's sake,* I became his devoted disciple.
>
> (*Vita* 2.10–12)

Jews had many reasons to associate the wilderness with purity and proximity to God. It had been the site of foundational events in the life of the nation: the place of Israel's wandering after the Exodus, the place where God had given his revelation to Moses, and his torah, or instruction, to his people. Other prophets of this period also called their hearers to follow them into the desert, "there to receive the signs of their redemption" (*BJ* 2.259; *AJ* 20.168). It was a place that fused historic and spiritual significance, which John himself, by baptizing there, may have deliberately wished to recall.

John's emphases—repentance for sin, purification—were hardly exotic concerns within Second Temple Judaism. The particular emphasis that John evidently placed on his own role as agent of this purification rite, however, *is* unusual. Other purificatory immersions or ablutions, whether performed by sectarians (Pharisees, Essenes), diaspora Jews (who occasionally improvised water-purification rituals such as "sprinkling"), or observant Jews generally, were self-administered: The person dipped or sprinkled himself. But John apparently immersed penitents—hence his sobriquet "the Baptizer." What was his point?

Here we briefly detour from Josephus and Mark to take in, as well, the teaching material attributed to John. According to Q, John's message of the impending arrival of the Kingdom came with fire-and-brimstone warnings of judgment. Addressing those coming to him for immersion, John says:

> Who warned you to flee from the wrath to come? Bear fruits that befit repentance, and do not begin to say to yourselves, "We have Abraham as our father"; for I tell you, God is able from these stones to raise up

children to Abraham. Even now the ax is laid to the root of the trees. Every tree therefore that does not bear good fruit is cut down and thrown into the fire.   (Lk 3:7–9//Mt 3:7–10)

John's teaching as related in Q repeats what Josephus said of him: His baptism or immersion would not be acceptable (that is, to God) unless preceded by the inner purification of repentance. Repentance leads in turn to deeds of piety (toward God) and justice (toward one's fellows) in Josephus' language; to "fruits befitting repentance" or "good fruit" in Q's.

By "piety" and "justice," Josephus intends more than general virtues. These are code words for the Torah, and most specifically the Ten Commandments. Piety (Gk. *eusebeia*) defines one's relationship to God, spelled out in the "first table" of the Law; justice or righteousness (Gk. *dikaiosynē*), one's relationship with others, the Law's "second table."

First Table: Piety toward God	Second Table: Justice toward Others
1. Worship no other gods	6. No murder
2. No graven images (idols)	7. No adultery
3. No taking God's name vainly	8. No theft
4. Keep the Sabbath	9. No lying
5. Honor father and mother	10. No coveting

John's call to moral renewal in the face of the coming Kingdom meant, precisely, keeping Torah—hardly unique themes in Jewish moral exhortation. What characterizes his particular preaching is his connecting observance specifically with bodily purification and apocalyptic warnings. Until and unless one repents and changes, he taught, bodily purification itself would aid nothing. Hence Q's characterization of those coming to John who have not already changed their ways: a "brood of vipers," these people do not yet "bear fruits that befit repentance." If the final judgment comes before they have produced "good fruit" (the good deeds befitting true repentance), their being part of Israel (children of Abraham) will avail them nothing; they will be condemned to the fire and "burn."

Several observations here, before speculating on John's reasons for so emphasizing his own agency in his rite of purification. First, this concern to attend to the inner (what we would designate "moral") dimension of repentance before addressing the external protocols of atonement (purity, offerings, and the like) is a stock theme of Jewish penitential tradition in all periods. In the first century, we find it stated in the Dead Sea Scrolls, in Philo, in Josephus, and of course (recalling that New Testament documents are first-century Jewish texts) in the Gospels as well. Scripturally, we find it in the classical prophets from the time of the First Temple. Thus,

> I hate, I despise your feasts,
>> and I take no delight in your solemn assemblies.
> Even though you offer me your burnt offerings
>> and cereal offerings, I will not accept them. . . .
> Take away from me the noise of your songs;
>> To the melody of your harps I will not listen.
> *But let justice roll down like waters,*
>> *and righteousness like an ever-flowing stream.*
>> (Am 5:21–24)

The prophet is not stipulating an "either-or" choice here—either make burnt offerings (which God hates) or pursue righteousness (which God loves and prefers). The man who is pious toward God and righteous toward his fellows does *both*. However, Christian writers both ancient and modern have often read the prophets as somehow speaking against ritual itself, valuing (inner) "moral purity" over (mere, external) "ritual" purity, as if the two were somehow mutually exclusive, or as if true inner piety, in the prophets' view, annulled any need for the purifications, rites, and offerings that in biblical narrative are also commanded by God. But here John's emphasis precisely on immersion seems to make the opposite case. The person who would be saved on the last day needed more than repentance and amended behavior: He also needed to be purified in his flesh.

We do not know much else about John's mission and message. What little more we have in the Gospel sources is suspect. All four Gospels present John as an Elijah-figure who functions primarily to prepare Israel for the Messiah/Jesus. John subordinates himself, speaking of "one mightier than I who comes," and who "will baptize you with the Holy Spirit" (Mk 1:7–8)—more dramatic foreshadowing for the Gospels' prime subject. Such pronouncements flatly fail a claim to authenticity based on the criterion of dissimilarity, for they present John enunciating precisely the later Christian community's own beliefs about him, and about Jesus' superiority to him. Again, the evidence of Josephus seems to imply that the opposite was the case in their own lifetimes (late 20s to early 30s C.E.) and even a half-century thereafter: His notice on John in *Antiquities* is substantially longer than his notice on Jesus (see p. 248).

Nor can much more be known from either the Gospels or Josephus about John's purifications. Could the penitent immerse as many times as he saw fit, or again if and when he again sinned (as with other Jewish immersions for purification)? Or could he immerse only once (on the analogy of much later Christian baptism)? Again, the sources say nothing one way or the other; but if the later practice of Christian baptism did not cast such a shadow over John's activity, there would be scarce reason to think of his immersions as a one-time event. Multiple immersions better fit John's native religious context.

Finally, nothing in John's message or in his practice of ritual purification presupposes criticism of or hostility toward the Temple, though New Testament scholars will assert that they see this "implied." This implication seems to me to rely more on our knowledge of the way that Christianity eventually evolved than on anything in the ancient texts. Absent evidence, we could indeed make the opposite argument based on the strong positive link between purity and cult in the period up to 70 C.E. Having repented, acknowledged his sin, mended his ways, and then through John purified his body, the former sinner may very well have completed the biblically mandated rituals of atonement when next he went to Jerusalem. Such would be consistent with John's message of piety toward God. We do not know, because we have no evidence either way. In light of the later evangelists' complex and occasionally outright hostile attitude toward the Temple, however—one that they impute as well to Jesus—we may be certain that they would have gladly used such traditions about John, had they known any.

What then can be known from these reports? First, that John seems to have emphasized his own role in immersing penitent sinners: They came to him for baptism; they did not (as with more traditional Jewish purification rites) immerse themselves. Perhaps his prominence in this ritual is related to his message of the impending Kingdom. As prophet of the End and summoner of Israel to repentance, John had a singular authority: Reception of his message meant, at the same time, acceptance of John as the Kingdom's authoritative prophet. I am speculating, but with reason: We shall see the same pattern repeated in the traditions about Jesus.

Second, while both Josephus and the Gospels say that John was executed by Antipas, it is hard to see why. Mark and, following him, Matthew relate a story of John's criticism of Herod's marriage to Herodias. The story folkloricly relates how Antipas was essentially tricked by his own incautious promise to Herodias' daughter into killing John (Mk 6:17–29//Mt 14:3–12). It sheds little light on Josephus' report: Afraid of John's effect on the people—"eloquence that had so great an effect on mankind might lead to some form of sedition, for it looked as if they would be guided by John in everything they did"—Antipas did away with him in a sort of preemptive strike.

But a message of "piety" and "righteousness" does not sound like a summons to sedition. Searching for an adequate explanation for John's execution, historians typically combine the Gospel stories and Josephus' text. Perhaps John, who truly was concerned with purity, criticized Antipas for making a union disallowed by Leviticus 18:16: marriage to his brother's (former) wife. Such a union was "impure" (Lv 20:21). Perhaps Antipas feared that John's condemnation of his marital impurity would undermine his authority with his subjects—especially (if we can rely on Luke's report that the Baptizer addressed in particular "tax collectors and soldiers," 3:10–14) with those subjects upon whose labors his power particularly depended. Or perhaps John's apocalyptic message, predicting as it did the imminent arrival of God's kingdom, was "implicitly" critical enough or threatening enough to current power relations that Antipas felt he had to act swiftly. The puzzle here would be why the Romans, in whose territory (the Judean west bank of the Jordan) John also worked, would not have executed him themselves. (Perhaps the fact that John's followers came and went, and were never massed at one time, was enough in Roman eyes to make him seem innocuous; but then, why not to Antipas too?) All we can know for certain is that this manifestly prophetic figure died at the hands of a secular ruler.

JOHN, JESUS, AND REPENTANCE

What we do know past doubting is that John had a crucially important impact on Jesus. According to the synoptic tradition, Jesus in some sense received his calling during or just after his baptism. The voice from heaven proclaims him "beloved son" as he emerges from the Jordan (Mk 1:9–11 and parr.); shortly thereafter, the spirit of God drives him, too, out into the wilderness for a solitary period before he begins his own mission (Mk 1:12–13 and parr.). On the evidence of Q, Jesus held John to be a prophet "and more than a prophet. This is he of whom it is written, 'Behold, I send my messenger before thy face, who shall prepare thy way before thee' " (Mal 3:1; Lk 7:26–27//Mt 11:9–10). The

Fourth Gospel presents John and Jesus as immersing in tandem: "Jesus and his disciples went into the land of Judea, and there he remained with them and baptized. John also was baptizing" (Jn 3:22–23, though cf. the later disclaimer added at 4:2). And in Q, Jesus links their two missions together:

> John the Baptizer has come eating no bread and drinking no wine, and you say, "He has a demon." And the Son of Man has come eating and drinking, and you say, "Behold a glutton and a drunkard, a friend of tax-collectors and sinners!"   (Lk 7:33–34//Mt 11:18–19)

Finally, the Gospels suggest that the priests in Jerusalem—Jesus' ultimate antagonists in the Passion narratives—were also unfriendly toward John. Contesting with the chief priests, scribes, and elders in the Temple in the days before Passover, Jesus embarrasses them by asking them publicly whether they thought that "the baptism of John was from heaven or from men? Answer me." The rest of the story gives an interesting index of John's appeal and authority even after his death:

> They argued with one another, "If we say, 'From heaven,' he will say, 'Then why did you not believe him?' But shall we say, 'From men'?— they were afraid of the people, for all held that John was a real prophet. So they answered Jesus, "We do not know."   (Mk 11:30–33)

Matthew's Jesus more pointedly condemns these men for not "receiving" John. In his retelling of this scene at the Temple, Matthew has Jesus reprimand the chief priests, saying that harlots and toll collectors will enter the Kingdom before them. "For John came to you in the way of righteousness, and you did not believe him, but the tax collectors and the harlots believed him; and even when you saw it [i.e., the effects of John's preaching], you did not believe" (21:32).

So who was John to Jesus? A mentor of some sort: They both shared the message of the coming Kingdom. A model? Yes and no. If we can rely on John 3:22, cited above, Jesus also baptized, at least for a while; but clearly that activity was not as central a part of his mission, and it left no trace in the Synoptics at all. Similarly, this datum would indicate that bodily purity was also important to Jesus, but that he did not orient his mission and message around it.

Some of their ethical instruction was similar: John's directions to the "multitudes," the toll collectors, and the soldiers coming to him (uniquely reported in Lk 3:10–14)—to share clothing and food with the poor, desist from graft, violence, lying, and greed—echo traditions also attributed to Jesus ("Give to everyone who begs from you," 6:29; cf. much of the instruction given in Matthew's Sermon on the Mount). As befits a mission of repentance, both addressed themselves especially to sinners (cf. Mk 2:17, "I came not to call the righteous, but sinners").

But their modus operandi differed. John lived as an ascetic; Jesus clearly did not, as the Q-saying quoted above attests. He evidently was no enthusiast for voluntary fasting. "People came to him and said, 'Why do John's disciples fast and the disciples of the Pharisees fast, but your disciples do not fast?" (Mk 2:18 and parr.). Biblically mandated fast days, however, such as Yom Kippur—*the* fast, in Jewish tradition— were another matter, and Matthew's Jesus instructs his followers on the correct way to observe these ("And when you fast, do not look dismal . . . but anoint your head and wash your face, that your fasting may be seen not by men but by the Father," 6:16–17). John's "disciples"— were they simply people who received immersion from him and attempted to live by the precepts he set, or did something else distinguish them?—did not stay with him in the wilderness: The Gospels present them in the Galilee (e.g., Mk 2:18, cited above). Jesus seems to have traveled with an entourage and a specially designated group of twelve. And while John ranged around the banks of the Jordan, Jesus seems to have taken his message to villages, synagogues, and marketplaces in and around the Galilee, and to the Temple in Jerusalem (Mk 11:27–12:24 and parr.; many times in Jn, as we shall see).

Finally, both called Israel to repentance in the face of the coming Kingdom, though their styles and characteristic emphases differed. John's apocalyptic message seems to have encouraged reform particularly by the threat of harsh judgment. "His winnowing fork is in his hand," says John of the "mightier one" who will come after him; "and he will clear his threshing floor and gather his wheat into the granary, but the chaff he will burn with unquenchable fire" (another Q-tradition, Mt 3:12//Lk 3:17).

Gospel traditions also attribute many such threats to Jesus. He pronounces dire warnings against villages that do not receive his message. When the Kingdom comes, "it will be more tolerable on that day for Sodom than for that town" (Lk 10:12//Mt 10:15). He utters woes against Galilean cities—Chorazin, Bethsaida, Capernaum—that did not respond to his call to repentance, "for if the mighty works done in you had been done in Tyre and Sidon, they would have repented long ago, sitting in sackcloth and ashes" (Mt 11:20–24//Lk 10:13–15). He warns unrepentant sinners: "I tell you, on the day of judgment men will render account for every careless word they utter; for by your words will you be justified, and by your words you will be condemned" (Mt 12:36–37). "The men of Nineveh will arise at the judgment with this generation and condemn it; for they repented at the preaching of Jonah, and there is something greater than Jonah here" (Q again: Lk 11:32//Mt 12:41). In Matthew's parable of the weeds mixed with the wheat (13:24–30 and 36–43) and of the good and bad fish gathered into one net (13:47–50), Jesus dwells on the way that, "at the close of the age," the righteous will be separated from the evil doers, who will burn in the eschatological fire, weeping and gnashing their teeth (vv. 49–50). The rich man who does not give charity is rightly condemned to the flames (the parable of the rich man and Lazarus, Lk 16:19–31); the fig tree that does not yield good fruit will be cut down (Lk 13:9). Better to pluck out an eye, to cut off hand or foot, than to be led into sin by them, and so risk being thrown into hell, "where the worm does not die and the fire is not quenched" (Mk 9:42–48 and parr.).

Yet, to generalize from other sayings and parables also attributed to him, Jesus also spoke of surprising reversals of fortune that the Kingdom would occasion. Prostitutes and toll collectors would precede chief priests into the Kingdom (Mt 21:31). When the Kingdom arrived, many of the first would be last, and the last first (Mk 10:31 and parr.; Matthew attaches this saying to the conclusion of his parable of the laborers in the vineyard, where latecomers are paid the same full-day's wage as those there since morning, 20:1–16). Further—again on the evidence of the Gospel traditions ascribed to him—Jesus not only echoed John's theme of God's burning anger and judgment; he also called sinners to repentance by encouraging them to consider God's surpassing love, leniency, and compassion. "If you, who are evil, know how to give good gifts to your children, how much more will your Father who is in heaven give good things to those who ask him!" (Mt 7:11). Heaven rejoices over the repentant sinner, just as a woman rejoices over finding a lost coin, or a father over the return of a prodigal son (Lk 15:8–32). God does and will judge, Jesus, like John, urged. But unlike John, he added: God is compassionate as well as just; though he loves the righteous, he also loves the sinner and seeks him out (indeed, just as Jesus did, again unlike John, in his mission). Accordingly, the sinner who harkened to Jesus' call need not fear God's wrath—indeed, he should fear it less than should the righteous who did not receive Jesus' message.

More than the certainty of the coming Endtime prompts the synoptic Jesus to invoke God's justice against recalcitrant sinners, however. So, too, does the temperament and tendency of those who do repent. Jesus' first warning, to the sinner, is: God *judges*. But his consequent warning, to the repentant, is: *God* judges. Men therefore should not; and when they do, they should know that God will judge them by the same standard that they themselves applied to others. "Judge not, that you not be judged. For with the judgment you pronounce you will be judged, and the measure you give will be the measure you get" (Mt 7:1). As many times as one's brother sins against him, that many times should one forgive ("Not seven times, but seventy times seven," Mt 18:22). In other words, the call to repentance issued both by John and, subsequently, by Jesus, asserted that God would forgive the penitent sinner. But this great characteristic of the Father in heaven, Jesus also urged, established a principle of reciprocity between his sinful children on earth. They, too, should forgive one other, generously and sincerely—"from your heart" (Mt 18:35).

That God forgives those who repent would not come as news to John's or Jesus' audiences: Jews had been assembling scriptures, Psalms, and prayers praising God for his mercy and compassion for almost a millennium by the time they preached. Repentance for sin, further, was an integral feature of Jewish religion, woven into the pattern of the year. The entire people, wherever they lived, were to put aside the "the tenth day of the seventh month" as a day of atonement, as God had instructed them:

> It shall be for you a time of holy convocation, and you shall afflict yourselves and present an offering by fire to the Lord. And you shall do no work on this same day; for it is a day of atonement, to make atonement for you before the Lord your God. . . . It is a statute for ever throughout your generations in all your dwellings. It shall be to you a Sabbath of solemn rest, and you shall afflict yourselves; on the ninth day of the month beginning at evening, from evening to evening. (Lv 23:27–32)

The reason that the message of John and of Jesus sounded in the ears of their contemporaries as prophecy rather than as simply a call to reform was thus not its moral content—this was, to stress the point again, a deeply traditional theme in Jewish piety—but its urgency, the way that they both coupled their call to repentance with their authoritative pronouncement that the times were fulfilled and the Kingdom of heaven was at hand (Mk 1:15; Mt 3:2 [John], 4:17 [Jesus]). Those who came to John for baptism, seeking him out in the wilderness by the lower Jordan, would have already acknowledged the authority of his message: This, indeed, would be why they came. John then personally immersed them, purifying their bodies since they through their repentance had already purified their souls.

Jesus, by contrast, went looking for his hearers. According to the Gospels, he sought them out; they did not come first to him. Calling out to those who had not (as with John's hearers) already acknowledged him—or indeed, perhaps, even heard of him—he asserted *his* authority to pronounce this message through healings and exorcisms, performing "startling deeds" and "mighty works" (Josephus' and the Gospels' characterization); and he authorized his disciples to spread the gospel of the coming Kingdom by doing the same. According to the synoptic tradition, this strategy worked: When Jesus began his mission, people started to flock to him because of his power to cure. And he pointed to this power, according to Q, to legitimate his mission even to John, whose disciples inquired about him on account of his deeds.

> Go and tell John what you hear and see: the blind receive their sight and the lame walk, lepers are cleansed and the deaf hear, and the dead are raised up, and the poor have good news preached to them. And blessed is he who takes no offense at me.   (Mt 11:4–6//Lk 7:22–23)

Perhaps, too, this is why the evangelists present so many of his early exorcisms as occurring "in the synagogue" where people are gathered—which is to say, on a Sabbath. Since—again, unlike John—Jesus came upon people in their usual habitation, the only time (as he knew) that they would be assembled, and thus able to witness his deeds and hear his message, was on the Sabbath: Any other day would find them scattered among their various occupations. Rather than think that his appearances in synagogue assemblies on Shabbat were intended as confrontational (as commentators frequently conjecture), the choice may well have been simply and eminently practical. He could first preach ("on the Sabbath he entered the synagogue and taught," Mk 1:21), and then, when and if his hearers were startled by his teaching ("and they were astonished, for he taught them as one who had authority," v. 22), he could reinforce his message with a demonstration of power ("and immediately there was in their synagogue a man with an unclean spirit," whom Jesus heals, vv. 23–28). It was in this way, comment the evangelists, that his fame spread (e.g., Mk 1:28, 39).

What then, finally, was Jesus' relation to John? Did Jesus replace John, once the latter was arrested? Or was he in a sense John's junior colleague, working alongside him after his own baptism to likewise broadcast the message of the coming Kingdom? Mark presents the first scenario ("Now after John was arrested, Jesus came into Galilee, preaching the gospel of God and saying, 'Repent, for the Kingdom of God is at hand,' " Mk 1:14–15); the Fourth Gospel, the second ("Jesus and his disciples went into the land of Judea. There he . . . baptized. John also was baptizing at Aenon near Salim. . . . for John had not yet been put into prison," Jn 3:22–24). But whichever the sequence of their respective missions, whatever the differences in their strategies of presentation, Jesus shared with John the same urgent message to prepare for God's fast-approaching Kingdom.

JESUS AND PURITY

Given the strong association of immersions with the Baptizer's mission, we could equally well think of him as "John the Purifier." John was a key figure in Jesus' life and, in a sense, the starting point of Jesus' own mission. What then, if anything, can be inferred from their relationship, as well as from other evidence in the Gospels, about Jesus' own perspective on the biblical laws of purity?

The purity codes were intimately aligned with the ancient system of sacrifices, and both are distant from and often unfamiliar to most modern readers of New Testament texts. To complicate the issue, the term "impurity" in Jewish biblical texts can function in two different ways. The first had no moral content or implication, but rather expressed a specific, objective, contagious state: Scholars often refer to this as "ritual" or "levitical" impurity. Many of these impurities would be contracted involuntarily through bodily functions—menstruation, ejaculation, childbirth, genital flux, skin disease—though sometimes they could be the result of deliberate actions as well. (Burying the dead, or burning the red heifer to prepare the water of purification for corpse-pollution, are two divinely mandated activities that render their agents *tameh*—unclean or impure.) Most people, under normal circumstances, would be in this state of impurity most of the time.

The chief practical effect of many of these impurities in Jesus' period was to restrict access to the Temple. But most people (excepting, that is, the priests serving in Jerusalem) were not in the Temple most of the time. When they did enter, they would first resort to the various procedures—usually some combination of washing and waiting—prescribed in the Bible for removing such pollutions. The remedy for this type of impurity, thus, was purification, which might involve particular offerings as well. (We will see how when we consider a case of leprosy, below, Mk 1:40–44.)

Scholars designate the second type of impurity "moral" or "spiritual" to distinguish it from the first. Moral impurity has to do with the defiling nature of sin. Such defilements, since assumed to be contracted voluntarily, obtained exclusively to the individual sinner. Its remedy had a twin focus, which we might understand as both "moral" and "ritual." The moral remedy was repentance, the ritual remedy atonement. But the biblical prescriptions and, we might imagine, those ancient people who lived by them, envisage these as two aspects of a single movement of "return," of turning the heart back to God. It was the idea and activity of purification that bound inner/moral and outer/ritual into one process, as indeed Josephus' notice on John the Baptizer states: John immersed penitents for the purification of the flesh once they had already cleansed their souls through righteousness (*AJ* 18.117). Through the inner act of repentance the sinner put the defiling activity away from himself; through purification and atonement—some sort of offering, often scaled according to the sinner's economic means—the penitent removed the pollution of his sin from the altar of God, where it had accrued.

John the Baptizer had linked his apocalyptic warnings and his call to repentance to a ritual of purification. If Jesus in fact practiced immersing penitent sinners, as the Fourth Gospel states, then he did too. Even if he did not, however, both men, as Jews calling fellow Jews to repent, were summoning their hearers to return to "the ways of the Lord"—to God's instructions in piety and righteousness as conveyed in his Torah. Part and parcel of this instruction were the laws of purity.

This may seem like an uncontroversial observation. In fact, it has been vigorously contested in many recent reconstructions of the historical Jesus. These reconstructions have argued that, as part of his mission to Israel, Jesus took his stand precisely *against* the biblical laws of purity. Whatever moral content these scholars ascribe to Jesus' mission—an ethos and politics of compassion; a commitment to radical social egalitarianism; a repudiation of violent Jewish nationalism—the purity laws function to represent its opposite. Assessments of status, social and sexual hierarchy, unjust distribution of power crystallizing especially around the Temple in Jerusalem: The purity laws and the type of religion and society they supported, claim these scholars, literally embodied everything Jesus was against.

Such an understanding of the evidence gives added moral depth to the evangelists' depictions of Jesus' activity. What, during his mission, did Jesus actually do? He traveled, eating with people he encountered and sharing their table ("practicing commensality"). He healed the sick, frequently through touch. He called women as well as men to receive his message of the Kingdom. And finally, in the last week of his life, he challenged the priestly construction of correct worship by turning over the tables of the money changers in the Temple.

Encoded in this activity, these scholars argue, are the outlines of Jesus' vision. He fought against the social, economic, and gender stratifications of his society. Accordingly, he fought against the codes of purity as well. Eating with the poor, embracing outcasts and sinners, Jesus in effect ignored distinctions of purity. Touching and healing the sick—the leper, the demoniac, the hemorrhaging woman—"shattered" or "subverted" ritual law. And demonstrating his contempt for the monopoly on forgiveness proclaimed by the Temple with its system of atoning sacrifices, Jesus independently proclaimed the forgiveness of sin, knowing that God desired mercy and not sacrifices.

In these revisionist reconstructions, the Temple itself stands as the ultimate target of Jesus' critique. More than just the privileged location of the "purity elite" (that is, the priests), the Temple in this view supported exactly the economically and socially oppressive hierarchy that this Jesus fights to undermine. Enraged at its splendor, disgusted by its grandiose wastefulness, repulsed by the monopoly on forgiveness exploited by its sacrificial cult, or perhaps alarmed by the belligerent nationalism it focused and encouraged, Jesus symbolically threw over the Temple's—or perhaps the priests'—function when he overturned the money changers' tables. He thereby infuriated the priests and so courted his own death.

One virtue of this reading is that it can coherently unite Jesus' Galilean mission with his Judean death. The purity laws provide the traction for the entire movement of Jesus' public career, which accordingly must be reconstructed basically upon Markan lines, since his action in the Temple is what gets him killed. (John's Gospel, remember, presents a quite different chronology. His Jesus overturns the tables already in chapter 2 and subsequently makes multiple trips to Jerusalem.) Also, by so targeting the laws of purity, these reconstructions bind together what Jesus preached with why he died, or at least with the reason why the priests would want him dead: his antipurity stance, enacted as it were in their own front yard, undermined their authority and insulted their office.

Another virtue is the way that this reading closes the gap between Jesus' day and our own. Such a Jesus—caring, staunchly egalitarian, antinationalist—is immediately, comfortably relevant to our own concerns. Indeed, he battles the same social ills that bedevil thoughtful people in the modern West: economic inequality, racial and national prejudice, even sexism. And he does so—a third virtue—by energetically repudiating codes of religious behavior that have been largely irrelevant to the practice of Christianity since 70 C.E., namely, the rules concerning purity and the etiquette for approaching the sacrificial altar.

But this interpretation of the Gospels' material is compromised, first of all, by a failure to think concretely. If the evangelists' stories about Jesus indeed bridge the gap between the time of their composition (c. 75–90 C.E.) and his mission (c. 28–30 C.E.)—the presupposition of any quest for the historical Jesus—then they must be construed within the social context they purport to describe, namely early first-century Second Temple Judaism. Thus: Why suppose that Jesus, by touching someone (for example, a leper, Mk 1:41) or being touched by someone (the hemorrhaging woman, Mk 5:25) who was ritually impure, thereby "disregarded" and so "subverted" the purity laws? In his own time and culture, after such defiling contact, Jesus would simply undergo a ritual cleansing himself in order to be purified. Absent the presupposition of hostility to purity codes, why think that he would not or did not? Similarly with eating with known sinners and/or toll collectors: Jesus by so doing would be in no danger through such association of contracting (moral) defilement. Nor should his behavior have scandalized others. As the Gospels depict his mission, Jesus did not say, "Continue sinning and you'll get into my father's Kingdom anyway." Their putting aside sinful behavior, on the contrary, would be the measure of the degree to which such people had "heard" Jesus' message. In real life (to the degree that these Gospel stories approximate it), neither instance of his behavior constitutes a "flagrant violation" or "radical disregard" for purity rules, which for Jesus as for his contemporaries were God's law.

Understanding the purity rules within their own social context makes it difficult to see them as chiefly a cipher for Jesus' moral opposite. For instance, within the ancient Jewish system purity does not correspond to social class and therefore cannot coherently serve as a prime support of supposed class structures. The purity rules were incumbent upon all Israel; and the priests—in these reconstructions the supposed perpetrators and beneficiaries of this oppressive system—had *more* purity rules than anybody else because of their responsibilities in the Temple.

Since impurity and purity were states that one moved in and out of, they could hardly serve to stratify society along class lines. Indeed, one could argue the opposite: Since they affected everybody, their effect was radically equalizing. The lowliest peasant who had just completed the ritual of the red heifer was pure, the most aristocratic chief priest, having just buried a parent, was not. The fussiest Pharisee, the highest high priest, would be neither more nor less impure after sexual intercourse than the scruffiest Galilean fisherman. Furthermore, in all three of these cases, only the priest's normal social activity would be affected, because his workplace was the Temple. For the Pharisee or the fisherman, this impurity would have no social effect. To see impurity as a quasi-permanent state, then, or to imagine such a state as corresponding to social class, is simply wrong.

But what about the sexism of ancient Jewish society? According to the Jesus-as-feminist construct, first-century Jewish society and religion excluded and devalued women, and the purity laws were part and parcel of this oppression. But Jesus, by contrast (so goes the argument), famously reached out to women as well as men. He thereby shattered the conventions of purity, subverted its rules, and scandalized his contemporaries.

Upon reflection, this argument also seems strained. As we have already seen, the category "impure" is gender-blind. A healthy adult Jewish female would incur impurity on a regular basis, through menses; but so would her husband, through his own semen, after intercourse. Impurity is conveyed by menstrual blood and semen both. During her pregnancy, all things being equal, a wife would be pure while her husband, after a nocturnal emission, would not be. Some impurities are specific only to one gender, while others—leprosy, corpse-pollution—apply equally to both. As with class, so with gender: Purity rules were in principle binding on all Israel (though different Jews interpreted the various biblical injunctions differently). Observant men as well as women were equally affected. And the same means of purification were open to all.

To erect on the foundation of Leviticus and Numbers a superstructure of supposed Jewish sexism is one way, of course, to purchase immediate ethical relevance for Jesus. He can then exorcise this modern demon for us, conferring by his example approval of our own egalitarian agenda. Like oppressive class distinctions or gross inequalities of power and/or wealth, sexism bothers most or many of us in the modern West.

But before our own day, how universal or morally evident would such issues have seemed? We strain sometimes to understand our parents' views of things because their instincts and outlook can differ so markedly from our own—a gap of a mere generation. We are charmed or alarmed by the social world of Jane Austen's Elizabeth Bennet and Mr. Darcy because it is so distant and different from ours—a gap of less than two centuries within an arguably continuous culture. We are struck by the brutality and repugnance of chattel slavery and child labor—though most Americans, a short 150 years ago, were not. How much more different from ours, then, must the instincts and outlook of an ancient people in a completely different culture be? How then can we presume to import our values or political agendas across millennia to serve as an explanatory construct for their actions?

In brief, the more facile the ethical or political relevance that a particular construct of Jesus presents, the more suspect its worth as history. Only ancient evidence, not modern agendas, can reveal what might have mattered to ancient people. Whatever Jesus taught, however he lived, the fact that his mission gave rise to a movement means that he had to make sense first of all to his own contemporaries. We have to understand them to understand him. And while class struggle or sexism or an intense and immediate association of religion and "nationalism" may weigh heavily on the minds of twentieth-century First World liberals, we gain little insight into ancient societies by projecting our political sensibilities onto and into them. And finally, though we may have difficulty—unlike ancient people—in finding religious or spiritual meaning in the concept of purity, or in ritual generally, our difficulties tell us nothing about theirs.

At several points in this study, I have urged that the person in search of the past must affect an innocence of the future. Our knowledge of how events ultimately worked out too easily gives us a false perspective on how they came to be. In search of the historical Jesus and, thus, Christian origins, this is particularly so, because we so easily use what the movement shortly became as the interpretive framework for how it started and why. Its post-Temple future—the matrix for all New Testament writings save Paul's—thus interprets its past. Jesus (as indeed also John the Baptizer) thus ends up opposing his own native Judaism, its sole human context, the Jewish people, its ancient rites and ritual protocols, and its own chief holy site. The movement's post-Temple, post-Torah-observant gentile future, we all know, lay just around the corner, so that must be the direction in which Jesus left it heading.

But in fact the Gospel narratives should be read with the opposite presumption in mind. We must begin from the premise that Jesus was truly a Jew of his own time—had he not been, he would not have had first-century Jewish followers. Absent specific instructions on purity in what we can reconstruct of his teaching, we should assume *not* that Jesus ignored or opposed Jewish purity codes, but rather that he took them for granted as fundamental to the worship of the God who had revealed them, uniquely, to Israel. Indeed, read without the future impinging on their interpretation, the Gospels themselves, though products of a later period, nevertheless still present a Jesus embedded securely and coherently in the religious world—and, hence, the purity laws—of late Second Temple Judaism.

A manifest example of this embeddedness of purity rules is a story related in Mark 1:40–44, where Jesus cures a leper by touching him.

> A leper came to him beseeching him, and kneeling said to him, "If you will, you can make me clean." Moved with pity, he stretched out his hand and touched him and said to him, "I will; be clean." And immediately the leprosy left him, and he was made clean. And he sternly charged him, and sent him away at once, and said to him, "See that you say nothing to any one; but go, *show yourself to the priest, and offer for your cleansing what Moses commanded,* for a proof to the people."

"What Moses commanded" appears in some detail in Leviticus 14 when God, speaking to Moses, says, "This shall be the law of the leper for the day of his cleansing" (Lv 14:1). After a thorough examination by the priest, the (former) leper is given "two clean living birds and cedarwood and scarlet stuff and hyssop" (v. 4). One bird is slain in an earthenware vessel over running water, and the other elements of the sacrifice (living bird, cedar, scarlet stuff, hyssop) dipped in its blood. The ex-leper is next sprinkled seven times with the slain bird's blood. He is then pronounced clean, and the living bird released (vv. 5–7). After washing his clothes, shaving off all hair, and bathing, the ex-leper waits seven days, and then shaves again (beard, eyebrows, everything, the text specifies, v. 9). Again he bathes, "and he shall be clean."

But then a longer list of offerings "on the eighth day" ensues: two male lambs without blemish, one perfect, year-old ewe, a cereal offering of fine flour mixed with oil, and a unit of oil itself. The priest uses these to follow a detailed protocol of slaughter, anointing, sprinkling, and burning (vv. 11–20). "Thus the priest shall make atonement for him, and he shall be clean" (v. 20). Other details follow: an alternative list of offerings ("But if he is poor and cannot afford so much," v. 21) scaled to the means of the worshiper. "This is the law for him . . . who cannot afford the offerings for his cleansing" (v. 32). God then moves on to explain the procedure for diagnosing leprosy in houses (vv. 33–53).

There is no way to know whether anything like this exchange between Jesus and a leper ever actually took place. But that is not the point. Rather, it is Mark's story itself. His Jesus invokes an elaborate ceremony of purification here. Its details are unknown to most modern readers. But for any of Mark's Jewish hearers, and perhaps for those Gentiles associated with his diaspora community through the synagogue, these protocols of the law for the cleansing of a leper would have been familiar, a matter of public knowledge: Not once but many times through the years they would have heard it read aloud, discussed its interpretation, and related it by comparison or contrast to other such commands. This communal, oral learning of the Law was a standard part of synagogue culture, the chief reason for communal gatherings on Shabbat.

Mark elsewhere, of course, is perfectly capable of presenting Jesus, or interpreting him, as controverting purity laws. In chapter seven, his Jesus criticizes Pharisaic extensions of these codes (ritual hand-washing before meals, purifications after returning from market, immersing eating utensils, 7:3–4), and Mark interprets him as refuting the food laws generally (7:19; cf. Mt 15:17–20). But when Mark does not belabor some controversy between Jesus and his Jewish contemporaries, he presents a normally Law-observant character. Even the procedures for the ex-leper alluded to at Mark 1:44, though they strike us as elaborate, in antiquity would have constituted "normally Law-observant." And that is how an ancient audience would have understood Jesus in this story.

Jesus' observance of biblical purity codes lurks at a latent level in evangelical accounts, too. "Latent" here refers to those incidents in

Gospel narrative obliquely touching on a purity issue that does not in itself figure prominently, but does unobtrusively shape the story. Consider the instruction Matthew's Jesus gives his followers during the Sermon on the Mount:

> So when you offer your gift at the altar, if you remember that your brother has something against you, leave your gift there before the altar and go; first be reconciled to your brother, and then come and offer your gift. (Mt 5:23–24)

Think: In this culture, a worshiper would have to be in a state of purity in order to stand "before the altar." (Even the eventual, formerly pagan gentile hearers of Matthew's Gospel would assume this, since pagan religious etiquette also required purification before offering a sacrifice.) Why would Matthew's audience presuppose that Matthew's believer who worships at the Temple's altar would disregard the biblical laws of purity (which would require his having immersed before entering the area), while observing what they were linked to, the laws of offerings? More likely, Matthew's original ancient audience would suppose that this worshiper would have prepared properly to approach the altar; and that, therefore, is what they would have heard the evangelist's Jesus saying, too.

So, too, with the Gospel traditions about Jesus' pilgrimages to Jerusalem, related in both the Synoptics and John. John mentions four such journeys: twice for Passover (2:13; 11:55), once for an unspecified feast (5:1), and once for Sukkot (7:10), when Jesus lingers in the city from early autumn through winter until the extrabiblical Feast of Dedication celebrating the Maccabees' purification of the Temple (10:22). Entry into the Temple at festivals required special purification; entry at other times, at least immersion before nightfall of the day before entering the area to make an offering. Worshipers had access to immersion pools near the Temple compound specifically for this purpose. Implicit in these stories of Jesus' going to the Temple for these holy days is Jesus' observing the biblically mandated purity protocols to enter. The evangelists' ancient audiences would have no reason to think otherwise. Without the presupposition of an antipurity Jesus, neither would their modern audience.

The Passion narratives, finally, provide two more instances where Jesus' observance of purity rules is obliquely assumed by the shape of the story. In the first, the Gospels portray Jesus entering the city together with many other pilgrims. These pilgrims account for the celebrating crowds who usher Jesus into Jerusalem (the so-called Triumphal Entry; Mk 11:7–10 and parr.; Jn 12:12–15) and who later gather to hear him preach in the Temple in the days before the feast (Mk 14:1; Mt 11:15 ff.; Lk 19:45 ff.; cf. Jn 2:13–17). What are he and they all doing there?

The paschal meal had to be eaten in a state of purity, including and especially purity from corpse contact (Nm 9:6). This required that pilgrims be in the city at least seven days in advance of the beginning of the feast, the evening of 14 Nisan, in order to undergo the weeklong rite of purification. God through Moses gave the details in Numbers 19:11–12: "Those who touch a dead body shall be unclean seven days. They shall purify themselves with *the water* on the third day and the seventh day, and so shall be clean." The "water" in question was mixed with the ashes of the immolated red heifer. Pilgrims in Jerusalem for the festival would receive this sprinkling of special water on the designated days. If Jesus indeed entered the city with these other pilgrims, and if he indeed taught the holiday crowds during the days before the feast from within the Temple compound, then he would have been there, as they were, to be purified through this special rite. This is the presupposition of the story; and, if the story has any relation to actual fact, this would have been Jesus' purpose too.

The second and last example of a purity observance presupposed by the Passion narratives—observance specifically of this rite of corpse-purification—comes in traditions of the Last Supper. The Passover meal that Jesus and his disciples celebrate in the synoptic Gospels presupposes that they all had been purified in order to eat the meal. And at least one of their number would have gone to the Temple late in the afternoon of that same day in order to slay the corban Pesach, the goat or lamb, or they could not have held the biblically mandated commemorative meal.

All these details go unmentioned in the evangelists' stories. They inform the shape of their narratives nonetheless. This may seem to some readers like an argument from silence, and in a way it is: No evangelist states, "And while Jesus and his disciples were all gathered in the Temple for the rite of purification in the days before the feast" (though cf. Jn 11:55). But the loudness of this silence in this instance gives the measure of our own *un*familiarity with and distance from the ancient world of both Jesus and these early Christians, whether Jews or Gentiles. We stand outside the religious context that they all shared, and so must work to recapture what they and their ancient audiences would have presumed.

THE CLEANSING OF THE TEMPLE

If this argument is correct—that the historical Jesus of Nazareth kept the biblical purity laws, and that the original audiences of the evangelists, hearing their stories, would have no reason to think otherwise— then what sense can be made of the evangelists' report of Jesus' action in the Temple? This is Mark's version of the incident:

> And they came to Jerusalem. And he entered the Temple and began to drive out those who sold and those who bought in the Temple, and he overturned the tables of the moneychangers and the seats of those who sold pigeons; and he would not allow anyone to carry anything through the Temple. And he taught and said to them, "Is it not written, 'My house shall be called a house of prayer for all the nations?' But you have made it a den of robbers." And the chief priests and the scribes heard it and they sought a way to destroy him; for they feared him, because all the multitude was astonished by his teaching.
>
> (Mk 11:15–19)

John's version, more dramatic and elaborate, comes at the beginning of his Gospel, also just before Passover.

> The Passover of the Jews was at hand, and Jesus went up to Jerusalem. In the Temple he found those who were selling oxen and sheep and pigeons, and the moneychangers at their business. And making a whip of cords, he drove them all, with the sheep and oxen, out of the Temple; and he poured out the coins of the money-changers and overturned their tables. And he told those who sold pigeons, "Take these things away; you shall not make my Father's house a house of trade."
>
> (Jn 2:13–16)

This scene is inscribed in church tradition as the "Cleansing of the Temple." Cleansed of what? The quotations from the prophets adduced by the synoptic evangelists, who combine Isaiah 65:7–8 ("a house of prayer for all the nations") and Jeremiah 7:11 ("den of robbers"), provide one interpretation. Jesus, in upsetting the tables of "those who sold," protested against such commerce within the Temple precincts: Apparently he considered it dishonest. The Johannine Jesus' remark also touches on this theme.

Until recently, modern commentators had followed the evangelists' lead. Such commercial enterprise, they have argued, did indeed pollute the Temple, or compromise its religious function. In driving the traders and money changers out, Jesus was therefore restoring its purity of worship, "cleansing" the holy site of commerce.

Within the last two decades, however, as scholars have increasingly interpreted the New Testament within a context of actual first-century Jewish practice, the coherence of this traditional view has dissolved. For one thing, it makes no historical sense. The function of the Temple—as indeed, of any temple in the ancient Mediterranean—was to serve as a place for offering sacrifices. In Jerusalem since the days of Solomon it had never been otherwise. Only unblemished pigeons or animals would do, and this is what these support services supplied. Pilgrims—such as Jesus' parents in Luke's nativity story—could thus purchase such offerings once they arrived at the Temple area (Lk 2:24). And since the Temple relied on the Tyrian shekel (its silver content was stable and reliable), money changers—doubtless for a fee—converted the various currencies of wayfaring worshipers to this standard coinage. Pigeon vendors and money changers, in other words, facilitated the pilgrims' worship of God as he had commanded Israel through Moses at Sinai. Jesus' gesture therefore could not have encoded "restoring" Temple service to some supposed pristine ideal, because there had never been a time when its service did not involve offerings.

Jews throughout the empire and beyond voluntarily contributed the half-shekel Temple tax precisely toward the support of these sacrifices. "To think of leaving off those sacrifices is to every Jew plainly impossible," says Josephus. The people would "rather give up their lives than the worship which they are accustomed to offer God" (*AJ* 15.248). The priests, too, took their mandate no less seriously. Josephus relates how, in 63 B.C.E., when the Roman general Pompey successfully besieged Jerusalem, the priests continued making offerings even as Pompey stormed the Temple (*AJ* 14.65–68). "At the very hour when the Temple was taken, when they were being massacred about the altar, they never desisted from the religious rites for the day" (*BJ* 1.148). Even more incredibly, in light of the greater social chaos and extreme suffering and famine that prevailed in the city during Titus' final siege, both priests and people collaborated to continue with the daily offerings almost to the very end (*BJ* 6.93–95).

How then do we fit this report of Jesus' action into the solid evidence we have that Jews everywhere overwhelmingly supported the Temple service? If by this gesture he were repudiating the sacrifices themselves, he would be utterly unique among both Jews and even Gentiles of his own period: In antiquity, worship entailed offerings. Even the Essenes, alienated from the current priesthood and keeping their distance from the Temple, did not repudiate the sacrifices per se: They thought, rather, that the service should be run by their own lights, and they looked forward to doing exactly that once God established them in Jerusalem. Such a repudiation on Jesus' part, further, would be tantamount to rejecting the five books of Torah, where God had revealed the protocols and purposes of these sacrifices to Israel.

If, however, Jesus targeted not the offerings themselves but commerce within the Temple precincts—the support services facilitating these offerings—what then? His action would have no practical significance. Were pilgrims coming in from Egypt or Italy or Babylon supposed to carry their own birds with them? pick them up anywhere? have their own supply of Tyrian coinage, or hope that they would get some somehow during their trip? And on either construction, antisacrifice or antisupport service, even if we look to Christian evidence alone, such a Jesus appears a resounding failure. Those closest to him, his own disciples, evidently failed to grasp this revolutionary religious idea. On the evidence of Paul's letters, the Gospels, and the Acts of the Apostles, these earliest Christians chose to live in Jerusalem, to worship in the Temple, to keep the festivals, the Sabbath, and the food laws, and to regard Torah as the revealed word of God. If Jesus had indeed acted and taught against the Temple service, then his immediate followers completely missed his point.

In light of all these considerations, scholarly opinion on the meaning of the Temple incident has changed. Attention has focused not on what Jesus supposedly said (most scholars regard the lines from Isaiah and Jeremiah as evangelical additions), but on what he did. Without those later guidelines culled from the prophets that the Gospel writers provide, how are we to interpret his gesture, overturning tables?

Scholars read this incident against the immediate backdrop of other evangelical reports about Jesus and the Temple, and against a more general backdrop of traditions about the Temple in Jewish apocalyptic writings. In the Gospels, Jesus shortly after this first incident predicts the Temple's utter destruction when teaching about the End of the Age ("Do you see these great buildings? There will not be left here one stone upon another that will not be thrown down," Mk 13:2 and parr.). A little while later, at his hearing before Jewish authorities, he is accused by "false witnesses" of having threatened to destroy the Temple and to rebuild it—Mark adds, "not with hands"—in three days (Mk 14:57–60; cf. Mt 26:60–62; Acts 6:14). The relevant Temple theme in other Jewish writings—the Dead Sea Scrolls, various other Apocrypha and Pseudepigrapha—is the expectation that, in the new age, in God's kingdom, God would splendidly renew the current Temple or establish a new and more glorious one ("a glorious building for all generations forever," Tb 14:5). Combining all these data with the report of Jesus' action, a different, symbolic meaning emerges. By overturning the tables, Jesus was symbolically enacting an apocalyptic prophecy: The current Temple was soon to be destroyed (understood: not by Jesus, nor by invading armies, but by God), to cede place to the eschatological Temple (understood: not built by the hand of man) at the close of the age.

This interpretation has the benefit of uniting Jesus' gesture with his proclamation of the coming Kingdom of God. And it reintegrates what we know of his disciples' religious behavior after Jesus' death with Jesus' mission beforehand. As a matter of course they would have continued to worship at the Temple: Jesus had never said not to. The Temple incident had nothing to do with any supposed "cleansing," criticism, or condemnation. In symbolizing (apocalyptic) destruction, it pointed ahead to eschatological renewal and rebuilding. Jesus' gesture was simply a dramatic performance of the chief message of his mission, that the Kingdom was, indeed, at hand.

In research on the historical Jesus, however, no single consensus interpretation ever commands 100 percent of the scholarly opinion. Some commentators still hold to some version of the older, traditional view. Other critics, rightly observing the crucial role played by the Temple incident in Mark's rendition of Jesus' story—without it, Mark would have difficulty bringing Jesus to the attention of the priests—question whether it ever happened at all. Actual history rarely obliges narrative plotting so exactly: Perhaps the whole scene is Mark's invention. (Such a view, however, requires that the Fourth Evangelist either knew Mark's Gospel or else this tradition springing from it, since the Temple incident, albeit reinterpreted, also appears in Jn 2.) Still others have ringingly endorsed the position that Jesus' disruption actually symbolized destruction. But since they champion a nonapocalyptic Jesus, they have to redefine what this prophecy of destruction would mean.

Thus Jesus the Jewish peasant Cynic who preaches radical egalitarianism and uses Kingdom language as a way to speak about unmediated ("unbrokered") religious community was a Jesus who ignored and so subverted purity laws. He himself, as impresario of this Kingdom movement, stood in fact as the Temple's opponent, alternative, and substitute. The Temple represented exactly the opposite of what Jesus preached. When he overturned the tables in its courtyard, Jesus symbolically enacted its destruction. Not its apocalyptic destruction—this Jesus is not an apocalyptic prophet—but its religious destruction. Inspired by a radically different view of what society could and should be, Jesus through his symbolic action repudiated Temple worship. The ethical Kingdom he preached would give no place to it.

Or consider Jesus the ethical, egalitarian Spirit-Person. He preached and urged an ethic of compassion; and he, too, used Kingdom-language not apocalyptically but metaphorically, as a way to conjure the vision of a new, kinder society. But purity rules distinguish and discriminate. They reinforced the steep grade of the Second Commonwealth's power pyramid, with large, landholding, aristocratic priestly families at the pinnacle, and their retainers—scribes, lawyers, Pharisees—clustering as near to them as they could get on the higher slopes. At the bottom of this social heap lay the disenfranchised masses, peasants whom the purity elite viewed as degraded, expendable, impoverished, and impure. Jesus the social prophet, engaged in radical social criticism, preaching a universal ethic of love and compassion, subverted these rules in his mission and teaching. The elites preached a politics of purity; Jesus championed the politics of compassion. Thus, when he went up to Jerusalem that fatal Passover, this Jesus overturned the tables, symbolically indicting the Temple and the religious system it stood for. His gesture symbolized not the Temple's destruction, but its rejection. Jesus' action in the Temple repudiated purity and all its works: the political, social, and spiritual oppression that it embodied and enforced.

Or consider the antinationalist Jesus. This Jesus sought to reform his native religion in part by targeting specifically the purity laws. These laws discriminated against the ill, holding them to be ritually unclean and thus cut off from the people of God. But Jesus, with the message "God loves you," went out to the sick. He welcomed the poor and the outcast. He rejected his coreligionists' obsessions with exclusiveness and purity (be it ritual or racial; this last buttressed distinctions between Jew and Gentile, thus shoring up Israel's threatened identity). The Temple stood for all these things, and for that alone Jesus would have condemned it. But worse: It stood as the symbolic center of Judaism's violent nationalism. When he went up to Jerusalem that last Passover, Jesus enacted a prophecy of the Temple's destruction. If Jews did not give up their nationalist obsessions, the Temple would be destroyed. Not by Jesus, certainly, but by God, working through the agency of a foreign army, Rome, as he had in the days of the Babylonian Exile. (And alas, Jews did not listen; and so Jesus' prophecy was fulfilled.) Jesus denounced military action; he radically urged that one love one's enemies. Israel should be a light to the nations, not a religiously arid, unkind, xenophobic national power. In one highly condensed gesture, then, Jesus both enacted God's judgment upon the Temple and predicted its actual military destruction.

These views have been advanced, restated, reasserted, and repeatedly published in academic tomes and in popular format again and again since the mid-1980s. As I write, uncorrected proofs of the latest popular, coauthored version sit on my desk. But in seeing Jesus' gesture as some sort of negative judgment on or action hostile to the Temple and the purity laws, these revisionist proposals recapitulate the essence of the traditional view of Jesus' "cleansing of the Temple," and so are subject to the same criticisms. They misconstrue purity. They remove Jesus from his native context, both religious and social. They shift the emphasis of his message from apocalyptic prophecy to some kind of abstract ethical stance—egalitarianism, compassion, antinationalism—which, though immediately meaningful to us, has little purchase on antiquity. And they render incomprehensible the continued and well-documented Law-observance of Jesus' earliest followers.

But perhaps the most serious problem with any proposal that so focuses on a clash between Jesus and "Judaism" however construed—high-priestly interests, purity and/or "nationalism," or Temple sacrifice, any or all of which Jesus through his mission and finally through this prophetic gesture purportedly challenged or condemned—is that it cannot, finally, account for two of the bedrock facts about Jesus: that at some point he was called "messiah"; and that Rome put him to death.

The term "messiah" did have great interpretive range in Jesus' period. This figure could be a priest, a prophet, a royal warrior, perhaps even an angelic, nonhuman figure (see pp. 123ff.). While all these can encode a symbolic critique of current power arrangements—especially regarding the Hasmonean combination of the two separate offices of priest and king—they also serve as eschatological markers, personages to appear at the End of Days. Does this knowledge help to close the gap between the supposed antipurity Jesus and the term "messiah"?

Of these interpretive possibilities, we can rule out the hazy figure of the nonhuman heavenly or angelic messiah at once: the pre-Resurrection, human Jesus cannot be made to match. The existence of this type of messiah in near-contemporary Jewish sectarian texts cannot account for Jesus' having been identified with the term. The Messiah Son of David—the figure most securely attested in biblical texts—functions eschatologically as a warrior king (he destroys the enemies of Israel) and, subsequently, the prince of peace. A Jesus who refutes purity rules on any grounds—antihierarchy, antidiscrimination, and especially antinationalism (this redeemer-king is precisely "nationalist": the king of *Israel*)—has little to do with such a figure. And the Endtime prophet-messiah seems to function most as a teacher of righteousness. The historical Jesus might reasonably have been interpreted as such, but the term's appropriateness would have little to do with the supposed symbolic action in the Temple, unless we assume that he thought purity rules were intrinsically unrighteous.

The most plausible choice among these various figures, then, might seem to be the priestly messiah. Qumran's sectarians were alienated from the Temple in Jerusalem and hostile to its priesthood (as Jesus, in these reconstructions, is thought to be), and they accordingly held that the Temple's offerings were impure. An eschatological priestly messiah serving in the mammoth Temple that they envisaged for the End of Days would, finally, make "pure" offerings, because he would follow the purity codes of the sect. The Essenes' "remedy" for the Jerusalem Temple's impurity, in other words, was not to jettison purity laws, but to intensify them. This seems a poor fit with the modern antipurity Jesus.

What about Rome's involvement in the revisionist Jesus' death? The proposals surveyed here all claim that Jesus' stance on purity, construed as they understand it, was intrinsically "political" because it and he thereby challenged those in power within his society. And they observe correctly that ancient Jews would not have distinguished between "political" and "religious" as we do.

But "political" within a Jewish context does not translate immediately into "political" in the Jewish-Roman context. Tribute, domestic order, secure boarders, military support in time of war: These were Rome's demands of its subject provinces and allies, and this is the context that matters for understanding Jesus' execution. A Jesus who contests the current understanding and operation of purity codes is utterly irrelevant to these Roman concerns. Why should Pilate have cared about any of these peculiar, intra-Jewish debates? And if it were for a personal reason—namely, because of his long and we must suppose friendly association with Caiaphas—that Pilate agreed as a favor to cooperate in Jesus' death, why then specifically death by crucifixion?

Speculation on what purity might have meant to Jesus cannot help here. But consideration of one more contextual aspect of his mission might provide more purchase on the question of his status as "messiah" for his movement and, immediately linked to this, on the question of his death. What can be known about Jesus' followers?

The Followers of Jesus

WE HAVE ALREADY met some of Jesus' followers in the list that Paul gives of the earliest witnesses to the Risen Christ: "the Twelve," "the brethren" ("more than five hundred"), and "the apostles" (1 Cor 15:5–7; the text is cited in full on p. 90). The synoptic Gospels, however, give the impression that Jesus collected a much larger following than this during his mission in the Galilee. "The whole city" gathers about Jesus after his Sabbath debut in Capernaum (Mk 1:33). People come to him "from every quarter," so that he can no longer enter towns but must meet them out in the countryside (1:45). Great "crowds" gather about him whenever he speaks (2:13, 3:7 "a great multitude," cf. v. 9, 3:20, 4:1 "a very large crowd," 5:21 "a great crowd," and so on). We should therefore probably distinguish between those whom Paul names—they most likely represent a committed core group—and those Jews from various Galilean towns and villages who "followed" Jesus in the sense of going out to hear his teaching and/or solicit cures.

Both groups matter substantially to the later movement. Of those Paul mentions, James and Peter settle in Jerusalem, establishing the new community's "headquarters" (Gal 1:18, 2:1–10; and the opening chapters of Acts). Others (we might include Peter in this group, too) spread Jesus' gospel as itinerant teachers, as perhaps they had during his lifetime; still others from among the brethren, women and men both, may have been householders who supported those wandering. The crowds in the Galilee, on the other hand, form the local communities of villagers, tenant farmers, and other agricultural workers whom scholars see as the human matrix for the (similarly peopled) Q-traditions.

Perhaps, as well, these served eventually as the communities of origin for the Gospel of Mark. If these groups bridge the gap between the later movement and the historical Jesus, then clearly they must have been involved with him, somehow, before his death.

Earlier, when reviewing the traditions in Paul and the Gospels that identify Jesus as Messiah, we came to the conclusion that ascription of the title must have come first during Jesus' mission (see p. 154), which is to say, among his followers, and at some point prior to his death. But when? And why? Here again, we have only the Gospels to turn to, and their double status as products of the post-Resurrection movement as well as reservoirs of historical tradition complicates their use. We have to "look through" the evangelists' theologizing depictions of Jesus as Messiah—the Messiah as one who heals (Mt 12:22–23) or who specifically is crucified and rises in three days (Lk 24:46)—to find what they might tell us about his mission and his followers that can help us with our questions.

The synoptic Gospels' depictions of huge numbers of people coming out to Jesus in the Galilee need to be weighed against what we know did not happen: Antipas never moved against him. Gatherings of four or five thousand people, assembled at one time in one place, would certainly have come to the attention of the tetrarch (Mk 7:44, the miracle of the loaves and fish feeding five thousand men; 8:9, the repeat miracle, feeding four thousand. Mark stages the first miraculous feeding on the western shore of the Sea of Galilee—on the same side, that is, as Antipas' capital, Tiberias). At that point, Jesus would start to look to Antipas the way that Theudas, or the Egyptian, or the signs prophets looked to Roman authorities, and we must assume that Antipas would have responded similarly. The Baptizer, without such standing crowds, had already made him nervous about sedition (*AJ* 18.116–19).

The evangelists' claims that Jesus gathered his enormous audience from all over the region—"a great multitude from Galilee followed; also from Judea and Jerusalem and Idumea and from beyond the Jordan and from about Tyre and Sidon a great multitude, hearing all that he did, came to him" (Mk 3:7–8 and parr.)—also seems dubious, and for the same reason. Also, these scenes are simply unrealistic. Journeys from these regions outside the Galilee would have taken days if not weeks; agricultural workers, villagers, and farmers would not have had the leisure time necessary for the trip. We should thus understand "huge crowds from everywhere" not as a factual description but as an evangelical trope, signaling significance. (Mark, for example, speaks similarly of the Baptizer, who drew "all the country of Judea and all the people of Jerusalem," 1:5). In reality, then, did Jesus attract crowds? Yes, he must have; surely, though, not these huge convocations—several thousands—all at one time.

Did Antipas ever deal with Jesus at all? Mark has him hear of Jesus because of the exorcisms that he and the Twelve work: "King Herod heard of it; for Jesus' name had become known" (Mk 6:14; cf. Lk 9:7). Mark uses this report to segue into his story about the Baptizer's death (vv. 16–29), and Antipas himself makes a connection between John's mission and Jesus'. ("He said, 'John, whom I beheaded, has been raised,' " v. 16). And in chapter 3, evidently aggrieved by Jesus' curing on the Sabbath, Mark's Pharisees hold "counsel with the Herodians against him, how to destroy him" (3:6). We are not told who these people are, and the episode goes nowhere in the story, though the Herodians do show up, again accompanied by Pharisees, on the Temple Mount to entrap Jesus with a (politically) tricky question about paying the Roman tribute (12:13). After this they drop from view.

Luke, uniquely, relates two more episodes connecting Jesus and Antipas. In the first, set in the Galilee, some Pharisees come to warn Jesus: "Get away from here, for Herod wants to kill you." Jesus responds defiantly, "Go and tell that fox, 'Behold, I cast out demons and perform cures today and tomorrow, and on the third day I finish my course . . . for it cannot be that a prophet should perish away from Jerusalem' " (13:31–33). In the second, set in Jerusalem, they do meet, though at Pilate's initiative.

> When he learned that [Jesus] belonged in Herod's jurisdiction, he sent him over to Herod, who was himself in Jerusalem at that time. When Herod saw Jesus, he was very glad, for he had long desired to see him, because he had heard about him, and he was hoping to see some sign done by him. So he questioned him at length; but he made no answer. The chief priests and the scribes stood by, vehemently accusing him. And Herod with his soldiers treated him with contempt and mocked him; then, arraying him in gorgeous apparel, he sent him back to Pilate.   (Lk 23:7–12)

We can base on these reports at least the bare supposition that, perhaps, Antipas was aware of Jesus when the latter was active in the Galilee. To move much beyond this with any confidence is difficult. Evidently Antipas never arrested Jesus, nor (if we put the silence of

Matthew, Mark, John, and Josephus against this single report in Luke) did he ever try to halt his mission. And this datum affords some perspective on the size of the crowds following Jesus. Given first of all the fact that he was crucified, and given also how quickly and widely the message of the movement spread throughout the region after his death, we must suppose that Jesus had more followers than just his core group of Twelve, or Twelve plus the Seventy (Lk 10:1); perhaps he had even more than the "more than five hundred brethren" mentioned by Paul. But huge followings drawn from everywhere in the region are extremely unlikely, again because we know what did not happen—the Galilean mission was uninterrupted—and also because we know what did: Jesus did not die *until* he went to Jerusalem.

This last fact can also help when evaluating a proposal occasionally (and currently) put forward that the reason that Jesus was so clearly and lastingly proclaimed "messiah" was that he had used the title of himself during his own mission. The appealing simplicity of this proposal must also be weighed against what else we know. If Antipas, fearing sedition, executed John when John preached (to combine Josephus and the Gospels) repentance, purity, and the coming judgment preceding the Kingdom, what would he have done with someone actually claiming to be the Messiah? Jesus would have been executed long before reaching Jerusalem. The counterclaim—that Jesus did indeed think of himself as Messiah, but he defined the term against its traditional meanings in a radically new and different way—is itself defeated, again, by what we know: He did have numerous followers. If he claimed the title for himself, its meaning would have had to make sense to them also, not just to him.

And finally, there is the tortuous ingenuity of Matthew and Luke, each in his own way introducing Jesus' messiahship back into the Galilean phase of his mission. They must work so hard in part because they draw on Mark, whose Jesus is notoriously reticent about his messianic identity. Had Jesus of Nazareth, while in the Galilee, ever claimed to be messiah, even if the crowds around him were small enough for Antipas (who nonetheless did know of his miracles?) not to have found out, could it really have left no trace at all in Mark? All the evangelists claim "christ" as a title for Jesus. Had Jesus used it of himself, they would not each have had to work so hard to make their respective, and various, cases.

This last consideration helps narrow the options for where and, thus, when "messiah" became attached to the figure of Jesus. Probably *not* during his mission in the Galilee, for the simple reason that he never ran into trouble there. This leaves Jerusalem as the venue for this claim. And if this acclamation was a factor contributing to Pilate's decision to crucify him, we must assume that its first source was his followers, not (sardonically) his executioners. Yet all the major sources for Jesus—Mark, Q, and the Gospel of John—convey the impression that Jesus' followers, overwhelmingly, were Galileans; Jerusalem, by contrast, seems either indifferent or hostile. This is the picture even in the Fourth Gospel, which uniquely presents Jesus as conducting repeated missions in the city, by comparison scarcely teaching in the Galilee at all.

GALILEANS AND JUDEANS IN JOHN

The Johannine Jesus appears in Jerusalem at Passover already by the second chapter of the Gospel. John sets the "cleansing of the Temple" then, linking it explicitly with Jesus' prediction of its destruction as an oblique Passion prediction. It occasions uncomprehending comment ("The Jews then said, 'It has taken forty-six years to build this temple, and you will raise it up in three days?' But he spoke of the temple of his body," 2:20–21), but no hostility, priestly or otherwise. (In the Synoptics, by contrast, this event, placed at the end of Jesus' mission, brings him to the fatal attention of the chief priests, who thereupon resolve to kill him.) On this particular Passover, John continues, "many believed in his name when they saw the signs that he did" (v. 23). Jesus then pursues his mission in Judea (3:22–4:2), passes through Samaria, where he seems to be proclaimed as Christ (4:3–43, cf. vv. 25, 29), and returns home to a warm welcome in the Galilee.

John's depiction leaves open the possibility that those in Jerusalem who "believed in his name when they saw" the signs Jesus worked (2:23) may have been Galileans themselves. "When he came into the Galilee the Galileans welcomed him, having seen all that he had done in Jerusalem at the feast, for they too had gone to the feast" (4:45). Shortly thereafter, the crowds in the Galilee want to "take him by force to make him king" (6:15). Judea, by contrast, is hostile territory, and Jesus begins to avoid going there. "He would not go about in Judea, because the Judeans [or "Jews": the word in Greek, *Ioudaioi,* can be translated either way] sought to kill him" (7:1; we are not told why).

Despite this absence of local support, Jesus does continue frequenting Jerusalem itself. Up once more, teaching in the Temple during Sukkot/Tabernacles, he again occasions controversy: The "people of

Jerusalem" debate whether he is "the christ" (7:25–31) or "the prophet" (7:40–42). Some Jerusalemites, in particular the Pharisees and chief priests, want to arrest him. No arrest occurs (vv. 43–48), and early the next morning Jesus is in the Temple again (8:2). After a classically lengthy, hostile, and theologically overwrought Johannine dialogue, the *Ioudaioi* take up stones to throw at him, but Jesus eludes them (8:59); meanwhile, they continue to debate whether he is prophet or christ (9:17, 22). Evidently Jesus stays in the city during the several months between Tabernacles in early autumn and the winter festival celebrating the Maccabean purification of the sanctuary, for we next see him again walking in the Temple during this latter feast (10:22). At this point the *Ioudaioi* importune him, "How long will you keep us in suspense? If you are the Christ, tell us plainly" (10:24). Another fraught theological dialogue between them ensues, the mood turns ugly, and they try to arrest him, again to no avail (v. 39).

Jesus leaves Jerusalem for Perea (10:40) and returns to Bethany in Judea to raise his friend Lazarus from the dead (11:1–44). This deed, inexplicably, motivates a gathering of "the council" back in Jerusalem. The chief priests and Pharisees are concerned that the "signs" that Jesus works will bring Rome down upon their heads and lead to the destruction of the Temple and the nation (vv. 45–48). They decide that he must die (vv. 50–53).

Jesus' final Passover, as in the Synoptics, begins with the Triumphal Entry: Celebrating pilgrim crowds welcome him with "Hosanna! Blessed is he who comes in the name of the Lord, *even the King of Israel!*" (12:12–13). And John, similarly to Matthew, quotes Zechariah 9:9 when Jesus rides into the city on an ass. "Fear not, daughter of Zion; behold, *your king is coming,* sitting on an ass' colt!" (12:15). Jesus tells the crowd that he must die by crucifixion; they counter that the Law says "that the Christ remains forever" (vv. 32–34).

This is the last time we see a large gathering of Jesus' followers in John's Gospel. Three long chapters of high Christology intervene between Jesus' entry into the city and his arrest the night before the night of the seder by a mixed group of Roman soldiers and officers of the Temple guard (18:1–11). They lead him to a brief interrogation before Annas, the former high priest; thence to the current high priest, his son-in-law Caiaphas (vv. 13–24); and then, finally, to Pilate. The dialogue between Jesus and Pilate, and the subsequent Crucifixion scene, redound with kingly titles, images, and language (18:33–19:21). The

Ioudaioi, gathered outside Pilate's praetorium, insist on Jesus' death. Jesus hangs under the titulus written by the Roman prefect himself: Jesus of Nazareth, King of the Jews.

To sum up: Despite the differences in their respective presentations of Jesus' itinerary, both the Synoptics and John clearly present that portion of the Jewish population sympathetic to Jesus as, for the most part, Galilean. His Judean followers were not nearly so numerous, though evidently he did have some. (The Fourth Gospel specifies Mary, Martha, Lazarus, and "many" of their acquaintances, 11:1, 18, 45; and Luke, who nowhere develops a Judean mission as John does, nonetheless has the council of chief priests and scribes complain before Pilate that Jesus "stirs up the people, *teaching throughout all Judea,* from Galilee even to this place [Jerusalem]," Lk 23:5.) John's Gospel thus makes explicit what Luke's states in passing and the other two only imply: Jesus took his mission south to Judea and also to Jerusalem as well as to the villages of the Galilee, and he drew a following from these places as well.

JOHN'S JESUS, MARK'S JESUS, AND THE CRUCIFIXION

To what degree can we rely on John for historical information about Jesus? Neither the evangelist's narrative nor his speeches inspire confidence as history. His Jesus' itinerary is choppy and occasionally nonsensical. (Most famously, at the "bump" between 5:47 and 6:1, Jesus goes directly from Jerusalem "to the other side of the Sea of Galilee," the de rigueur multitude already in tow.) And his dialogues and lengthy soliloquies, theologically freighted, are virtually impossible to imagine in a realistic setting. If the historical Jesus truly did have followers, he could not have been making speeches like this to them.

So congenial is theological symbolism to the author that he completely subsumes the import of Jesus' action in the Temple to Christology ("but he spoke of the temple of his body," 2:21). The scene is highly dramatic, but narratively it goes nowhere. No one objects to Jesus' action or grows hostile as a result. Indeed, despite the greater drama of this scene compared with Mark's—the whip of cords, the panicked sheep and oxen (vv. 14–15)—Jesus' action is utterly without consequence in the story. Even his own disciples fail to grasp what he means until "after he was raised from the dead" (v. 22).

Further, nothing as lowly as exorcisms occupies John's Jesus. He prefers dramatic signs: water into wine at Cana (2:1–11), long-distance cures (from Cana to Capernaum, 4:46–47), raising the *very* dead Lazarus, entombed already four days (11:17–44). Serene, untroubled, indeed otherworldly, this Jesus remains forever in control. Before Pilate, he essentially tells the prefect what to do (19:11). On the cross, he knowingly orchestrates his actions to fulfill Scripture (19:28–30) and expires with a tranquil "It is finished."

Small wonder, then, that most of the scholars currently engaged in research on the historical Jesus prefer the synoptic tradition to John. Mark (augmented variously by Q) and Mark's Jesus are simply more usable. Working cures through exorcisms, speaking in synagogues, proclaiming the coming of God's kingdom: Mark's Jesus, for all his peculiarities, is nonetheless, recognizably, a first-century Jew. And this preference for the substance of Mark's depiction has led, as well, to a pronounced preference for Mark's chronology in general (hence a view of Jesus' mission as focused extensively if not almost exclusively in the Galilee), and for Mark's presentation of Jesus' last week in Jerusalem in particular. Whether the Jesus of the modern scholar is an apocalyptic prophet, a Galilean Hasid, a social activist of whatever stripe, or an antipurity antinationalist, he remains chiefly in the Galilee, goes to Jerusalem and performs his action in the Temple on his last Passover, and dies in consequence thereof, having drawn the negative attention of the chief priests to himself.

This consensus on Mark's presentation is that much more striking when the question turns to assessments of the Jewish trial in the Passion narratives. Here again, most modern scholars stand together; but they unite in their opinion that, in this instance and on this issue—historical suitability—*John* is to be preferred.

The reasons are not hard to look for. Mark's account as it stands beggars belief. He presents two full sessions of "the council" (the high priest, chief priests, elders, and scribes), the first late into the night of the seder, the second early that morning (14:53, 15:1). "Many" witnesses perjure themselves with false and contradictory testimonies as the council seeks his death (14:55–59). And when Jesus finally responds to the high priest's question—"Are you the Christ, the son of the blessed?" saying, "I am. And you will see the Son of Man seated at the right hand of Power and coming with the clouds of heaven"—the high priest calls it blasphemy, and the council condemns him "as deserving death" (vv. 61–64). After a second plenum council "as soon as it was morning," they lead Jesus away to Pilate.

This scene is incoherent even in terms solely of Mark's own Gospel.

Mark had spent his foregoing chapters developing a picture of mounting menace on the part of scribes and Pharisees. After Jesus pronounces a paralytic pardoned of his sins, the scribes, "in their hearts" accuse Jesus of blasphemy (2:3–7). After he restores a man's withered hand, the Pharisees plot with Herodians "how to destroy him" (3:1–6). They dog his steps, put hostile questions, attempt to trick him. Up until 11:18, the Pharisees are clearly the villains of the piece. But with Jesus' action in the Temple court, the onus swings onto the priests, and there it stays. No Pharisees figure in the Jewish trial scene, whether as witnesses or as council members; none shows up to deride him on the cross. And the theme of legal violations (of the Sabbath, for example, or of purity rules), so carefully developed earlier, likewise disappears: No accusation relevant to these issues surfaces before the high priest.

How, further, did Mark's high priest know to ask his question? To this point in the story, Jesus has told no one that he was "messiah" and/or "son of God," demanding the silence of his disciples (8:30) and of unclean spirits (1:34, 3:11) when they so identified him. More to the point: The question has nothing to do with the ostensible reason for his arrest, namely, his action in the Temple. In the view of most commentators, the high priest's question coheres best with the Christian confession of faith in Mark's own community. The evangelist, at the moment of highest drama, presents Jesus confessing his own Christological identity, in effect dying for Christianity.

Mark's reason for the priests' necessary stealth in bringing Jesus before them—fear of popular outrage if they were seen arresting Jesus (14:1–2)—is itself undermined by Mark's use of "the crowds" before Pilate. In 15:8, they materialize at dawn of 15 Nisan literally out of nowhere; by 15:11 the chief priests, with little effort, have completely swung popular opinion around. So anxious is Mark's Pilate to please this mob that he even releases Barabbas, a known murderer and insurrectionist, condemning Jesus to death only because they insist (15:15). The vacillating allegiances of this crowd, implausibly developed, are nonetheless absolutely necessary to Mark's presentation: He otherwise would have no way of getting Jesus from the Jewish council to a Roman cross.

Removed from the framing of his Gospel and reflected on critically and historically, Mark's presentation grows increasingly unlikely. Take the climax of the Jewish hearing. Even if the high priest had reason to ask Jesus if he were the messiah (on the theory, for example, that he'd gotten wind of what the pilgrims had cried out when celebrating Jesus' entry into the city the week before), and even if Jesus (for some reason) had said "Yes," the claim itself would not count as blasphemy. We have ample record in Josephus of other messianic figures in the period leading up to and including the revolt; later, we have the example of Bar Kokhba. History had falsified these men's claims, but nowhere are the claims themselves seen as blasphemous. And Mark's scene before Pilate fares no better. For the prefect to release Barabbas, a known insurrectionist, would have been astoundingly incompetent. And the Pilate we know from other ancient sources, both Jewish (Philo, Josephus) and Roman (Tacitus), was never overly concerned about his popularity with his Jewish subjects (see p. 171f.).

Finally, according to Mark's chronology, the priests would have just barely finished with the most hectic, exhausting week and day of their year. (In fact, the day following the seder, which the dawn audience before Pilate on Friday morning marks, would have required the priests' presence before the altar for yet more service.) Responsible for preparing the Temple for this annual onslaught of pilgrims, they had spent the previous week supervising the necessary purifications. The Thursday day of Jesus' arrest, 14 Nisan, they would have overseen the slaughter of tens of thousands of lambs and goats in a few hours before sunset, the beginning of the night of the meal. They then would have ensured that the Temple—all courts of which had been used as a theater for sacrifice—had been washed down and cleaned for the next day's worship; and then they would have gone back to their own families to observe the mandated commemorative feast. After all this, that very night as Mark has it, they would *then* show up at the high priest's house not once, but twice, for two meetings of the full council, all to deliberate over someone they already intended to condemn, and who would have to be dispatched by Pilate anyway! It is hard to imagine. (Indeed, in editing Mark's version, Luke reduces the priests' meeting to a single council in the morning, Lk 22:66. He also drops the dialogue between Jesus and the high priest, the imputed threat to the Temple, and the charge of blasphemy.)

John's account of Jesus' hearing before the priests, parsimonious and plain, is also much more credible. The action of the evening, still a Thursday, is moved back in terms of the holiday: in John, 14 Nisan, the date of Passover, is Thursday night and all day Friday. (Jewish days begin at nightfall. In the synoptic chronology, 14 Nisan falls on Wednesday night and continues all day Thursday; Thursday after sundown begins the next day, 15 Nisan, with the paschal meal.) The combined Roman and Jewish arresting party lead Jesus over to Annas, the former high priest. Annas then questions Jesus "about his disciples and his teaching" (18:19). Jesus answers simply that his teachings have always been public, in the synagogues and in the Temple, and invites Annas to ask his hearers what he said. He is then passed on to Caiaphas (v. 24) and, without further ado, to Pilate (v. 28). No Christological confessions. No highly charged accusations of blasphemy. No dramatic press of fraudulent witnesses. And no unnecessary throng of chief priests.

Of course, neither of these accounts, Mark's or John's, may be true. Logically, it is hard to see how both could be true. But if only one is true, the more likely candidate is John's—which, indeed, is why so many scholars, their general preference for the Markan tradition notwithstanding, appeal to the Fourth Gospel for their reconstructions of Jesus' Jewish "trial."

This mingling of the two different Gospel traditions—Mark for Jesus' character and mission; John for Jesus' "trial"—helps when constructing a more credible account of Jesus' hearing before the high priest. However, it brings along the complication of highlighting, both narratively and logically, what precedes Jesus' arrest, but only in Mark, not in John: that is, Jesus' action in the Temple.

In recent reconstructions, this incident has borne the whole weight of explaining how and why Jesus ends up dying on this particular Passover. The Temple action serves to symbolically sum up the essential meaning of Jesus' mission, construed by most scholars as exclusively Galilean. And whatever core meaning scholars see in this gesture (apocalyptic, political, critical—the interpretations vary widely), that meaning then serves to explain what happens next: Jesus' arrest, "trials," and crucifixion. The message conveyed by turning over the tables and disrupting the pigeon sellers and money changers—whatever it is—thus must alarm or offend the priests so greatly that they not only want Jesus dead, but they also can and do persuade Pilate to do the job.

By so focusing on Jesus' gesture at the Temple as the immediate reason for his arrest and death, modern scholars have inconsistently blended the two, mutually exclusive Passion chronologies of John and Mark. Mark dominates; Jesus' putative gesture carries enormous interpretive freight; the weight of scholarly conjecture bears upon how Jesus must have affronted the priests. We can do better than this. By staying focused on what we actually do know—that Jesus was crucified, though his followers were not—we can think ourselves back behind the drama of Mark's presentation to the confusing picture we have of Jesus of Nazareth's final circumstances. Once more, then, we return to the Temple Mount, shortly after Jesus' initial entry into the city. What did he do there, and what did it mean?

THE TEMPLE, AGAIN

In modern reconstructions as in Mark's narrative, the scene at the Temple is the key to the rest of the story. Those historians who see Jesus' action as a prophetic gesture portending the apocalyptic destruction of the Temple then have to explain why this so upsets the priests. Did they perhaps construe his enactment of destruction as in fact some sort of prophetic threat? That would explain the recurrence of this theme, put in the mouths of "false witnesses" in later trial traditions. "We heard him say, 'I will destroy this temple which is made with hands, and in three days I will build another, not made with hands,' " Mk 14:58. This threat reverberates in later Christian tradition. In Stephen's trial in the Book of Acts, Luke writes of other "false witnesses" who claim to the council, "We have heard [Stephen] say that this *Jesus of Nazareth will destroy this place,*" that is, the Temple (Acts 6:14). On this last Passover of Jesus' life, then, perhaps insulted by Jesus' gesture, perhaps offended by the (implied?) threat, anxious to get through the holiday without incident, the chief priests and/or Caiaphas would have moved to arrest Jesus, hand him over to Pilate, and recommend his execution as a potential troublemaker.

Those scholars who see Jesus' gesture as a nonapocalyptic prophetic act cinch their interpretation into their reconstruction of his mission more generally. Jesus' opposition to the Temple or whatever he took it to stand for in these reconstructions—a wrongful monopoly of atonement, spiritual and economic hierarchy, the oppressions of purity culture, the home base of power elites, the center of virulent nationalism— becomes, in fact, *the* defining clue not only to his view of his mission, but also to his view of himself. From this point, the enacted acme of his mission, it can be a short leap directly into Jesus' head. "Jesus must have thought that. . . ." or "If he did this, Jesus could only have meant that. . . ." Thus the Jesus who performs the action in the Temple is a Jesus who in effect—and according to some scholars, in intent—proffers himself and/or his movement as the Temple's alternative or replacement. No wonder the priests were so angry.

(Too bad that they did not stop for a moment and reflect concretely. Was their beloved Temple endangered in the slightest by Jesus' daring interpretive move? Were the Jewish communities throughout the Mediterranean world really going to start understanding the Torah differently, and cease coming to Jerusalem to worship? Would the caravans from Babylon now deposit their huge burdens of half-shekel donations from the pious directly in Capernaum? If Jesus thought of himself or the community of his followers as the Temple's alternative, what, practically, would he have meant? And who, outside his group, could possibly have grasped it? And if his meaning were so idiosyncratic to his mission, how dangerous could it be?)

The fundamental problem with focusing in this way on the Temple incident is that, on any construction, it leaves the meaningful business between Jesus and the priests. But viewing the matter as primarily between the priests and Jesus only increases the difficulty in seeing why Pilate would have executed him by crucifixion. It is time, I think, to reconsider the significance of Jesus' overturning the vendors' tables in the Temple, the putative linkage of this with predictions of the Temple's destruction, and the likelihood that his teaching about the Temple, whether by word (Mk 13:2, "no stone upon another that will not be thrown down") or by deed (overturning the tables, as interpreted by modern scholars) led directly to his execution.

In light of the way that the Gospel writers understand and present Jesus' action in the Temple, we must first of all ask, Who would have understood the symbolism of this gesture? If Jesus, by overturning the money changers' tables, had intended to symbolize coming destruction—be it of the Temple itself or some aspect of its symbolic universe (purity, hierarchy, nationalism, and so on)—how well could others divine his meaning? Both the Synoptics and John, evidently independently of each other, construe Jesus' imputed action as a condemnation of the Temple's support services. Mark's Jesus quotes Isaiah 56:7 and Jeremiah 7:11 to this effect ("My house shall be called a house of prayer for all the nations; but you have made it a den of robbers"); John's Jesus, stern and uncharacteristically direct, says simply, "Take these things away; you shall not make my Father's house a house of trade" (Jn 2:16; cf. Mk 11:17). If Jesus' gesture had actually symbolized destruction, his meaning was so obscure to the writers of the Gospels that they consistently misconstrued it, missing this opportunity to have their hero's action state what they otherwise put forthrightly into his mouth, namely, that the Temple would be destroyed. How many of Jesus' own contemporaries, especially those outside his own circle, would have understood him? And if the symbolic meaning of the gesture could not be readily, publicly grasped, how could it in turn have gotten Jesus into any trouble at all?

Also complicated is the relation of Jesus' gesture (especially if by it he prophetically enacted destruction, Mk 11 and parr.); his prophecy of the Temple's coming destruction (Mk 13 and parr.); the report of this prophecy as a threat, repeated by false witnesses, at his trial before the priests (Mk 14:57–58); and the way that all these Markan motifs fit in with the fact that the Romans indeed destroyed the Temple in 70. Our problems begin with the fact that we cannot know when the Gospels—Mark in particular—were written. Academic consensus, not uncontested, dates all four Gospels to the last third of the first century. Some scholars place Mark's composition slightly before the Jewish War with Rome, explaining his apocalyptic tone as the measure of his anxious anticipation of trouble; others think that all four were composed (or redacted) sometime after 70.

A post-70 setting can account very nicely for those parts of the Synoptics that predict the Temple's destruction. Luke's revision of Mark ("When you see Jerusalem surrounded by armies, then know that its desolation has come near," 21:20) seems clearly updated in light of the war. Further, ancient prophetic writings often "predict" an event that had in fact already occurred. The accuracy of their predictions only enhances the authority of the text. And, finally, it is standard scholarly practice to date the composition of such texts to some period shortly after but no earlier than the "predicted" event. We have already seen these characteristics, ancient and modern, come together around the text of Daniel. The author's pseudonym locates the prophecy in the sixth century B.C.E., with the generation of the Babylonian Captivity. The decoding of the text's symbolic references points to events in the late Seleucid period. Scholars, orienting their estimates from Daniel's "abomination of desolation" (Dn 12:31), date the text to no earlier than 167 B.C.E., when Antiochus Epiphanes desecrated the altar in Jerusalem.

Against such arguments, those who see these Markan themes as predating the actual Temple's destruction, perhaps even as arising from authentic teaching traditions of Jesus, can point to two facts supportive of their case. First, Jewish apocalyptic literature to either side of Jesus' lifetime also speaks of the current Temple's destruction, and occasionally, too, of its replacement by a superior, final Temple (cf. the Temple "not made with hands" in Mk 14:58). The existence of this traditional apocalyptic motif enhances the possibility that Jesus, preaching the coming Kingdom, may also have thought in terms of the Temple's destruction. Second, in Josephus, we find secure evidence of an irre-futably genuine prophecy of the Temple's destruction in the bizarre his-tory of another Jesus—Jesus son of Ananias.

During the festival of Sukkot in the autumn of 62 C.E., "when the city was enjoying profound peace and prosperity," Josephus writes, this Jesus, standing in the Temple, suddenly began to cry out,

> "A voice from the East! A voice from the West! A voice from the four winds! A voice against Jerusalem and the sanctuary, a voice against the bridegroom and the bride, a voice against all the people!" Day and night he went about all the alleys with this cry upon his lips. Some of the leading citizens, incensed at these ill-omened words, arrested the fellow and severely chastised him. But he, without a word on his own behalf or for the private ear of those who smote him, only continued his cries as before. Thereupon the magistrates, supposing (as was indeed the case) that the man was under some supernatural impulse, brought him before the Roman governor. There, although flayed to the bone with scourges, he neither sued for mercy nor shed a tear but merely . . . responded to each stroke with "Woe to Jerusalem!" . . . Albinus [the Roman procurator] pronounced him a maniac and let him go. During the whole period up to the outbreak of the war . . . he repeated his lament. . . . His cries were the loudest at the festivals. So for seven years and five months he repeated his wail, his voice never flagging nor his strength exhausted, until in the siege . . . he found his rest.   (BJ 6.300–309)

Finally, in defense of the authenticity of Jesus' prediction in Mark, scholars note that Mark's description is insufficiently exact, whereas *post facto* predictions are typically very exact, precisely because they can be. "Do you see these great buildings?" asks Mark's Jesus. "There will not be left here one stone upon another that will not be thrown down" (13:2). Not exactly, as any modern tourist can tell you. The retaining walls of Herod's Temple still stand. Though a mosque now dominates the top of the mount, Jews pray before the Kotel, or Western Wall. And besides, the Temple itself was destroyed by fire, which this prophecy—a tribute to its authenticity—fails to mention at all.

This argument seems less compelling than the first two (prior and posterior apocalyptic tradition; the unarguably authentic prophecy of Jesus son of Ananias). Read Josephus' description of the Temple's demise in Book 6 of his history, *The Jewish War.* True, the fire features prominently, but his overall theme, quite simply, is total devastation.

From Josephus' eyewitness account, in other words, you still would not know that the retaining walls of Herod's man-made mountain stood. Mark, not an eyewitness, can perhaps be excused. Also, even according to Josephus' account, Mark's Jesus foresaw accurately: None of the *buildings* on the mount remained standing.

If Jesus' prediction of the Temple's destruction, articulated clearly in Mark 13, is indeed after the fact, a product of events in 70, then the likelihood of the same prophecy's being encoded in Jesus' Temple action—obscured by the evangelists, revealed through scholarly interpretation—diminishes accordingly. But still to be accounted for is the appearance of this scene in two independent witnesses, Mark and John.

The presumption of a postdestruction date of composition speaks precisely to this point. Both evangelists, writing in the postwar period, knew that the Temple had, dramatically, ceased to exist. Its nonexistence is an overwhelming religious datum that they have to address.

Other Christians in the late first century speak of the Temple variously. The Epistle of the Hebrews devalues the earthly Temple, saying it had all along been a mere shadow cast by the heavenly Temple, where Jesus now serves as perfect priest and perfect sacrifice. The author of Revelation, by comparison, envisaging the imminent descent of the heavenly Jerusalem after the apocalyptic travails, specifies that "I saw *no temple in the city, for its temple is the Lord God almighty and the Lamb,*" that is, the apocalyptic Christ (Rv 21:22). The actual Temple in the earthly Jerusalem is nugatory in the first view, unnecessary in the second. The pseudonymous letters that make their way into the New Testament canon written in the name of first-generation figures—"Peter," "James," and the "Paul" of the pastoral epistles, Ephesians, Colossians, and 2 Thessalonians—cannot speak of the Temple's destruction without compromising their false authorship. But all early Christian communities as types of Jewish communities had to make sense of this terrible loss.

One way was to have Jesus already "know" the fate of the Temple and predict its demise as one of the events that must precede his glorious return. The tradition given in Mark 13, followed by Matthew and Luke, makes this move in one way; John's linking of the Temple's destruction to Jesus' resurrection (Jn 2:19–21) makes it in another. Still another way is to have Jesus pronounce the sacrifices performed at the Temple a lower way to worship God (safe statement, since after 70 it was no longer possible in any case); prayer, by comparison, like right conduct, could be practiced anywhere. This theme weaves in and out of all the Gospels, and the scene in the Temple is one of the ways the evangelists make this point.

John clearly knew some version of the tradition that stands in Mark 11. But how? As usual, we cannot know. To assume that John actually read Mark is one way to answer this question, but it leaves dangling the much more difficult one: Why then would the fourth evangelist use so little and disregard so much of Mark? I find it less difficult to suppose that this episode of Jesus' upsetting the vendor's tables in the Temple was a story that floated freely, circulating orally and, thus, without a fixed context. This can explain its different function in the two Gospels (in Mark, it sets up the Passion; in John, it serves as a vehicle for Christology), its contrasting locations (Mark's finale, John's debut), while accounting for Jesus' two different speeches that nonetheless point a similar meaning, namely condemnation of the Temple's support services (thus "domesticating" the Temple's destruction).

Evidence of other such "floating" stories exists. The most ancient manuscript authorities for the Gospel of John, for example, omit John 7:53–8:11, the story of Jesus and the woman caught in adultery. Other, later manuscripts place the story after John 7:36; still others after John 21:25. And sometimes the story appears in manuscripts of Luke, after Luke 21:38. Apparently this story traveled freely—that is, orally—for some time after the Gospels attained their written form. As it became known in communities that had (a) written Gospel(s), it was incorporated variously. Such a history says nothing about the story's authenticity, but it can account for its appearance in different Gospels.

In the instance of the story about Jesus' action in the Temple, Matthew and Luke clearly drew on Mark. They use it the same way as he does, to begin the events leading to the Passion by bringing Jesus to the hostile attention of the chief priests; and they adduce the same quotations from Isaiah and Jeremiah. John and Mark, by contrast, share only the story's bare bones: Passover, some violent gesture against Temple vendors, some condemnation of trade in the Temple precincts. The story itself may be authentic, that is, dating to Jesus sometime c. 30, and Mark and John accordingly each know some version of it. Or it may have crystallized along with other traditions likewise developing the theme of Jesus' purported hostility to certain forms of traditional Jewish worship and practice, sometime during the period between his execution and the composition of these two Gospels. Or it may be original to Mark, a dramatic plot device to bring his story to its climax, which John, reading Mark, later adopted and adapted to his own purposes. We simply cannot know. And we have no compelling evidence either way.

If Jesus did in fact predict the Temple's destruction and, thus, if he symbolically encoded that destruction by some action in the Temple, then two problems still remain. The first is Paul's absolute silence on the issue. Here was Jesus, making a spectacular prophecy at a key moment in his mission. Here were Peter, John, and probably others of the original disciples, who must have known the prophecy and who certainly knew Paul (Gal 1:18, 2:9). And here was Paul himself, speaking frequently in his letters about the coming Kingdom. Why did he not say anything about Jesus' prophecy at all?

We only have seven letters from Paul—six if you look at Philemon as more of a memo. He was an active apostle for close to thirty years. Clearly he wrote more than seven letters in all that time. The far greater part of his correspondence is lost—among which, for all we know, his definitive description of Jesus' prophecy of the Temple's imminent apocalyptic destruction.

Still, there are plenty of places in the few letters we do have where he might have brought up this impressive, foreseen sign of the End of the Age. Consoling his unhappy Thessalonians, somewhere after 4:15, "For this we declare to you by the word of the Lord" that the Temple will be destroyed and established by God as part of the Endtime events. Or after Philippians 4:5, "The Lord is at hand! Once the Temple is no more, as he said, then it will be rebuilt and glorious by the Father." Or somewhere in 1 Corinthians 15, where he again rehearses the sequence of events at the End. Or at least in Romans—chapter 8, when he talks about the transformation of the universe? After chapter 11, when Israel is reincorporated into redemption, and all are saved? In chapter 15, when he takes the offering of the Gentiles to Jerusalem as if he were in priestly service "not to this earthly Temple, which as you know the Lord said will soon be no more, but to the Eternal Temple." But, of course, he says nothing of the sort. Anywhere. Given the happenstance of historical evidence surviving from this period of the movement, one should not make too much of Paul's "silence." But there it is.

And, finally, there is the problem of the Temple courtyard itself. This last point is really an exercise in thinking concretely. Please turn to the drawing of the Temple Mount on pages 56–57. Note the size of the human figures ascending the steps on the south side. The money changers and pigeon sellers were most likely located either in the Royal Portico or under the stoa and along the colonnade: out of the rain in the winter, out of the broiling sun, reflecting back up off the stone facing of the courtyard, in spring and summer. (Another point against John's depiction at 2:14: No large sacrificial animals like sheep and oxen would have been kept within the courtyard itself. They would have fouled the precincts. Rather, they would have been sold in the market area below the Temple, beneath the western side of the area, and oxen in any case would have been in demand only very rarely.)

Now imagine the place absolutely jammed with humanity—tens of thousands of people—during the days between the eighth and fourteenth of Nisan. Now imagine Jesus walking over to the tables of some of these vendors and overturning them. Now ask yourself, How many people would have even been able to see him? How many would or could have noticed? Let's say that at best the people immediately around Jesus would or could have seen him. Would people on level ground have noticed, even twenty feet away? Could they even have heard the disruption? What about people fifty feet away? Or in the middle of the courtyard, or even under another section of the stoa?

The Temple area enclosed by the wall was enormous: approximately 169,000 square feet. An archaeologist has estimated that twelve soccer fields could fit neatly into the space. Its very size prompts the question: If Jesus had made such a gesture, who would have seen it? Those in his retinue and those standing immediately around him. Otherwise the people with the clearest view—*if* Jesus were positioned close to the edge of the roof of the west or east colonnades rather than farther toward the interior—would have been, ironically, those Roman soldiers patrolling from the roof of the stoa on the *opposite* side of the courtyard. The effect of Jesus' gesture at eye-level—where everyone else was— would have been muffled, swallowed up by the sheer press of pilgrims. How worried, then, need the priests have been?

WE ARE STILL looking for a reason why Pilate would have executed Jesus by crucifixion. The scene in the Temple courtyard, if historical, still leaves a gap in the picture: If Caiaphas wanted Jesus out of the way for whatever offense his action encoded, and Pilate consented to do the job, why not a simple, private murder? And if the scene in the courtyard is not historical—many considerations call it into question— then how do the priests become involved at all?

At this point, recall Josephus' description of the fate of Jews fleeing

Photograph of the heel bone of the crucified Yehochanan, from Givat ha-Mivtar

Crucifixion was the method of execution reserved by the Romans particularly for those they thought guilty of sedition. It was intended as much as a spectacle for the edification of those watching—an effective warning against harboring thoughts or committing acts similar to the victim's—as a slow, ugly, and even humiliating mode of death for the insurrectionist. In 1968, just outside Jerusalem, archaeologists discovered a first-century ossuary, or bone box, containing the remains of one Yehochanan, a young man between the ages of twenty-four and twenty-eight who had died by crucifixion. His arms had been tied rather than nailed to the crossbar; his legs nailed through the heel to either side of the upright. The nail securing his right heel had struck a knot in the wood and bent, and so remained with the body when it was taken down.

Jerusalem during the siege, and Titus' thoughts on the matter. Once they were caught, he writes, they

> were accordingly scourged and subjected to torture of every description before being killed and then crucified opposite the walls.... [Titus'] main reason for not stopping the crucifixions was *the hope that the spectacle might perhaps induce the Jews to surrender, for fear that continued resistance would involve them in a similar fate.*   (BJ 5.450)

Crucifixion was a Roman form of public service announcement: Do not engage in sedition as this person has, or your fate will be similar.

The point of the exercise was not the death of the offender as such, but getting the attention of those watching. Crucifixion first and foremost is addressed to an audience.

I suggest that is where we should look for the explanation for Jesus' death. Not to a supposed protest or enacted prophecy in the Temple, which even if it did occur cannot explain his fate. Not to Jesus' psyche or to his innermost convictions about himself and his identity, to which we have no access in any case. Even if for some reason Jesus had been convinced that he were the messiah, but in some radically new and unanticipated way, his self-image would not have mattered to anybody in power, and would scarcely have made sense to anybody outside himself. Not to his program such as we can reconstruct it from the traditions about his mission: If that were dangerous, somehow threatening, or even implicitly threatening to established powers, Antipas would have gotten to him first. We should look, instead, to the crowds in Jerusalem. They are the audience whom Pilate addresses. In that sense, they are the reason for Jesus' death.

Jewish pilgrims hailed Jesus as messiah in Jerusalem. Pilate killed him as a messianic pretender—not, again, because *Jesus* thought he was messiah (would Pilate have cared about Jesus' self-identity?), but because others thought and proclaimed that he was. But Pilate knew better than they did, or knew that they were wrong, because he executed nobody else from this group other than Jesus himself. What is the import of these facts? Where do the priests come in? And why Jerusalem at Passover—indeed, on this particular Passover?

Chapter 5

THE DAYS IN JERUSALEM

THE GOSPELS' patchy account of events surrounding Jesus' final Passover in Jerusalem offers no clear view of what happened. At some point, other Jews acclaimed him messiah. Pilate struck; the high priest or chief priests were somehow involved. Pilate executed Jesus by crucifixion but did not pursue anyone else from Jesus' group. On or around Passover, Jesus died on a cross as King of the Jews.

But shortly thereafter, various groups of his followers were convinced that they saw him again, raised from the dead. And the mission that Jesus had taken over from John and carried to Israel went forward again, spread now by these followers, whose message differed slightly but significantly from Jesus' own. The Kingdom of God is at hand, they said; but they added that Jesus himself, the Risen Christ, would return to inaugurate it. Spreading throughout the villages of Judea and the Galilee, running up the coast to cities ringing the Mediterranean through the network of Greek-speaking synagogue communities of Asia Minor, now taking on significant numbers of Gentiles as well as Jews, the movement that had crystallized around Jesus continued to spread in his name. In his name, too, his apostles baptized Gentiles into these tiny new communities, and in his name Jew and Gentile together prayed to the God of Israel for the speedy establishment of his Kingdom and the return from heaven of his Son.

The developments *from* Jesus' mission seem more visible in the evidence than the developments that led up to it; but they all form a single trajectory along which we can trace the origins and growth of this particular Jewish messianic movement. Orienting ourselves from the endpoint once again—these mixed congregations of Jews and Gentiles in the communities of the Diaspora—we need to reimagine the mission and message of Jesus, that period of his life that fell between John the Baptizer on the one hand and Pilate on the other.

The Call to Israel

FOR REASONS that are forever lost to us, Jesus of Nazareth responded to the charismatic call to repentance and purification sounded by the ascetic holy man John. How had John's message penetrated so far north of where he lived, taught, and practiced his mission, baptizing by the Jordan River in the desert wilderness between Judea and Perea? How had his message traveled inland from the river to other parts of Judea and even to Jerusalem? Penitents from all these areas flocked to him; perhaps, returning to their homes, they spoke to neighbors, who then were moved likewise to seek him out. Alone of all the Jews John immersed, the single one about whom we have any knowledge is Jesus. Sometime after receiving John's purification, Jesus began his own mission to Israel, calling Jews to repentance in the face of the coming Kingdom.

Within just five years of Jesus' death, evidence abounds of this new movement's wide and rapid dissemination. *Ekklēsiai,* small gatherings of its members, appear in the villages of Samaria and Judea as well as in the Galilee (Acts 8, 9:31; Gal 1:22; Bethany in Judea, Jn 11:18); in Lydda and, on the coast, Joppa (Acts 9:32, 42) and Caesarea (Acts 10); farther north, in the Syrian cities of Damascus (Gal 1:17; Acts 9:10 ff.) and Antioch (11:20). Jerusalem, meanwhile, had become home to many of the original disciples (Gal 1:18, 2:1). According to Luke, the core community had been there continuously since the final pilgrimage of Jesus for Passover (Lk 24:53; Acts 1:3–8 and passim).

Whether because of these apostles themselves, or the prestige and holiness of the city, the community in Jerusalem seems from early on to have exercised tremendous authority. When Paul joins the movement, perhaps within three years of Jesus' execution, he consults with the Jerusalem apostles on several occasions. "Then after three years [from his divine call to be an apostle], I went up to Jerusalem to visit Cephas [Peter]. . . . But I saw none of the other apostles except James the Lord's brother" (Gal 1:18–19). "Then after fourteen years I went up again to Jerusalem . . . and laid before them (but privately before those who were of repute) the gospel which I preach among the Gentiles, lest somehow I should be running or had run in vain" (2:1–3). Paul clearly contacts these earlier apostles—his insistence on his own authority in Galatians notwithstanding—to confirm the validity of his preaching. James sends men from Jerusalem to Antioch to look in on, perhaps supervise, the community there (2:11). And Paul solicits contributions from his Gentile communities in Macedonia and Achaia for the support of the "poor among the holy ones in Jerusalem" (Rom 16:25–26; cf. 1 Cor 16:1–4; 2 Cor 8–9).

What bridges this gap between Jesus coming into his own mission sometime shortly after his contact in Judea with John the Baptizer and this network of *ekklēsiai* of mixed sizes and ethnicity in tiny villages, in great urban centers, and in Jerusalem—*the* Holy City—all within, perhaps, a decade? Scholars who concentrate on the Galilean roots of the movement see that northern region as its true matrix: chief arena of Jesus' preaching and teaching; home to the Q-communities, groups who preserved or valued primarily teachings from Jesus, not stories about him. The origins of the Jesus movement, they say, bear the stamp of the Galilee religiously (in its indifference to Temple-oriented purity rules), politically (it articulates the historic, independent Israelite identity vis-à-vis aristocratic, priestly Judea), and sociologically (formed and based in small towns, it was intrinsically peasant and rural). Jerusalem, in this light, only *seems* important because of the theological emphasis of Luke's Gospel and the Acts of the Apostles. Intensive regional studies of the Galilee are the best way, they argue, to understand the earliest, and in a sense the most authentic, phase of the Jesus movement.

This orientation reflects the current scholarly preference for the synoptic Gospels in historical Jesus research. Part of this preference rests on the greater historical plausibility of the image of Jesus as healer, teacher, and prophetic figure found in Mark, Matthew, and Luke. Part also rests on the accidents of documentation: Three of the four canonical Gospels share a literary relationship, and thus seem to converge upon the same picture. Despite knowing full well that Matthew and Luke most likely derive their portrait of Jesus and their narrative chronologies from Mark, scholars easily slip into thinking of them as three different witnesses ("In all three Gospels we find. . . ."). Consequently, the Synoptics combine to outweigh the authority of traditions in John.

Of course the Galilee and Judea were two different regions with their own particular histories and traditions. Of course their respective political realities diverged significantly, especially once Judea fell under direct Roman rule and the Galilee retained its Jewish ruler, client of Rome though he was. And of course Jerusalem was not like any place else.

But Jesus does not seem to have plotted his course thinking in our political, sociological, and religious terms. He entered into his sense of his own mission through John, by the Jordan in the south; and he took his message north to the villages of his native Galilee, through villages in Judea and, repeatedly, to Jerusalem as well. His mission was a mission to *Israel*.

The evidence for this more broadly based and widely disseminated mission is scattered in the Synoptics, but it's there. Once he approaches Jerusalem, Mark's Jesus acts as if he already has contacts in the area. "And when they drew near to Jerusalem, to Bethphage and Bethany, he sent two of his disciples, and said, 'Go to the village opposite you, and immediately you will find a colt' " (Mk 11:1–2). "His disciples said to him, 'Where will you have us go and prepare for you to eat the Passover?' And he sent two of his disciples and said to them, 'Go into the city, and a man carrying a jar of water will meet you. Follow him; and wherever he enters, say to the householder, "The Teacher says, 'Where is my guest room?' " ' " (Mk 14:12–14). The point, of course, is not that anything like these exchanges actually happened: How could we ever know? The point, rather, is that even Mark, the evangelist whose portrait of Jesus' itinerary matters so much to the message of his Gospel, the writer most invested in the dramatic, one-way, Galilee-to-Jerusalem trajectory—even Mark knows when the story cannot proceed without somebody or somebodies in Jerusalem facilitating Jesus' actions.

That is a literary point, resting on an analysis of Mark's narrative. John's narrative, such as it is, conveys much less concern than does Mark's with the shape of Jesus' missionary itinerary. John invests his concern in his Jesus' bel canto soliloquies on his own theological identity. John's attention to itinerary is haphazard at best, and occasionally unbelievably sloppy. That does not make the details of his presentation of Jesus' itinerary ipso facto any more reliable than Mark's as history. But it does mean that since he is less invested in Jesus' itinerary, since he does not subordinate it to his theology the way Mark does his, the impression of the shape of Jesus' mission his Gospel gives may be more reliable, because it is less reworked. John conveys explicitly what Mark only implies, and what Luke suggests but does not depict (see Lk 23:5), namely, that Jesus and his mission—like John the Baptizer and his—encompassed the Galilee *and* Judea, specifically Jerusalem, as well.

This observation based on Mark's story—a literary argument—can be amplified by appeal to historical data. Other ancient sources, Josephus not least of all, claim that Galileans frequently made the pilgrimage to Jerusalem: That Jesus would do so, too, is not remarkable. (Even Luke, who follows Mark's once-to-Jerusalem chronology for the adult Jesus, nevertheless depicts Jesus as a child going up annually to Jerusalem, specifically for Passover, with his parents, Lk 2:41.) Quite the opposite: Given Jesus' evident religious intensity, his commitment to the faith and traditions of Israel, it would be very odd if he had not. Further, shortly after his death, his movement spread quickly and broadly in both regions, the Galilee and Judea, and in town and country. Why insist then on some sort of rural quintessence to this movement that makes its well-attested widespread growth so much harder to account for? Jesus' message was heard, and people responded, in both venues.

This is not to deny the rural stamp that many of the traditions in Q and in Mark bear. Jesus himself was a Galilean and thus, as those scholars particularly committed to regional studies urge, the Galilee could well have played an essential role in shaping his temperament, his thought, and thus his teaching. In the narrative incidentals of the parables we can still glimpse that world of village marketplaces and small farms. But in constructing, indeed conceiving, his mission, Jesus seems to have drawn deeply on a much broader, and more broadly shared, universe: the world of the *Sh'ma* and of the covenant, of the prophets and the Ten Commandments; the world of redemption, revelation, and realized promise encoded in the seasonal holy days of Pesach, Shavuot, and Sukkot; the world of the Bible and the Bible's God, the God of the universe, the God of Abraham, Isaac, and Jacob. Jesus issued a call to repentance, moral renewal, ethical purity, commitment, community, to preparation for God's kingdom. It could be and was heard by city dwellers and country people both. Jesus called out, not just to or even primarily to Galilean peasants, but to *Israel*.

(A random detail, which Mark provides: the names of the sons in Jesus' family [6:3]. They hark back to the heroic age of the nation, the patriarchal narratives of the Bible: James/Ya'acov, the name of Isaac's son, Abraham's grandson, who wrestled with the angel and was given the name Israel; Jose/Yosef, in Genesis one of the twelve sons of Jacob, arguably the greatest, a savior to his people; Jude/Yehudah and Simon/Shimon, in the Genesis narrative two more of Jacob's sons, founders of two of Israel's twelve tribes; finally Jesus' own name, Yehoshua, the biblical Joshua, successor to Moses, leading his people out of the wilderness, over the Jordan, into the Land. It's a little like naming a string of sons Washington, Jefferson, Hamilton, Franklin: The names themselves convey a close identification with the nation's foundational past.)

Finally, this impression, based on John's Gospel, of a back-and-forth mission, established both in the Galilee and in Judea from the beginning, not only accounts for why the movement is likewise established in both regions so soon after Jesus' death. It also explains the paradox that has driven this investigation, namely, that when Pilate moved against Jesus, Jesus was the sole one of his movement to die.

According to this view of his missionary itinerary, Jesus had been up to the city many times during his mission, most likely for the pilgrimage holidays. The most natural place to find a crowd during those times was precisely where the priests and the Romans also were, which is to say, the Temple. On this, both Mark and John agree: When Jesus taught in Jerusalem, he taught in the Temple's court.

The Passover that Mark depicts, in other words, was most likely *not* the first time that Jesus had been teaching about the Kingdom of God in Jerusalem during the days before a feast. The sorts of encounters that Mark relates between Jesus and the chief priests, the scribes, the Sadducees and Pharisees, may have happened whenever Jesus was there (11:27–12:44). By the time Jesus was arrested during what would be his last Passover in the city, he was a known quantity—to the priests, surely, *and* to Pilate. For if Jesus had been up to Jerusalem repeatedly for the festivals, he had always been in town when the prefect was, too.

Pilate crucified Jesus. He executed him, that is, specifically as a political insurrectionist. But Pilate knew perfectly well that Jesus was *not* an insurrectionist, and thus that he had no need of rounding up others in his movement as well. The experience of the post-Resurrection community in Jerusalem makes this same point. Pilate continued as prefect for another three to six years after Jesus' execution. In that time, we hear no whisper of his harassing this group. But if Pilate—or any later Roman prefect or procurator—had suspected them of any kind of active political opposition, the original disciples never could have formed a community and continued to reside in the city. Thus, also, this particular Passover: Neither after the Triumphal Entry nor after Jesus' arrest were the disciples pursued. Even more to the point, they were tremendously confused and dismayed by Jesus' arrest—an impression preserved in all accounts, despite the way such distress belies the detailed Passion predictions that the evangelists repeatedly depict Jesus delivering. His arrest caught his followers utterly by surprise, probably because he had always been able to state his message during the holidays without any interference.

By the time he finally executed Jesus, Pilate probably had plenty of information about him, because Jesus had taught openly in Jerusalem for years. In terms of the realpolitik of Roman concerns, Jesus was harmless, and Pilate knew it. So only he died. But then the questions remain: Why, especially if Pilate knew he was harmless, did Jesus die at all? Why specifically by crucifixion? And why then?

The Crucified Messiah

ONCE THE floating story of Jesus' overturning the tables in the Temple court is bracketed out, the same narrative structure for Jesus' final trip to Jerusalem emerges in both Mark and John. On his way up to the city, festive crowds of pilgrims hail Jesus as the harbinger of the messianic Kingdom ("Blessed is the kingdom of our father David that is coming!" Mk 11:10), perhaps even as a Davidic king ("Hosanna to the *Son of David!*" Mt 21:9; "*Blessed is the King* who comes in the name of the Lord!" Lk 19:38; "Blessed is he who comes in the name of the Lord, *even the King of Israel!*" Jn 12:13). He enters the city like messianic royalty, riding on a donkey to conform to the prophecy in Zechariah 9:9: "Behold, *your King is coming to you,* humble, and mounted on an ass" (the Triumphal Entry, Mk 11:1–10 and parr.; Mt 21:5 and Jn 12:15 cite Zec explicitly). He goes to the Temple and teaches there daily before the holiday begins, so popular with the crowds of pilgrims that the priests decide they cannot risk arresting him openly. After a final meal with his disciples on or just before the night of the Passover meal (the Last Supper), Jesus is arrested by stealth, heard before priestly authorities, and handed over to Pilate, who crucifies him that morning as *King of the Jews*. Before nightfall, the onset of the Sabbath, Jesus is dead.

The italicized phrases should help visually underscore the interpretive point: A straight line connects the Triumphal Entry and the Crucifixion. A pilgrim crowd noisily proclaiming the coming of the Kingdom, not to mention the coming of their King, would certainly provoke Pilate's attention and concern: With much less provocation, he had swung into bloody action before. Instead, however, and oddly, the Gospels depict him as doing nothing. Jesus' Triumphal Entry calls forth no police action either from the Temple guard or from Roman troops, and Jesus is left to teach to crowds in the Temple every day as the holiday approaches.

What are the chances, then, that something like this excited demonstration actually occurred? Some scholars hold that the evangelists relate accurately even the details of Jesus' entry into the city, specifically the tradition that he came riding on a donkey in deliberate imitation of this line from Zechariah. The virtue of this opinion is that it would permit a glimpse into Jesus' mind, or at least his intentions: Redefining this title around himself, Jesus would thereby at least implicitly declare himself King or Messiah. But in light of the absence of Roman response—inexplicable, since such actions and proclamations would easily constitute sedition—the demonstration, they say, must have been quite modest, with Jesus making a relatively unobtrusive entrance, performing this symbolic act (riding the donkey) only for insiders.

Thinking of this scene with the criterion of dissimilarity in mind might clarify the question. To have Jesus self-consciously redefine the meaning of "messiah" as a meek and humble king—as, in fact, himself—fails this criterion cold. Such a reconstruction would have Jesus of Nazareth as the self-consciously intentional origin of the Christian definition of Messiah. Impossible? Hard to say: Criteria of authenticity only help to sort out data along a gradient of lesser or greater probability. Having Jesus script his actions quite precisely by symbolic appeal to explicit verses of ancient prophecy seems implausible to me: That sort of scriptural proof-texting usually signals the activity of the Gospel writers. And little in these Gospel traditions—though the evangelists would have liked it—points to Jesus' putting himself forward as messiah in any way. Had he actually done so here, when entering Jerusalem for Passover, it would have come out of nowhere. And the speculation that Jesus uttered this triumphant messianic symbolic act sotto voce to a small group of insiders goes against both the tone of the scene's depiction in these narratives and its historical finale, namely, the Crucifixion itself.

But if Jesus had taught many times in Jerusalem, and thus if Pilate already knew that Jesus in every practical way was harmless, then this scene's basic historicity—pilgrim crowds hailed Jesus as messiah as they all coursed into Jerusalem the week preceding his last Passover—can stand without whittling down its scale or significance. The crowds' action called forth no Roman response precisely because Pilate knew that the message of Jesus' movement posed no threat to Roman power.

The independent testimony of Paul and the Synoptics converges on and confirms this point. Whatever its ultimate hopes for the revelation of God's justice against the forces of sin and evil, in the short run, before the Kingdom came, evil was to be met with nonresistance, the enemy with love rather than hatred (Mt 5:38–6:4//Lk 6:27–36). Persecutors should be blessed, vengeance eschewed, injustice tolerated (Rom 12:9–13:14; cf. 1 Cor 6:7, on enduring injustice rather than taking a fellow Christian to law). Pay taxes; honor civil authorities (Mk 12:17 and parr., on rendering to Caesar; Rom 13:6–7, on paying taxes; 13:1–5, on honoring authorities more generally). The explanation for the Christian's passive resistance—or, perhaps more accurately, active nonresistance—to evil and oppression closes Paul's hortatory section in Romans and is embedded in the gospel narrative: *God* was about to step actively onto the scene to defeat evil, right injustice, punish the wicked, redeem the suffering. In the brief time remaining until that moment, the believer's only obligatory preparation was to harken to Jesus' summons to repent and, thus, reform.

The early Christian message of nonresistance was not a call to tolerate injustice or endure aggression indefinitely. On the contrary, it enunciates the conviction that motivated the entire movement: The Kingdom was at hand; God would give the wicked their comeuppance soon. Thus to Christians at Rome, Paul concludes his exhortation to respect all governing authorities and to pay taxes by invoking precisely the nearness of the End. "You know what hour it is, how it is full time now for you to wake from sleep. For salvation is nearer to us than when we first believed; the night is far gone, the day is at hand" (Rom 13:11–12; see the preceding ten verses for Paul's teaching). And after surveying the persecutions that his followers will suffer ("they will deliver you up to councils; and you will be beaten in synagogues, and you will stand before kings and governors for my sake"), the Jesus of Mark's apocalyptic soliloquy concludes, "Then they will see the Son of Man coming in clouds with great power and glory. . . . Truly, this generation will not pass away before all these things take place" (Mk 13:9, 26, 30). If Mark, sometime after 70 C.E., and Paul, midcentury, stand gripped by their conviction of the imminent turning of the age, then surely Jesus, the source of this conviction, proclaimed his message with no less urgency.

But the Kingdom Jesus preached would be brought about by an act of God, not by human effort or force of arms. Pilate knew that Jesus taught this. Other prophets—Theudas, the Egyptian, signs prophets— would proclaim similar messages in their turn: It was God, not men, who would cause the Jordan to part, or the walls of Jerusalem to crumble, or "signs of deliverance" to be tendered (AJ 20.97–98, 168–170; cf. p. 150). But these men called out huge crowds, convening mass rallies in the desert. No matter how supernaturally they expected to see their message realized, Rome found their immediate effect disruptive and potentially incendiary. The army cut them down. Jesus, by contrast, did his teaching in situ: in village synagogues or at the Temple, where people would have already congregated in any case and, in the instance of Jerusalem during the holidays, where Roman surveillance was already in place. "Day after day I was with you in the Temple teaching" (so Mark's Jesus, at the point of his arrest, 14:49). "I have always taught in synagogues and in the Temple, where all Jews come together; I have said nothing secretly" (so John's Jesus to Annas, 18:20). So again here. Despite his tumultuous entry, Jesus was left unmolested by both Jewish and Roman authorities to preach in the Temple, as he usually had, in the days before the feast.

What was he teaching? That the Kingdom of God approached. What made this Passover different from all the other holidays when he had taught the same message? This time crowds of pilgrims, exuberantly and with conviction, proclaimed Jesus the messiah. What prompted their acclaim on this particular Passover? The acuteness of their expectation of the Kingdom. Here, before going farther, three prevening factors that affect the story from this point onward must be considered: the identity of these crowds; their reasoning in proclaiming Jesus messiah, and the role of the chief priests during Jesus' final week in Jerusalem.

Who were these people? Mark identifies them simply as "many" (*polloi,* 11:8). Going both before and following Jesus, they praise him as coming "in the name of the Lord," and they bless the advent of "the kingdom of our father David" (11:9). Luke, uniquely, shrinks this throng to "the whole multitude *of the disciples*" (Lk 19:37). Matthew and John simply imply that the crowd is a large group of pilgrims. Matthew says that "most of the crowd" hail Jesus (presumably they are pilgrims entering the city, 21:8–9). John suggests that these people had already arrived in Jerusalem, then collected and gone out again specifically to celebrate Jesus' entry. "The next day a great crowd who had come to the feast heard that Jesus was coming to Jerusalem . . . so they went out to meet him" (12:12–13).

The Gospels at this point depict this crowd hailing Jesus himself as "son of David," hence Messiah (Mt 21:9) and King (Lk 19:38; Jn 12:13). Were these people those Galileans and Judeans already familiar with Jesus and his teaching? Perhaps, though precisely because they did know him, they would have little reason to initiate the claim. More likely, I think, Jesus' authoritative proclamation of the Kingdom's immediately imminent arrival triggered for those pilgrims relatively new to his mission the conviction that, were the Kingdom on its way, Jesus himself would be its leader. Enthusiasm for the coming Kingdom, racing within this combustible mix of excited new hearers and faithful followers (who reflected back, perhaps, on their own witness to Jesus' authority, and the healings and exorcisms that underscored it), would transmute quickly into enthused acclamation of Jesus as messiah. And enthusiasm infectiously spreads.

Why should it have started at all? Because of the way that the idea of the messianic age or Kingdom, in Jewish tradition generally and in *Christian* Jewish tradition in particular, is so linked to the idea of the coming of the messiah. This conviction was not universally shared, as a quick review of intertestamental texts reveals. The Judaism of the late Second Temple period was marked by vigorous and vociferous variety, and some Jews were perfectly capable of conceiving God's kingdom without associating any special human figure with its establishment. In the apocalyptic writings of this period, messiah is optional both as a term and a concept.

But clearly, early Christians numbered among those Jews who did link the coming of the messianic age with the coming of the messiah. The evidence on this point is abundant and multiply attested: The pressures of more traditional Jewish messianic thought are precisely what prompt the early Christian revisions of it, expressed in the expectation of Jesus' *Second* Coming. In Paul, in Q, in Mark, the Kingdom's definitive arrival is put off until the Son returns in glory. Leading armies of angels, descending to the sounding of trumpets, gathering in the elect: Jesus of Nazareth, in life the least military of figures, transforms in traditions of his own Second Coming into a recognizably—thus traditional—messianic figure, whose advent will establish the Kingdom of his Father.

How widespread such hopes were among Jews in the Second Temple period cannot be known, but the very birth and growth of the post-Resurrection Christian movement is itself evidence of its vigor. Josephus and, interestingly, two Latin historians, Tacitus (*Histories* 5.13) and Suetonius (*Vespasian* 4), independently report that popular commitment to a messianic prophecy fanned the flames of Jewish rebellion in the period just before and during the revolt. "What more than all else incited them to war," wrote Josephus of his countrymen, was

> an ambiguous oracle, likewise found in their sacred scriptures, to the effect that at that time one from their country would become ruler of the world. This they understood to mean someone of their own race, and many of their wise men went astray in their interpretation of it. The oracle, however, in reality signified the sovereignty of Vespasian, who was proclaimed emperor on Jewish soil. (*BJ* 6.312–313)

The strength of this messianic expectation lingered in Jewish circles long after the devastation of 66–73, even after the debacle of the Bar Kokhba revolt in 132–135. Centuries later, a rabbinic writing depicts Jochanan ben Zakkai, the great authority of the generation of the Jewish War, teaching caution in the face of messianic fervor. "If there was a plant in your hand, and you are told, 'Behold, the Messiah is here,' go and plant the plant, and then go forth to welcome him" (*Avot de-R. Natan* 39, 33b–34a). And even the great Rabbi Akiva is held up as a negative example of what messianic enthusiasm can do. Responding to his identification of bar Kokhba as the Messiah, a colleague observes, "Akiba! Grass will grow through your cheekbones, and the Son of David still will not have come" (*yTann* 68d).

These cautions notwithstanding, the fundamental Jewish prayer known as the Eighteen Benedictions (*Shemoneh Esreh,* "the eighteen"), probably redacted into its final form sometime between 70 and 100 C.E., explicitly praises (and thus petitions) God for the resurrection of the dead, the reunion of dispersed Israel, the restoration of national independence, the destruction of the godless and reward of the just, the rebuilding of Jerusalem, the sending of the Messiah, and the restoration of Temple worship. Pious Jews, including women, slaves, and children (usually exempt from such requirements), were expected to say the prayer three times a day. It embodies in liturgical form the key hopes of apocalyptic eschatology:

Proclaim our liberation with the great trumpet, raise a banner to gather together our dispersed, assemble us from the four corners of the earth. *Blessed are you, Lord, who gathers the banished of your people Israel....* And to your city, Jerusalem, return with mercy and dwell in its midst as you have spoken; build it up soon in our days to be an everlasting building, and raise up quickly in its midst the throne of David. *Blessed are you, Lord, who builds Jerusalem.* Cause the shoot of David to shoot forth quickly, and raise up the horn of his salvation ... bring back the worship into the Holy of Holies of your house. *Blessed are you, Lord, who causes your presence to return to Zion.*

Messianic hope in Jesus' period was neither uniform nor universal, but it was certainly well established and articulate. In many traditional forms of Judaism as in its Christian forms, the coming of the Kingdom was immediately linked with the coming of the messiah. This is the general context we must presuppose in order to understand what survives in the Gospel traditions of the Triumphal Entry, and how that event led to the crucifixion of Jesus. For it was during his entry into the city on this particular Passover that Jesus was first proclaimed messiah.

Again, based on the impression the Gospels convey, Jesus himself was not the source of this messianic identification, though his message was its cause. Did he attempt to dissuade the crowds, even argue against them? There is no way to know. On the evidence of the Crucifixion itself, however, and thus apparently even after their festive entry into Jerusalem around the eighth of Nisan, they continued their acclaim. Jesus, the focus of this popular conviction, had in essence lost control of his audience. Nor, with language like "Kingdom of God" and "messiah son of David" flying around, could he control the crowd's interpretations of his message or their expectations about him. As he continued to teach about the Kingdom in the Temple area during the week, their excitement would only have mounted as the feast approached.

Josephus, writing toward the end of the century, has this to say:

> About this time there lived Jesus, a wise man. He worked surprising
> deeds and was a teacher of such people as accept the truth gladly. He
> won over many Jews and many of the Greeks. When Pilate, upon
> hearing him accused by men of the highest standing among us, con-
> demned him to be crucified, those who had come to love him did not
> give up their affection for him. And the tribe of Christians, so called
> after him, has not disappeared to this day.   (*AJ* 18.63–64)

Josephus here characterizes Jesus as a wise man (*sophos*), a worker of
marvelous deeds (*paradoxa*), and a teacher (*didaskalos*). His characterization conforms strongly to the picture in the Synoptics. The only hint
of anything messianic about Jesus in Josephus' notice here is the way he
designates his followers: They are *Christianoi*. The stem, *Christ-*, points
to the Greek word for messiah, *christos*. Elsewhere in *Antiquities*,
describing events in the year 62 C.E. when the high priest Annas executed James by stoning, Josephus identifies him as "James the brother of
Jesus *the so-called Christ*" (*AJ* 20.200). In other words, Josephus neither
called Jesus *Christos* nor did he say that Jesus claimed the title for himself. Nor do the "men of highest standing" (*protoi*, the "first men")
accuse Jesus of claiming to be Messiah: In fact, Josephus does not say
what the first men accuse Jesus of, or why. His report, independent of
the Gospels, reveals only that Jesus was a wonder-working wise man
and teacher whom Pilate crucified. Josephus relegates the messianic
designation either to Jesus' followers, the *Christianoi*, or to hearsay
("Jesus the so-called Christ").

Josephus' brief discussion fits together with the reticence and ambi-
guity of the Gospels' account, which also never portrays Jesus forthrightly propounding his own messianic identity, but puts the claim only
in the mouths of others. Similarly, in the Passion narratives, Pilate
refers to "Jesus who *is called* the Messiah" (e.g., Mt 27:17, 22). "What do
you wish me to do with the man *you call* the King of the Jews?" (Mk
15:12). It seems mostly likely, then, that this identification of Jesus as
Messiah did *not* come from Jesus himself. Had he claimed this title and
role for himself, Antipas would surely have acted long before Pilate did.
Further, nothing in the traditions about his mission would make him a
plausible messianic candidate in the eyes of his contemporaries. He was
not, like Judah the Galilean or Athronges before him, or bar Kokhba
long after, advocating armed struggle against the Romans (see p. 166);
nor was he even, like some of the later signs prophets, gathering huge

Testimonium Flavianum:
Josephus' Notice on Jesus of Nazareth

In *Jewish Antiquities* 18.63–64, Josephus gives a short summary statement on Jesus. Scholars have debated the historical merits of this passage, some (few, now) maintaining that the whole is authentic, others (another minority), that the whole is a Christian interpolation, that is, a passage written into the manuscript by a later Christian scribe. Most scholars currently incline to see the passage as basically authentic, with a few later insertions by a Christian scribe. The passage as rendered below follows the editorial judgments and English translation of John Meier, *A Marginal Jew,* vol. 1, pp. 60–61. I give the Christian insertions in italic, the Josephan substratum in roman. Note, too, that even with the additions, Josephus' passage on Jesus is less than half the length of his description of John the Baptizer in *Jewish Antiquities* 18.116–119—a clear indication of his view of their relative importance.

At this time there appeared Jesus, a wise man, *if indeed one should call him a man.* For he was a doer of startling deeds, a teacher of people who receive the truth with pleasure. And he gained a following both among many Jews and among many of Greek origin. *He was the messiah.* And when Pilate, because of an accusation made by the leading men among us, condemned him to the cross, those who had loved him previously did not cease to do so. *For he appeared to them on the third day, living again, just as the divine prophets had spoken of these and countless other wondrous things about him.* And up until this very day the tribe of Christians, named after him, has not died out.

masses of people at one time in anticipation of a miraculous token of liberation (see p. 150).

Nor does Jesus seem to have urged that he was the Messiah, though in some special, utterly unprecedented, and previously unknown way. Such a message would have had to make sense to his contemporaries, or he would not have had followers; but, as later Christian tradition a half-century or more after his death shows, the evangelists were still struggling to articulate such a concept themselves. Had any such tradition already existed, they would gladly have availed themselves of it. Instead, they must work hard to make their (respective) cases.

Can anything of Jesus' self-claim be reconstituted from the Gospels? The man they portray teaches and acts with authority. He works exorcisms and healing miracles to reinforce his authority to teach and appears to have utter confidence in his message and in his authority to pronounce it. Those who hear *him,* Jesus taught, will assuredly have a high place in the coming Kingdom; those who fail to heed *his* call will gnash their teeth in the outer darkness once the Kingdom comes. Like his mentor the Baptizer, Jesus presented himself as the authoritative spokesman for his message. He acted, in short, like a prophet.

The title and role of "prophet" and "christ" seesaw in the fourth evangelist's crowd scenes. "This is indeed the prophet!" cry the Galilean multitudes (6:14). In Jerusalem, "some of the people said, 'This is really the prophet!' Others said, 'This is the Christ' " (7:40). The blind man cured by Jesus says, "He is a prophet" (9:17). "If you are the Christ, tell us plainly!" the crowd in the Temple demands (10:24). This theme of Jesus as prophet appears, mixed in with messianic acclamation, in the other Gospels as well. Just after the Triumphal Entry where they had proclaimed him "Son of David," upon entering the city, the pilgrim crowds explain to inquiring Jerusalemites, "This is the prophet, Jesus of Nazareth from Galilee" (Mt 21:11). And Jesus in Q laments, "O Jerusalem, Jerusalem, killing the prophets and stoning those who are sent to you!" (Lk 13:34//Mt 23:37). Luke's Jesus prefaces this lament with a remark, pointing toward the Passion, that applies this identification to himself. "I must go on my way today and tomorrow and the day following; for it cannot be that a prophet should perish away from Jerusalem" (Lk 13:33). And after the Crucifixion, two of his disciples speak of "Jesus of Nazareth, who was a prophet mighty in deed and word before God and all the people" (Lk 24:19).

Later evangelical tradition will settle on "Christ" as the most appropriate designation for Jesus. But the evangelists stand in the developing post-Resurrection tradition, and they have redefined the term, tailoring it to fit what they know of Jesus' life or vice versa. But what about this messianic acclamation before the Resurrection, during Jesus' lifetime? The best evidence we have—unambiguously from the Gospel stories of the Triumphal Entry; upon reflection from their descriptions of Jesus' final Passover in the city—is that the crowd around Jesus was the first to proclaim him Messiah. In the Galilee? No; on the way into Jerusalem. His closest followers? No: The disciples seem to witness the acclaim but not initiate it. Pilgrims, not close associates, are the ones who initiate the cry. Routinely? No; *only* on that final Passover. Because Jesus himself, acting in such a way—riding into town on a donkey, or upsetting the money changers' tables in the Temple—in effect proclaimed himself messiah for those who had eyes to see, and his follow-

ers just echoed his self-claim? Not likely. The ride into the city via
Zechariah 9:9 looks much too much like evangelical proof-texting. And
in light of the support service that the money changers provided, as well
as the sheer size of the Temple court and the post-70 redaction of the
Gospels, it seems at least uncertain whether Jesus demonstrated against
them at all. And in any case, such a gesture would hardly have been
generally understood as "messianic": The messiah battles Israel's enemies, not Israel's traditional worship.

So why, then, on this particular Passover, would the crowds in
Jerusalem have proclaimed Jesus as messiah? Left looking at this
record—Gospel accounts, Josephus' notice, the subsequent outcome of
events—historians are like newscasters observing a muddy football
field several days after the game, trying to imagine from the "record" in
the ground the sequence of specific plays. What causes, invisible or
obscured, could conceivably have led to the known results?

Imagine once again Jesus' preaching, both in the Galilee and in
Judea, that the Kingdom of God approached. Imagine that he conducted such a mission for years before his final encounter with the
priests and Pilate in Jerusalem. Every time that he goes up to the city, he
prophesies this event and speaks of its nearness; perhaps, as Matthew
and John especially depict, he demonstrates his prophetic authority
with "mighty acts," "spectacular healings" (Josephus' *paradoxa*). "And
the blind and the lame came to him in the Temple, and he healed them"
(Mt 21:14; cf Jn 5:1–9, where Jesus by the pool of Bethzatha heals the
man who had been paralyzed for thirty-eight years). After the holiday,
he returns to the Galilee and resumes teaching and healing there. As
the next holiday approaches, he turns south, to Judea, then up to
Jerusalem, and then back again. And the same the next season, and the
next—how many times we cannot know.

But perhaps at the beginning of the cycle of preaching and pilgrimage that ended in what turned out to be his final trip to the city, Jesus
announced that this Passover would be the last before the Kingdom
arrived. God would come in power to establish his rule at or as the climax of Jesus' mission. This news would have spread throughout the
movement's human network, linking villages from the Galilee through
Judea and up to Jerusalem. Pilgrims gathering in the city for Passover,
hearing the news in advance of Jesus' own arrival, consequently greeted
him, when he appeared, as the human agent of God's coming kingdom—perhaps, indeed, as its king. Absent explicit evidence, what sup-

ports this conjecture? The traditions about Jesus' Triumphal Entry the last time he came to Jerusalem, which may preserve a genuine echo of the singular enthusiasm and excitement of this particular pilgrimage. The stories about the behavior of the Twelve, his closest followers, where traces of a huge expectation lie submerged beneath reports of their confusion and despair at Jesus' arrest. At that point, "they all forsook him and fled" (Mk 14:49). Their actions show—evangelical Passion predictions notwithstanding—that they were utterly unprepared for what happened. When they all went up to Jerusalem with Jesus that Passover, Roman dominion was not what they expected to see triumph. Instead, they were expecting the triumph of God.

And finally, the traditions about the Resurrection appearances that grow in the wake of this black moment display the power of his closest followers' commitment to Jesus' message that the Kingdom really *was* at hand. That Passover, in Jerusalem, they were expecting an eschatological event, the arrival of God's kingdom. What they got instead was the Crucifixion. But then, an *unexpected* eschatological event occurred: God, they became convinced, had raised Jesus from the dead. Two of the prime promises of the messianic age—the resurrection of the dead and the vindication of the righteous—these men believed they now saw realized in the person of their executed leader.

The traditions of the Last Supper, further, might provide a glimpse of Jesus' own sense that he had lost control of the situation, that the crowds had gotten out of hand. Aware of the danger that their own mounting enthusiasm placed him in, he had a last meal specifically with his committed core group. In the course of this meal Jesus evidently spoke frankly about the danger he was in. If worse came to worst, if he were killed, he told the Twelve to see in his death a confirmation of the truth of his mission: "Take, this is my body. . . . This is my blood of the covenant, which is poured out for many" (Mk 14:22, 24). No matter what happened to him, Jesus taught, the truth of his prophetic message stood: The Kingdom was near. "I shall not drink again of the fruit of the vine until that day when I drink it new in the Kingdom of God" (14:25).

"It is on these festive occasions"—that is, during the high holidays of the pilgrim festivals—"that sedition is most apt to break out" (*BJ* 1.88). The chief priests of Jesus' period were every bit as aware of this tendency as Josephus was some four decades later. Jesus teaches in the Temple courtyard; the excited pilgrim crowds collect there. As the holiday nears, the nervous energy, on both sides, mounts. The chief priests know what Pilate knows: Jesus himself is not dangerous. But for the first time, this Passover, the crowds who swarm around him are. In the intensity of their expectation—that the Kingdom was literally about to arrive? That Jesus was about to be revealed as messiah? That the restoration of Israel was at hand?—they are restive, potentially incendiary. These chief priests are the ones so positioned to know both the temperament of the holiday crowd, and—because they share a common tradition—the disruptive potential of a lively messianic expectation. And in reality these men, and the high priest in particular, were caught in the middle between their own people and Rome, responsible to the prefect, the Syrian legate, and ultimately the emperor if domestic peace faltered. If any incident erupted, they were accountable.

This pattern emerges clearly from Josephus' reports of such incidents. After protesters had hacked down the golden eagle built over one of the Temple's gates, Herod not only executed the guilty parties, he deposed the high priest too: It had been on his watch that events had careened out of control (*BJ* 1.651–55; *AJ* 17:149–67; above, p. 166). And after Pilate's bloodletting in Samaria when crowds followed a prophet to Mount Gerizim, Vitellius the Syrian legate not only sent Pilate to judgment in Rome but relieved Caiaphas of office and appointed a new high priest as well (*AJ* 18.85–89; above, p. 172). So, too, after the murder of Galilean pilgrims on their way through Samaria to reach Jerusalem in the year 50 C.E., when the resulting conflagration threatened to engulf the region. After exercising local justice, the Syrian legate sent Ananias the high priest, the chief priest Jonathan, and other high-ranking citizens to Rome to be heard by the emperor, though none of these men had been personally involved in the violence (*BJ* 2.232–44).

The priests were held responsible not only by Rome; they felt their responsibility acutely themselves. Thus in the final turmoil before the city declared open revolt in 66 C.E., the aristocratic priests tried hard to deter their people from their bloody undertaking. Advising the populace to submit to the procurator Florus,

> The chief priests, having assembled the multitude in the Temple, exhorted them to meet the advancing Romans and to prevent any irremediable disaster. . . . The factious party refused to listen. . . . Then it was that every priest and every minister of God, bearing in procession

the holy vessels and wearing the robes they usually wore when performing their priestly duties, and the harpers and choristers with their
instruments, fell on their knees and earnestly implored the people not
to provoke the Romans. . . . Even the chief priests might then have
been seen heaping dust upon their heads, their breasts bared, their garments rent. [These are all signs of mourning.] . . . By these remon-
strances they succeeded in soothing the multitude.   (*BJ* 2.320–325)

The excitement of the crowds around Jesus that Passover might easily have spilled over into riot, or been perceived as about to do so by the
Roman troops staring down at them from the roof of the Temple stoa.
The priests were perfectly positioned both to know their mood and the
likely Roman response. If this is what Caiaphas feared, then as the
highest Jewish leader responsible for preserving the peace, he would
have alerted Pilate.

What then? Here again, where the evidence thins, we must speculate. Perhaps Caiaphas said something to Pilate like, "You know about
the rumor spreading this week that Jesus of Nazareth is messiah. Some
people actually expect him to reveal himself this Passover. The crowd
seems restless." Pilate would know what to do. Working in conjunction
with the high priest's Temple guard, who knew the city infinitely better
than his own troops did, he would move swiftly, arresting Jesus by
stealth, at night, to keep these noisy enthusiasts quiet as long as possible.
Let them wake up to their messiah already on a cross by the next morning. Killing Jesus publicly, by crucifixion, would go a long way toward
disabusing the crowd. Let him hang indicted by their own belief: KING
OF THE JEWS. A nice touch—an insult to the idea itself as well as to their
convictions.

Or perhaps Caiaphas himself was the one who decided that Jesus'
death was the only effective way to deflate the wild hopes growing
among the city's pilgrims. Again, Caiaphas also, like Pilate, knew that
Jesus himself was harmless. But if this mob started anything—a
demonstration, a riot; if they simply disrupted the normal course of
events in the holiday-swollen city—bloodshed would surely follow.
Caiaphas by this point had some twelve years' experience with Pilate's
techniques of crowd control. "It is expedient for you," the Gospel of
John has him say, "that one man should die for the people, and that the
whole nation should not perish" (11:50). If he himself moved to arrest
Jesus, he might then have simply handed him over to Pilate with a rec-
ommendation to execute. That Pilate chose specifically crucifixion as

Jesus' manner of death, however, suggests once again that the prefect also, and not just the high priest, really did have the crowds first and foremost in view.

This reconstruction is sketched primarily from John. Mark's picture of two Jewish trials at night and again at dawn on 15 Nisan, for all the reasons reviewed (see p. 223), is just too implausible to credit. The virtue of drawing Jesus' mission from John, with his repeated sojourns in Jerusalem, is that it can account for Pilate's already knowing who Jesus is. This datum alone, from all the other traditions the Gospels offer, can explain the core historical anomaly of the Passion stories: Jesus was crucified, but his followers were not.

So also for Pilate's first question to Jesus when Jesus is led before him: "Are you the King of the Jews?" (Mk 15:2//Mt 27:11//Lk 23:3//Jn 18:33). In three of the four Gospels—Mark, Matthew, and John—the question is utterly unprepared for by the narrative *except* by reference back to the Triumphal Entry. Otherwise, Pilate has no information on which to base such a question. Luke alone, smoothing over this omission in Mark, provides a bridge. "We found this man perverting our nation and forbidding us to give tribute to Caesar and saying that he himself is Christ a king" (Lk 23:2). In our reconstruction, Pilate already knows who Jesus is, and thus already knows that he and, by extension, his immediate followers pose no first-order political threat. And from reports of the crowd's acclamation when they entered Jerusalem with Jesus on 8 Nisan, at the beginning of the preparatory week before the feast, Pilate knows, too, that Jesus has been hailed as king.

Both the Jewish trial scenes and the hearing before Pilate, as they now stand in all the Gospels, are shaped by later Christian apologetic concerns. The evangelists place the burden of incriminating Jesus and insisting that he die on priestly leadership in Jerusalem—defunct at the point that they write. The "crowds," too, "the people" in Jerusalem who howl before Pilate for Jesus' death, are also ashes in the recent past. Indeed, the avowal Matthew puts in the mouth of these people as they demand Jesus' death—"His blood be upon us and upon our children!" (27:25)—the evangelist knew had already come due: The city and its residents had been utterly destroyed within a generation of Jesus' execution. Pilate, who in these later stories represents Roman justice, in contrast seeks to set Jesus free. Urging Jesus to defend himself against the chief priests' accusations ("for he perceived that it was out of envy that the chief priests had delivered him up," Mk 15:10), he makes every effort to free him, finally giving in to the priests' demand only because he is anxious "to satisfy the crowd" (15:15).

Is the hostile crowd, then, solely the (apologetic) invention of the evangelists? We cannot know for certain, but logically it need not be. The presence in the city during the holiday of a crowd violently opposed to Jesus, as well as a crowd energetically enthused, in fact sharpens Pilate's decision: by one act, he can appease one while simultaneously deflating the other. Other reconstructions are less plausible. The evangelists' vague designation ("the crowd") cannot refer to the *same* group of people because of the way they so condense the action: The priests do not have enough time to swing popular opinion around in the course of this single, highly packed interval between evening (when Jesus is so popular that he must be ambushed to be arrested without incident) and morning (when the crowd demands his death). Nor could the hostile crowd have been "most of the people." Had Jesus been so unpopular, Pilate may indeed have moved to kill him (thus appeasing Jesus' numerous opponents), but would scarcely have had reason to crucify him. The one group historically necessary in any of these scenarios, however, is the numerous, vocally enthusiastic crowd. Without them, Pilate would have had no reason to crucify.

The rest of the Gospels' Passion accounts, once Jesus goes from Pilate to the cross, is thickly overlaid with theological themes and obviously shaped by biblical testimonies. The evangelists quarry the descriptive details of Jesus' death from Isaiah, Psalms, Zechariah. Thus Jesus submits in silence to calumny (Is 53:7) and abuse (Is 50:6). He refuses wine and myrrh (Prv 31:6?) or wine and gall (Ps 69:21). His garments are divided (Ps 22:18); he cries from the cross (variously Ps 22:1 or 31:5). Once he is dead, the soldiers do not break his bones (Ps 34:20), though one does pierce his side (Zec 12:10). These narratives serve a theological rather than historical purpose. They demonstrate that Jesus, quite literally, died "according to the Scriptures." They cannot be made to yield much historical information past the bare fact that his crucifixion followed rapidly upon his arrest

Modern reconstructions of these events often place much of the burden of Pilate's decision to execute Jesus, or the priests' motivation for recommending that he do so, on Jesus' own self-claim. Pilate kills Jesus as a messianic pretender because he knew that Jesus thought of himself in some sense as King of the Jews. Pilate, in this view, thus teaches Jesus a lesson. Or perhaps—so run these arguments—the priests were angry because they knew that Jesus thought of himself as having superior authority, perhaps because he never reminded those whose sins he pronounced forgiven to offer a sin sacrifice in Jerusalem (hence undermining the Temple's function), perhaps because he overturned the money changers' tables (thereby signaling his disapproval, for one reason or another, of the entire system). Accordingly, the priests then ask Pilate to teach him a lesson. True, were it not for the crowds, neither party might have much cared what Jesus thought about himself. But on either of these constructions, the reasons for Pilate's decision to crucify shrink to something either private (Jesus' thoughts about himself) or personal (the chief priests' grudge against Jesus' *lèse majesté*).

The reconstruction offered here places the burden of these events where the cross in any case points to: the intended audience for the spectacle, the holiday crowds. Jesus and his mission had been part of Jerusalem's landscape for years. His teachings about the coming Kingdom, like the Baptizer's before him, were well known. His pinpointing the arrival of the Kingdom for *this* particular Passover was the spark that ignited all the rest. The tinder had long been laid: hopes for the coming Kingdom, the message of liberation woven into the story of Passover itself, the excitement of pilgrimage, the swollen city population, the singular authority with which Jesus taught and acted in proclaiming his message. And more fundamental to all this: the biblical traditions and pilgrim psalms lauding Jerusalem forever as the city of the Great King, the city of God and of his chosen one, his beloved son, scion of David's line, the Messiah.

Jesus' authoritative announcement of the Kingdom's imminent arrival spiked popular commitment and enthusiasm on this last trip to Jerusalem, and this popular enthusiasm is the origin of Jesus' identification as the son of David. Messianic speculations, definitions, expectations had multiplied in this period. Their various esoteric permutations stand in the sectarian literature of the time. But the most fundamental definition, the one scripturally attested and therefore generally available, the one already manifest in Paul's letters, in the Gospels of Matthew and of Luke, in later rabbinic piety and even synagogue prayer, is the idea of the Messiah son of David. Jesus' closest followers, and Jesus himself, never claimed this title or role for him. The crowds whose hopes he fanned and fed did. Their fervor led directly to his death.

What happened next? Whether the night of the seder (15 Nisan;

Mark) or the night before (14 Nisan; John), Jesus would have been apprehended surreptitiously, perhaps by a mixed posse of Temple guards and Roman soldiers led to the place of ambush by a disaffected disciple (Jn 18:2, 3, 12). Caiaphas and Pilate would have arranged things together, needing to move swiftly, effectively, and in secret for precisely the reason the Gospels state: Any public move against Jesus would risk riot (Mk 14:1–2; for this reason, too, as a precaution, it is an armed contingent that goes out to make the arrest). The crowd's excitement had mounted as the night of Passover approached, as the ancient story of God's redemption of the children of Israel from their oppressive bondage to Pharaoh resonated with the wild conviction that they now shared: *This* was the Passover of their redemption; *this* was the hour when God would reveal his Messiah, redeem and restore Israel, vanquish unrighteousness, wipe away every tear. . . .

Mark's chronology at this point is more dramatic than John's. The nightfall transition from 14 to 15 Nisan builds a stop-action into the swift sequence of events. No matter how gripped with excitement the holiday throng, no matter how agitated their hopes, in the declining hours of the day certain things, no matter what, had to get done. The corban Pesach, the lamb or goat for the sacred meal, had to be brought to the Temple, slaughtered, prepared; the evening prayers said; the biblical story recalled and feast begun once night fell. The necessary busyness would create exactly the sort of distraction that would give Pilate and Caiaphas their opportunity. Late that night, while some in the city still feasted and others, finally, slept, their soldiers found Jesus, who offered (just as they thought) no resistance.

Perhaps Jesus was led before the High Priest or his father-in-law, though this is unlikely. Between their duties at the Temple and their festive meals at home, these men would have put in a long day already; and besides, what need? Perhaps Jesus was interrogated briefly by Pilate, though this, too, is unlikely. There was no point. His death warrant had already been signed by the very crowd that had clamored around him, responding to his message of impending redemption. Pilate's soldiers had their orders, and they knew what to do.

Day would have dawned. Gradually, sleepily, the city within the walls and the pilgrim city encamped in tents and booths in the valley below would have stirred to life. Slowly at first, somehow, then spreading, then blazing rapidly, the news would have traveled. Perhaps then—astonished? shocked? bereft?—crowds of Jesus' followers together with the pilgrim throng would have streamed out of the city to the hill just outside, to the Place of the Skull, Golgotha. There they would have beheld the man, dying on a cross. Jesus of Nazareth. King of the Jews. As far as Pilate was concerned, that was the end of the matter.

Afterword

JESUS, CHRISTIANITY, AND HISTORY

I N   T H E   W A Y S that counted for him, Pilate was right. With Jesus dead, the city swung back under control. The turbulent holiday crowds ceased their agitated anticipation of the coming Kingdom and God's imminent revelation of Jesus as his messiah. Chastened, demoralized, they quieted down again. The rest of the holiday probably passed without incident.

For Jesus' closest followers, however, it was otherwise. Panicked by his arrest, most had fled. What happened next we cannot know for certain, because our different sources tell us different stories: Only the broadest lines are clear. Absolutely certain that Jesus was dead, some members of this small group began to perceive, and then to proclaim, that Jesus lived again. God, they said, had raised him from the dead.

What these disciples actually saw or experienced is now impossible to say. Paul, whose testimony is late (some twenty years after these events) and admittedly secondhand ("I delivered to you as of first importance what I also received"), teaches that the Risen Christ appeared in a *pneumatikon sōma,* a "spiritual body." Whatever this might be, Paul insists that this body was *not* flesh and blood. "I tell you this, brethren: *flesh and blood cannot inherit the Kingdom of God,* nor does the perishable inherit the imperishable" (1 Cor 15:3, 44, 50). The still later traditions in Luke and John speak to the contrary. "See my hands and my feet," says Luke's Risen Christ, directing his startled disciples to look at the wounds he still bears. "It is I myself. Handle me, and see; for *a spirit has not flesh and bones as you see that I have*" (Lk 24:39–40). "Put your finger here, and see my hands," John's Risen Christ orders doubting Thomas. "And put out your hand, and place it in my side. Do not be faithless, but believing" (Jn 20:27).

Strictly speaking, these reports tell us nothing of Jesus of Nazareth. His story ended on a Roman cross. And these reports tell us very little about what the actual disciples might have seen. Written considerably after the events of that Passover, they diverge significantly between themselves.

What these Resurrection stories do give us is a glimpse into the convictions of Jesus' closest disciples, who are their ultimate source. The resurrection of the dead was one of the redemptive acts anticipated in Jewish traditions about the End of Days, when God would redeem Israel and bring them back to the Land. If his disciples believed that they had seen Jesus raised—whatever it was that they experienced, however we choose to interpret it now—then they were continuing to function within the apocalyptic paradigm established by his mission.

Resurrection within more traditional forms of Judaism had been imagined as a communal experience, one of the saving acts anticipated at the Endtime. "I will open your graves and raise you from your graves, O my people," God promises in the prophet Ezekiel. "I will bring you home into the land of Israel" (Ez 37:12). "Many of those who sleep in the dust of the earth shall awake," prophesies Daniel (12:2). "Blessed are you, O Lord," runs the text of the Eighteen Benedictions, "you who revive the dead." The significance for Jesus' apostles of his individual resurrection was that it heralded this nearing general one: Jesus was "the first fruits of those who have fallen asleep" (1 Cor 15:20). His resurrection thus confirmed for his followers that the Kingdom, and so the resurrection of all the dead, was on the way; indeed, very near. Their experience of his resurrection confirmed for them both Jesus' own authority and the authority of his message.

Yet still the Kingdom did not come. Meanwhile, evidently, these Resurrection appearances continued for some time. Paul lists a series of such epiphanies (1 Cor 15:5–8). Luke closes his Gospel and opens his history, the Acts of the Apostles, with the Risen Christ speaking to the disciples: "To them he presented himself alive after his passion by many proofs, appearing to them during forty days, and speaking of the Kingdom of God" (Acts 1:3). The closest followers of Jesus—"Cephas, and then the Twelve"—responded to their experience of these appearances by returning to Jerusalem. Did they gather back in the city in anticipation of the Kingdom's coming? Were they waiting, having construed Jesus' resurrection as itself a signal of the approaching End? If so, then eventually the continuation of time pushed them to a new conclusion, and a different interpretation of the significance of Jesus' resurrection. Bursting into energetic, committed, and sustained missionary activity, these disciples looked forward to the Risen Christ's *definitive* reappearance soon, at his Parousia. In the brief time they thought was remaining, they dedicated their lives to spreading this good news, the *euangelion* of Jesus, to all Israel.

It was in this post-Resurrection stage, as the movement spread to synagogue communities along the coast and into the Diaspora, that these disciples began to encounter significant numbers of sympathetic Gentiles. How many is "significant"? Enough so that, by the late 40s, various apostles assembled together with the leaders of the Christian community gathered in Jerusalem in order to decide what should become of these Gentiles, and how they were to be integrated into the *ekklēsiai* of followers of Christ (Gal 2:1–10; for a different description of recognizably the same assembly, Acts 15). Were these Gentiles more like Godfearers, that is, voluntary Judaisers, and so free of any obligation to Torah? Or were they more like converts, thus "bound to keep the whole law" (Gal 5:3) including, for males, circumcision?

The position taken by this assembly gives us, again, the measure of the movement's continuing apocalyptic commitment and the need for social improvisations that their unprecedented situation called for. Gentiles-in-Christ, they agreed, need not convert to Judaism. Shunning idolatry and the sins associated with it would suffice. The only context within Jewish tradition native to such nonpagan Gentiles was the Kingdom spoken of by the prophets. This new, Gentile Christian population thus gives us another measure of the earliest community's apocalyptic orientation. The rest of the world might still be in the old age, laboring under the forces of darkness and decay, but those inside the *ekklēsia* already lived according to the new age, empowered by God's Spirit (Rom 8:1–39; see p. 133). And as the prophets had long ago foreseen, when the Kingdom came—as in a sense it already had for these communities whose members worked miracles and prophesied, whose Gentiles voluntarily relinquished their native religious allegiances to make a sole commitment to the God of Israel—God would gather in not only Israel, redeemed from sin, but also the nations, redeemed, at last, from their slavery to false gods. Thus Paul to his Gentiles in Galatia (note the tense of his verbs): "Formerly, when you did not know God, you were in bondage to beings that by nature are no gods; but now *you have come to know* God" (Gal 4:8–9).

The disciples' conviction that they had seen the Risen Christ, their permanent relocation to Jerusalem, their principled inclusion of Gentiles *as* Gentiles—all these are historical bedrock, facts known past doubting about the earliest community after Jesus' death. They fall into a pattern. Each marks a point along the arc of apocalyptic hope that passes from Daniel to Paul, from Qumran's Scrolls to the synagogue's Eighteen Benedictions, from the prophets of the Jewish canon to the Book of Revelation, which concludes the New Testament: the conviction that God is good; that he is in control of history; that he will not countenance evil indefinitely. All the many and various themes in all these different writings unite around this fundamental belief that, at the End, God will prevail over evil, restoring and redeeming his creation.

We can also locate along this arc particular prophets of God's coming kingdom: John the Baptizer, Theudas, the Egyptian, the signs prophets reported by Josephus. And, of course, Jesus of Nazareth, whom the disciples, after his death, proclaimed Christ. The form their proclamation took reveals to us the power in this period of specifically messianic traditions about the coming Kingdom. Their experience of Jesus' resurrection did not require his disciples either to impute the charged title "Christ" to him, or to link their belief in the approaching fulfillment of his message of the Kingdom to an expectation of his return. But they did. The *Second* Coming of Jesus—Christianity's singular contribution to the variety of messianic expectations in late Second Temple Judaism—resonates precisely with the Davidic paradigm. To the sound of trumpets, leading angelic hosts, defeating the powers of evil, the Risen Christ would return as a warrior.

It was the crowds assembled for Pesach in Jerusalem, I have argued, and not these close associates of Jesus, who first proclaimed Jesus messiah. They did so in part because they were swept up by their enthusiasm for his authoritative message that the Kingdom was at hand: The Kingdom would be accompanied by the Son of David. And they could do so precisely because they did *not* know him. Unlike those in the core group who had followed him during his mission, and thus who knew perfectly well how distant Jesus was from anything like a recognizably messianic candidate, these pilgrims had no other context to place Jesus in save the one in which they had first met him: during the pilgrimage feast in the city of David at Passover, in all the excitement, panoply, and ritual reenactment of the holiday that commemorated the liberation and redemption of their people. Their enthusiasm for Jesus and his message had led directly to his death on the cross.

Jesus' crucifixion as King of the Jews had come as a shock to his core followers. Their experiences of his continued presence after his death, on the evidence of the Gospels, surprised them, too. Seeking to understand what they had witnessed, they turned to Scripture. It was there that they found various ways to conceive of their vindicated leader. Paul's letters, the Gospels, Acts of the Apostles, and the other writings that would eventually comprise the New Testament—all these record the creative meditations of this first apostolic generation and those of believers who came into the community after them. In these texts Jesus still stands as his earliest followers during his mission had perceived him: a true prophet, commissioned by God. Through Isaiah, they saw Jesus as God's Suffering Servant: "He was wounded for our transgressions; he was bruised for our iniquities. . . . The Lord has laid on him the iniquity of us all" (Is 53:5). The language of Leviticus offered images of sacrifice upon the altar of God: Jesus, then, might be understood as a sacrifice, a corban: "Behold the Lamb of God!" (Jn 1:36). He was the Son of Man appearing at the End of the Age, at first suffering, but later returning with the clouds of heaven. "To him was given dominion and glory and kingdom. . . . His kingdom shall not be destroyed" (Dn 7:14; Mk 13:26). And he was God's anointed one, champion of the Kingdom, his messiah.

This last designation was born specifically of events surrounding the disciples' final Passover with Jesus—the jubilant popular acclaim, the ugly execution as King of the Jews. But their experience of Jesus' resurrection cast all these foregoing events in a new light. In the post-

Resurrection retrospect of Jesus' core followers, "messiah"—variously modified, to be sure, in light of this retrospection—came to figure as the most fitting title of all.

THE JESUS ENCOUNTERED in the present reconstruction is a prophet who preached the coming apocalyptic Kingdom of God. His message coheres both with that of his predecessor and mentor, John the Baptizer, and with that of the movement that sprang up in his name. This Jesus thus is *not* primarily a social reformer with a revolutionary message; nor is he a religious innovator radically redefining the traditional ideas and practices of his native religion. His urgent message had not the present so much as the near future in view.

Further, what distinguished Jesus' prophetic message from those of others was primarily its timetable, not its content. Like John the Baptizer, he emphasized his own authority to preach the coming Kingdom; like Theudas, the Egyptian, the signs prophets, and again like the Baptizer, he expected its arrival soon. But the vibrant conviction of his followers even decades after the Crucifixion, together with the unprecedented phenomenon of the mission to Israel and the inclusion of Gentiles, suggests that Jesus had stepped up the Kingdom's timetable from *soon* to *now*. By actually naming the day or date of the Kingdom's coming, perhaps even for that very same Passover that proved to be his last, Jesus galvanized crowds gathered in Jerusalem who were not socialized to his mission—its pacifist tenor, its emphasis on divine rather than human action—and who in praising the approaching Kingdom proclaimed him Son of David and Messiah. It was this combustible mix of factors—the excited popular acclaim, in Jerusalem at its most densely populated pilgrim festival, when Pilate was in town specifically to keep his eye on the crowd—*not* his teaching as such, nor his arguments with other Jews on the meaning of Sabbath, Temple, purity, or some other aspect of Torah, that led directly to Jesus' execution as King of the Jews.

Finally, a Jesus whose itinerary is sketched primarily not from the Synoptics but from John—a Jesus, that is, whose mission extended routinely not only to the Galilee but also to Judea, and specifically Jerusalem—can speak to the anomaly that has propelled this investigation, namely, that Jesus alone was killed as an insurrectionist on that Passover, but none of his disciples were. A repeated mission in Jerusalem, especially during the pilgrimage holidays when the prefect, too, of necessity, was there, explains how Caiaphas and Pilate would both already know who Jesus was and what he preached, and thus know as well that he was not in any first-order way dangerous. Just as the crowd's enthusiasm for Jesus as messiah accounts for the specific manner of his death, so Jesus' dual focus—Judea, especially Jerusalem in and around the Temple, as well as the Galilee—accounts for the high priest's and the prefect's familiarity with his mission, and thus explains why Jesus was the sole focus of their action.

Essential questions, nonetheless, remain unanswered. Why did Jesus respond to John the Baptizer's call to repentance and purification in the face of the approaching Kingdom? Why did his immediate disciples, in their turn, make such a commitment to follow him as they did? Why was his apocalyptic message so compelling? Why did his disciples, alone of all those who followed charismatic prophet-figures in this period, claim that Jesus had been raised from the dead? Why did they eventually infer from this experience that they should continue Jesus' mission by extending it out to the Diaspora?

Here the explanatory nature of historical investigation must cede both to our own ignorance and to its own limitations. In the end, history itself is more a descriptive than an explanatory enterprise. It runs more on coherent narrative than on strictly testable propositions. While the reconstruction of a sequence of events permits, indeed invites, speculation on the causal links between them, history offers not so much explanation as close description of a particular sort. We cannot hope to measure the truth of an historical proposition with the certainty that we could test or prove an experimental hypothesis in the empirical sciences. No historical reconstruction can be *proven* to be true. The best it can do, once interpretation has woven as much of the evidence as it can into a meaningful, coherent, and plausible pattern, is persuade.

The current welter of work on the Jesus of history reflects the confusions of competing interpretive narratives. One historian's apocalyptic prophet is another's radical social reformer, another's pious, individually oriented Hasid, another's political critic, another's Cynic-like sage. But all narratives are not created equal, and the reasons for choosing between them, for deciding which is persuasive, are not arbitrary. This is so because, even if the focus of a historical narrative is an individual, that individual, be it Jesus or anyone else, lived in a social context. This social context is the historian's critical promontory.

This means that the search for the historical Jesus must be, of necessity, a search for his first-century audience, too. This might seem like asking for trouble: After all, if Jesus seems an elusive subject, those who heard him seem even more so. At least we have documents that are about him; about them, by comparison, precious little.

Yet upon reflection, all the information in our sources actually speaks more directly about them than about him, for Jesus left us no writings. Paul's letters, the Gospels—and, from an outsider's perspective, Josephus—testify less to Jesus directly than to the effect he had on others. These ancient documents, then, must be read no less in an effort to reconstruct them as to reconstruct him. It is this great cloud of witnesses—Jesus' anonymous audiences; his disciples; his sympathizers, and his opponents—that provides a point of purchase in the swirl of competing historical reconstructions. The prime goal of the historian is to find a first-century Jesus whose mission would make sense to his contemporary first-century Jewish hearers. It was on his fundamental intelligibility to them that the whole rest of the history of Christianity depended.

The challenge of placing Jesus coherently within his native, early first-century environment is aided by the handful of indisputable facts that have served as the touchstones for this reconstruction: his encounter with John the Baptizer, his popular following, his proclamation of the Kingdom of God, his crucifixion by Pilate in Jerusalem, the survival of his core followers, who took up his proclamation of the Kingdom while identifying Jesus as Christ, risen from the dead, and extending the mission out from its Jewish matrix to also include Gentiles. No reconstruction of the historical Jesus can persuade if it cannot meaningfully accommodate, as well, this handful of sure facts.

These facts—some corroborated by outside sources—come chiefly through the medium of early Christian writings. *All* of these texts are written from a post-Resurrection perspective, which in turn refracts what historical reminiscences they contain. And, Paul excepted, all the other Christian authors write with the knowledge that the Temple in Jerusalem was no more. This knowledge, no less than their beliefs about Jesus, affects how they tell their stories about him. The approach to a credible approximation of the historical figure of Jesus of Nazareth lies through these stories, traversed and in effect, through a critical knowledge of Jesus' environment, corrected for these later points of view.

In the end, the person we seek stands with his back turned toward us, his face toward the others of his own generation. For Jesus of Nazareth, as any person, lived intact and entirely within his own culture and period, innocent of what the future held. And while he and his message do relate to the various forms of Christianity that ultimately resulted from his mission, their interpretations of Jesus as Christ are identical neither with his own religious beliefs, nor with each other's. The historical figure of Jesus does stand as the starting point of the later Christian interpretations of him. For this reason, an accurate appreciation of his actual historical context does matter to theology. Bad history will result in bad theology. (Try to imagine a Christianity centered on a sixth-century Norse Jesus slain by invading Finns. It won't work. Neither should more subtly inappropriate "historical" contexts—"urbanized" Galilees, warring classes, misogynist Pharisees.) But the correspondence between the historical Jesus and later Christian confessions of faith about him is indirect rather than direct, mitigated rather than immediate.

The evangelists themselves amply demonstrate this point. The "historical" Jesus—that is, Jesus as they imagined him during his lifetime, among his contemporaries—was their common focal point. But they each viewed him from the perspective of their own time and place, which, though some nineteen centuries closer than ours is, inevitably affected their view. Through their various interpretations the evangelists "updated" Jesus, bringing him into their own historical and religious environments—post-Temple, anti-Pharisee, mixed Jewish and Gentile. Mark arranged and thus interpreted prior traditions. Matthew both edited and augmented Mark. So did Luke, although differently. John is outstandingly different from these three. If we consider the range of later noncanonical Gospels—the Gospel of Thomas; the Gospel of Peter; the Gospel of the Egyptians, and still others—these differences of interpretation only multiply. While each Gospel relates stories and teachings that are clearly variations on a common theme, each evangelist, nonetheless, in a certain sense creates and presents his own Jesus, one who serves to establish and so legitimate the beliefs and practices of the evangelist's own, later community.

The task of the current quest for the historical Jesus is fundamentally different, and its points of principle distinguish it from theology both ancient and modern. A theological construction of Jesus can appropriately strive to relate this foundational figure to the concerns and customs of the modern believing community. As many different theological interpretations will result as there are churches—Roman Catholic, Greek Orthodox, Pentecostal, Baptist, Presbyterian, and on and on. The goal of that effort is to find what Jesus *means* to those who gather in his name, within that church. But a historical construction of

Jesus looks for what Jesus *meant* to those who followed him in their own lifetimes, and his. It in principle works in the opposite direction, not pulling Jesus into a modern context but placing him, as coherently and compellingly as possible, in his own.

Such an effort must respect the distance between now and then, between his concerns and commitments and ours. The historical Jesus of Nazareth was never and can never be our contemporary. To drape him in garments borrowed from current agendas while asserting that these agendas were actually his only distorts and so obscures who he was.

If modern believers seek a Jesus who is morally intelligible and religiously relevant, then it is to them that the necessary work of creative and responsible *re*interpretation falls. Such a project is not historical (the critical construction of an ancient figure) but theological (the generation of contemporary meaning within particular religious communities). Multiple and conflicting theological claims inevitably result, as various as the different communities that stand behind them. But this theological reinterpretation should neither be mistaken for, nor presented as, historical description.

To regard Jesus historically requires releasing him from service to modern concerns or confessional identity. It means respecting his integrity as an actual person, as subject to passionate conviction and unintended consequences, as surprised by turns of events and as innocent of the future as is anyone else. It means allowing him the irreducible otherness of his own antiquity, the strangeness Schweitzer captured in his poetic closing description: "He comes to us as One unknown, without a name, as of old, by the lakeside." It is when we renounce the false familiarity proffered by the dark angels of Relevance and Anachronism that we see Jesus, his contemporaries, and perhaps even ourselves, more clearly in our common humanity.

ABBREVIATIONS

Jewish Scriptures

Gn	Genesis	Ez	Ezekiel
Ex	Exodus	Am	Amos
Lv	Leviticus	Mi	Micah
Nm	Numbers	Zep	Zephaniah
Dt	Deuteronomy	Zec	Zechariah
Jos	Joshua	Mal	Malachi
Sm	Samuel	Ps	Psalms
Kgs	Kings	Prv	Proverbs
Is	Isaiah	Dn	Daniel
Jer	Jeremiah	Chr	Chronicles

Apocrypha

Mc	Maccabees	Tb	Tobit

New Testament

Mt	Matthew	Jn	John
Mk	Mark	Acts	Acts of the Apostles
Lk	Luke	Rom	Romans

Cor	Corinthians	Pt	Peter
Gal	Galatians	Thes	Thessalonians
Phil	Philippians	Rv	Revelation

Dead Sea Scrolls

| 1 QS | *Community Rule* or *Manual of Discipline* | 1 QM | *War Scroll* |

Josephus

| AJ | *Antiquitates Judaicae, Jewish Antiquities* | *c. Ap.* | *contra Apionem, Against Apion* |
| BJ | *Bellum Judaicum, The Jewish War* | *Vita* | *Life* |

OTHER

//	parallel (similar verses, usually between two sources)	Lat.	Latin
cf.	compare	LXX	Septuagint, the Jewish translation of the Scriptures from Hebrew into Greek
f.	and the following verse, in biblical citations; and following, in notes		
ff.	and the following verses, in biblical citations; and following, in notes	parr.	parallels (similar verses in the three synoptic Gospels)
Gk.	Greek	RSV	Revised Standard Version (of the Bible)
Heb.	Hebrew	SBLSP	*Society of Biblical Literature Seminar Papers*
HJP	Schürer-Vermès, *History of the Jewish People in the Age of Jesus Christ*	v.	verse
		vv.	verses

NOTES

INTRODUCTION
THE HISTORY OF THE HISTORICAL JESUS

Scholarship on the historical Jesus is currently in a period of fruitful confusion. Reconstructions of his life polarize around two basic options, namely, whether or not Jesus was some sort of apocalyptic teacher.

Those who hold to the first option define the important phrase "Kingdom of God" as a dramatic, divine intervention that would forever change the nature of human existence, when God would exercise his power to eradicate evil and extend his reign of peace and justice throughout the earth. Various ideas cluster around this concept, among which we find the resurrection of the dead, the reward of the just, and the punishment of the wicked; the eradication of injustice, and death itself; the restitution of Jerusalem, the twelve tribes of Israel, and the Temple; and, sometimes, the coming of the messiah. For a brief discussion of this concept and its roots in the historical experience of the nation of Israel, see my earlier book *From Jesus to Christ*, pp. 70–86; on this term itself, see Sanders, *The Historical Figure of Jesus*, pp. 169–88. For lengthier critical discussions orienting the reader in current scholarship as well as ancient sources, see Meier, *A Marginal Jew*, vol. 2, pp. 237–88 (Jewish traditions), 289–397 (Jesus and the coming Kingdom), and 398–506 (the Kingdom as already present); and Schürer-Vermès, *The History of the Jewish People in the Age of Jesus Christ* (hereafter cited as *HJP*), vol. 2, pp. 488–554.

273

Sanders' *Jesus and Judaism* was the major work of the 1980s on Jesus as an apocalyptic prophet, and it established a sort of plumb line for subsequent studies placing Jesus within this context. The most recent programmatic statement is Allison's *Jesus of Nazareth;* he includes an excellent bibliographical essay on the comparative social study of millenarian movements, pp. 78–94. Older and still valuable, Dunn, *Jesus and the Spirit;* and Koch, *The Rediscovery of Apocalyptic.* In *Jesus the Jew* and *The Religion of Jesus the Jew,* Vermès' charismatic Galilean "Hasid" ("pious man") also functions within this apocalyptic worldview, though his spirituality is chiefly individual and existentialist.

A nonapocalyptic Jesus necessarily requires a redefinition of "Kingdom of God," since the phrase itself (or its Matthean equivalent, "Kingdom of Heaven") is all but universal in the earliest strata of tradition—Mark, Q, and, less frequently, in Paul. In recent North American scholarship, this position has been most associated with the Jesus Seminar; for a representative statement, see Funk, *Honest to Jesus.* The seminar publishes its conclusions in its journal, *Foundations and Facets Forum.* Versions of the nonapocalyptic Jesus include Jesus as Cynic sage, on whom especially the work of Downing, *Christ and the Cynics* and *Cynics and Christian Origins;* see also the major study by Mack, *A Myth of Innocence.* Crossan has offered a massively argued portrait of Jesus as a type of Jewish peasant Cynic sage in *The Historical Jesus,* reprised in popular format as *Jesus: A Revolutionary Biography.* "Kingdom," in this context, refers to new social practices such as radical egalitarianism, enacted by people in the present: That is to say, it is a noneschatological social or ethical concept. Crossan accordingly speaks of a "sapiential" kingdom and "ethical" eschatology. Another nonapocalyptic Jesus: Borg, e.g., *Jesus in Contemporary Scholarship.* His Jesus is a culturally subversive, boundary-shattering Spirit-person who preaches kinder interpersonal relations (the "Kingdom") and teaches in principled opposition to the Temple in Jerusalem and its laws of purity. (Allison offers a clearly written analysis and critique of this last position, contrasting it to Sanders', in *Jesus of Nazareth,* pp. 95–130.)

Last but by no means least, Wright's *Jesus and the Victory of God* offers an antipurity, antinationalist Jesus who *is* apocalyptic, but who (in Wright's view) so radically redefines all the traditional terms that he contrasts sharply with those of Sanders et al. While insisting that his Jesus is thoroughly Jewish, his controversies intra-Jewish ones, Wright ends by presenting a Jesus who preaches an anti-Zionist, essentially post-Jewish (that is, "antinationalist") Judaism, with the ("nationalist"?) terms "Kingdom" and "messiah" accordingly redefined. Wright reviews the work of Mack (pp. 35–44), Crossan (pp. 44–65), those who reconstruct a Cynic Jesus (pp. 66–74), and Borg (pp. 75–78). All of these authors, Sanders and Wright included, I review in "What You See Is What You Get."

PRELUDE I
JERUSALEM

This briefly recasts Josephus' gripping description of the destruction of Jerusalem and the Temple in Book 6 of *Jewish War (BJ).* Josephus had been a principal in this rebellion and was an eyewitness to the siege. For the dimensions of Herod's Temple and the estimates of Jerusalem's population during the feasts, see Sanders,

Judaism, pp. 47–145. His first four chapters, pp. 3–43, provide an excellent quick tour through the tangled political and religious history just preceding Jesus' period. For the deaths of the priests Meir and Joseph, *BJ* 6.280; the deforestation of the countryside, 6.5–8; the oracle of the world ruler, 6.312–13. Of the people standing on the colonnade of the burning Temple, Josephus writes:

> Next [the Roman soldiers] came to the last surviving colonnade of the outer court. On this women and children and a mixed crowd of citizens had found a refuge—6,000 in all. Before Caesar [Titus] could reach a decision about them or instruct his officers, the soldiers, carried away by their fury, fired the colonnade from below. As a result some flung themselves out of the flames to their deaths, others perished in the blaze. Of that vast number there escaped not one. Their destruction was due to a false prophet who that very day had declared to the people in the City that God commanded them to go up into the Temple to receive the signs of their deliverance.   (*BJ* 6.283–286)

Finally, on the fate of civilian captives once the city capitulated, 6.414–34. Josephus comments just prior to this passage that the glut in people sold into slavery from Jerusalem considerably lowered retail prices, "as supply was far in excess of demand," 6.384. "They make a desert," is an observation on the Roman pacification of Britain, Tacitus, *Agricola* 30. It suits Judea too.

CHAPTER I

GOSPEL TRUTH AND HISTORICAL INNOCENCE

Any effort to reconstruct the Jesus of history must begin with a consideration of the problems with our sources. Among the many handbooks for the canonical texts that treat the standard problems of date and place of composition, authorship, key theological concepts, and so on, is Kümmel, *Introduction to the New Testament.* Crossan, *The Historical Jesus,* argues for redating some of the noncanonical writings (Gospel of Thomas, Gospel of Peter) and integrating them into research—see pp. xxvii–xxxiv and his appendices, pp. 427–50 and 454–60, for argument and examples; he extends the argument, with reference to the Gospel of Peter and the canonical Passion narratives, in *Who Killed Jesus?* For a different perspective on the same issue of sources and method, see Meier, *A Marginal Jew,* vol. 1, pp. 41–55, 112–66 (on *not* using apocryphal gospels), and 167–95 (criteria of judgment); vol. 2 includes a nice summary of these issues as "Rules of the Road," pp. 4–13. See also Allison, *Jesus of Nazareth,* pp. 1–74, with a critical consideration of Crossan's proposals, pp. 10–33.

Problems of terminology compound a comparison of Mark and John on the chronology of Passover. Sanders offers an extremely clear discussion of these complicated issues, *Historical Figure,* pp. 249–251, 282–286, and this note reiterates the points he makes there. The ancient festival actually combined two holidays, Passover on 14 Nisan (during which, in the afternoon, the animals were slaughtered), and Unleavened Bread on the fifteenth (during which, in the evening immediately following, the commemorative meal was held). Strictly speaking, "Passover" means precisely evening and the following day, 14 Nisan; the sacrificed animal, also called "the passover," is eaten the following evening, the first night of Unleavened Bread (Ex. 12:6; Lv. 23:5); but ancient Jews could also refer to the whole holiday as Passover (cf. Mk 14:1, Lk 22:1; *AJ* 18.19). Thus for Mark, Wednesday night begins 14 Nisan, the lambs are slaughtered Thursday afternoon, and Thursday evening, 15 Nisan, Jesus has the paschal meal/Last Supper with his disciples. For John, Jesus is arrested Thursday night, 14 Nisan, and dies on the cross Friday afternoon, still 14 Nisan, while the lambs are slaughtered in the Temple. In my text, for convenience, I refer to the commemorative meal 15 Nisan as "the seder," though that term and the traditions now associated with it come from a later period.

Specifically on the gospel material, Sanders, *The Historical Figure of Jesus,* pp. 57–97; on methods for proceeding, *Jesus and Judaism,* pp. 1–22, and a review of the classic scholarship on this issue at an earlier point in the quest for the historical Jesus (Schweitzer, Bultmann, Bornkamm, et al.), pp. 23–58. In the closing pages of that work he also discusses the anomaly that stands at the center of my argument here—that Jesus was crucified, but none of his followers were killed—though he draws different conclusions, pp. 294–306. See, too, my book, *From Jesus to Christ,* pp. 3–8 (the nature of the documents), 205–211, on the evangelists' social contexts as these affected their respective depictions of Jesus.

PRELUDE 2
THE TEMPLE

In chapter 7 of *Judaism,* after having presented the reader with an enormous amount of historical and archaeological information on Herod's Temple, Sanders incarnated his academic discussion in a brief narrative description of an imaginary family's routine of sacrifice when in Jerusalem for one of the three pilgrimage festivals. The device made his points with such clarity and vigor that it emboldened me to write my fictional vignette here. "Joseph's" sacrifice is modeled on Sanders' discussion of the guilt offering, p. 113; his explanation to Yehoshua about death, God's altar, and purity, on Sanders' interpretation, p. 71f.; see, too, his discussion of terms translating the various kinds of offerings, pp. 107–110. The names of Jesus' brothers are given in Mark 6:3, his sisters (at least two) alluded to in the same place. Without the (different) virgin birth stories in Matthew and Luke, we would have no reason to suppose Jesus was the eldest of his parents' brood, so I juggled the birth order: Here, he is tucked in between three older brothers, a younger and an older sister, and baby Shimon.

On the dimensions of Herod's Temple, the ways he extended the earlier building, and the ways that the new architecture improved the flow of the huge volume of foot traffic through the Temple courtyard, see Sanders, *Judaism,* pp. 55–69. Shanks, *Jerusalem,* pp. 137–213, has beautiful photographs of archaeological artifacts from the Jerusalem of Herod and Jesus. On Gentiles and purity within Jewish law, Sanders, *Judaism,* pp. 72–76; on supplying worshipers with sacrificial victims, pp. 85–92. For the way that sacrifice worked as atonement, pp. 107–12. For the extreme unlikelihood of large quadrupeds for sacrifice being kept within the Temple area (Jn 2:15 notwithstanding!), pp. 86–88. How priests and tens of thousands of worshipers managed to sacrifice the Passover corban within a few hours on the afternoon of 14 Nisan is controversial: see pp. 135–39.

Somewhere beneath what we now call Robinson's Arch, Yehoshua recites what will become the sixteenth benediction of the *Shemoneh Esreh* or *Amidah,* along with the *Sh'ma* ("Hear O Israel . . ."), the chief prayer of Judaism.

CHAPTER 2
GOD AND ISRAEL IN ROMAN ANTIQUITY

The study of purity rules in ancient religions, pagan or Jewish, has a huge bibliography, and much of the scholarly discussion is unavoidably technical. Part of our difficulty in understanding purity rules arises from their intrinsic complexity and particularity; part, from their utter foreignness to modern Western post-Enlightenment sensibilities. The anthropologist Douglas has written several important and accessible books on the idea of impurity and the ways that it functions within certain cultures: see *Purity and Danger* and *In the Wilderness.* She comments astutely on the basic difference in mentality between Western and traditional cultures. Whereas in all previous civilizations, religion has shaped reality and purity codes have shaped the world, "for us," she notes,

> a long scientific liberal tradition has made our culture secular and pluralist. The effort of tolerance so needful for living in a plural society leads us to repudiate the drawing of moral lines and social boundaries; but it is the essence of impurity to draw sharp lines. This may be why [the study of] comparative religion [as a discipline within the secular, liberal Western academy] starts with a prejudice against impurity and finds defilement hard to understand. *(Wilderness,* p. 24)

The "otherness" of purity codes accounts for some of the difficulties when placing the still culturally central figure of Jesus back into his native ancient context: He becomes not "too Jewish," but too different. We will examine the consequences of purity's foreignness for the study of the historical Jesus in later chapters.

Lane Fox provides a meticulously researched and narratively accessible glimpse into the religious world of the majority culture in *Pagans and Christians.* He relates that "in many pagan cults, rules of sexual purity governed entry into a temple and sometimes participation in worship. Generally they excluded people who had recently had sex or specifically committed adultery, but the exclusion was usually brief. Before sleeping in Pergamon's great shrine of Asclepius, clients were expected to have abstained from sex for two days; elsewhere, one day, or a quick wash, sufficed. . . . The rules for a public cult in Pergamon demanded a day's interval after sex with one's wife, two days' after sex with someone else's" (p. 347).

On Jewish purity regulations (which evolved considerably, and variously, between the biblical period and late Second Temple times) see inter alia Milgrom, *Leviticus;* and Neusner, *The Idea of Purity in Ancient Judaism.* The biblical legislation clusters in Leviticus and Numbers. For detailed examination and analysis for Jesus' period, see Sanders, *Jewish Law from Jesus to the Mishnah,* pp. 29–41, 131–254 (Pharisees), 258–71 (Diaspora communities); see also his useful table of biblical impurities, correlated to means of purification and zones of affected activity, p. 151. Schürer-Vermès, *HJP,* vol. 2, pp. 475–78, gives copious bibliography and references to Mishnaic texts; pp. 555–90 (Essenes, whose spirituality was especially articulated through their development and interpretation of the purity code).

On the question of sin and impurity, see Klawans, "The Impurity of Immorality in Ancient Judaism"; on Gentiles as "common" but not, in any levitical sense, "impure," his essay, "Notions of Gentile Impurity in Ancient Judaism," which cites the relevant earlier discussions of Alon and Büchler. His important full study of impurity is forthcoming from Oxford University Press (2000). Another important recent discussion: Hays, "The Impurity of Gentiles in Biblical Law and Late Antique Judaism" (unpublished MS).

On specific Jewish practices (prayer, *mezzuzot,* tefillin, and Sabbath), see Sanders, *Judaism,* pp. 119–235. Note his comments on intra-Jewish polemic and the way that the priests—since their function in the Temple meant that they were "the employees of the nation for the purposes of maintaining the worship of God in the temple, and teaching and judging the people" (p. 182)—were therefore a universal target of criticism for any other individual or group with an opinion, pp. 182–89. All of these topics, discussed with full bibliography, may be found under their appropriate entries in Schürer-Vermès. On synagogues in this period, see again Schürer-Vermès. Readers unfamiliar with any of these terms will find the *Oxford Dictionary of the Jewish Religion* (eds. Werblowsky and Wigoder) a convenient quick-reference tool.

General discussion of Josephus' three "Jewish philosophies"—Sadducees, Pharisees, Essenes—may be found in Cohen, *From the Maccabees to the Mishnah.* Those wishing to be oriented in the issues swirling around the Dead Sea Scrolls will find a superb popular introduction in Shanks, *Understanding the Dead Sea Scrolls.*

CHAPTER 3
TRAJECTORIES: PAUL, THE GOSPELS, AND JESUS

Often, scholars who work on the historical Jesus see Paul as a sharp contrast rather than a corroborating witness to the early Jesus traditions: The more Jesus of Nazareth is fit into a first-century Jewish culture, the more Paul is seen in some sense as the actual inventor of Christianity, contributing to the "de-Judaization of the pristine gospel in the Graeco-Roman world" (so Vermès, *The Religion of Jesus the Jew,* p. 213, characterizing the joint effect of Paul and John the Evangelist on developing Christian tradition). Paul was certainly read this way—that is, as anti-Judaizing, indeed as anti-Jewish—by later Gentile Christians in the second century and beyond (Marcion, Justin Martyr, Origen, Jerome); but he cannot be held responsible for such misinterpretations. On Paul and his later interpreters on precisely this issue, see most especially Gager, *Origins of Anti-Semitism.*

On Paul's apocalypticism, and the ways that it unites his message with that of the historical Jesus, my works *From Jesus to Christ,* pp. 156–76; and "From Jesus to Christ: The Contribution of the Apostle Paul." On Mark and his use of the destruction of the Temple to proclaim the nearness of the Christ's Second Coming to his own generation of believers, *From Jesus to Christ,* pp. 177–87; and "Jesus and the Temple, Mark and the War."

Consideration of apocalyptic traditions from and about Jesus invariably involve two complex issues: the interpretation of the phrase "Son of Man," and the role played by the text of Daniel, where the phrase significantly appears. See especially the seminal discussion of the Aramaic context and syntax of "Son of man" in Vermès, *Jesus the Jew,* pp. 160–91; and his follow-up essay, "The Present State of the Son of Man Debate," in *Jesus and the World of Judaism,* pp. 89–99. See also Crossan, *The Historical Jesus,* pp. 238–59 (distancing Jesus from any apocalyptic usage); Sanders, *Jesus and Judaism,* pp. 142–46 (the opposite conclusion); N. T. Wright, *Jesus and the Victory of God,* pp. 510–19 (Jesus did use the phrase, but it was his way of calling himself "messiah," p. 519). For a lucid discussion of these complex issues within the Dead Sea Scrolls and other ancient Jewish literature, with generous notes to the recent debate, see Collins, *The Scepter and the Star,* pp. 173–94; also Allison, *Jesus of Nazareth,* p. 65 and his lengthy bibliographic survey in n. 242, p. 65. On continuing Christian apocalypticism after this period, see Gager, *Kingdom and Community;* and my essay, "Apocalypse and Redemption in Early Christianity."

On traditions concerning the Twelve Apostles, see Sanders, *Jesus and Judaism,* pp. 98–105 (the tradition is authentic and indicates Jesus' apocalyptic orientation in that the number recalls the twelve tribes of Israel); Crossan, *Revolutionary Biography,* pp. 108–10 (the tradition is inauthentic, i.e., it speaks to the later Christian community's view of itself as the "true Israel"). Relevant, too, is Allison's discussion, *Jesus of Nazareth,* pp. 141–45, on the restoration of Israel. On the broader resonances between traditions of Israel's restoration and the content of Jesus' mission, see especially Sanders, *Jesus and Judaism,* pp. 61–119.

Radical ethical demands frequently accompany millenarian movements. We see them in the earliest Jesus traditions, too, aligned with the proclamation of the coming Kingdom. See Sanders, *The Historical Figure of Jesus,* pp. 196–204; and the comments on his argument by Räisänen, "Jesus in Context." Crossan, *The Historical Jesus,* sees Jesus' entire mission as a radical ethical message but unallied with apocalyptic, pp. 225–353; on the later tradition, see Crossan, *The Birth of Christianity,* pp. 305–16 (negating apocalyptic eschatology) and 317–44 (affirming ethical eschatology). Allison, *Jesus of Nazareth,* pp. 172–216, argues that Jesus himself should be viewed as an ascetic. On the long history of Christian asceticism and its meaning in Mediterranean societies in periods of diminished apocalyptic expectation, see Brown, *Body and Society;* Lane Fox, *Pagans and Christians,* pp. 336–74. Voluntary poverty is another piece of this puzzle. On the Essenes, who perhaps provide another example of eschatology-inspired asceticism, see Schürer-Vermès, *HJP,* vol. 2, p. 578; on Jewish sexual asceticism in this period more generally, Meier, *A Marginal Jew,* vol. 1, pp. 336–49.

The question of Jesus' ethics leads us directly to the question of his attitude toward the Law. New Testament scholars frequently draw a distinction between the Law's "ritual demands" (and segue from there to purity codes, sacrifices, and the Temple) and its "ethical demands" (love of others, care for the poor, and so on), and argue that Jesus (and Paul, and early Christianity generally) rejected or discarded the former, favoring as of greater importance the latter. See Sanders, *Jesus and Judaism,* pp. 55–58, 245–69, and 325–39, for an analysis of modern Christian scholarship's difficulties with ancient Jewish law: He notes that "ritual" becomes associated with "mere externality," and therefore with inauthentic religion, "ethics" with "internal" and thus "authentic" religion. These ways of thinking, he observes, trace back partly to the existentializing analyses of Bultmann in the earlier part of this century, partly to the Protestant critique of Catholicism embedded in New Testament scholarship more generally, given the discipline's birth in the late Renaissance, which coincided with the Protestant Reformation. Perhaps needless to say—but I will say it anyway—such a reading is hopelessly anachronistic and, to the extent that doing history requires sympathetic imagination, only obscures the ancient people whose lives and values we seek to reconstruct.

For the continued Torah-observance of Jesus' followers after his death: worshiping in the Temple, Luke 24:53; Acts 3:1, 5:12, 42, 21:26 ff. (Paul), 22:17 (again); specifically on sacrificing at the altar, Matthew 5:23–24; we might infer this from the apostles' relocation to Jerusalem, Galatians 1:18–19, 2:1; Luke 24:52; Acts 1:12 and passim; Sabbaths, e.g., Mark 16:1 and parr. (cf. Lk 23:56b, making the point specifically: "On the Sabbath day they rested according to the commandment"); fasts, Matthew 6:16–18; festivals, Acts 2:1 (Pentecost, i.e., Shavuot; cf., perhaps, 1 Cor 16:8); food laws, Acts passim and especially Peter's vision 10:10–16; Galatians 2:12, for the controversy more generally. Acts 9:32–35 tells the story of Peter's bringing "all the residents of Lydda" to belief in Christ in the earliest period of the post-Resurrection movement; Josephus mentions that this same town fell to the procurator Cestius during the troubles before the outbreak of the war in the fall of 66 "because the whole population had gone up to Jerusalem for the Feast of Tabernacles [Sukkot]," *BJ* 2.515. If both stories are true, this is further evidence that early Christians observed traditional Jewish practice. On the confusions inherent in conflating Paul's message to Gentiles with the earliest Christians' attitude toward their own native religious culture, i.e. Judaism, see Fredriksen, *From Jesus to Christ*, pp. 102–112.

Meier considers the issue of Jesus' miracles at length in *A Marginal Jew*, vol. 2, pp. 509–1038; see (more briefly) also Sanders, *The Historical Figure of Jesus*, pp. 132–68. Crossan exorcises the supernatural by regarding the miracle traditions as a *façon de parler:* "healings" and "exorcisms" are the tradition's way of speaking about social reenfranchisement. Illness is really about ostracism, demonic possession about colonial oppression (*Revolutionary Biography*, pp. 75–101, esp. 82, 91). I sympathize with Crossan's effort but can't buy it: "What You See Is What You Get," pp. 84–85.

On the meanings of messiah, see especially Collins, *The Scepter and the Star;* and the various essays collected in Neusner et al., *Judaisms and their Messiahs at the Turn of the Christian Era*. Collins discusses four basic messianic paradigms (kingly, priestly, prophetic, heavenly) passim and concludes that the "concept of the Davidic messiah as the warrior king who would destroy the enemies of Israel and institute an era of unending peace constitutes the common core of Jewish messianism around the turn of the era," p. 68. On the dim figure of a heavenly messiah, pp. 136–53. Collins emphasizes that Jesus' identification as Messiah must be "grounded in some way before the crucifixion" (p. 204), and speculates that his followers' enthusiasm during the Triumphal Entry might have led to his execution by Rome (pp. 206–7), an argument I will develop further here.

On the political and cultural turmoil of the Seleucid/Hasmonean period, and the ways that Herod represents a resolution of sorts, see Sanders, *Judaism,* pp. 13–43; more detailed discussions in Cohen, *From the Maccabees to the Mishnah,* and Schäfer, *The History of the Jews in Antiquity.* Hengel's now-classic study, *Judaism and Hellenism,* sets the discussion of the cultural and religious issues arising in the aftermath of Alexander the Great. Cohen sums up well: " 'To Hellenize or not to Hellenize' was not a question the Jews of antiquity had to answer. They were given no choice. The questions that confronted them were 'how?' and 'how far?' " (p. 45).

Gruen's essay "Hellenism and the Hasmoneans," in his volume *Heritage and Hellenism,* pp. 1–40, acquaints the reader with the complexities of the Hasmonean/Seleucid political symbiosis. He points out that after 159 B.C.E. — which is to say, more than a decade after the successful Maccabean revolt—the office of high priest remained vacant for seven years: The Seleucids, who normally would have appointed the candidate, hesitated lest they offend Jewish sensibilities, and so involve themselves in more military engagements; and the Hasmoneans did nothing, because their local popularity was too precarious to permit a usurpation. Civil war in Antioch finally settled the issue when one contestant for power, Alexander Balas, bought the Hasmonean Jonathan's support by appointing him to the high priesthood (pp. 14–16; cf. 1 Mc 10:17–22; *AJ* 13:45–57). Gruen observes:

> Jonathan's ready acceptance of his role needs to be understood in proper context. It was neither a sell-out nor a betrayal of the Maccabaean cause. Judas had raised a revolt against Antiochus IV [Epiphanes]'s perverse policy [i.e., the pollution of the Temple] but not against the Seleucid kingdom. And his campaigns directed themselves as much at indigenous foes as at the armies of the king. He had never claimed as objective the eradication of Hellenic power in Palestine, let alone of Hellenism. The arrangement between Jonathan and Alexander Balas basically reinstated the system as it had operated since the beginning of the century: the Jewish High Priest held sway in Jerusalem under the patronage of the Seleucid ruler. . . . The greater the Hasmonean hold on [local] power, the greater their dependence on Seleucid favor. (pp. 16, 18)

It was precisely the ambiguities of the Hasmonean political enterprise, as Collins brings out, that fed the multivocality of messianic speculation in this period.

On apocalyptic expectation as an expression of the idea of Israel, see Fredriksen, *From Jesus to Christ,* pp. 70–93; on the ways that Paul's mission to the Gentiles conforms to this apocalyptic theme of Gentile inclusion (*not* conversion), pp. 156–176; with fuller bibliography and primary references, my essay, "Judaism, the Circumcision of Gentiles, and Apocalyptic Hope." Two excellent discussions of Gentile interest in the synagogue: McKnight, *A Light among the Gentiles;* Reynolds and Tannenbaum, *Jews and Godfearers at Aphrodisias.* The Jewish inscription at Aphrodisias (third century C.E.) presented in this last essay reveals a surprising amount of comfortable interaction between members of the Jewish community there and its pagan gentile neighbors. The inscription gives the names, inter alia, of fifty-four *theosebeis* (pagans who also worshiped the God of Israel), nine of whom are listed as members of the city council who would thus, Tannenbaum observes, be present "at public pagan sacrifices (e.g., at the opening of all council meetings)," p. 58; for his entire discussion of Godfearers, pp. 48–66. Further, on the Jewish reception of converts, absent any policy or practice of active proselytizing, see Goodman, *Mission and Conversion*; and Schäfer, *Judeophobia*.

Others were less charmed by Judaism and pagan interest in it, as evinced by their sarcastic and occasionally hostile comments. These are collected in Whittaker, *Jews and Christians: Graeco-Roman Views,* pp. 3–103; and exhaustively in Stern, *Greek and Latin Authors on Jews and Judaism*. In their view, such voluntary Judaizing was dangerous, because it might too easily slip into full conversion. Thus the Roman satirist Juvenal (c. 60–130 C.E.), who comments that those who have "a father who reveres the Sabbath" themselves end up worshiping the sky (an allusion to aniconic Jewish worship), avoiding pork, "and in time they take to circumcision," *Satires* 14; Stern, pp. 102–7.

Greeks and Romans generally viewed circumcision with disgust and those converts who received it voluntarily as, in a sense, traitors to their own culture. Schäfer, who comments that "the distinction between 'politics' and 'culture/religion' is untenable for the ancient world" (*Judeophobia*, p. 159), notes:

> Juvenal accuses only the Jews—not any other ethnic group . . . —of proselytism. And it is precisely the combination of proselytism [receiving converts] and exclusiveness [the convert must eschew traditional gods to worship *only* the God of Israel] that alarms him. One can hardly think of a more serious attack on the customs of Rome's ancestors than the Jewish insistence that one has to abandon the "laws of Rome" . . . in order to follow the "Jewish law." . . . That the one had to be substituted for the other, could not be integrated into the other, was completely alien to a Roman; that this strange superstition could become successful in the very heart of the Roman empire was intolerable. . . . [A] way of life particularly alien and hostile to Roman (and Greek) culture succeed[s], strangely and ominously enough, in entering Roman society and converting Romans to their religion of arrogant exclusiveness.   (*Judeophobia*, p. 185)

How many Gentiles in antiquity were attracted to the synagogue? And of that number, how many went even further and made an exclusive commitment, wrenching themselves out of their native social and religious context and actually converting to Judaism, which for men entailed as well receiving circumcision? We cannot know. But if the emperor Domitian, toward the end of the first century C.E., did extend the mandatory payment of the former Temple tax to include recent converts to Judaism, we have some measure: enough to have a noticeably positive effect on tax revenue. For the argument, *Judeophobia,* pp. 113–17 and nn., pp. 259–60.

If converts to Judaism—an ancient, traditional, legally recognized, and legally protected religion—could be the object of the sort of fear and contempt Juvenal represents, how much stranger and more dangerous would an exclusive allegiance to the God of Israel *absent* conversion to Judaism seem? Yet this is what Paul and other Jewish Christian apostles call Gentiles to do. The utter novelty and radical social instability of their circumstance provides us, I think, with an index of these apostles' time frame: Christ would return and the Kingdom would come *soon,* thus resolving the anomaly.

On "messiah" in the Gospels, the essays by MacRae ("Messiah and Gospels," pp. 169–85) and Kee ("Christology in Mark's Gospel," pp. 187–208) in Neusner et al., *Judaisms and Their Messiahs at the Turn of the Christian Era.* Ashton, *Understanding the Fourth Gospel,* analyzes the uses of this term in the Gospel of John but includes much by way of comparison to the Synoptics and Acts as well: see especially pp. 238–79 and 292–308. On the signs prophets and others mentioned by Josephus, see Gray, *Prophetic Figures in Late Second Temple Jewish Palestine.*

CHAPTER 4
CONTEXTS: THE GALILEE, JUDEA, AND JESUS

The quest for the historical Jesus has opened up into the quests for the historical Galilee and the historical Temple. The arguments and/or descriptions I give here are contested as well as supported by recent work.

On ritual immersion pools, and the way that they attest to a common Jewish concern with purity, see especially Sanders, *Judaism,* pp. 222–30, and the photos after p. 220. The archaeologist Ronny Reich has excavated and interpreted many of the ancient *mikvaot* in Israel, not without being challenged: An accessible summary of his position may be found in his note, "The Great Mikveh Debate," *Biblical Archaeological Review* 19 (1993): 52–53. The issue—when is a stepped pool a *mikveh?*—is controversial for two reasons: (1) sometimes a stepped pool might be simply a Roman *frigidarium,* a cold-water pool without ritual significance; and (2) later rabbinic halakah, which mandates a particular kind of construction, is not always evidenced in the excavated first-century material. Where the stepped pools are dug into bedrock, however, their ritual status seems indisputably established: a pool for recreational or hygenic purposes would not need to be built in such an arduous way. Nor should variety in first-century *mikvaot* surprise us, since the rabbinic, or Pharisaic, halakah certainly was not universal in that period (if ever). Finally, for an overview of the issues and interpretive options, see B. Wright, "Jewish Ritual Baths."

Social theory has been applied to ancient material in order to reconstruct the world of Jesus and of the Gospels. For the Gospels, see particularly the work of Theissen, *The Gospels in Context* and *Social Reality and the Early Christians;* and Richard Horsley's critical appraisal, *Sociology and the Jesus Movement.* Works frequently cited by those New Testament scholars drawn to sociology and social anthropology include: J. Kautsky, *The Politics of Aristocratic Empires* (Chapel Hill: University of North Carolina Press, 1982) and G. E. Lenski, *Power and Social Privilege: A Theory of Social Stratification* (New York: McGraw-Hill, 1966): These understand peasant-elite power relations in terms of exploitation and class antagonisms. On the peasant, political nature of banditry, E. J. Hobsbawm, *Primitive Rebels: Studies in the Archaic Forms of Social Movement in the Nineteenth and Twentieth Centuries* (New York: Norton, 1956). Crossan's two biographies (1991 and 1994) see Jesus as appealing particularly to the radically impoverished and the destitute; both he and Borg construe the purity laws as one of the ways elite culture imposed itself on peasant society. Meier and Freyne both argue against the view that the Galilee, or its village culture, lived in radical poverty; see Meier, *A Marginal Jew,* vol. 2, pp. 278–85. Freyne notes that "the gospels presume that adequate provisions for a sizable crowd can be procured in the surrounding villages (Mk 6:36)," *Galilee, Jesus and the Gospels,* p. 145: In a destitute village economy, they could not. For an incisive consideration of the larger economic picture in re taxes and tithes in Judea and the Galilee in the period before the revolt, see Sanders, *Judaism,* pp. 157–69, specifically in response to the estimates of Borg and Horsley, which he considers poorly calculated and significantly exaggerated.

Using theories of class struggle to understand the dynamics of ancient societies is hazardous for any number of reasons, the chief one being the appropriateness of the model to antiquity. Goodman comments on the absence of an identifiable class consciousness in ancient Judea, which in turn hampered the Jews' organizing a collective political opposition to oppression, whether local or foreign:

> There were no social categories to correspond to the function of different groups in economic production. Neither free peasants nor tenant farmers nor craftsmen, nor indeed rich landowners and rich merchants, used such labels to identify themselves or recognized that as groups they were separate classes with identifiable interests and rights. Important social categories for them were based on religious status: a man felt himself to be an Israelite, a Levite or a priest, a proselyte or a natural-born Jew. He felt no tug of solidarity with others in his economic class. The resentment of the poor at exploitation by the rich remained unfocused. . . . [Because giving charity was mandated by Torah as a religious obligation], when a poor man received charity from someone with money to spare, no social conventions insisted that he should be grateful. *The relationship between patron and client which was fundamental in, for instance, Roman culture was not found among the Jews. (The Ruling Class of Judea,* p. 67; for the whole discussion, 51–75 and 77).

Similarly, the word "peasant" as an analytic category is problematic, especially as a term for understanding Jesus, whom the Gospels depict as a craftsman, not an agricultural worker: see Meier, *A Marginal Jew,* vol. 1, pp. 278–84, with useful remarks on the modern perception of ancient poverty. "In one sense, therefore, Jesus certainly belonged to the poor who had to work hard for their living. And yet our imagination, rhetoric, and desire for instant social relevance can get carried away in depicting the grinding poverty Jesus supposedly endured. . . . The problem with us modern Americans speaking of the 'poor Jesus' or the poor anybody in the ancient Mediterranean world is that poverty is always a relative concept," p. 282. Also, we as moderns tend to measure economic categories in terms of standards of living. By that last measure, virtually anybody farther than two generations behind us lived lives of acute material deprivation!

Finally, to see ancient Roman society as split absolutely between a tiny economic elite and a mass of exploited peasants and subsistence-level workers ignores the effects of markets in complicating the picture. Thus the archaeologist Strange, on the lower Galilee in Jesus' period:

> [F]rom archaeological surveys in Galilee it is possible to posit another dimension of social reality. It seems that there are more farmers on small plots of land than those plots will support. This suggests that the small land owner had [also] to work for wages for somebody else at least part of the time, or else develop a specialty on the side which could be marketed. *Thus the simple designation "peasant" for this social stratum is misleading, since these people appear to have also been artisans and small entrepreneurs as well as agricultural laborers.* ("First-Century Galilee from Archaeology and from the Texts," p. 89.)

In sketching the historical Galilee I have found myself leaning much more toward the reconstructions of Freyne (1980 and esp. 1988) than of Horsley (1995). Horsley's consistent revisionism, in my view, puts too much strain on what we have in our texts. According to Horsley, the Temple and its Torah were not *Jewish* so much as *Judean* (the Greek word *Ioudaios* can in fact denote either). Where Galileans seemed to share a religion with Judeans (the "Great Tradition"), they actually drew on a prior stock from their common Israelite heritage (the "Little Tradition"). Josephus, he says, overestimates the numbers of Galileans worshiping at the Temple (p. 145). Torah, in the Galilean view and experience, was really the Law of the Judeans (pp. 147, 155–57, and passim). To think of Sepphoris and Tiberias as primarily Jewish misses the fact that they "must have been dominated by an urban political culture superimposed upon the Galilean towns and villages" (p. 169; for the whole argument, pp. 163–85). As for the massive protest staged by Galilean peasants in the spring of 41 C.E., he says, it was the sight of Roman troops moving through their country, and their own economic distress, not Caligula's statue headed toward the (Judean) Temple, that mobilized their action (p. 279). Nothing in Josephus' text supports such an interpretation, but then, given Horsley's analytic categories, the priestly, aristocratic, Judean Josephus is too highly suspect to serve as a reliable source.

Ancient demographics are elusive; unsurprisingly, numbers can vary widely between modern scholars. To estimate the population of an ancient village, scholars map out the excavated area of settlement, subtract an estimate of the noninhabited space (roads, market squares, and so on) from the total area, agree on something like an average number of persons per domestic housing unit, factor in the amount of arable land needed to support X number of people over Y amount of time, and thus come up with some approximation of a reasonable number. Meyers and Strange, *Archaeology, the Rabbis, and Early Christianity,* pp. 48–61, give the reader a good sense of this type of reasoning in their discussions of Jerusalem, Nazareth, and Capernaum. On ancient Nazareth, see Meier, *A Marginal Jew,* vol. 1, p. 280 and n. 77 on p. 300 f.; for Capernaum, Sanders, *The Historical Figure of Jesus,* p. 103; for generally lower figures and a different argument about the population of Galilean villages, Horsley, *Galilee,* pp. 189–95.

For an excellent essay on the Samaritans, see the article by James Purvis in vol. 2 of the *Cambridge History of Judaism,* pp. 591–613. On the question of the continuing Jewish or Israelite identity of the population of the Galilee in the years between the Assyrian conquest and the Hasmonean *reconquista* of the mid–second century B.C.E., scholarly opinion is divided. Here, exceptionally, Freyne and Horsley agree: cf. Freyne, *Galilee from Alexander the Great to Hadrian,* pp. 35–44, 392; Horsley, *Galilee,* pp. 40–46, as against *HJP* vol. 1, pp. 207–18; and Millar, *The Roman Near East,* pp. 344–47, who presumes the forced Judaization of the Galilee at the same time that this policy was exercised on the Itureans to the north.

On the vexed question of urbanization, both the material evidence and its social construal, see the articles by Strange, Horsley, Reed, and Oakman in the 1994 *Society of Biblical Literature Seminar Papers,* cited in full in the bibliography. Edwards in his 1992 essay describes how cities and villages in the lower Galilee— the primary region of Jesus' activity—created a web of reciprocal, and usually mutually beneficial, economic relations. Together they were "linked to a vibrant regional market network" (p. 72). See also Meyers, "Jesus and His Galilean Context." It helps to remember, too—despite the images of alienated masses and exploited workers that the combination of class analysis and "urbanization" can conjure—that early first-century Tiberias or Sepphoris was not mid-nineteenth-century industrial Manchester.

Did Jesus speak Greek? See especially the comprehensive consideration of the evidence and arguments in Meier, *A Marginal Jew,* vol. 1, pp. 255–68. He concludes, "Scholarship must rather proceed with the most probable opinion, viz., that Jesus regularly and perhaps exclusively taught in Aramaic, his Greek being of a practical, business type, and perhaps rudimentary to boot. In a quadrilingual country [Aramaic, Hebrew, Greek, and Latin], Jesus may indeed have been a trilingual Jew [Aramaic, Hebrew, and Greek]; but he was probably not a trilingual teacher" (p. 268). See, too, Sanders' remarks on the cultural penetration of Hellenism into Galilean village life, *The Historical Figure of Jesus,* p, 104.

Was Jesus very like a Cynic? Burton Mack makes the case in *A Myth of Innocence,* pp. 66–77. Not coincidentally, he sees the Galilee as "worldly-wise and accustomed to diversity" (p. 65), in fact "an epitome of Hellenistic culture on the eve of the Roman era" (p. 66). Crossan refines the picture: Jesus is a Peasant Jewish Cynic, *The Historical Jesus,* pp. 72–88 and 421–22. I have argued against the likelihood of the first characterization and the usefulness of the second in "What You See Is What You Get," pp. 79–85; cf. also N.T. Wright's remarks, *Jesus and the Victory of God,* pp. 66–74.

Why, finally, did Jesus (apparently) never go to Sepphoris and Tiberias? My speculation here echoes Freyne's, *Galilee, Jesus and the Gospels,* p. 140: Perhaps, with the example of John the Baptizer so clearly before him, Jesus was simply attempting to stay out of harm's way by avoiding Antipas. Of course, had Antipas wanted to arrest and execute Jesus, too, he presumably could have done it even if Jesus stayed exclusively in villages: Avoiding Sepphoris or Tiberias had not helped the Baptizer.

For the religious and political realities of Judea, especially as concerns the Temple and the various obligations of the high priest, see the excellent overview in Sanders, *Judaism,* pp. 35–43; on the Temple and the way it ran, pp. 77–102, specifically on the high priest's vestments and their significance, pp. 92–102. For a lucid description of Judean political realities from Rome's point of view, see Millar, *The Roman Near East,* especially pp. 43–69; for the numbers of men in Roman military units, p. 71. He comments, "Many different items of evidence . . . tend to suggest how comparatively tenuous and uncertain Roman control of the southern region [Judea] was, and how much it depended on diplomacy and on the erratic effects of personal presence," p. 55. Lastly, on the man who stands behind the Jerusalem of Jesus' day, Herod the Great, see the recent biography by Richardson, *Herod.* Richardson's combined knowledge of history and architecture enables him to read closely Josephus' descriptions of the Temple. See especially his analysis of the "golden eagle affair," pp. 15–18. Scholars (Crossan, Horsley) frequently assume that this was a Roman eagle, symbolizing Herod's political allegiances. In fact, Josephus does not say (*BJ* 1.648–55; *AJ* 17.149–67), and Richardson conjectures that the figure was in fact a "Nabatean" eagle: p. 16, n. 4.

Roman religious tolerance was partly indigenous to paganism, partly practical in terms of ruling over so many different peoples with their different cults. Judaism itself was a *religio licita,* a recognized legitimate cult, within the empire; consequently, its unimpeded practice was the ultimate responsibility of the emperor in his role of *pontifex maximus,* "highest priest." So firmly were Jewish "religious rights" established, so definitely was conversion to Judaism (especially for men, with the dramatic and consequential decision to be circumcised) a known social fact, that, according to the fourth-century Christian writer Eusebius, during Rome's anti-Christian persecutions a gentile Christian could consider converting to Judaism to avoid harassment (*Ecclesiastical History* 6.12, 1). See *HJP,* vol. 1, pp. 1–149, for a thorough discussion of diaspora Jewish communities, their civic and religious rights, and their routine and strong ties with the Jewish homeland. On the persecution of Christians, see Lane Fox, *Pagans and Christians,* pp. 419–92. For Roman laws affecting Jewish communities, see Linder, *The Jews in Roman Imperial Legislation.* On the social and religious significance of the Temple tax, see Sanders, *Judaism,* pp. 52, 84–85, and 156; and *HJP,* vol. 2, pp. 270–72, 282. Sanders gives calculations for the value of the required half-shekel or two-drachma donation, paid by males before the revolt, extended to women and children as well by Vespasian. He notes, "This is not a large sum: approximately two days' pay for a day labourer, a man at the bottom of the pay scale. That it was paid is one of the things about first-century Judaism that is most certain," p. 156. Finally, for the sequence of events surrounding Caligula, his statue, and Petronius—one of the great cliff-hangers of this period—see *HJP,* vol 1, p. 397; for the whole episode, and the ways that it links with the troubles in Alexandria, pp. 390–98.

Two of the most recent full studies of John the Baptizer are Taylor, *The Immerser,* and Meier's book-within-a-book, *A Marginal Jew,* vol. 2, pp. 19–233. On John's peculiar clothing, see Taylor, pp. 35–41; on his location in the desert, pp. 42–48; see also Meier, pp. 42–49. On John's desert setting Meier observes, p. 46:

> The desert naturally conjured up for Jews of any stripe the founding events of the exodus from Egypt, the covenant at Sinai, and the forty years of wandering in the wilderness. . . . Closely connected with the wandering in the desert was the Jordan, for it was by crossing the Jordan that Joshua put an end to the desert-wandering and led Israel into the promised land. The Jordan was also connected with some of the legends about the

prophets Elijah and Elisha (2 Kgs 2:1–18, 5:1–15). The obvious natural qualities of both desert heat and river water only reinforced the OT [Old Testament] traditions of testing and judgment in the wilderness and the gift of new life at the Jordan. The fierce radicalism of the Baptist, as well as his threat of judgment by fire for the nation's apostasy, found its perfect backdrop in the Judean wilderness and the Dead Sea, at the southern end of which lay the traditional sites of Sodom and Gomorrah.

If the sequence John the Baptizer–Jesus–Pilate sets the trajectory of Jesus' mission, then the sequence Baptizer-Jesus-Paul sets the trajectory of early Christianity. John preached the imminent coming of God's kingdom; so, too, did Paul. Those who argue that Jesus, the middle term on this trajectory, was *not* an apocalyptic prophet must thus argue that he changed his mind about John's message at some point after his immersion, and that the apocalyptic elements in post-Resurrection tradition then come in later, as a result of Jesus' followers altering *his* message: see, e.g., Crossan, *The Historical Jesus,* pp. 227–64; *Revolutionary Biography,* pp. 29–53, esp. 47. On Josephus' characterization of John's preaching "piety toward God and justice toward men," and the ways that these terms stood as a summation of the "two tables" of the Law, Sanders, *The Historical Figure of Jesus,* p. 92; more discursively, *Judaism,* pp. 192–95, also pp. 257–60.

Meier argues that John's purifications were a one-time event, *A Marginal Jew,* vol. 2, p. 56, and that John's mission "implicitly calls the traditional cultic means of atonement and sanctification in Israel, notably the temple sacrifices, into question," p. 75, n. 52. Here I follow Taylor, who argues the opposite: "Nothing in our sources connects purification rituals with an anti-Temple stance. Immersion was never a substitute for Temple sacrifice," *The Immerser,* p. 31; see also pp. 95, 111. These issues touch on the delicate question on how we as historians should use silence as a datum. Just because John, for instance, does *not* in our documents specifically say, "And now be sure to offer an atonement sacrifice the next time you go to Jerusalem," should we assume that either he or his hearers would have thought otherwise? In a context where certain behavior is customary and well established (such as availing oneself of sacrificial atonement the next time one was in Jerusalem for, e.g., a festival: People were not required to immediately make special trips!), does silence indicate dissent from or compliance with common custom? I would assume the latter. See further Sanders, *Jesus,* pp. 55–58, on arguments about "implicit opposition" to the Law.

Taylor notes, too, that we simply cannot know from the evidence whether John's immersions were repeatable (p. 70). I would add to her arguments that even in much later gentile Christianity, where the activity of baptism had been long invested with sacramental, specifically Christian import (initiation into the body of Christ; dying and rising with Christ, dying to sin, and so on), debates about second or multiple baptisms raged, ultimately to be settled (in the case of North Africa's Donatists) only by the force majeure of Imperial intervention. My point: If multiple immersions were the case even when single immersions would have been desirable in principle (later ones were to remedy the enormous sin of apostasy in time of anti-Christian persecution), then in John and Jesus' own time and context, when multiple or repeatable immersions were the norm, absent evidence, we should not assume the contrary.

Sanders has argued at length that Jesus, unlike John, did not preach a mission of repentance, *Jesus and Judaism,* pp. 204–8. "The novelty and offence of Jesus' message was that the wicked who heeded him would be included in the Kingdom even though they did not repent as it was universally understood—that is, even though they did not make restitution, sacrifice, and turn in obedience to the law," p. 207; see also *The Historical Figure of Jesus,* pp. 230–37. I find his position unconvincing and adduce my reasons for seeing Jesus as preaching repentance in the text. Räisänen, commenting on Sanders, observes that we have no evidence for the claim that Jesus ran into serious opposition for his behavior with sinners, nor any "that this behaviour had anything to do with the arrest of Jesus," "Jesus in Context," p. 15. Cf. Crossan, *The Birth of Christianity,* pp. 337–42.

The view that Jesus was against purity, and that this opposition informed his action in the Temple court (Mk 11: 15 and parr.), is the leitmotiv of Crossan's, N. T. Wright's, and most particularly Borg's works. Against this, my essay "Did Jesus Oppose the Purity Laws?" The idea that purity laws particularly discriminated against women and that Jesus, by opposing these laws, also opposed the misogynist culture of his day is a recent restatement of an old theme in the Christian study of Judaism, where Jesus' singular moral excellence is contrasted with that of his native culture, which in turn is viewed as his moral opposite. In its classic form, the Christian-Jewish contrast was "grace" as opposed to "works." We now see "egalitarianism" (Jesus, Christianity) opposed to "hierarchy" (the priests, the Temple, or anything to do with purity regulations); "compassion" (Jesus) as opposed to "purity" (the Jewish context; this last slogan is Borg's particular contribution); and "inclusiveness" against ethnically exclusive "nationalism" (N. T. Wright). A Jesus who champions some version of equal rights for women, and who accordingly combats patriarchal Judaism to do so, is of a piece with such polarizing "analyses."

The social historical question of women in the early Jesus movement is complex and difficult, not least of all because we know so little of women's lives in this period generally. For an excellent survey of the latest scholarship and the state of the question, see the essays in Kraemer and D'Angelo, *Women and Christian Origins.*

Who wrote the Gospels, Jews or Gentiles? No one knows, though scholars, on the basis of internal evidence, will venture "ethnic" identifications. The author of Matthew is universally regarded as Jewish; for the last thirty or so years, so also the author of John. Arguments for Luke go either way, though the author's fluency with the Septuagint, combined with the probable date of composition (late first century) incline me to suppose that he, too, was a Jew: The Bible was a bulky collection of books—scrolls actually—that would not have been circulating or accessible outside of a synagogue context in this early period.

What about Mark? Again, any answer is speculative. Many scholars presuppose that he was a Gentile; he demonstrates little of the familiarity with Jewish traditions and scriptures that Luke and Matthew so conspicuously display, nor does he evince close (if hostile) relations with his local synagogue communities in the way that John does. If Mark was a Jew, one colleague has observed to me, he was an extremely ignorant one. True. Ignorance of course is no respecter of persons or ethnic groups, and not everyone in the early movement could have Paul's education. The very early date of the Gospel's composition (some time shortly post-70), its scriptural underpinnings (evident especially in the Passion narrative), and the stimulus to compose given (I think) by the Temple's recent destruction, all incline me to think that its author, too, was Jewish.

Why does it matter? In part, because the implied social and religious location of the author gives us a jumping-off point for speculations about his community—whether it, too, was Jewish, gentile, or some mix—and about what they might have understood when hearing the Gospel. My argument here, however—that the Gospels bespeak an understood etiquette of purification—requires only that the evangelists' audiences be ancient. Nobody in antiquity, especially on a cultic holy day designated sacred to the god, did the equivalent of park-the-car-and-run-into-the-sanctuary. Proximity to an altar universally required (some sort of) preparatory purification. Jewish hearers (Matthew's certainly; Luke's and John's probably; and I think also Mark's) would have specific associations through their biblical culture with what this would have entailed, as would those gentile hearers who had been associated with the synagogue. Gentiles of a purely pagan background, however, would presuppose purifications too.

Sanders works out the chronology of Jesus' entry into Jerusalem in light of the necessary purification protocols in *The Historical Figure of Jesus,* pp. 250–52.

From time to time, scholars have raised the issue of historical tradition in John's Gospel: the classic studies are Dodd, *Historical Tradition in the Fourth Gospel;* and Robinson, *The Priority of John.* These studies proceed by close technical analysis of particular words, phrases, or episodes in the Gospel, sifting the text to detect particular traditions that may be independent of and ultimately prior to what we have in the Synoptics. Coakley, "Jesus' Messianic Entry into Jerusalem," analyzes the four canonical accounts to argue finally that Jesus was the unwilling participant in this demonstration of messianic enthusiasm. On the question of whether John drew on Mark, cf. Barrett, *The Gospel According to St. John* (yes, probably, pp. 14, 34–37); and R. Brown, *The Gospel According to John* (no, probably not, pp. xliv–xlvii). Innumerable other combinations of literary dependence between the four Gospels have been proposed and defended with conviction and ingenuity.

The argument I make here is much simpler. Given what we know about Jesus, the sort of itinerary that John presents makes much more sense than the one-year, one-way itinerary in Mark (followed by Matthew and Luke) that itself so much obliges Mark's distinctive theology. I do not defend the historicity of particular words, phrases, or the exact details of John's itinerary per se. As all the conflicting erudition shows, the evidence is simply too problematic to yield any unarguable conclusions.

The preference for Mark's chronology over John's, and especially the explanatory importance of Jesus' action in the Temple for his arrest and subsequent execution, provides so far as I know the unique point on which Sanders, Vermès, Crossan, Borg, and N. T. Wright all agree. This is partly due to the force and clarity with which Sanders made his argument in *Jesus and Judaism,* where to escape the endless bog of uncertainty over authentic or inauthentic sayings of Jesus, he chose to concentrate on deeds. Jesus' action in the Temple was his starting point. He concluded that Jesus did indeed overturn tables; that the traditional interpretation of his action as "cleansing" was historically impossible; and that by this gesture Jesus had intended to symbolically enact the Temple's impending apocalyptic destruction—hence its apocalyptic restoration or rebuilding—with the approaching advent of the Kingdom. After his arrest, unsympathetic outsiders (such as the priests) interpreted his gesture as a prophetic threat to the Temple. Other scholars take Sanders' point that Jesus' gesture was symbolic, but differ on the meaning of the symbolism. They unite on its import: the action led to Jesus' arrest and subsequent crucifixion.

Let's say that, for whatever reason, Jesus did perform this action more or less as Mark describes during his final Passover in Jerusalem. How does this account for his execution by Pilate specifically by crucifixion? Sanders argues that Jesus thought of himself as God's viceroy, which is to say, as a king. (The French word enables Sanders to insist that Jesus did not claim the title "messiah" for himself [p. 308], though functionally "viceroy" and "messiah" seem the same to me.) Jesus also deliberately managed the Triumphal Entry, including riding on an ass in knowing recollection of Zechariah 9:9, in order to proclaim his kingship (pp. 306–8). Why then did the Romans not move in at this point? "Perhaps the event took place but was a small occurrence which went unnoticed. Perhaps only a few disciples unostentatiously dropped their garments in front of the ass . . . , while only a few quietly murmured 'Hosanna,' " p. 306 (see, too, his summary paragraph, p. 308).

Jesus' action in the Temple, overturning tables, was "the crucial act which led to his execution" (p. 334). The priests and also the Romans then assumed that Jesus was a threat to public order (pp. 302, 304). Thus "he was executed by Pilate at the behest of the Jewish leadership" (p. 318; Sanders notes the superiority of John's version of the Jewish "trial": "The vaguer account of John seems better to correspond with the way things actually worked," p. 318). More clearly and dramatically, *The Historical Figure of Jesus,* p. 273: "Why did Pilate order Jesus' execution? Because the high priest recommended it and gave him a telling charge: Jesus thought he was king of the Jews. [Sanders' high priest infers this from Jesus' Triumphal Entry and his teaching about the Kingdom, however, *not* from the Temple act, which simply drew Jesus to his attention, p. 272, cf. p. 269.] Pilate understood that Jesus was a would-be king without an army, and therefore he made no effort to run down and execute Jesus' followers. He probably regarded him as a religious fanatic whose fanaticism had become so extreme that it posed a threat to law and order."

Crossan's Jesus had thought of himself as the Temple's "functional opponent, alternative, and substitute," *The Historical Jesus,* p. 355. (Meaning what? People could offer their Passover sacrifices in front of Jesus? Give him their two drachmas? Go to him for Sukkot?) His action at the Temple symbolized his destruction of its religious function (p. 359). This angered the priests, so they used their connections with Pilate to engineer Jesus' death. How? Why? And why specifically by crucifixion? Not clear. Crossan concludes, "I think that the symbolic destruction [overturning the tables] was but the logical extension [of the message of Jesus' mission: unbrokered religion] . . . ; I think that it actually happened and, *if* it happened at Passover [Crossan's anti-Temple Jesus has little use for pilgrimage holidays], *could* easily have led to arrest and execution," p. 360.

One last example: N. T. Wright's Jesus overturns the Temple's tables to symbolize its approaching military destruction by Rome if it does not cease to be the center of Jewish nationalist aspirations: Jesus thus "pronounces judgment," *Jesus and the Victory of God,* p. 333–36; also pp. 406–28. (Wright's specifying Rome—or inferring that Jesus did—enables him to credit Jesus with an extremely accurate prophesy that was in fact precisely fulfilled; but he thereby creates a further difficulty: Why would the evangelists, after the fact, so obscure Jesus' correct prognostication? They nowhere claim that Jesus had Rome in mind when he spoke of coming judgment or destruction.)

According to Wright, Jesus also "saw himself, and perhaps also his followers with him, as the new Temple," pp. 426 and 612–54. This is no stretch since, says Wright, Jesus also thought of Jerusalem as Babylon and his group alone as Israel. Further, his actions both at the Triumphal Entry and in the Temple were self-consciously messianic, but in a new, nonnationalist way (pp. 490–91 and passim). All this is political stuff, and it was as a political leader that Pilate killed him (though both Jesus' accusers and Pilate knew he was not a "normal revolutionary," p. 544). In a display of hermeneutical virtuosity, Wright also seems to affirm the historicity *both* of the Markan trial narrative (p. 517) *and* of the Johannine narrative (pp. 549–51).

Wright's argument is dense, lengthy (well over twelve hundred pages, if we include his setup volume, *The New Testament and the People of God,* in the count), and learned. His Jesus, who enjoys a detailed command over so many scriptural and extrascriptural verses and allusions that he must have been the envy of the scribes and Pharisees he tangled with, essentially creates Christianity, which in turn is faithfully preserved in the canonical texts of the New Testament. I find this picture impossible in whole and in part.

CHAPTER 5
THE DAYS IN JERUSALEM

Was Jesus in fact political in a recognizably militarily revolutionary way? This was the position of Brandon, *Jesus and the Zealots;* see the essays in response to his thesis in Bammel and Moule, *Jesus and the Politics of His Day.* For an extremely carefully argued consideration of the trial narratives in the Gospels, see Millar, "Reflections on the Trial of Jesus." He notes that, since "no Gospel represents Pilate's decision as a formal verdict, there is a very clear sense in which the entire notion of 'the trial of Jesus' is a modern construct," p. 378.

On the charged question of the historical reliability of the Gospels' accounts of Jesus' arrest, hearings, and execution, see R. Brown, *The Death of the Messiah;* and Crossan's impassioned rejoinder, *Who Killed Jesus?* Hengel's brief monograph, *Crucifixion,* is extremely informative. However, his argument that Jews would find death by crucifixion offensive, and *eo ipso* would view anyone so killed as "accursed" (and thus be particularly offended by the idea of a *crucified* messiah) draws on later Christian theology, not ancient Jewish history. Paul in Galatians—the letter where he rails against his congregations' harkening to other Christian missionaries who urge them to receive circumcision—refers in passing to Deuteronomy 21:23, "Cursed of God is every man hanged from a tree" (Gal 5:11). Outside of assertions in Christian writings and modern New Testament scholarship, however, we have no evidence of actual Jews looking at crucified compatriots this way. Josephus says nothing of the sort when relating the story of the eight hundred Pharisees crucified by a Hasmonean king (*BJ* 1:97; *AJ* 13:380–83), or the crucifixion of two thousand rebels in Judea by Varus in 6 C.E.—and he himself was politically antipathetic to the latter movement. Finally, the earliest apostolic community lived in Jerusalem until at least the outbreak of the revolt against Rome in 66 C.E.: For decades, unmolested by supposedly offended Jerusalemites, it proclaimed Jesus as crucified messiah. Romans, who particularly exercised this mode of execution, might very well have supposed that anyone crucified had probably been a slave, a rebel, and/or a criminal (e.g., Tacitus, *Histories*, 2.72). Jews would probably see a fallen patriot. So, too, Brandon, "The cross was a symbol of Zealot sacrifice long before it was transformed into the Christian sign of salvation," *Jesus and the Zealots*, p. 145. See further Fredriksen, *From Jesus to Christ*, pp. 146–48; on the relative calm of the Jerusalem church, pp. 143–45.

Within millenarian groups, a specifically named Endtime date often works to concentrate and raise popular attention and to spur fence-sitters to commit to the movement. The shape of the Passion story in these Gospels prompted my speculation here. Such "spiking" of apocalyptic enthusiasm is endemic to Christian culture throughout late antiquity and the Middle Ages; the various agitations we see now around the year 2000 are part and parcel of a long cultural predisposition. On the millenarianism of the early movement, both around Jesus and shortly after his death, see Allison, *Jesus of Nazareth;* on the repeat pattern in late antiquity, Fredriksen, "Apocalypse and Redemption in Early Christianity." For a fascinating and well-documented nineteenth-century version of a similar phenomenon, see O'Leary's discussion of the Millerites in *Arguing the Apocalypse*, pp. 99–133. Miller's prediction of the End for March 1844 (also known as "The Great Disappointment") stimulated great interest in his group, increasing its membership. Once his prophecy failed, the movement itself went on to flourish as the Seventh Day Adventist Church. Another good recent study of the apocalyptic mentality: Boyer, *When Time Shall Be No More*.

AFTERWORD
JESUS, CHRISTIANITY, AND HISTORY

See Sanders' reflections on this material about the resurrection of Jesus, *The Historical Figure of Jesus*, pp. 276–81. Crossan does not take these traditions as intending a historical description; rather, he says, Jesus' followers composed the Resurrection stories to serve as narrative metaphors for their existential experience of his continuing "presence," i.e., the effects of his teaching and example, *Revolutionary Biography*, pp. 123–58, 197.

My reconstruction of events here presupposes that Pilate's action against him caught Jesus by surprise. This position is not universally shared. N. T. Wright's is the most recent portrait of a Jesus who knowingly planned—and to that degree intended and orchestrated—his own death in service to his particular theological message. "Jesus, then, went up to Jerusalem not just to preach, but to die. . . . Jesus believed that the messianic woes were about to burst upon Israel, and that he had to take them upon himself, solo" (*Jesus and the Victory of God,* p. 609; for the whole argument, pp. 553–611). Against this point of view I can argue no more eloquently than Sanders, who notes,

> All the sayings which attribute to Jesus the will to die correspond so closely with what happened, and with early Christian doctrine, that the case for their creation by the early church is overwhelmingly strong. The criterion of dissimilarity is by no means infallible, but here it must come into play. One might as well attribute to Jesus the doctrine of the Trinity or of the Incarnation. Further, a historian must be uncomfortable with an explanation which leaves other actors in the drama out of account. When pushed to its limit, this view means that Jesus determined in his own mind to be killed . . . [and] then imply that he pulled this off by provoking the authorities. It is not historically impossible that Jesus was weird, and I realize that my own interpretation of his views may make twentieth-century people look at him askance. But the view that he plotted his own redemptive death makes him strange in any century and thrusts the entire drama into his peculiar inner psyche. The other things we know about him make him a *reasonable* first-century visionary. We should be guided by them.   (*Jesus and Judaism,* pp. 332–33)

Amen.

The current reconstruction emphasizes Pilate's role in the events leading to Jesus' crucifixion. Two earlier Jewish sources—Paul and, a generation later, Josephus—instead emphasize the role of Jewish leaders. Josephus says, vaguely, that as a result of "an accusation made by the leading men among us," Pilate condemned Jesus to the cross (*AJ* 18.63). Paul, by contrast, seems to speak in anger:

> You, brethren, became imitators of the *ekklēsiai* of God in Christ Jesus which are in Judea; for you suffered the same things from your countrymen as they did from the *Ioudaioi* [Jews? Judeans?] *who killed both the Lord Jesus and the prophets, and drove us out, and displease God and oppose all men by hindering us from speaking to the Gentiles that they may be saved—so as to fill up the measure of their sins. But God's wrath has come upon them at last!*   (1 Thes 2:14–16)

Scholars divide on the question of whether this passage is actually by Paul or put in by a later interpolator. In favor of its authenticity is the fact that no manuscript tradition preserves a reading that stands without it, and also that the intemperate tone can be matched to other passages, especially in Galatians. Against, the uncharacteristic way that Paul speaks of his own people ("the Jews"), the attribution of the murder of all the prophets to them (a prominent theme only in the later Gospels, and certainly nowhere else in Paul), and the complaint that the Jews hinder Paul's gentile mission (a theme, again, in the much later Acts of the Apostles, but nowhere else in the Epistles). Finally, the tense of the final line, indicating past completed action—"God's wrath *has come* upon them!"—most readily calls to mind the later Christian view of the meaning of the destruction of the Temple, an event outside Paul's lifetime. These arguments are assembled in Pearson, "1 Thessalonians 2:13–16." Even were this passage authentic—I am undecided—the fact that Jesus was crucified rather than executed or killed in any other way still indicates that no one other than Pilate made the actual decision, and that in so doing he had a particular objective in mind.

GLOSSARY

Alenu (Heb. "to us"): A prayer, now part of the synagogue service, that praises God for his revelation to Israel. It proclaims his kingship and expresses hope for the establishment of his kingdom, when the rest of humankind will be redeemed from spiritual error, cease worshiping idols, and turn piously to the Creator. Rabbinic tradition ascribes its composition to a third-century authority, Rav; but its original provenance may go back to the service of the Second Temple, since it makes no mention of restoring the Temple and specifically alludes to the Temple practice of prostration during worship.

Antiochus Epiphanes: Greek Seleucid ruler, descendant of one of Alexander the Great's generals. In the 170s B.C.E., Antiochus supported the reforming efforts of Jerusalem's Hellenizing priestly families; by 167, he had erected a pagan altar in the Jerusalem Temple (the "abomination of desolation" of Dn 13:14), thus triggering the Maccabean revolt.

apocalyptic eschatology: A mood or tradition within Judaism particularly marking the period between c. 200 B.C.E. and c. 200 C.E. that looked to the imminent realization of God's promises for the redemption of Israel and, ultimately, all Creation.

Apocrypha: Religious writings of unknown or spurious authorship that have authority but not canonical status in Jewish and, later, Christian tradition, e.g., Tobit.

apostle (Gk. "messenger" or "envoy"): An emissary, someone who travels to give a message. In earliest Christianity, the term may designate the core group of Jesus' intimate followers, or later followers such as Paul who traveled to spread the message of the Christian movement.

Decius: The Roman emperor who in 250 C.E. initiated the first empirewide legal action against (Gentile) Christians by insisting that they also participate in Rome's traditional cult.

Diaspora (Gk.; Lat. "dispersion"; Heb. *galut,* "exile"): Jewish designation for any place where Jews live outside the Land of Israel.

ekklēsia (Gk. "assembly"): A gathering or assembly of people, perhaps for religious purposes. In later Christian circles the term came to designate particularly those gathered around the message of the gospel, thus, eventually, "church" (Fr. *église*).

halakah (Heb. "to go"): Jewish interpretation of biblical laws, both their application and the methods or means to fulfill them.

Hasmoneans: The priestly family who led the war against the Seleucids and those Hellenizing Jews supporting them in 167 B.C.E., and who subsequently established a ruling dynasty of kings and high priests who led the country and served in the Temple until the ascendancy of Herod the Great in 37 B.C.E. In the period of the anti-Seleucid rebellion, the family is also known as the Maccabees, from the battle name of one of the leaders of the revolt, Judah Maccabee ("the Hammer").

Herod family: *Herod the Great,* the greatest and most powerful Jewish king of postbiblical Israel, ruled as governor of the Galilee from 47 to 37 B.C.E., and as king of the region until 4 B.C.E. He consolidated power by marrying into the Hasmonean family, then killing off most of his in-laws, eventually even his wife, Mariamne (28 B.C.E.). Of all of Herod's splendid and ambitious architectural projects, the Temple in Jerusalem was the crowning glory. He began enlarging and beautifying the Temple in c. 20 B.C.E. The completion of this project in 63 C.E. left some eighteen thousand men out of work. Herod died in 4 B.C.E., leaving Judea, Idumea, and Samaria to the rule of his son *Archelaus,* and dividing up northern areas between his sons Philip and Antipas. Equally brutal but much less effective than his father, Archelaus was deposed by Augustus in 6 C.E., and his lands passed directly under Roman authority. His brother *Antipas,* the Herod of the Gospel stories about Jesus' mission, ruled the Galilee and Perea for the most part peacefully and well. He was deposed by Caligula after a family intrigue in 39 C.E. *Herod Agrippa I* (see Acts 12), nephew of Antipas and grandson of Herod the Great, was named king of Perea by Caligula (37 C.E.); later, Claudius extended his sovereignty to include Judea and Samaria (41 C.E.). Agrippa died suddenly in 44 C.E., and his territories reverted to the status of Roman province. His son, *Agrippa II,* ruled some of the family's traditional holdings in the north from c. 50 C.E. The country erupted in revolt in 66, and he sided with Rome throughout the war. Dying childless c. 100, he was the last of Herod's line to rule.

Josephus (37–100 C.E.): Born and raised in Jerusalem of a well-to-do priestly family, Josephus as a young man was put in charge of the defenses of the Galilee when revolt against Rome broke out in 66 C.E. He surrendered to the Romans, prophesying that Vespasian would become emperor, and so entered the general's entourage, from which vantage point he witnessed the subjugation of Judea and the siege and destruction of Jerusalem. His works include the invaluable *Jewish War* (*BJ*), the *Antiquities of the Jews* (*AJ*), an apology *Against Apion* (*c. Ap.*), and a sketchy autobiography, *Life of Josephus* (*Vita*). Josephus died in Rome, where he had spent the remainder of his life since the war under the patronage of Vespasian and Titus.

kerygma (Gk. "preaching"): With reference to earliest Christianity, the oral proclamation of traditions from and about Jesus.

L: Academic designation for material appearing uniquely in the Gospel of Luke.

M: Academic designation for material appearing uniquely in the Gospel of Matthew.

Maccabees: The name applied to the Hasmonean family who successfully led the war against Hellenizing Jews and the Seleucid king Antiochus Epiphanes in 167 B.C.E. The word also designates four books of Jewish Apocrypha, 1 Mc and 2 Mc being histories of the war, 3 Mc, a sort of historical novel, and 4 Mc, philosophical reflection.

messiah (Heb. "anointed"): A term in the Hebrew bible designating "king" (in particular, David or one of his line), by Jesus' lifetime "messiah" had come to mean an Endtime figure who played a part in the apocalyptic redemption of God's people. As such, it was interpreted variously, even within single communities: the Dead Sea Scrolls speak of two messiahs, one priestly, one military ("the messiah of Aaron and David," 1 QS 9.1), and allude both to a prophetic messiah and to a dim, heavenly figure. Not all apocalyptic texts mention a messianic redeemer figure, but where it does appear, it most often refers to a figure of David's line who leads to final victory the forces of good.

mezzuzot (Heb. "doorposts"): Small parchment pages on which biblical passages are written, *mezzuzot* were (and are) attached to the doorposts of Jewish houses as a way to fulfill the prescription in Deuteronomy 6:9, "And they [God's words] shall be as a doorpost upon your house and your gates."

mikveh (Heb.; pl. *mikvaot*): Stepped pools used for ritual immersion to cleanse the user of impurity.

Mishnah (Heb. "repetition, instruction"): A compilation of oral law interpreting the commands of biblical (i.e., written) law. It dates from c. 200 C.E., though strains of the traditions it contains are considerably older.

Parousia (Gk. "presence"): A Christian term used for the Endtime appearance or Second Coming of Christ.

Pesach/Passover: The Jewish festival commemorating the liberation of Israel from Pharaoh as described in Exodus. While the Temple stood, Jerusalem was a center for pilgrims during this holiday, one of the three biblically mandated pilgrimage feasts.

Philo of Alexandria (c. 20 B.C.E.–50 C.E.): Jewish Hellenistic philosopher and community leader in Alexandria, Philo participated in the delegation sent to Caligula in 40 C.E. over the anti-Jewish violence that had erupted in that city. His main body of work was philosophizing, heavily allegorical interpretations of the Septuagint.

pontifex maximus (Lat. "highest priest"): One of the titles and functions of the emperor of Rome, whose duty it was to ensure and support the practice of all legitimate cults within the empire.

priest; high priest; chief priests (Heb. *cohen, cohanim*): Biblically, the priests were a subgroup of the tribe of Levi, the clan designated by God to serve at his altar. The high priest had special responsibilities, particularly on the High Holy Days and on Yom Kippur, to sacrifice on behalf of the entire community. In principle a life appointment, by the late Hellenistic period, and later under the Hasmoneans and especially under Herod (170s B.C.E. through the war with Rome in 66–73 C.E.), the position was subject to political riptides in Jerusalem. The designation "chief priests" probably refers to priests in the aristocratic families from whose number the high priest was appointed. Outside the Temple, the priests also served their communities as teachers and interpreters of Torah.

province: a Roman colonial administrative unit.

Pseudepigrapha (Gk. "false writing"): The name given to extracanonical religious works written under the name of another, usually very ancient, authority. False authorship enhanced the authority of the new teaching.

Q (from German *Quelle,* "source"): Material in Greek, mostly sayings but some story, common to Matthew and Luke that does not appear in Mark. Scholars divide over whether Q was a (now lost) document or a body of tradition that circulated orally.

Seleucids: The name of the Hellenistic family of one of Alexander the Great's generals whose power centered in Syria. They contested with the Ptolemies, another such family whose power base was Egypt, for control of the lands lying between them. Territorial Israel figured prominently in their ongoing border disputes.

Septuagint: The Greek translation of Jewish Scripture originating out of Alexandria. The translation was completed by the second century B.C.E.

Shavuot/Pentecost: One of the three biblically mandated pilgrimage holidays, Shavuot (Heb. "weeks") is observed fifty days after Passover in the very late spring or early summer. According to rabbinic tradition, it commemorates the giving of the Law on Sinai fifty days after the Exodus (cf. Ex 19:1).

Shemoneh Esreh (Heb. "eighteen," for the number of benedictions contained in the weekday prayer): Also known as the *Amidah* ("standing") and simply "the Prayer" (*ha-tefillah*), now the core of the synagogue service, this prayer praises God for raising the dead (number 2), delighting in repentance (number 5), redeeming Israel (number 7), and also gathering in the exiles (number 10). It also petitions him to have mercy on the righteous, on converts, and on all who trust in him (number 13), to rebuild Jerusalem, reestablish David's kingdom, and renew the Temple service (numbers 14–17). It concludes with a prayer for peace. The prayer preserves a stratigraphic record of Jewish piety, with some parts predating, others clearly postdating the Roman destruction of the Temple.

Sh'ma (Heb. "hear"): One of the prime prayers of Judaism, the *Sh'ma* repeats passages from Deuteronomy 6:4–9, 11:13–21; and Numbers 15:37–41. Its recitation was part of the Temple service, which the synagogue continued. It was and is also recited morning and evening. The synoptic Jesus recites the first line of the *Sh'ma* in response to the scribe's query about the greatest commandment (Mk 12:28–31 and parr.).

Sukkot/Tabernacles or Booths: The fall pilgrimage festival that marks the end of the holy season begun with Rosh haShanah and Yom Kippur. Later tradition associates the holiday with the period when Israel wandered in the desert after the Exodus, living in temporary dwellings.

synagogue (Gk. "to bring together" or "assemble"): An institution of Jewish communal life, primarily for hearing and instruction in the Torah, and later also as a place for public prayer. In Jesus' period, a synagogue might simply designate the assembly of worshipers, not a particular building, though Jews in urban areas might construct large buildings to serve as community centers as well as places for religious instruction and study.

synoptic Gospels (Gk. *syn-*, "together," *opsis*, "view"): The term applied to the first three Gospels in the Christian canon (Matthew, Mark, and Luke) because they share a common narrative chronology and many verbal details.

Talmud (Heb. "teaching"): The compendium of Jewish law that contains the Mishnah (collected c. 200 C.E.), and discussion and interpretation of the Mishnah, called the Gemara (collected c. 500 C.E.).

tefillin/phylacteries: Two black cubical boxes made of leather that contain verses from the *Sh'ma* and, in antiquity, perhaps other biblical passages. One box is bound to the head "between the eyes" (i.e., on the upper forehead), the other (usually) to the left arm. This custom or practice seems well established by the first century: Tefillin have been found at Qumran, and Matthew's Jesus implicitly instructs his followers on the correct size for their tefillin (they should not be as broad as those of the Pharisees, 23:5).

Titus: Son of Vespasian and himself a Roman general, Titus fought at Vespasian's side during the Jewish War. When political crisis called his father away, Titus pressed on with the siege of Jerusalem, eventually burning the city and destroying the Temple in the summer of 70 C.E.

Torah (Heb. "teaching"): The first five books of the Bible, authorship of which is traditionally ascribed to Moses. More particularly, Torah also refers to those teachings and religious principles enunciated in the revelation at Sinai.

Vespasian: The Roman general who subdued the Galilee during the Jewish War against Rome. Vespasian succeeded as emperor after the period of turmoil marked by Nero's death, and established the line of Flavian emperors.

SELECT BIBLIOGRAPHY

JEWISH TEXTS

I usually cite biblical or intertestamental texts from the *Oxford Annotated Revised Standard Version with Apocrypha*. A larger collection of intertestamental Jewish writings can be found in *The Old Testament Apocrypha and Pseudepigrapha,* 2 vols., ed. J. H. Charlesworth (New York: Doubleday, 1985).

Josephus
BJ   Bellum Judaicum   The Jewish War
Loeb Classical Library, 2 vols. (Cambridge, MA: Harvard University Press, 1927–1928).

AJ   Antiquitates Judaicae   Jewish Antiquities
Loeb Classical Library, 7 vols. (Cambridge, MA: Harvard University Press, 1930–1965).

Vita   Life
Loeb Classical Library (Cambridge, MA: Harvard University Press, 1926).

c. Ap.   contra Apionem   Against Apion
Loeb Classical Library (Cambridge, MA: Harvard University Press, 1926).

The Loeb editions print the Greek text with facing English translation. For *BJ,* I also use the revised edition of Penguin English translation, *The Jewish War* (Harmondsworth, UK: Penguin, 1981).

Philo, Loeb Classical Library, 10 vols. (Cambridge, MA: Harvard University Press, 1929–1943).

The Dead Sea Scrolls in English, trans. Geza Vermès (Harmondsworth, UK: Penguin, 1962).

CHRISTIAN TEXTS

I usually cited the Oxford RSV translation for New Testament writings, occasionally emending to clarify my own interpretive point. For the Greek text, *Novum Testamentum Graece et Latine,* ed. E. Nestle et al. (Stuttgart: Deutsche Bibelgesellschaft, 1984). Specifically for the Gospel texts, *Synopsis of the Four Gospels,* ed. K. Aland, 8th ed. (Stuttgart: German Bible Society, 1987). For translating specific terms or words, *A Greek-English Lexicon of the New Testament and Other Early Christian Literature,* ed. W. Bauer, with F. W. Gingrich and F. W. Danker (Chicago: The University of Chicago Press, 1979).

Eusebius, *Ecclesiastical History.* Loeb Classical Library, 2 vols. (Cambridge, MA: Harvard University Press, 1953).
Justin Martyr, *Apology.* Ante-Nicene Fathers, vol. 1 (Grand Rapids, MI: Eerdmans, 1973).
Tertullian, *Apology.* Ante-Nicene Fathers, vol. 3 (Grand Rapids, MI: Eerdmans, 1975).

OTHER ANCIENT TEXTS

Pliny the Elder, *Natural History,* Loeb Classical Library, 10 vols. (Cambridge, MA: Harvard University Press, 1938).
Seutonius, *Lives of the Caesars.* Loeb Classical Library, 2 vols. (Cambridge, MA: Harvard University Press, 1924).
Tacitus, *Annals; Histories.* Loeb Classical Library, 4 vols. (Cambridge, MA: Harvard University Press, 1932).

MODERN WORKS

The following list is highly selective. I have named here only those works that have significantly affected my own interpretation, whether positively or negatively, as well as books whose reconstructions of Jesus and his mission differ sharply from my own. I also include several studies that I consider both accessible and valuable to the nonspecialist.

Alexander, P. S., review of *Jesus and Judaism,* by E. P. Sanders. *Journal of Jewish Studies* 37.1 (1986):103–6.
Allison, Dale C., *Jesus of Nazareth: Millenarian Prophet* (Minneapolis: Fortress Press, 1998).
Alon, G., "The Levitical Uncleanness of Gentiles," in *Jews and Judaism in the Classical World* (Jerusalem: Magnes Press, 1977), 146–89.

Ashton, John, *Understanding the Fourth Gospel* (Oxford: The Clarendon Press, 1991).

Bammel, E. and C. F. D. Moule, *Jesus and the Politics of His Day* (Cambridge: Cambridge University Press, 1984).

Barrett, C. K., *The Gospel According to St. John* (London: SPCK, 1962).

Borg, Marcus, *Jesus in Contemporary Scholarship* (Valley Forge, PA: Trinity Press International, 1994).

———, *Meeting Jesus Again for the First Time* (San Francisco: HarperSanFrancisco, 1994).

Boyer, Paul, *When Time Shall Be No More* (Cambridge, MA: Harvard University Press, 1992).

Brandon, S. G. F., *Jesus and the Zealots* (Manchester, UK: Manchester University Press, 1967).

Brown, Peter, *Body and Society: Men, Women, and Sexual Renunciation in Early Christianity* (New York: Columbia University Press, 1988).

Brown, Raymond E., *The Gospel According to John,* 2 vols. (Garden City, NY: Doubleday, 1970).

———, *The Death of the Messiah,* 2 vols. (Garden City, NY: Doubleday, 1994).

Büchler, A., "The Levitical Impurity of the Gentile in Palestine before the Year 70," *Jewish Quarterly Review* 17 (1926):1–81.

Casey, Maurice, *Son of Man: The Interpretation and Influence of Daniel 7* (London: SPCK, 1979).

Chilton, Bruce, *The Temple of Jesus: His Sacrificial Program within a Cultural History of Sacrifice* (University Park, PA: Pennsylvania State University Press, 1992).

———, *Judaic Approaches to the Gospels* (Atlanta: Scholars Press, 1994).

———, *Pure Kingdom: Jesus' Vision of God* (Grand Rapids, MI: Eerdmans, 1996).

Coakley, J. F., "Jesus' Messianic Entry into Jerusalem (Jn 12:12–19)," *Journal of Theological Studies* 46 (1995), 461–82.

Cohen, Shaye J. D., *From the Maccabees to the Mishnah* (Philadelphia: Westminister Press, 1987).

———, "Respect for Judaism by Gentiles According to Josephus," *Harvard Theological Review* 80 (1987):409–30.

———, "Crossing the Boundary and Becoming a Jew," *Harvard Theological Review* 82 (1989):14–33.

Collins, John J., *The Scepter and the Star: The Messiahs of the Dead Sea Scrolls and Other Ancient Literature* (New York: Doubleday, 1995).

Crossan, John Dominic, *The Historical Jesus: The Life of a Mediterranean Jewish Peasant* (New York: HarperCollins, 1991).

———, *Jesus: A Revolutionary Biography* (San Francisco: HarperSanFrancisco, 1994).

———, *Who Killed Jesus? Exposing the Roots of Anti-Semitism in the Gospel Story of the Death of Jesus* (San Francisco: HarperSanFrancisco, 1995).

———, *The Birth of Christianity: Discovering What Happened in the Years Immediately after the Execution of Jesus* (San Francisco: HarperSanFrancisco, 1998).

Dahl, Nils, *The Crucified Messiah and Other Essays* (Minneapolis: Augsburg, 1974).

Dodd, C. H., *The Interpretation of the Fourth Gospel* (Cambridge: Cambridge University Press, 1953).

———, *Historical Tradition in the Fourth Gospel* (Cambridge: Cambridge University Press, 1963).

Donahue, John R., *Are You the Christ? The Trial Narrative in the Gospel of Mark* (Missoula, MT: Scholars Press, 1973).

Douglas, Mary, *Purity and Danger* (London: Routledge and Keegan Paul, 1966).

———, *In the Wilderness: The Doctrine of Defilement in the Book of Numbers* (London: Sheffield, 1993).

Downing, Gerald F., *Christ and the Cynics: Jesus and Other Radical Preachers in First-Century Tradition* (Sheffield, UK: Sheffield Academic Press, 1988).

———, *Cynics and Christian Origins* (Edinburgh: T. & T. Clark, 1992).

Dunn, James D. G., *Jesus and the Spirit* (Philadelphia: Westminister, 1975).

Edwards, Douglas, "The Socio-Economic and Cultural Ethos of the Lower Galilee in the First Century: Implications for the Nascent Jesus Movement," in *The Galilee in Late Antiquity,* ed. Lee I. Levine (New York: Jewish Theological Seminary, 1992), 53–73.

Evans, Craig A., "Jesus' Action in the Temple," *Catholic Biblical Quarterly* 51 (1989) 237–70.

———, "Predictions of the Destruction of the Herodian Temple in the Pseudepigrapha, Qumran Scrolls, and Related Texts," *Journal of Social Psychology* 10 (1992): 89–147.

Finegan, Jack, *The Archaeology of the New Testament,* rev. ed. (Princeton, NJ: Princeton University Press, 1992).

Fredriksen, Paula, *From Jesus to Christ: The Origins of the New Testament Images of Jesus* (New Haven, CT: Yale University Press, 1988).

———, "Jesus and the Temple, Mark and the War," *SBLSP* 29 (1990): 293–310.

———, "Apocalypse and Redemption in Early Christianity: From John of Patmos to Augustine of Hippo," *Vigiliae Christianae* 45 (1991): 151–83.

———, "Judaism, the Circumcision of Gentiles, and Apocalyptic Hope: Another Look at Galatians 1 and 2," *Journal of Theological Studies* 42 (1991): 532–64.

———, "Vile Bodies: Paul and Augustine on the Resurrection of the Flesh," *Biblical Interpretation in Historical Perspective: Studies in Honor of Karlfried Froehlich,* ed. M. Burrows and P. Rorem (Grand Rapids, MI: Eerdmans 1991), 73–85.

———, "From Jesus to Christ. The Contribution of the Apostle Paul," *Jews and Christians Speak of Jesus,* ed. A. E. Zannoni (Minneapolis: Fortress Press, 1994), 77–91.

———, "Did Jesus Oppose the Purity Laws?" *Bible Review,* XI.3 (1995), 20–25, 42–47.

———, "Torah-Observance and Christianity: The Perspective of Roman Antiquity," *Modern Theology* 11.2 (1995): 195–204.

———, "What You See Is What You Get: Context and Content in Current Research on the Historical Jesus," *Theology Today* 52 (1995): 75–97.

Freyne, Sean, *Galilee from Alexander the Great to Hadrian, 323 BCE to 135 CE* (Wilmington, DE: Michael Glazier, Inc., 1980).

———, "Vilifying the Other and Defining the Self: Matthew's and John's Anti-Jewish Polemic in Focus," in *To See Ourselves as Others See Us: Christians, Jews,*

"Others" in Late Antiquity, ed. J. Neusner and E. S. Frerichs (Chico, CA: Scholars Press, 1985), 117–43.

———, *Galilee, Jesus and the Gospels: Literary Approaches and Historical Investigations* (Philadelphia: Fortress Press, 1988).

Funk, Robert W., *Honest to Jesus: Jesus for a New Millennium* (San Francisco: HarperSanFrancisco, 1996).

Gager, John G., *Kingdom and Community* (Englewood Cliffs, NJ: Prentice Hall, 1975).

———, *The Origins of Anti-Semitism: Attitudes toward Judaism in Pagan and Christian Antiquity* (New York: Oxford University Press, 1983).

Goodman, Martin, *The Ruling Class of Judaea: The Origins of the Jewish Revolt against Rome, AD 66–70* (Cambridge: Cambridge University Press, 1987).

———, *Mission and Conversion: Proselytizing in the Religious History of the Roman Empire* (Oxford: The Clarendon Press, 1994).

Gray, Rebecca, *Prophetic Figures in Late Second Temple Jewish Palestine* (Oxford: Oxford University Press, 1993).

Gruen, Erich S., *Heritage and Hellenism: The Reinvention of Jewish Tradition* (Berkeley and Los Angeles: University of California Press, 1998).

Hays, Christine, "The Impurity of Gentiles in Biblical Law and Late Antique Judaism," unpublished MS.

Hengel, Martin, *Judaism and Hellenism: Studies in Their Encounter in Palestine during the Early Hellenistic Period,* 2 vols. (Philadelphia: Fortress Press, 1974).

———, *Crucifixion in the Ancient World and the Folly of the Message of the Cross* (Philadelphia: Fortress Press, 1977).

Horbury, William, "The Messianic Associations of 'Son of Man,' " *Journal of Theological Studies* 36 (1985): 34–55.

Horsley, Richard A., "The Death of Jesus," in *Studying the Historical Jesus: Evaluations of the State of Current Research,* ed. Bruce Chilton and Craig A. Evans (Leiden, Netherlands: E. J. Brill, 1994), 395–422.

———, "The Historical Jesus and the Archaeology of the Galilee: Questions from Historical Jesus Research to Archaeologists," *SBLSP* 33 (1994): 91–135.

———, *Sociology and the Jesus Movement* (New York: Continuum, 1994).

———, "Wisdom Justified by All Her Children: Examining Allegedly Disparate Traditions in Q," *SBLSP* 33 (1994): 733–51.

———, *Galilee: History, Politics, People* (Valley Forge, PA: Trinity Press International, 1995).

Jonge, Marinus de, *Jesus, the Servant-Messiah* (New Haven, CT: Yale University Press, 1991).

Juel, Donald, *Messiah and Temple: The Trial of Jesus in the Gospel of Mark* (Missoula, MT: Scholars Press, 1977).

Kee, Howard Clark, "Christology in Mark's Gospel," in *Judaisms and Their Messiahs at the Turn of the Christian Era,* ed. J. Neusner, W. S. Green, and E. S. Frerichs (Cambridge: Cambridge University Press, 1987), 187–208.

Klawans, Jonathan, "Notions of Gentile Impurity in Ancient Judaism," *Association of Jewish Studies Review* 20.2 (1995): 285–312.

———, "The Impurity of Immorality in Ancient Judaism," *Journal of Jewish Studies* 48.1 (1997):1–16.

————, "Idolatry, Incest, and Impurity: Moral Defilement in Ancient Judaism," *Journal for the Study of Judaism* XXIX, 4 (1998): 391–415.

————, *Impurity and Immorality in Ancient Judaism* (New York: Oxford University Press, forthcoming 2000).

Koch, Klaus, *The Rediscovery of Apocalyptic* (London: SCM, 1972).

Kraemer, Ross, and Mary Rose D'Angelo, eds., *Women and Christian Origins* (New York: Oxford University Press, 1999).

Kümmel, W. G., *Introduction to the New Testament,* rev. English ed. (Nashville: Abingdon, 1975).

Lane Fox, Robin, *Pagans and Christians* (New York: Alfred A. Knopf, 1987).

Linder, Amnon, *The Jews in Roman Imperial Legislation* (Detroit: Wayne State University Press, 1986).

Mack, Burton, *A Myth of Innocence: Mark and Christian Origins* (Philadelphia: Fortress Press, 1988).

MacRae, George, "Messiah and Gospel," in *Judaisms and Their Messiahs at the Turn of the Christian Era,* ed. J. Neusner, W. S. Green, and E. S. Frerichs (Cambridge: Cambridge University Press, 1987), 169–85.

McKnight, Scot, *A Light among the Gentiles: Jewish Missionary Activity in the Second Temple Period* (Minneapolis: Fortress Press, 1991).

Meeks, Wayne A., "Breaking Away: Three New Testament Pictures of Christianity's Separation from the Jewish Communities," in *To See Ourselves as Others See Us: Christians, Jews, "Others" in Late Antiquity,* ed. J. Neusner and E. S. Frerichs (Chico, CA: Scholars Press, 1985), 93–115.

Meier, John P., *A Marginal Jew: Rethinking the Historical Jesus,* vol. 1: *The Roots of the Problem and the Person,* vol. 2: *Mentor, Message, and Miracles* (New York: Anchor Bible Reference Library, Doubleday, 1991–1994).

Meyers, Eric M., "Jesus and His Galilean Context," in *Archaeology and the Galilee,* ed. Douglas R. Edwards and C. Thomas McCollough (Atlanta: Scholars Press, 1997).

————, and James F. Strange, *Archaeology, the Rabbis, and Early Christianity* (Nashville: Abingdon Press, 1981).

Milgrom, Jacob, *Leviticus 1–16* (New York: Doubleday, 1991).

Millar, Fergus, "Reflections on the Trial of Jesus," in *A Tribute to Geza Vermès,* ed. Philip R. Davies and Richard T. White (Sheffield, UK: University of Sheffield Press, 1990) 355–81.

————, *The Roman Near East, 31 BC–AD 337* (Cambridge, MA: Harvard University Press, 1993).

Neusner, Jacob, *The Idea of Purity in Ancient Judaism* (Leiden, Netherlands: E. J. Brill, 1973).

————, W. S. Green, and Ernest S. Frerichs, eds., *Judaisms and Their Messiahs at the Turn of the Christian Era* (Cambridge: Cambridge University Press, 1987).

Newton, Michael, *The Concept of Purity at Qumran and in the Letters of Paul* (Cambridge: Cambridge University Press, 1985).

Oakman, Douglas E., "The Archaeology of First-Century Galilee and the Social Interpretation of the Historical Jesus," *SBLSP* 33 (1994): 220–51.

O'Leary, Stephen, *Arguing the Apocalypse: Toward a Theory of Millennial Rhetoric* (New York: Oxford University Press, 1994).

Pearson, Birger, "1 Thessalonians 2:13–16: A Deutero-Pauline Interpolation," *Harvard Theological Review* 64 (1971): 79–94.

Purvis, James, "The Samaritans," *The Cambridge History of Judaism,* vol. 2, ed. W. D. Davies and L. Finkelstein (Cambridge: Cambridge University Press, 1989), 591–613.

Räisänen, Heikki, "Jesus in Context," *Reviews in Religion and Theology* 2 (1994): 9–18.

Rajak, Tessa, *Josephus: The Historian and His Society* (Philadelphia: Fortress Press, 1984).

Reed, Jonathan L., "Population Numbers, Urbanization, and Economics: Galilean Archaeology and the Historical Jesus," *SBLSP* 33 (1994): 203–19.

Reynolds, Joyce and Robert Tannenbaum, *Jews and Godfearers at Aphrodisias* (Cambridge, UK: Cambridge University Press, 1987).

Richardson, Peter, *Herod: King of the Jews and Friend of the Romans* (Columbia: University of South Carolina Press, 1996).

Robinson, J. A. T., *The Priority of John* (London: SPCK, 1985).

Sanders, E. P., *Jesus and Judaism* (Philadelphia: Fortress Press, 1985).

———, "Jewish Association with Gentiles and Galatians 2:11–14," in *Studies in Paul and John,* ed. R. T. Fortna and B. R. Gaventa (Nashville: Abingdon, 1990), 170–88.

———, *Jewish Law from Jesus to the Mishnah* (Philadelphia: Fortress Press, 1990).

———, *Judaism: Practice and Belief, 63 BCE–66 CE* (Philadelphia: Trinity Press International, 1992).

———, *The Historical Figure of Jesus* (London: Penguin Press, 1993).

Schäfer, Peter, *The History of the Jews in Antiquity* (Luxembourg: Harwood Academic Publishers, 1995).

———, *Judeophobia: Attitudes toward the Jews in the Ancient World* (Cambridge, MA: Harvard University Press, 1997).

Schürer, Emil, *The History of the Jewish People in the Age of Jesus Christ (175 BC–AD 135),* rev. and ed. Geza Vermès et al., 3 vols. in 4 parts (Edinburgh: T. & T. Clark, Ltd., 1973–1987).

Schwartz, Daniel R., *Studies in the Jewish Background of Christianity* (Tübingen, Germany: Mohr-Siebeck, 1992).

Segal, Alan F., *Rebecca's Children: Judaism and Christianity in the Roman World* (Cambridge, MA: Harvard University Press, 1986).

Shanks, Hershel, *Jerusalem: An Archaeological Biography* (New York: Random House, 1995).

———, ed., *Christianity and Rabbinic Judaism: A Parallel History of Their Origins and Early Development* (Washington, DC: Biblical Archaeological Society, 1992).

———, ed., *Understanding the Dead Sea Scrolls: A Reader from the Biblical Archaeological Review* (New York: Random House, 1993).

Smallwood, E. Mary, *The Jews under Roman Rule* (Leiden, Netherlands: E. J. Brill, 1976).

Smith, M., "What Is Implied by the Variety of Messianic Figures?" *Journal of Biblical Literature* 78 (1959): 66–72.

Spence, Jonathan D., *The Memory Palace of Matteo Ricci* (New York: The Penguin Group, 1984).

Stern, Menachem, *Greek and Latin Authors on Jews and Judaism,* vols. 1–3 (Jerusalem: The Hebrew University Press, 1974–1984).

Strange, James F., "First-Century Galilee from Archaeology and from the Texts," *SBLSP* 33 (1994): 81–90.

Taylor, Joan E., *The Immerser: John the Baptist within Second Temple Judaism* (Grand Rapids, MI: William B. Eerdmans Publishing Co., 1997).

Theissen, Gerd, *The Gospels in Context: Social and Political History in the Synoptic Tradition* (Minneapolis: Fortress Press, 1991).

———, *Social Reality and the Early Christians* (Minneapolis: Fortress Press, 1992).

——— and Annette Merz, *The Historical Jesus: A Comprehensive Guide* (Minneapolis: Fortress Press 1988).

Vermès, Geza, *Jesus the Jew: A Historian's Reading of the Gospels* (Philadelphia: Fortress Press, 1973).

———, *Jesus and the World of Judaism* (Philadelphia: Fortress Press, 1981).

———, *The Religion of Jesus the Jew* (Philadelphia: Fortress Press, 1993).

Werblowsky, R. J. Zwi, and Geoffrey Wigoder, eds., *Oxford Dictionary of the Jewish Religion* (New York: Oxford University Press, 1997).

Whittaker, Molly, *Jews and Christians: Graeco-Roman Views* (Cambridge, UK: Cambridge University Press, 1984).

Wright, Benjamin G., "Jewish Ritual Baths—Interpreting the Digs and Texts: Some Issues in the Social History of Second Temple Judaism," *The Archaeology of Israel,* ed. N. A. Silberman and D. Small, *JSOT* Supplement Series 237 (1997): 190–214.

Wright, N. T., *The New Testament and the People of God* (Minneapolis: Fortress Press, 1992).

———, *Jesus and the Victory of God* (Minneapolis: Fortress Press, 1996).

INDEXES

INDEX OF SCRIPTURAL PASSAGES

JEWISH SCRIPTURES

Name Index

Aaron, 69
Abraham, 33, 65, 72, 113, 127, 187, 188, 239, 240
Adam, 79
Agrippa I, 169, 171, 174, 179
Akiva, Rabbi, 123, 246
Albinus, 228
Alexander, 177
Alexander the Great, 19, 85, 121, 159, 160
Allison, Dale C., 274, 275, 279, 293
Alon, G., 278
Ananias, 253
Andrew, 83, 91, 92
Annas, 9, 25, 219, 224, 244, 248
Anna the prophetess, 147
Antiochus Epiphanes, 85–6, 121, 161, 170, 227
Apion, 178, 180
Apollonius of Tyana, 113
Archelaus, 123, 165, 166, 167, 168, 180
Aretas, 152, 173, 174
Aristobulus, 177
Artaxerxes, 178
Asclepius, 113
Ashton, John, 283
Athronges, 166, 167, 249
Augustus, 3, 23, 103, 122–3, 166, 167, 168, 170,
    171, 172, 173, 175, 177, 179, 180, 243, 255
Austen, Jane, 202

Bammel, E., 292
Bannus, 186, 187
Barabbas, 222, 223
Bar Kokhba, 123, 124, 223, 246, 249
Barnabas, 129, 136
Barrett, C. K., 290
Bartholomew, 91
Bartimaeus, 140
Beelzebub, 112
ben Belgas, Meir, 13–14
ben Dalaeus, Joseph, 14
ben Dosa, Hanina, 113
ben Hanan, Jesus, 14
Benjamin, 36
ben Zakkai, Jochanan, 246
Borg, Marcus, 274, 284, 289, 290
Boyer, Paul, 293
Brandon, S. G. F., 292, 293
Brown, Peter, 279
Brown, Raymond E., 290, 292
Büchler, A., 278

Caiaphas, 3, 9, 18, 25, 33, 173, 214, 219, 224, 225,
    232, 253, 254, 258, 267
Caligula, 65, 86, 173, 174, 180, 181
Cephas, 136, 263

Claudius, 174, 175, 177
Coakley, J. F., 290
Cohen, Shaye J. D., 278, 281
Collins, John J., 279, 280, 281
Constantine, 135
Crossan, John Dominic, 274, 275, 279, 280, 283,
    284, 286, 287, 288, 289, 290, 291, 292, 293
Cumanus, 149
Cyrus, 119–20

D'Angelo, Mary Rose, 289
Daniel, 27, 84, 85, 89, 227, 264
David, King, 29, 56, 95, 120–6, 137, 140–7, 149,
    153, 159, 213, 241, 245, 247, 257, 265, 266
Decius, 175, 176
Dodd, C. H., 290
Douglas, Mary, 277
Downing, Gerald F., 274
Dunn, James D. G., 274

Eleazar, 13, 113
Elijah, 22, 113, 138, 139, 147
Elisha, 113, 147
Enoch, 35
Ezekiel, 27, 89, 120, 262

Fadus, 150
Felix, 150, 151
Florus, 150, 253
Fredriksen, Paula, 273, 276, 278, 279, 280, 281,
    293
Freyne, Sean, 284, 285, 286
Funk, Robert W., 274

Gabriel, 146
Gager, John G., 278, 279
Gallio, 8
Goodman, Martin, 282, 284
Gruen, Erich S., 281

Hanan, 113
Hasid, 7, 8, 267
Hasmonean family, 63, 85, 122, 123, 124, 159,
    160, 161, 168, 213
Hays, Christine, 278
Herod Antipas, 23, 123, 152, 153, 161, 165, 167,
    173, 176, 190–1, 215, 216, 217, 234, 249
Herodias, 190–1
Herod the Great, 3, 14, 18, 23, 38, 48, 56, 63, 64,
    93, 122, 123, 160, 161, 166, 167, 168, 171, 172,
    174, 177, 180, 190, 216, 228, 229, 253
Hobsbawm, E. J., 283, 285
Honi the Circle-Drawer, 113
Horsley, Richard A., 284, 286, 287

Subject Index

Page numbers in *italics* refer to illustrations.